THE
ABOMINATION
OF
DESOLATION
IN
BIBLICAL ESCHATOLOGY

Desmond Ford

THE
ABOMINATION
OF
DESOLATION
IN
BIBLICAL ESCHATOLOGY

Desmond Ford

University Press
of America™

Dedicated

To the memory of Gwen Ford, who encouraged this project
though aware she would not live to see it; and to Gill
Ford, whose whole-hearted help made the hope a reality.

ACKNOWLEDGEMENTS, etc.

The writer is deeply indebted to Avondale College, Cooranbong, New South Wales, Australia, which granted him two years leave-of-absence for study purposes, and to Professor F. F. Bruce, whose learning, kindness, and unstinted help made "the rough places plain" and "the crooked things straight".
The writer would also like to thank the following publishers for permission to include quotations used in this volume. These are listed in alphabetical order of publisher's names -- p. 90, fn. 24, Lectures on the Last Things, p. 24, by William Hendriksen, (copyright by William Hendriksen, 1951 -- used by permission of Baker Book House); p. 288,-9, fn. 122, The Revelation of St. John the Divine, p. 131, by G. B. Caird, used by permission of Adam and Charles Black; p. 132, fn. 9, The Servant of the Lord, p.280, H. H. Rowley, used by permission of Basil Blackwell, publishers; p. 85-86, fn. 8, The Parousia in the New Testament, pp. 178,-9, by A. L. Moore, used by permission of Brill, Leiden; p. 95, fn. 61, No Stone on Another, pp. 453,-4, by Lloyd Gaston, used by permission of Brill, Leiden; p. 303, fn. 147, The Revelation of St. John the Divine, p. 178, by A. Farrer, used by permission of Clarendon Press; p. 41, fn. 30, The Last Judgment, p. 87, by James P. Martin, used by permission of Wm. Eerdmans; p. 172-3, fns. 167, 168, The Theological Dictionary of the New Testament, ed. Gerhard Kittel and Gerhard Friedrich, article by Foerster, vol. 1, p. 598, used by permission of Wm. Eerdmans; p. 152, fn. 51, "De 'Gruwel der verwoesting', Mt. 24:15, par.," GerThT, LX (1960), pp. 1-5, by G. C. Aalders, used by permission of Free University, Amsterdam; pp. 103-106, fn. 86, Der Weg Jesu, p. 444-448, (Berlin, 21968), by E. Haenchen, used by permission of De Gruyter; pp. 13, 164, 164, fns. 62, 112, 115, Documents of the Primitive Church, pp. 14-15, 18-19, 32, by C. L. Torrey, used by permission of Harper and Row, Publishers; p. 242, fn. 153, The Apocalypse of John, p. 396, by Isbon T. Beckwith, (copyright 1919 by Isbon T. Beckwith, used by permission of MacMillan Publishing Co., Inc.); p. 283, fn. 90, "Johannesapokalypse", RGG, Tübingen, 31956-65, col. 829, by Otto Piper; used by permission of J. C. C. Mohr (Paul Siebeck) Verlag, Tübingen; p. 97, fn. 68, Naherwartung, Tradition und Redaktion in Mk. 13, pp. 142-3, by R. Pesch, used by permission of Patmos Verlag, Düsseldorf; p. 84, fn. 2, Das Evangelium nach Markus, (Das Regensburg Neues Testament), p. 233, by J. Schmid, used by permission of Verlag Friedrich Pustet, Regensburg; p. 39, fn. 18, "Le Discours de Jesus sur la ruine du temple d'après Mc. XIII et Luc XXII", RB LVI (1949), pp. 70-71, by A. Feuillet, used by permission of Révue Biblique, Jerusalem; p. 70,71, fn 53, Ibid,RB. LV,(1948), 486-489 and p. 87, 88, fn. 16, Évangile selon saint Matthieu,pp. 334-335, by M-J. Lagrange, used by permission of Révue Biblique, Jerusalem; p. 92ff. fn. 41, 42, Évangile selon

saint Marc, pp. 462-3, by M-J Lagrange, used by permission of Révue Biblique, Jerusalem; pp. 52, 53, fns. 131, 132, Introduction to the New Testament, pp. 132, 136, by W. G. Kümmel, used by permission of SCM Press Ltd., London; pp. 282-3, fn. 86, Commentary on the Revelation of St. John (ICC), I, p. cvi-cvii, by R. H. Charles. Used by permission of Charles Scribner and Sons, New York; p. 44, fn. 61, Jesus and the Kingdom, p. 97, by George E. Ladd, used by permission of The Society for Promoting Christian Knowledge; from the same publisher, p. 108, fn. 97, The Son of Man in Mark, p. 156, Morna Hooker; p. 183, fn. 83, "Der gruwel der verwoesting (Mt. 24,15 = Mc 13,14)", StCath XX (1944), 135, by Van Dodewaard, used by permission of St. Cath; p. 240, fn. 140, The Background of the New Testament and Its Eschatology, pp. 415-16, by W. D. Davies, used by permission of Cambridge University Press; from the same publisher, p. 108, fn. 101, The Temple and the Community in Qumran, p. 129, 130, by B. Gärtner; p. 54, fn. 149, "Parusie-verzögerung und Urchristentum", TLZ LXXXIII (1958), p. 12, used by permission of Theologische Literaturzeitung, Berlin; p. 138, fn. 54, The Faith of Israel, pp. 15, 16, H. H. Rowley, used by permission of the Westminster Press.

ABOUT THE WRITER

Born in Townsville, Queensland, Australia, the writer's first articles were published by Associated Newspapers of Sydney, where he was employed from 1944-46. Following four years of ministerial training at Avondale College, he engaged in pastoral and evangelistic work for seven years in New South Wales. After completing his B.A. in 1957, the writer attended Potomac University, Washington D. C. for the M.A., and the Michigan State University for a Ph.D. in Rhetoric. From 1961-70 were spent or the Faculty of Avondale College, Australia, in the Department of Theology. 1971-72 were spent in research at Manchester University on the present topic and a Ph.D. in New Testament received. Since then, he has resumed his chairman's duties at Avondale's Theology department, but consequent to July, 1977, has been a visiting professor at Pacific Union College, Angwin, California, in the department of Religion. He is married, has three children, and is the author of Discovering God's Treasures (Review and Herald), Answers on the Way (Pacific Press), and a commentary, Daniel (Southern Publishing Association).

PREFACE

The present investigation aims at determining the origin and significance of the mysterious βδέλυγμα τῆς ἐρημώσεως allusion in Mk. 13:14, and in discovering its relationship to similar canonical references. The study necessarily involves the nature and place of apocalyptic and its links with eschatology, and therefore the Olivet discourse as recorded in the Synoptics, Daniel, Revelation, and 2 Thessalonians are primary sources.

Chapter one shows the importance of the study as acknowledged by many exegetes, and highlights the issues comprehended by any exhaustive study of Mark 13, a chapter which has provoked more scholarly controversy than perhaps any other in the Synoptic Gospels. The contradictory opinions extant in this area suggest that presuppositions and prejudices have often deflected the true intent of exegesis.

Chapter two offers an exegetical survey of Mark 13, analyzing the four chief positions taken on the chapter. These positions are:

1. Application to the fall of Jerusalem only,
2. Application to the end of the Age only,
3. Application to both events (though understood in the Gospel as distant in fulfillment from each other) on the basis that either Christ or the Evangelist blended the themes,
4. Application to both events, regarding such as promised by Christ to the generation contemporary with Him. This view makes the fall of Jerusalem a part of the predicted end of the Age.

It is pointed out that the first two schools depend heavily upon reading metaphorically an important section of the chapter, and taking literally that which the opposing school refuses so to construe. Each therefore shows its weakness and its strength, for error is more often manifested in what is denied than what is affirmed. The third position seems to have been adopted for apologetic purposes and can hardly be said to spring from thorough exegesis. Only the fourth position can survive close examination. An excursus discusses whether Christ, in common with other Hebrew prophets, may here have delivered a contingent prophecy in whole or in part. A further excursus discusses the scope of the tribulation mentioned in Mark 13, and whether it is limited to the confines of Jerusalem and Judea.

Chapter three illustrates the fact that Mark 13 is a midrash of Daniel, and therefore seeks to discover the basic theme of that book, the place of the שמם שקוץ, the relationship between the כבר אנש and the שקוץ שמם, and the קדש and the שקוץ שמם.

vii

It is stressed that the kingdom of God and the vindication of
its heirs is the primary motif. Prior to Daniel the religious
world made little use of מלכות but this book gives a more precise
delineation of the divine kingdom than hitherto offered in the
Old Testament. The sanctuary is presented as a microcosm of the
kingdom of God, and the writer has skillfully interwoven
references to the sanctuary as background to the promises of the
establishment of Yahweh's kingdom of glory. These references
occur in both the narrative and prophetic sections of the book.
In many respects, Dan. 8:14, with its promise of vindication for
the sanctuary and its worshippers, is the key verse of the book.
This passage marks a distinct literary division, for it
terminates the usage of visionary symbols requiring interpretation. Hereafter, all is explanation. Thus Dan. 8:14 is the
climax of the symbolic "forecasts" of the book. The vindication
promised there is expanded in Dan. 9:24 and also in 12:1-3, and
parallels 7:22, 27 and 2:44. Even the narratives of Daniel
stress vindication. In each story we see the righteous rewarded
or the wicked punished. The servants of the true God triumph
over all opposition despite their apparent helplessness before
the might of their heathen oppressors. The historical passages
inevitably link with the prophetic. The introduction by Daniel
pictures a northern invader marching upon Jerusalem to ravage its
temple and worshippers. The theme of the treading underfoot of
the sanctuary and the host begins here and reaches its high-point
in the Old Testament Antichrist. Even in chapter nine, the
narrative helps interpret the vision, with references to sin,
transgression, iniquity, Jerusalem, sanctuary, desolation,
righteousness, etc., being found in both. All the key characteristics of Antichrist -- pride, blasphemy, idolatry, and oppression -- are represented in the stories as well as the visions.
The use of the key-word "deliver" in both sections of the book
illustrates the artistry of the author. For the purpose of the
present study the most important fact is that all the primary
factors in the message of Daniel are found also in the Olivet
discourse, and in each case the presentation is true to the
original Old Testament picture in form, though the substance is
augmented. Particularly is this true of the theme of vindication
by the Son of Man. The coming of the Son of Man in Mk. 13:26 is
the counterpart of the rise of the βδέλυγμα τῆς ἐρημώσεως as is
also the case in Daniel 7. Even in a number of minute particulars the eschatological discourse echoes the very wording of
Daniel, as well as by its stress on the major themes of the
advent of the kingdom and the exaltation of its heirs.

Chapter four offers textual criticism and exegesis of Mk. 13:14
itself. Particular attention is paid to the various interpretations offered for defining the βδέλυγμα τῆς ἐρημώσεως. Those
viewpoints which see in the invading Roman army with its idolatrous ensigns, and in the final Antichrist the fulfillment of

Christ's prophecy, receive the closest scrutiny. The reason why
most modern commentators see only the Antichrist and no fulfillment in history is indicated. Again the commentator's position
on the origin of Mk. 13:14 is shown to be often determinative of
his exegesis.

Chapter five shows the close relationship between Paul's
prediction in 2 Thess. 2 and Christ's in Mk. 13:14. The main
elements requiring interpretation, ἡ ἀποστασία, ὁ ἄνθρωπος τῆς
ἀνομίας, ὅ ναος, τὸ κατέχον are analyzed in relationship to
their context and other passages. The usual positions taken on
ὅ κατέχον are examined and rejected as incomplete. In their
place is offered a Gestalt comprehending the strengths of each
and avoiding their inadequacies. Some linguistic connections
between the βδέλυγμα τῆς ἐρημώσεως and key-terms of 2 Thess. 2
are indicated as well as conceptual parallels. It is pointed out
that what we have here in Paul is an echo of a genuine tradition
of Christ's words.

Chapter six pursues the Antichrist motif throughout the last
half of the book of Revelation. The βδέλυγμα τῆς ἐρημώσεως has
its seed in the book of Daniel, its "blade" in the Olivet
discourse, its "ear" in 2 Thess. 2, but the "full grain" is to
be found in what is pre-eminently the Apocalypse. Comparisons
are made between the various Antichrists of this book and those
of Daniel, Mk. 13, and 2 Thess. 2. Suggestions are made regarding the hermeneutic to be applied to the passages studied. This
consideration of a special hermeneutic is made necessary by the
existence of such contrary assessments of the value of Revelation
and of its significance. The exegete's own Weltanschauung can
too easily interpenetrate his application of the laws of grammatico-historical exegesis. Thus the array of interpretations
is practically as bewildering as the puzzling book itself.
Supplementary hermeneutic principles for the Apocalypse spring
from the fact that its basic symbolism springs primarily from
the Old Testament and the life and eschatological teachings of
Christ. While this symbolism and the language expressing it
is heavily Hebraic, the Seer evidently considers the Christian
church to be the heir of literal Israel. Minor principles which
help to guide exegesis include such stylistic forms as contrast,
prolepsis, and recapitulation. The first-named is the most
important and is vital for correct interpretation of many of
the symbols associated with the Antichrist figures. Chapter 11
is considered in some detail, thus illustrating the type of
hermeneutical approach advocated.

The Antichrist visions embody not only the familiar features
of the שׁקוץ שׁמם but also many less obvious borrowings from
Daniel. The "war" and "flood" terminology of the latter
reappears, particularly in the climactic plagues concerning

Armageddon and Euphrates. Dan. 11:45 is seen as part of the Old
Testament background for the last battle described in Rev. 16.
The Babylon of the Apocalypse is, of course, also reminiscent of
Daniel. The whore stands in obvious contrast to the woman
clothed with the sun, and while Rome stands at the centre of the
Seer's vision, it does not exhaust the significance of his
symbol. Rev. 17 is an excellent illustration of the necessity
of beginning with local and historical meaning before enquiring
further. The flight out of Babylon, according to many interpreters, echoes Mark 13:14f. as surely as Rev. 13 rings the
changes afresh on that same passage. Rev. 17-20 contain several
allusions to the concept of desolation, and the related abomination theme is also present in the closing chapters. The final
application of Mk. 13:14 is in the twentieth chapter where the
last manifestation of Antichrist's surrounding of the sanctuary
occurs. At that point, as in Dan. 7,8,9,11-12, vindication
takes place, and the kingdom of God materializes in glory.

The conclusion summarizes convictions that have arisen from
the investigation, and emphasizes the necessity of recognizing
Mk. 13:14 as part of Christ's creative interpretation of Daniel.
The suggestion is made that Mark 13 and Daniel, because of the
light they cast on the Scriptural teaching of the kingdom of
God, merit continued study along the lines begun in the present
work.

TABLE OF CONTENTS

		Page
Preface		iv
List of Abbreviations		vii

PART I. PROLEGOMENA

.Chapter

I.	Issues Concerning Mark Thirteen:	1
	The Presuppositions of Exegetes	6
	Definitions of Eschatology and Apocalyptic	11
	The Origin of the "Olivet Discourse"	14
	The Apparent Contradiction of Q Materials by Mark 13	27
	The Problem posed by the Congruence (or Incongruence) of vv. 28-30 with v.32, and other "Inconsistencies"	29
	The Composition Dates of the Synoptic Gospels	31
	The Specific Purpose, or Purposes, of Mark's Gospel, and of Chapter 13 in particular	33
	The Contextual Setting of Mark 13 -- Literary and Chronological	36

PART II. MK. 13:14 -
ITS CONTEXT, BACKGROUND, AND EXEGESIS

II.	Exegetical Survey of Mark Thirteen	59
III.	Relationship of Daniel to the Olivet Discourse	111
IV.	Exegesis of Mk. 13:14	141

PART III. MK. 13:14 -
SUBSEQUENT DEVELOPMENTS

V.	Relationship between II Thess. 2 and the βδέλυγμα τῆς ἐρημώσεως	193
VI.	The Apocalypse and the βδέλυγμα τῆς ἐρημώσεως	243

Conclusion	307
Select Bibliography	315

ABBREVIATIONS

AB	Analecta Biblica
AG	Arndt, W. F., and Gingrich, F. W., edd., A Greek English Lexicon of the New Testament and Other Early Christian Literature (E.T., Cambridge-Chicago, 1957)
ATD	Das Alte Testament Deutsch
ATR	Anglican Theological Review
β.τ.ἐ.	βδέλυγμα τῆς ἐρημώσεως
BDB	Brown, Driver, Briggs, Hebrew Lexicon
CBQ	Catholic Biblical Quarterly
CB	The Cambridge Bible
CGTC	The Cambridge Gk. Testament Commentary
ed.	editor
EB	The Expositor's Bible
EQ	The Evangelical Quarterly
E.T.	English Translation
ET	The Expository Times
GerTht	Gereformeerd Theologisch Tijdschrift
HAT	Handbuch zum alten Testament
HNT	Handbuch zum Neuen Testament
ICC	The International Critical Commentary
JBL	Journal of Biblical Literature
JThCh	Journal for Theology and Church
JTS	Journal of Theological Studies
KAT	Kommentar zum Alten Testament

LXX	The Septuagint
MM	Moulton and Milligan's <u>Vocabulary of the Greek</u> Testament, London, 1930
MNTC	Moffatt's New Testament Commentary
n. d.	no date
NLCNT (and NIGHT)	The New London Commentary on the New Testament (the English version of the American series, the New International Commentary on the New Testament)
<u>NovT</u>	<u>Novum Testamentum</u>
n.s.	new series
NT	New Testament
NTD	Das Neue Testament Deutsch
<u>NTS</u>	<u>New Testament Studies</u>
<u>RB</u>	<u>Revue Biblique</u>
<u>RGG</u>	<u>Die Religion in Geschichte und Gegenwart</u>, Galling, K., ed., Tübingen, 31956-65
<u>RSR</u>	<u>Recherches de Science Religieuse</u>
RSV	The Revised Standard Version of the Bible
<u>SJTh</u>	<u>Scottish Journal of Theology</u>
<u>StCath</u>	<u>Studia Catholica</u>
TBC	Torch Bible Commentary
<u>TBNT</u>	<u>Theologisches Begriffslexikon zum Neuen Testament</u>
<u>TDNT</u>	<u>Theological Dictionary of the New Testament</u>, ed. G. Kittel and G. Friedrich, E.T. by G. W. Bromiley (Grand Rapids, 1964--)
Th	Theodotion
<u>ThBl</u>	<u>Theologische Blätter</u>

ThViat	Theologia Viatorum
TLZ	Theologische Literaturzeitung
TNTC	Tyndale New Testament Commentary
TT	Theology Today
TWNT	Theologisches Wörterbuch zum Neuen Testament, ed. by G. Kittel and G. Friedrich (Stuttgart, 1933--)
TV	Theologia Viatorum
TZ	Theologische Zeitschrift
WC	Westminster Commentaries
ZAW	Zeitschrift für die Alttestamentliche Wissenschaft
ZNW	Zeitschrift für die Neutestamentliche Wissenschaft

CHAPTER ONE

ISSUES CONCERNING MARK THIRTEEN

The βδέλυγμα τῆς ἐρημώσεως phrase is the enigmatic heart of the most puzzling chapter in the primary book of the New Testament. As such, in its setting of Mark 13, it challenges continuing attention for purposes of criticism and exegesis.[1]

The context of the βδέλυγμα phrase is particularly rich thematically. It reflects not only two of the master teachings of Christ, the Kingdom of God and the Son of Man, but associated themes such as the Remnant, Antichrist, the Tribulation, and the Parousia.

The βδέλυγμα τῆς ἐρημώσεως is not an isolated allusion, but a refrain repeatedly occurring in eschatological passages. In concept it is sometimes present even when the precise terminology is absent. In the New Testament it is found not only in the Synoptic Gospels, but in 2 Thessalonians and the book of Revelation. Apart from the Olivet discourse, its most familiar setting is that cited by Matthew, namely Daniel, the book which above all others influenced the theological climate of Judaism in the first century. And as surely as Daniel itself sometimes reflects earlier books of the Old Testament, so it is in this instance. The constituent elements of the phrase under consideration are found first in the Pentateuch, and subsequently throughout the Old Testament writings, being particularly clustered in the books of Jeremiah, Ezekiel, and Isaiah, books from which the writer of Daniel freely draws.[2]

There are good grounds for believing that this cryptic phrase does not embody a tenuous abstraction merely, but rather reflects concrete historical events considered pivotal in the experience of Israel old and new. Major crises are thereby referred to, crises which became the sources of apocalyptic formulations.[3]

The βδέλυγμα τῆς ἐρημώσεως is ever linked with the temple, the symbol of the ancient theocracy and of the New Testament community. Bible writers make the variegated experiences of the temple a microcosm of all salvation history. Initially it represented God's coming in grace to dwell with men, and illustrated the Covenant promises, "I will make my abode among you . . . I will walk among you, and will be your God, and you shall be my people."[4] The same terminology is used in the climactic picture of consummation and glory entrusted to the new Israel. See Rev. 21:3. The profanation of the temple and its devastation under the Babylonian woe, provided the imagery for picturing the catastrophe of the Maccabean era, that of 70 A.D., and also the eschatological crisis finally to be precipitated by the Antichrist. The reconstruction of the temple after the exile, and the cleansing by Judas Maccabeus, became to Daniel's readers shadows of the ultimate "anointing of the most holy", the establishment of the Messianic temple, when "everlasting righteousness" would be brought in, and atonement made for all iniquity. The theme of attack upon the kingdom of God by its idolatrous desolators, plus the compensating vindication of those loyal to Yahweh, constitutes the essence of the holy war, and enshrines the basic dangers and hopes of the remnant in all ages.[5]

Our study seems contributory to the ongoing debate over eschatology and kindred issues. The nature of the kingdom spoken of by Christ, the place of apocalyptic, the significance of the temple imagery in the New Testament, exegetical issues associated with the destiny of both Israels, the Parousia -- its supposed premonitory symtoms and delay, the historical and exegetical approach to New Testament studies versus the philosophical existential mode -- all these and others are involved in the attempted unravelling of the significance of the βδέλυγμα τῆς ἐρημώσεως.

Because Mark 13 as the primary New Testament source in this study has long been considered as the passage in the Gospels most "replete with critical and exegetical difficulties",[6] and because its unique nature has specially challenged source, form, and (more recently) redaction critics,[7] another investigation is not without justification.[8]

The approach here made is that of Biblical Realism, "the effort to understand the New Testament writings from within the mind of their authors, to stand where the biblical writers stood, rather than to force the biblical message into modern thought forms."[9]

We are not now concerned with the relevance or irrelevance of the biblical world-view or views. Thus the modern concept of the universe as a closed system wherein neither miracle or other supernatural manifestations such as revelation or prediction are possible, or the opposing view of primitive theological orthodoxy, are not considered pertinent to the exegetical problem, except for their prejudicial impact.

ISSUES PERTINENT TO THE EXEGESIS OF MARK 13

Relationship of Mark 13:14 to the Rest of the Chapter

Our purpose in this section is to indicate the relationship between Mark 13:14 and the rest of the chapter, in order to show the necessity for an early glance at problems relating to the chapter as a whole.

The βδέλυγμα τῆς ἐρημώσεως referred to in v. 14 is not something isolated in significance from the remainder of Mark 13. Scholars, in commenting upon the verse, have used such expressions as the "Wendung"[10], "Hohepunkt"[11], "Angelpunkt"[12], "Crescendo"[13], pointing out its crucial position in the chapter.

Marxsen has a particular case to support by his estimate, but the
same is hardly true of the others. J. Schmid suggests, "For the
understanding of the whole discourse, this passage is of the
greatest importance."[14] Haenchen values it as "ausserst merkwürdig"[15], while Suhl summarizes, "Das Wort vom Greuel der Verwüstung . . . ist für das Verständnis der synoptischen Apokalypse
von entscheidender Bedeutung."[16]

The beginning, middle, and we believe the end,[17] of Mark 13
involve allusions to the temple. The chapter opens with a reference to the sacred building and its threatened destruction, and
it closes with warnings to be ready for the coming of the Son of
Man. The scene depicting the latter intimates the eschatological
fulfillment of the temple-dominating Shekinah.[18]

In Dan. 7, by the symbolism of the "Son of Man" being given the
kingdom, the suffering remnant of Israel was promised vindication.
This sufficed in the days of Antiochus Epiphanes, as Ezekiel 1,
with its vision of the heavenly glory, met the anguish of soul of
the captives who had been torn from their holy city. Mk. 13:26
implies the ultimate restoration of that new temple promised
since the days of Ezekiel when "the dwelling of God" shall be
"with men".[19]

The Son of Man is pictured as coming μετὰ τὴν θλῖψιν , after
the days of the tribulation created by the previous advent of the
βδέλυγμα. There is no legitimate way of separating the Parousia
from the threat to the temple.[20] That the expression βδέλυγμα
τῆς ἐρημώσεως refers to the temple is made certain by the fact
that in Daniel the βδέλυγμα is ever associated with the sanctuary.[21]

The obvious relation of v. 14 to the first half of the chapter
is also shown by the literary crescendo present in this section.

v. 7 ὅταν δε. . .ἀκούσητε πολέμους. . .μὴ θροεῖσθε

v. 11 ὅταν ἄγωσιν ὑμᾶς παραδιδόντες μὴ προμεριμνᾶτε

v. 14 "Οταν δὲ ἴδητε τὸ βδέλυγμα. . .τότε. . .φευγέτωσαν

Thus these verses picture the preliminary agitations which are
not to cause mental distress, as contrasted with the situation
when the βδέλυγμα appears. In this setting the δὲ must be given
its full adversative force.

The necessity for flight spoken of in v. 14 is linked with the
tribulation pictured in prior and succeeding verses. Vv. 9-13
picture oppression of believers and following the allusion to the
βδέλυγμα, the same picture reoccurs but in deeper colors. Even

4

the false Christs seen preceding the θλῖψις occur again, but in more scarlet hue as with the persecution itself. They now work miraculous signs and wonders. Christ is described as coming ἐν ἐκείναις ταῖς ἡμέραις μετὰ τὴν θλῖψιν. Thus verses 9-27, from yet another angle, are seen to constitute a whole.

The fact that the fundamental Old Testament allusions in this chapter come from Daniel and are to be found at the beginning, middle, and close, also indicate that we have here a unified presentation. Indeed, Mark 13 has been recognized as a Mahnrede on the temple-prophecies of Daniel.[22] None dispute that the references to the βδέλυγμα τῆς ἐρημώσεως and to the θλῖψις etc., are taken from the ancient apocalypse, but it seems almost sure that συντελεῖσθαι of v. 4 is from the same source.[23]

Mark 13:14 not only matches the earlier and later portions of the chapter by its reference to the temple and its use of Daniel, but it also is strongly parenetic in nature, as are these other sections. Watchfulness is demanded. Ὅταν δε ἴδητε . . . .Insight is called for. νοείτω. . . .And lastly, action appropriate to the attitudes of watchfulness and careful attention is urged. φευγέτωσαν . . . .

These seem to be sufficient grounds for regarding the chapter in its present form as an ideological unity, and therefore we approach the exegesis of τὸ βδέλυγμα τῆς ἐρημώσεως by attempting first to reach some conclusions on issues relating to the nature, origin and significance of Mark 13 as a whole.

Issues Concerning Mark Thirteen
1. Definitions of apocalyptic and eschatology. Is Mark 13 an apocalypse?
2. The origin of the Olivet discourse.
a. Place of apocalyptic in the teachings of Christ.

b. The "Little Apocalypse".

c. The framework of the discourse, Mark 13:1-4.

d. Parenthesis of Mark 13:14b.

e. The relationship between Mark 13 and 1 and 2 Thessalonians. The primary collection and circulation of the logia now found in Mark 13:5-37.

f. The relationship between Mark 13 and other Synoptic parallels such as Luke 12:35-46; Luke 17:24-37; Luke 21; Matthew 10:17-22; Matthew 24.

g. Relationship to the apocalypses of Judaism.

5

3. The apparent contradiction of Q materials by Mark 13.

4. The problem posed by the congruence (or incongruence) of vv. 30 and 32 of Mk. 13. Other "inconsistencies".

5. The composition dates of the Synoptic Gospels.

6. The specific purpose, or purposes, of Mark's Gospel, and of chapter 13 in particular.

7. The setting of the Olivet discourse within Mark's Gospel as a whole.

8. The presuppositions of exegetes.

It is recognized that each of these issues could demand a thesis in entirety. Nevertheless, significant conclusions regarding Mark 13:14 cannot be made without some enquiry regarding these matters. Of necessity we will but offer a summary of what seems to be the evidence in each case.

The Presuppositions of Exegetes

Certain it is, that the last item on the list is the most important, and therefore in dealing with the issues suggested, the last shall be first. It has been placed last because the other matters are frequently discussed, but this one only rarely, though it usually determines the exegete's conclusions throughout. So much is this the case that one can almost predict an exegete's positions on most of this problem's facets, if the exegete's school is known. Whether he be of Bultmannian persuasion, or a fundamentalist, may have much more to do with the results of his investigation than any other factor.

F. W. Farrar has written at length to prove that the history of exegesis is a history of error,[24] and if black and white really mean different things, then the statistics are in favour of the one-time Dean of Canterbury. H. Riesenfeld asserts:

> . . . it is inevitable that the innumerable contributions devoted to Gospel research are stamped to a greater or lesser degree by the attitude of the writer in question toward the person and character of Jesus. The fatal thing is that there is no such thing as research without presupposition. The more emancipated a scholar thinks he is, the less he is in actual fact.[25]

One of the best illustrations of these words is found in the history of the theology of Baur. Despite his protestations to the contrary, it does seem that the influence of Hegel's dialec-

tical triad worked as a leaven amidst all his research. Stephen
Neill suggests that:

> . . . it is in the field of its presuppositions, which
> in themselves have nothing to do with critical or his-
> torical method, that the whole great structure of the
> work of Baur comes to grief. Again, and again, when
> the presuppositions are exercising their unfortunate
> influence, critical method is for the time being aban-
> doned.[26]

No one who has read Mark Pattison's delineation of Warburton as
a Baur-like scholar can readily forget the beacon light offered
by the "brilliant example of a false method".[27]

And who, reading the following from Albert Schweitzer, being
aware also of Weiffenbach's main thesis on eschatology, can fail
to ask himself significant questions regarding the brilliant work
of scholars such as Bultmann, Dibelius, Martin Werner, Hans
Conzelmann, T. F. Glasson, and J. A. T. Robinson?

> The whole history of Christianity, down to the present
> day, that is to say, the real inner history of it, is
> based on the delay of the Parousia, the non-occurrence
> of the Parousia . . . [28]

A. L. Moore blames presuppositions for what he believes to be the
wrong stance of many scholars regarding the topic of his choice.
At the opening of his work on a topic similar to the present one.
He says:

> Behind these views one can discern the pressure of
> evolutionistic materialism and of the whole secular
> climate of thought. Even more apparent is the pressure
> of a secular philosophy behind the re-interpretation of
> eschatology in terms of existentialism.[29]

Just a few years previous to Moore's statement, James Martin set
out to study history of Protestant thought with reference to
eschatology and came to the same conclusions.[30]

On the other hand, there are grounds for believing that both
Moore and Martin began their research with presuppositions basically contrary to those they criticize. Riesenfeld does rightly
in reminding us that the freer of assumptions we each hold ourselves to be, the more in slavery to such we are. It would seem
that Philosophy and not Theology has become the Queen of the
sciences, Weltanschauungen determining Bibelerklärungen. Inasmuch as Epistemology assures us that no man can even begin to
think without presuppositions and that to some extent all

thinking is done in a circle, it becomes important at the outset
of any study to remind ourselves of our own personal prejudices
and then to seek to counterbalance the distortion of these as far
as possible. The present writer, remembering Riesenfeld's caveat, confesses that his own prejudicial entanglements are legion.

This issue is best illustrated by displaying the diametrically
opposed positions that some scholars have held regarding the
value of what has been called "the Olivet discourse", or sections
thereof. The extreme, one could almost say emotional, statements
in some of the following estimates suggest the presence of a
factor or factors other than the facts. If several people survey
the same scene or object and report it as possessing opposite
characteristics, the fault probably does not lie with that which
is beheld.

> D. Strauss: Such a thing as He has here prophesied of
> Himself cannot happen to a man. If he prophesied the
> like of Himself and expected it, then to us He is a
> fanatic; if He uttered it of Himself without any real
> conviction, then He was a braggart and a deceiver.[31]

> C. H. Weisse (re: Mark 13:24-27): an utterance con-
> structed out of the most narrow and superstitious belief
> in the symbolic sayings of a fantastic book (Daniel)
> which ignorance or deceit attributed to a renowned old
> prophet, and out of the most extravagant, half-insane
> imagination.[32]

> Timothy Colani: It contains the eschatology of Jewish
> Christians . . . Jesus could not have shared their
> opinions.[33]

> Wellhausen: It can safely be asserted that if Jesus
> did not once speak beforehand to His disciples of His
> suffering and resurrection, He certainly did not of
> His parousia.[34]

> C. G. Montefiore: It has very slight interest for us
> today, and little or no religious value.[35]

> Francis A. Henry: So then: Jesus, whose Good Tidings
> told of the heavenly Father and forgiveness of sin, who
> called men to the higher righteousness of love and a new
> life in union with the Divine, whose religion was so in-
> ward and spiritual, so pure from all earthly alloy --
> crowns all with an eschatology so gross and so grotesque!
> Jesus, . . . can only repeat when he touches on mankind's
> destiny what the vulgarest rabbi had long been preaching
> in the synogogue! Jesus, . . . whose outlook on the world

was ever sane, calm, clear-eyed -- yields to these fantastic dreams of his misguided people, and solemnly predicts as close at hand a startling series of preternatural events which have never come to pass! One who can believe that will believe anything.[36]

T. Francis Glasson: . . . this picture of a mistaken fanatic bringing the message that millions now living will never die.[37]

F. C. Grant: For any human being to identify himself with the Son of Man of the visions of Enoch, taken literally and without reinterpretation, could suggest little else than an unsound mind -- certainly not the supreme and unquestioned sanity of the Man of Galilee.[38]

Hölscher: Any specifically Christian element is lacking in the discourse. The whole derives from Daniel.[39]

J. A. T. Robinson (re: Mark 13:24-27): . . . a secondary compilation reflecting the expectation of the early Church.[40]

C. C. Torrey: The great eschatological discourse of Jesus, which we see reported by the three Synoptics, is a marvellously perfect composition in its detail and its conciseness, solidly and skillfully constructed by a writer who was worthy of His task. The Second Gospel, with all its planned brevity, could not more condense here than in the subsequent chapters. There was nothing in the discourse that could be omitted, and it was adapted entire.[41]

D. Schenkel: The most impressive and powerful utterance that Jesus made.[42]

J. Schniewind: . . . jedes einzelne Wort hat eine solche Prägung, wie sie nur von der Wirklichkeit "Jesus: her möglich ist . . . [43]

B. Vawter: That Jesus actually made such a prophecy, in view of his consistent eschatological teaching on the soonness of a divine visitation on Jerusalem and Judea, his conviction of the decisiveness of his own role in the workings of salvation history, and his reading of the temper of the times, there is absolutely no reason to question. His words are in the tradition of Israel's prophecy (cf. Jer. 7:1-15; Ezek. 24:15-23) and have not been simply made up by Christian writers in the light of later events.[44]

9

D. E. Nineham: . . . the climax to that whole part of
the Gospel he [Mark] was responsible for composing.
As such it brings out the infinite significance the
Evangelist saw in the events of the ministry.[45]

Lambrecht: Das 13 Kapitel hat im Mk-Evangelium einen
ganz besonderen Platz; am Ende des öffentlichen Lebens
Jesu and vor dem Beginn der Passion. Dieses Kapitel mag
eine geschlossene Einheit bilden; doch kann man nur
schwer a priori unterstellen, dass diese apokalyptische
Rede rein zufällig und ohne besondere Gründe und Absichten
an diese Stelle gesetzt wurde . . . auf diesem Höhepunkt
des Evangeliums?[46]

Beasley-Murray: It has long been recognized that the discourse holds a significant place in the Gospel of Mark
in that it forms both a conclusion to the teaching ministry of Jesus and an introduction to the passion narrative
immediately afterwards. The horror of the betrayal and
execution is not minimized, but the proportion of the
tragedy is changed. The cross for Jesus is the pathway
to glory; he knows whither he goes, and the shadow of
impending judgment falls upon the people that reject
their King.
    This has been admitted by writers as different as
Loisy and Dodd, Guignebert and Lightfoot.[47]

E. F. K. Muller: Dann aber stehen wir wieder vor der
Frage, ob nicht dieses christliche eschatologische System,
das sich trotz zahlreicher Einzelparallelen zur judischen
Apokalyptik als ein Neubau mit originaler Grundlage aus-
weist schliesslich auf Jesus selbst.[48]

John Peter Lange: The eschatological speech of the Lord,
the germ of John's Apocalypse; the New Testament exposition and form of the Old Testament ideas and symbols;
the opposite and corrective of all apocryphal Apoca-
lypsism.[49]

J. J. Van Oosterzee: We should have good right to wonder
at the eschatological conceptions which are found, for
instance, in Paul's Epistles to the Corinthians and
Thessalonians, if they had not the least Christian historical foundation in just such sayings of our Lord as
we meet with in this discourse.[50]

These quotations are significant for their illustration of
the contention underlying this discussion of presuppositions,
namely, that the exegesis of Mark 13 has been determined more
by the prior assumptions of the exegetes than perhaps any other

10

<u>passage of Scripture.</u>[51] To pursue without this awareness the close study of the chapter in question by a review of commentators can only lead to frustration and the suspicion that further effort must be fruitless in an area where so many great minds have come to diametrically-opposed conclusions.

The evidence is abundant that the Rabbinical method of reliance upon authorities is not absent from modern research, and much that poses as exegesis must only be eis-egesis. McCown's statement used by Beasley-Murray at the beginning of his volume, needs ever to be kept in mind. "No matter how original a scholar's imagination, no matter how penetrating and critical his judgement, society does far more of the writing of any book that lives than the author himself."[52]

1. Definitions of Eschatology and Apocalyptic

Various writers[53] claim so much for apocalyptic and eschatology that definitions are essential, but reading on these topics in modern works can be confusing because of the present diverse use of the terms. "'Eschatological' is used by scholars in half a dozen senses, often without definition . . ."[54] Similarly, Gerhard von Rad says of apocalyptic: "it is necessary to remember that no satisfactory definition of it has yet been achieved."[55]

In this study "eschatology" holds its traditional meaning, the doctrine of the "last things", and the emphasis given is that by which the term applies to the "last things" of the world rather than those pertaining to the individual. The consummation of the divine purposes for this earth are contemplated. That this had a "springing and germinant accomplishment" in the work of Christ at His first advent is recognized, but not here stressed. Existential eschatology, decision-in-depth in response to the call of the gospel, is not under discussion.

"Apocalyptic" is commonly used to signify the sudden catastrophic intervention of God in the affairs of earth to right all wrongs and to terminate history. When Albert Schweitzer wrote his <u>Quest</u> he unfortunately selected the term "eschatology" for the description of his main thesis.[56] "Apocalyptic" may have been better, and led to less confusion thereafter, for whereas eschatological has been diversely interpreted, and not always with reference to the catastrophic, apocalyptic when applied to events <u>ever</u> has the sense of dramatic intrusion by suprahistorical forces.

"Apocalyptic" in most modern technical discussions is used with reference to two different phenomena: a type of literature, and the special kind of eschatology therein embodied.[57] As a liter-

11

ary genre apocalyptic separates from prophetic literature in several respects, but nevertheless, no sharp break exists between the two.[58] Isa. 24-27, Joel 2-3, Zech. 9-14 embody certain aspects of apocalyptic, but not others.

Apocalyptic literature has the following characteristics.[59] (1) It is revelatory in a special sense. By means of dreams, visions, or heavenly journeys, the apocalyptist is given knowledge of the future, and other matters not normally accessible to human knowledge. (2) Usually, the visions or dreams described in apocalyptic are a mere literary form, that is, they are fictitious, not real. (3) Pseudonymity is a typical characteristic of apocalyptic, but not necessarily of biblical apocalyptic.

As Ladd points out, Daniel is not akin to most apocalypses at this point. Apart from the stories of the book itself, he is not known in the Old Testament, unless Eze. 14:14,20; 28:3 are interpreted as applying to the Jewish hero of exile. Similarly, the authorship of the last New Testament book is still a matter of dispute, and can hardly be used to support or deny this characteristic. (4) Pseudo-prophecy usually stamps apocalyptic. Not only names from the past, but historical facts are borrowed to be used in the guise of prophecy. The writer poses as living in the distant past, and history is rewritten from that period to the actual present, at which time it becomes vague, except for its portrayal of the imminent kingdom of God. (5) The use of symbolism is a further characteristic implied by the previous reference to visions. The metals and animals, employed by the writer of Daniel to represent empires, is the classic example.

When we turn our attention from the characteristics of apocalyptic literature to those of the apocalyptic eschatology found therein,[60] the following must be included. (1) That kind of dualism which contrasts the present age of suffering and incompleteness with the perfect age to come. The future glory is promised as vindication for all who now are unjustly ravaged. (2) A non-prophetic concept of history. The future is related to the present only by way of contrast. The God who now seems to sleep will "awake" with dramatic suddenness to turn the tide of earthly existence. Once more, the book of Daniel is atypical at this point. It stands nearer to the prophets, with considerable affinity to Wisdom literature, and thus indicates that a sharp division between apocalyptic and prophetic literature is not always possible. (3) Pessimism and determinism. This age with its cast of evil must run its course to a predetermined end. Ethical passivity often grows from such a viewpoint. (4) Apocalyptic eschatology is usually cosmic in scope, rather than restricted to Israel or neighboring powers.[61]

G. E. Ladd, D. S. Russell, and H. H. Rowley are agreed on the main characteristics of apocalyptic, except that Rowley does not always carry through his own recognition of the distinction between apocalyptic as a type of literature and a kind of eschatology.

Is Mark 13 an Apocalypse?

Unfortunately few commentators query the term "apocalypse". C. C. Torrey did, and with some acidity wrote as follows:

> N. P. Williams, in <u>Oxford Studies in the Synoptic Problem</u>, p. 416, concludes: "I cannot feel that the theory which sees in Mk. xiii a Jewish or Jewish Christian Apocalypse . . . rests upon any sure foundations." He adds, however: "It cannot of course be denied that Mark xiii is thoroughly apocalyptic in tone and colour, reproducing the conventional signs of the end which were commonplaces of the current eschatological literature."
>
> This last quotation gives the key to current error of terminology, in its assumption that "eschatological" and "apocalyptic" are synonymous terms, whereas in fact they are quite distinct. The confusion of the two in the present case is especially misleading and mischievous.
>
> The term "apocalypse" has long been employed to designate a definite type of literature, late Jewish or early Christian. The writings of this class possess certain characteristics which are sufficiently distinct to justify the classification. The Greek word ἀποκάλυψις meaning "revelation, unveiling, disclosure," and the like, is in itself vague and capable of a great variety of usage; the literary term, on the contrary, has its own restricted sense, derived from the outstanding features uniformly present in the typical examples of this peculiar literature. The "apocalypse" is a direct revelation of divine truth hitherto unknown, or of future events or conditions not capable of merely human prediction, disclosed by God to some one of his favored servants. This unveiling of secrets is given in the form of a vision or a dream; it could not be given in any other way. The recipient, in his ecstatic condition, may hear the voice of the Most High himself, as in 2 Esdras, chap. 14; but far oftener the disclosure is made through the instrumentality of angels. By the scene itself, or by some strange accessories, there is created an atmosphere of mystery and of the unseen world. No apocalypse, Jewish or Christian, is without these features.[62]

13

Torrey further affirms that when a writer proceeds to foretell the future, particularly naming the signs which are to mark the end of this age he does not become an apocalyptist thereby; especially not if the "signs" given are "an old story". This remark has particular relevance for the study of verses 24-27 of Mark 13 which, of all the chapter, seems closest to apocalyptic.63

The application of the term "apocalypse" to Mark 13 (particularly vv. 5-27) by a large number of commentators may suggest either that exegesis of this chapter has long been characterized by a considerable fuzziness and the tendency to parrot preceding writers without independent thought, or that the term "apocalypse" is being used with considerable latitude, and in the sense of literature containing apocalyptic eschatology.

Closely connected with the matter of defining eschatology and apocalyptic is the question of the relationship existing between prophecy and apocalyptic. What has been said of the characteristics of apocalyptic is here pertinent. We ought not to set forth a complete contrast between the two types of eschatology -- prophetic and apocalyptic. Apocalyptic is a development, frequently an exaggeration, of elements already present in the prophetic presentation of the future. The characteristic difference is often a minus quality rather than a plus. Old Testament prophecy teaches that the Kingdom of God will be ushered in by divine intervention rather than through the natural processes of history,64 and it is this viewpoint which is indispensable to apocalyptic eschatology. Jesus shared this outlook, unless we assume with Vincent Taylor et al. that apocalyptic elements have been inserted into Christ's teachings by an apocalyptic-minded church.65 Nevertheless, Christ did not partake of apocalyptic pessimism regarding history, and herein He stood closer to the prophets.

2. The Origin of the "Olivet Discourse".

a. Place of Apocalyptic in the teachings of Christ

A review of a century of exegesis on Mark 13 shows the pendulum tendency operating. To start with, the prim Victorian era in England, and the Continent with its optimistic sister Weltanschauung, could not view apocalyptic eschatology with anything other than raised eyebrows. An age which boldly affirmed:

> God's in His heaven,
> And all's right with the world

could see little meaning in apocalyptic nightmares. Then came Albert Schweitzer interpreting Jesus in harmony with his understanding of the Sitz im Leben of Palestine in the first century. The result was Christ as an apocalyptic deluded figure, obsessed with the imminent end of the world. The pendulum did not cease to move at this point. Thirty years later it was being strongly contended that the idea of a parousia preceded by signs had been wrongly distilled from Christ's teachings by an apocalyptically-minded church, contrary to Christ's personal beliefs. The Eschaton had already come in Christ, and that was that.[66]

Thus the viewpoint changed as personalities like Harnack, Schweitzer, and moderns such as C. H. Dodd gave place each to the other and dominated the theological scene, at least in certain geographical areas. Thus in answer to the question: "did Jesus hold apocalyptic views?" the answer comes "No", (Harnack); "Yes", (Schweitzer); "No", (Dodd); "Yes", (Bultmann);[67] . . . and so on, according to which scholar answers the question. The Spirit of the Age is at fault, and if spirits could be clothed, the dress of this particular one would best be described as chameleon. More ways than one exist for eviscerating apocalyptic, and not the least persuasive is the suggestion that Christ's mythological expectations for the future are merely incidental, and it is His timeless existential demand that should be recognized and proclaimed.[68]

We need reminding still that we cannot have the same thing both ways. The cake refuses to remain present with us, though eaten. Thus while some would insist that Christ cherished apocalyptic concepts by reminding us that he must have been a child of His time, others assure us that His authentic logia are recognizable only if dissimilar to those of his contemporaries. We shall have to be content with the facts presented in the Gospels if we wish to arrive at a conclusion that will be accurate still when cosmologies and Weltanschauungen change again. We are reminded of Dean Inge's saying that "he who marries the Spirit of the Age will soon be a widower."[69] Attitudes to eschatology have had some revision since 1945[70] but this should not influence us either.

Plummer reminds us that the words ascribed to Jesus in Mark 13 have as good a claim to authenticity as those elsewhere in the Gospels which are accepted by most.[71]

Secondly, it should be recognized that Christ's attitude to the Old Testament presupposes His acceptance of the prophetic and apocalyptic concepts reflected there. There is nothing in Mark 13 that would seem foreign to one who knew the Old Testament well.

Thirdly, the ideas present in Mark 13 are also scattered throughout the Synoptic Gospels in places other than the records

15

of the Olivet discourse. Any criticism which seeks to eradicate
all these is questionable.[72] See Luke 11:49-51; 13:23,27,35;
17:23-37; 18:8; 19:15,43; 20:16; Mt. 7:22; 10:23; 19:28;
21:44; 22:7; 25:31; 26:64; Mk. 14:25,62; 9:1; 8:38; 12:24
ff.

   Possibly the main scandal of apocalyptic is that referred to by
Sanday, five years after the appearance of Schweitzer's book.

   The great point about Apocalyptic, and the great
   value of its recognition to us at the present day, is
   that it postulates throughout a real manifestation of
   God upon earth, and not merely a teacher more eminent
   than the rest.[73]

Sanday also commented: "another great point about the insistence
upon Apocalyptic is, that it is true, by which I mean that it
finds in the Gospels something that is really there, and not
merely read into them from the outside."[74]

   Sanday, of course, made such comments without the insights that
form-criticism and redaction-criticism now offer. Nevertheless,
in essence his remarks remain relevant. Taking into account
form-criticism and redaction-criticism, we are still left with
the choice between believing that the Gospel accounts are the
result of the influence of the church upon Christ's teachings or
the influence of the teachings of Christ upon the early church.
The latter seems as likely as the former. Otto Piper has suggested it is high time that we did away with the myth of a creative community. Epochal concepts do not usually arise in this
way. Genius is inevitably lonely and rarely corporate. " . . .
creative thinking is rarely done by committees."[75] Nevertheless, the New Testament presentation of the Parousia and kindred
themes is not as clear-cut as some would like. There are difficulties which need to be acknowledged. Some scholars such as
C. K. Barrett, J. A. T. Robinson, and T. F. Glasson have suggested that it is unlikely that Jesus ever used the word Parousia
or uttered the equivalent of such expressions as "coming again".
Furthermore, though Jesus foretold (1) His resurrection and (2)
His advent as the Son of Man, there is no saying in which He
speaks of both together. Thus some have asked whether the two
events were, for Him, the one. Streeter pointed out that Q,
Mark, and Matthew provide an ascending scale in their tendency
to intensify Christ's apocalyptic sayings.[76] Did Matthew inject
his own second advent belief where it was not originally present?

   While a good case can be made for the foregoing, the evidence
earlier given of the wide spectrum of evidence from the Gospels
cannot be denied or accommodated to some other view. Christ's
references to His resurrection or return represent alternate ways

of denoting his confidently expected vindication. Very few
scholars indeed would question such clear statements as Luke 17:
26-30; Matthew 25:31-45, or Mark 13:32.

Secondly, it is the clear evidence of history that the early
Christians anticipated the Parousia of Christ. It is easier to
explain that fact on the basis claimed for it, than to explain
the fact away.[77] We must acknowledge that if Christ spoke of
His coming death, He probably did not leave it there. It would
be incredible if Christ knew His death was necessary for the
kingdom, and yet said nothing about His resurrection and Parousia. His death implied His resurrection, and His resurrection
implies His Parousia. This sequence of thought makes comprehensible one of the key claims made by Christ on which all four
Gospels stand in complete agreement: that He was the Son of Man,
the Judge and Saviour.[78]

b. The "Little Apocalypse"

The preceding consideration of the diverse attitudes taken by
exegetes to the eschatological and apocalyptic concepts found in
the Gospels may suggest the chief reason for that "sententia
recepta of synoptic criticism" (Moffatt)[79] that Mark 13 has at
its heart a borrowed Jewish apocalypse rather than authentic
logia of Christ. It is a matter of historical fact that the
hypothesis originated and gained ready acceptance as a result of
prejudice rather than exegesis.

When Timothy Colani wrote his most influential work, Jésus
Christ et les croyances messianiques de son Temps (1864), he did
so with obvious apologetic intent. Previously he had written a
series of articles published over a two year period, criticizing
the work of Renan who had pictured Christ as a puritanical
apocalypticist. Colani laboured to eradicate all evidences of
messianism and eschatology from the teachings of Christ. The
disciples, already indoctrinated with Jewish eschatology, were
the real culprits, Colani pointed out. As for Mark 13, it was
obvious that verses 5-31 were an interpolation inasmuch as the
real answer to the question of the disciples regarding the
temple was found in v. 32. Of course, "If any and every passage
which can be excised from a document without leaving an obvious
gap is therefore liable to be pronounced an interpolation, there
is an end of sane criticism . . . "[80] But, as Beasley-Murray has
shown, "The Little Apocalypse hypothesis is less the product of
an impartial criticism than the last stage of a developing
emotional reaction to a theological problem posed by agnos-
tics."[81] Nevertheless, because Colani's theory offered a welcome option for those embarrassed by the apocalyptic eschatology
of Mark 13, it found a ready, even non-critical, acceptance.
F. W. Beare spoke for many when he said that the controversial

chapter "consists of conventional commonplaces of Jewish apocalyptic literature which can certainly not be ascribed to the mind
of Jesus."[82]

Although such scholars as F. J. A. Hort, J. Weiss, G. Milligan,
A. Plummer, S. R. Driver, C. H. Dodd, E. Haenchen, G. W. Kümmel,
E. Lohmeyer, J. Schmid, L. Hartman, Vincent Taylor, and G. R.
Beasley-Murrey have pronounced the "fly-leaf" hypothesis untenable, it lingers on. Stephen Neill is bold enough to say that
"one of the curious features in German theology is that no ghost
is ever laid."[83] While this particular "ghost" began its haunt-
in France, the more theologically-minded country to the north
soon became its adopted home, coincident with the conferring
thereby of an ideological immortality. Rudolph Pesch[84] is perhaps the latest to rally this particular wraith of Gospel-criti-
cism.

Lars Hartman, in his study of Mark 13, views the "fly-leaf"
theory as an anachronism,[85] and a large number of major commentaries in recent years have either questioned or rejected it.

The only volume which contains an exhaustive treatment of the
subject, pronounces against the "Little Apocalypse" theory.[86]
Beasley-Murray set himself to read everything of note which had
been written on Mark 13 for approximately a century. Practically
every subsequent treatment of Mark 13 alludes to the work of
Beasley-Murray, but as one studies such treatments, the conclusion is forced upon one that the authors who cite Beasley-Murray
have not always read him closely. Suhl[87] refers to Beasley-
Murray but his comments on the "kleine jüdische Apocalypse" and
his use of Hölscher (though a cautious one) indicate that he
either has not read Beasley-Murray closely, or that he still
basically disagrees. Dr. Nikolaus Walter, writing thirteen years
after Beasley-Murray, mentions Hölscher repeatedly and refers to
the "fly-leaf" about ten times,[88] but suggests one thirty years
later than Hölscher does. It is difficult to understand how one
could read in Jesus and the Future the analysis of Hölscher's
article, and yet retain any confidence in Hölscher's position.

In England, the situation is similar to that on the
Continent, if the conflicting statements found in the recent
Peake can be considered typical.[89]

Regarding Beasley-Murray's work one may say, in considering its
reviews and the subsequent use made of it by scholarship, that
his main thesis is as proven as it is possible to prove any
contentious position. Loisy long ago saw the impossibility of
believing that this passage from Mark 13, which was reflected
elsewhere by Q had once existed as a self-contained and complete
entity.[90] Beasley-Murray has gathered and explained the doubts

of many on this subject.

Minor features of <u>Jesus and the Future</u> have been questioned
successfully. There is only inadequate support for the suggestion of textual emendation for Mark 13:14, for example. Some
writing more recently, such as Earle Ellis, would dispute the
interpretation given to Mark 13:34. But on the whole, Dr.
Beasley-Murray's thesis has recommended itself to a significant
range of New Testament scholars.[91] However, it should be
stressed that the abolition of the "Little Apocalypse" theory
does not disprove the composite nature of the discourse, or the
possibility that it contains some elements foreign to the teachings of Christ. Flückiger, in a recent study,[92] suggests that
the "discourse" has been moulded by the interweaving of three
groups of sayings including Jewish apocalyptic as one source.
Furthermore, the work of Marxsen, Conzelmann, and other redaction
critics has led to the viewpoint that considerable emendations to
early Christian traditions have been made by Mark himself.
Scholars, however, who have maintained the essential integrity of
the discourse include Johannes Weiss, Sir E. Hoskyns, Hort,
N. Davey, A. B. Bruce, J. Schniewind, A. M. Farrer, C. Cranfield,
etc.

c. <u>The Framework of the Discourse: Mark 13:1-4</u>

Since the days of Karl Ludwig Schmidt, form-critics, and more
recently redaction-critics, have regarded the majority of introductory statements of place and time in the Gospels as either
largely or solely framework devised by the Evangelists. The
fundamental difference in viewpoint between the form-critics and
the redaction-critics is that the latter have stressed the
theological significance which they believe these connections
possess.

In consequence, most modern commentators suggest that Mark 13:
1-4 is the product of editorial activity rather than a historical
narration.[93] The symbolic significance of the Mount of Olives,
the esoteric implications of private instruction, the seal of
trustworthiness in the names of the big four, the catechetical
question and answer form, all seem to argue for the position of
scholars such as Marxsen etc. If the reference to Jerusalem's
coming destruction is viewed as a <u>vaticinium ex eventu</u> then we
have stronger grounds still for contending that these opening
verses are purely redactional.

Probably this question can never be settled one way or the
other. The techniques of form and redaction criticism, though
undeniably useful, have their "clay feet" as C. F. D. Moule
recently reminded us. Several unproven assumptions underlie
such techniques.[94] In the present instance, perhaps all that

19

can be said is that the most likely reason for the speech being given this setting is that it happened just so.[95] It may be very well that someone in Mark's position possessed factual information which enabled him to rightly link together various pericopae. Furthermore, if there are grounds for viewing the preceding events of the Tuesday of Passion week as essentially historical, there does not seem to be any basic reason for denying the historicity of Mark 13:1-4.[96]

d. Parenthesis of Mark 13:14b

One of the reasons given by Colani and his successors for believing that a small Jewish apocalypse had been incorporated into Mark 13 was the existence of the parenthesis ὁ ἀναγινώσκων νοείτω. Colani asserted that obviously the <u>discourse</u> could not have been such -- the original must have been a <u>document</u>. One cannot say in the middle of a public address "whoso <u>readeth</u> . . . . "

Of course, even if Colani's contention be granted, this would not demonstrate the existence of part of Mark 13 as an independent Jewish apocalypse.[97] Some would suggest that it might indicate the early circulation of a compilation of Christ's genuine sayings, at some time of crisis such as A.D. 40.

On the other hand, prior to the "Little Apocalypse" theory, two independent explanations were available. One was that the parenthesis was the insertion of the Evangelist himself or the previous compiler of the "discourse". This remains the favored interpretation, as shown by the vast majority of commentaries. (Daube has made a good case for showing that Mark thus draws attention to the grammatical anomaly in his verse, the use of the personal participle ἑστηκότα in connection with the preceding neuter phrase.)[98]

The other explanation prior to Colani was that the parenthesis is an admonition by Jesus concerning the need for understanding the source from which He quotes, namely "Daniel the prophet". This view was held in former times by Chrysostom, Euthymius Zigabenus, Paulus, Fritzsche, Kaeuffer, Hengstenberg, Baumgarten-Crusius, Ewald, etc. It harmonized with the fact that the Jews contemporary with Christ believed Dan. 9:24-27 had not yet reached its complete fulfillment. In more recent times, J. Morison upheld this view, and some such as Lambrecht, Swete, Vincent Taylor and Cranfield believe it to be a possible explanation of the admonition in question.

A major objection to such a view is that Mark's version does not actually mention Daniel. In reply, however, it must be said that every intelligent Jew would have recognized the source of

20

the allusion.

> Es ist nicht nötig, das Sätzchen als Einlage
> von der Rede Jesu zu trennen, da mit Zitat aus
> Daniel ein heiliger Text in Sicht ist, den jeder
> Jünger liest.[99]

Jesus, according to Mark, has already used ἀναγινώσκειν three times before. See 12:10; 12:26; 2:25. Christ was in the habit of admonishing His hearers. (4:23 etc.) But we can hardly say Mark was in the habit of admonishing his readers. (Marxsen speaks of Mark 13:14b, as the only case of personal address in the book.) Some consider it unlikely that the Evangelist would be so impertinent as to interrupt the flow of Christ's words by inserting his own.[100] We must also explain why Matthew chose to retain the interpolation of Mark, though this is not insuperable. Furthermore it is doubtful that νοεῖν has the meaning of "note well" so often given to it. Its more probable reference is to intelligent comprehension of something not readily understandable.[101]

A point that needs to be stressed is that the word בין is a key word which recurs frequently in Daniel and is found in the very passage from which Jesus quotes. The angel admonishes Daniel to בין (Dan. 9:23) prior to his mention of the שקוץ (v. 27). See also, Dan. 9:2; 10:1; 12:9-12, and 8:27. The expression, or its equivalents, occurs more than twenty times in the book.

Daube remarks that the term is prominent in the Old Testament, and particularly so in Daniel. While he argues from Rabbinic usage of such expressions to Mark's likely usage, the argument could be made to run from the Old Testament and Rabbinic usage to Christ's.

The question must be left open as to whether we should regard the parenthesis as given by Jesus or inserted by Mark (or the original compiler).[102] But one thing is certain -- the parenthesis gives no support for Colani's hypothesis, and indeed sheds no definite light on the origin of Mark 13, unless we see in it another indication of Christ's masterly use of key Old Testament allusions.

e. The Relationship between Mark 13 and 1 and 2 Thessalonians

Beasley-Murray claimed that when the relationship between Mark 13 and the Epistles to the Thessalonians was more clearly seen, the "Little Apocalypse" theory would encounter heavy seas.[103] Several scholars have drawn up a table of comparisons between the Synoptic accounts of the Olivet discourse and the letters of Paul

21

to the Thessalonians,[104] and while no one today accepts Torrey's dating for Mark, his belief that Paul had access to the contents of Mark 13,[105] is agreed upon by many, as these tables and accompanying discussions show.

Some of the obvious parallels that have been noted are as follows:

Thessalonians	Synoptic Accounts
1 Thess. 4:15-17	Mk. 13:26-27 Mt. 24:31
" 5:1-5	" 13:32,33
" 5:6-8	" 13:35,36
" 5:4-10	" 13:22
2 Thess. 1:3-5	" 13:9-13
" 1:6-10	" 13:26-27
" 1:11-12	Lk. 21:36
" 2:1-2	Mk. 13:26-27
" 2:3	" 13:5 Mt. 24:12
" 2:4-6	" 13:14
" 2:7	Mt. 24:12
" 2:8-12	Mk. 13:22
" 2:13	" 13:27
" 2:15	" 13:23

We do not believe that Paul had access to Mark's Gospel as Torrey assumes, but the evidence is conclusive that he did have the same oral or written traditions which Mark later incorporated in his Gospel. Some form of Mark 13 circulated as an authoritative παράδοσις some years before 50 A.D. Paul knew it before his mission in Thessalonica, and had instructed the believers therefrom.[106]

There can be no real doubt that the early church specially cherished not only the record of the Passion and the Resurrection, but also its traditions regarding the Parousia. From the beginning these would have been circulated orally, and probably also in written form, to inspire and maintain hope among those who longed to behold their absent Lord. Particularly in crises, when the signs of the times seemed to shout with greater than usual urgency, would such traditions have done more than double work. A typical occasion would have been the time when Caligula's proud design to enshrine his statue in the temple provoked apocalyptic fever among both Jews and Christians. If the reference cited in Mk. 13:14 was considered as a logion of Christ, that logion would have dominated the thinking of thousands. Mk. 13 may well have originated at this time, as a compilation of the genuine sayings of Christ on the future.[107] This would explain its ready availability to Paul before his visit to Thessalonica.

f. The Relationship between Mark 13 and other Synoptic parallels such as Luke 12:35-46; Luke 17:24-37; Luke 21, Matthew 10:17-22, Matthew 24

The criterion of multiple attestation suggested by N. Perrin[108] for testing supposed words of Christ, has bearing on the study of the eschatological chapter in Mark. Therefore we ask: "Is the substance of the Olivet discourse attested by independent accounts?"

Obviously Matthew 24 and Luke 21 parallel Mark 13, but the issue is clouded because of the dependence of the first two Gospels on the third. Is there evidence that Luke and/or Matthew drew on transmitted traditions separate from Mark's Gospel?

Let us first consider Luke's account. F. C. Burkitt wrote long ago "What concerns us here is not that Luke has changed so much, but that he has invented so little."[109] Thus he speaks of Luke's use of Mark as a whole, but the comment has bearing on Luke's use of Mk. 13. Are the differences to be accounted for in terms of redaction?

Usually today it is affirmed that while Mark makes the fall of Jerusalem an eschatological event, Luke, on the contrary, historicizes it, separating it from the distant advent.

This, however, is an exaggerated picture. In Luke 21, the fate of the Holy City is still considered an eschatological event. As Mark described the tribulation associated with the βδέλυγμα as followed by cosmic signs and then the coming of the Lord, so does Luke.

Luke, indeed, does point to an interval before the Parousia by his phrase in ch. 21:9. οὐκ εὐθέως τὸ τέλος   But there is little difference between this statement and Mark's. οὔπω τὸ τέλος.   If, as Ellis argues, γενεά means the last generation as a term covering several lifetimes, then both Mark 13:30 and Luke

23

21:32 indicate that the readers live in eschatological time,[110] but the evidence for the position of Ellis is not impressive.

Luke sets forth a number of sayings in which the perils associated with the End are relevant for Christ's contemporaries. Luke 6:20-26; Luke 9:26; 12:8f., 40; 18:8; 11:29-32; 13:25-30; 14:14,15-24; 16:9; 18:24; cf. 19:11-27; 22:28-30; 18:8. Thus it does not appear correct to say that Luke, in ch. 21 or elsewhere, anticipates the future in a way different from Mark. Therefore, the grounds for saying that Luke has editorialized Mark 13 to make his special point are slight indeed. His καιροὶ ἐθνῶν are identical with the θλῖψις of Mark 13, and is an allusion to Dan. 8:13. This expression according to many commentators is part of Luke's key redaction, though this is not a necessary conclusion.

On the other hand, there is considerable evidence that Luke used a source other than Mark for this eschatological chapter.[111] A number of elements in Luke 21 are more easily explained on this basis than on any other.

1. The introduction in Luke assumes ignorance of the setting of the discourse, rather than a change. It is obvious that a discourse such as this would not have been publicly delivered.

2. Luke's omission of the mention of the Holy Spirit in the passage vv. 13-15 is uncharacteristic. The Gospel as a whole makes much of pneumatological allusions.

3. θρὶξ ἐκ τῆς κεφαλῆς ὑμῶν οὐ μὴ ἀπόληται would hardly have been devised by an editor after the Neronic persecutions, for it seems inevitable that his readers would have seen the promise as general even if first related to Christians in Jerusalem.[112]

4. Vv. 20-24 are poetic in form, and depend on Old Testament scriptures. It is not likely that Luke is the source of this format.

5. V. 28 is original with this account and seems an authentic saying placed appropriately.

6. If, as Perry believes, Luke's passion narrative had an independent source, it is possible that the eschatological narrative had likewise.[113]

Hartman suggests that only with some difficulty can the differences in 21:12-14,18,20,22,24-26a,28 be explained as editorial changes. He criticizes Conzelmann's attempted explanations as "not entirely successful", and gives an extended discussion. Luke's relationship with the Old Testament also

24

suggests a different version of the eschatological discourse, in addition to Mk. 13.[114]

Let us briefly consider Matthew's account. This Evangelist habitually groups sayings topically, and the conjunction of the advent parables in ch. 25 is not unexpected. Ch. 24 follows Mk. 13 more closely than does Luke 21. The most well-known issue regarding his version is the displacement of Mk. 13:11-13 by vv. 9-12, and his usage of the former passage in the mission discourse. See 10:17-22. Whether this is actually displacement, whether both discourses originally contained both sections, and other possibilities, are beyond proving.[115]

Bacon believes that for the most part the Matthaean variants have not the "slightest claim to be considered original" but . Beasley-Murray and others doubt whether the problem is quite so simple.[116]

Other parallel passages in Luke and Matthew such as Lk. 12:35-47 and Mt. 24:42-51; Lk. 17:23-37, and Mt. 24:37-41 confirm the evidence of the three major Synoptic accounts that more than a single tradition of the Olivet discourse lies behind the Synoptic accounts.[117] We probably have at least three which are in substantial agreement and which therefore strongly support the authenticity of the tradition. Time, place, and content factors for the most part are reinforced by a three-fold cord.

g. Relationship to the Apocalypses of Judaism

It has been too readily assumed that Mark 13 parallels typical Jewish apocalypses. He who takes this position, however, thereby shows he has read few such documents.[118] Mark 13 does indeed contain references to matters which are part of the "stock-in-trade" of Jewish apocalyptic writings, but, for the most part, the Gospel presentation is distinguished by its dissimilarity.

We footnote similarities, indicating from the Old Testament, the Apocrypha and the Pseudepigrapha similar references to the Synoptic account.[119]

1. . . .πολέμους καὶ ἀκοὰς.
Compare Isa. 19:2; Zech. 14:13. See also 1 Enoch 100:1-2; Testament of Judah 22:1-2; 4 Ezra 5:9; 6:24; 4 Ezra 9:3. Note particularly the Apocalypse of Baruch 70:3-7 which reads:

And they shall hate one another, and provoke one another to fight, and the mean shall rule over the honourable, and those of low degree shall be extolled above the famous . . . Then shall confusion fall upon all men, and some of them shall fall in battle, and

some of them shall perish in anguish, and some of
them shall be destroyed by their own.

2. . . . ὁ ἥλιος σκοτισθήσεται, καὶ ἡ σελήνη οὐ δώσει τὸ φέγγος
αὐτῆς, καὶ οἱ ἀστέρες ἔσονται. . .

Compare Amos 5:18-20; Zeph. 1:15; Joel 2:2; Isa. 13:10; Joel
2:30-31; 3:15-16. See also 1 Enoch 80:4-8; Sibylline Oracles
3:83-89, 796-806; Testament of Levi 4:1; Assumption of Moses
10:4-6; 4 Ezra 5:4. The last is representative of the rest when
it says: "Then shall the sun suddenly shine forth by night and
the moon by day . . . "

3. εἰς πάντα τὰ ἔθνη πρῶτον δεῖ κηρυχθῆναι το εὐαγγέλιον.

Compare Isa. 2:2-4; 45:20-22; 25:6-8; 49:6; 51:4; 55:5; 56:6-8.
See also 1 Enoch 48:4-5; Testament of Levi 18:5-9; Psalms of
Solomon 17:34; Sibylline Oracles 3:710-723.

4. ἐπισυνάξει τοὺς ἐκλεκτοὺς

Compare Isa. 11:11; 27:12,13; 1 Baruch 4:36-37; Pss. of Solomon
11:3.

5. ὁ υἱὸς τοῦ ἀνθρώπου . . .

Compare Gen. 1:26; Ps. 8; Dan. 7:13. Because the Similitudes
of Enoch is probably syncretistic, containing Christian elements,
its parallels to Mark 13:26 are not here cited. 4 Ezra 13, which
originated about the time of Mark's Gospel or within a matter of
decades, reinterprets Daniel 7 and presents the "Son of Man" as
the messianic deliverer.

6. τὸ βδέλυγμα τῆς ἐπημώσεως ἐστηκότα ὅπου οὐ δεῖ.

The parallels to this passage are enlarged upon in the subsequent chapters of this thesis. For the present we would point
out that Mk. 13:14 with its apparent reference to a personal
power (ἐστηκότα) standing in the holy place has been understood
by a large number of commentators to apply to Antichrist. While
this latter term first appears in 1 Jn. 2:18, the concept is much
earlier, being traceable not only to Dan. 7-12, but also to Eze.
38-39 and other O.T. passages. In non-canonical Jewish writings
the idea is probably present in such passages as The Assumption
of Moses 8:1ff; Pss. of Solomon 2:29; 2 Bar. 40:1ff; 4 Ez. 5:6;
Test. of Iss. 6:1; Test. of Dan 5:10; Test. of Judah 25:3; Sib.
Or. 3:63ff.

Despite the parallels existing between Mark 13 and the Pseudepigrapha, the contrasts are boundless. Mark 13 is chaste and

26

restrained when compared with much of Jewish apocalyptic material. The latter, in terms of the imagination, draws no punches. The Synoptic presentation of eschatological events is tantalizing in what it leaves unsaid. In Mark 13 we are not told what will happen to Antichrist and his hosts, neither is the reward of the righteous pictured in other than general terms.

The chief distinction, however, between Mark 13 and typical apocalyptic literature is the presence of parenesis. This is now an old story, that it is rare for paranesis to be embedded in apocalyptic material outside of Scripture. Even the use of the second person plural as the constant form of address is unusual![120]

The first word of Christ's discourse is βλέπετε . It is also the last, and rings like a refrain throughout the chapter. See vv. 7,9,11,23,33,35,37. Thus the motivation of this apocalypse, when compared with the non-canonical variety, is distinctive. It does not appeal to hope's cupidity, nor to the desire for vengeance. It calls instead for ethical alertness. Here is no precise time-table of events. In fact, the presentation seems exactly contrary to the main tenor that human nature would have prescribed. This cannot be said for Jewish apocalyptic in general.

3. The Apparent Contradiction of Q materials by Mark 13

Apart from the influence of presuppositions, the most important factor discrediting the authenticity of Mark 13 is its presentation of "signs" of the approaching end, in apparent contradiction to such passages as Lk. 17:20-37; 12:35-48, and Mt. 12:39.

Vincent Taylor declares that Mark views Christ's teachings "through the veil of apocalyptic."[121] Thus, Mark presents the advent as being preceded by visible signs of war, earthquake, famine, persecution, celestial portents, etc. But, says Taylor, "all this is so different from Luke xvii. 22ff., that we are entitled to suspect the transposition of the original tradition into another key."[122]

When T. W. Manson sets out to discuss the eschatological teaching of Jesus, we are first reminded that Mark 13 cannot be made the starting point of investigation. Because the "early Church was certainly obsessed by the idea of the imminent return of the Lord" there is nothing strange in the idea that a document purporting to give Christ's words regarding the advent should have circulated, and later been incorporated in Mark's Gospel. However, what Manson calls the vital point is the fact that the description given in Mark 13 "does not square with the account given by our other sources, notably Q, or with the other statements of Paul."[123]

27

The two pictures are declared "irreconcilable".[124]

   To the objections by Taylor and Manson can be added those of
T. F. Glasson, C. K. Barrett, and J. A. T. Robinson. Such writers
understood Mk. 13:27 as initially signifying Christ's vindication
by His resurrection and ascension. Dan. 7:13 seems to speak more
of an ushering into the presence of God than of a descent to
earth.[125] However, in this particular section we are concerned
with the major objection offered by Taylor and Manson, and this
primarily calls for an examination of Lk. 17:20ff.

   Two things should first be said. One, Jewish apocalyptic
already believed in an end that would come suddenly and yet be
preceded by signs. Montefiore witnesses to this,[126] although at
another time he seems to have forgotten the fact.[127] Obviously,
the two ideas are not irreconcilable. We must not confuse
immediacy and imminence. Signs can indicate a relative time,
without revealing the specific day or hour. Secondly, critics
have not balked at the fact that Paul and the writer of Revelation
have the same conjunction of ideas. I Thess. 5:1,2 reminds the
Thessalonians of the abruptness with which Christ shall come, but
it also takes it for granted that the believers have some
knowledge of χρόνων. . .καιρῶν.   2 Thess. 2 has the same
relationship present. The Thessalonians are reminded of the sign
of the apostasy which must precede the Lord's sudden appearance
in glory. In Revelation, we have a catena of signs and yet the
warning ἰδοὺ ἔρχομαι ταχύ.

   Loisy declared, "Cependant, savoir que la parousie est proche,
et ne pas savoir le jour où elle se produira, sont choses
conciliables".[128] Kümmel also affirms the same. " . . . both
conceptions -- the end comes suddenly, and it is historically
prepared for -- go together and are viewed together in the apocalypticism of Judaism and primitive Christianity."[129]

   One of the most interesting discussions of Luke 17 is given by
Rudolph Otto. He quotes from K. L. Schmidt's article in Kittel's
TWNT regarding "this much discussed and much tortured saying of
Jesus", and then adds concerning Schmidt, "He then continues the
torture. He says it has its point solely in the rejection of
calculation of omens."[130] Otto proceeds[131] by arguing that the
passage in Luke 17 is another example of paradox in the teachings
of Christ, and that the refusal to offer or promise signs was no
real contradiction of Christ's words elsewhere.[132]

   With great directness Otto adds:

      It would probably be impossible to find a better
      example than this exegete of one influenced by a
      prejudice which has grown to be a dogma, and which

compels the observer to see awry, and to fail to
appreciate the unique element of an original conception
which is plainly to be seen in this utterance of Jesus
besides others already examined.[133]

In Luke 17, to the Pharisees, Christ speaks of a kingdom already
in their midst,[134] but to His own disciples He speaks of the
future kingdom of glory. The point made is not that this kingdom
will come without signs, but that it will be sudden and unexpected
for a world which, like that of Noah's day, is given up to things
of the flesh. As destruction came suddenly to the inhabitants of
Sodom and Gomorrah despite warnings from Lot, who understood the
signs of the times, so will it be at the end of the age. This
explanation of Lk. 17 harmonizes with Mark 13:34 which admonishes
the disciples of the impossibility of pin-pointing the exact
moment of the Parousia, and yet urges them γρηγορῆσαι.

There is no real contradiction between Mark 13 and the teachings
of the Q materials or other passages of the New Testament.

4. The Problem posed by the Congruence (or Incongruence) of vv.
28-30 with v. 32, and other "Inconsistencies"

Those who see in Mark 13 a tissue of inconsistencies[135] assume
that the Gospel compiler nodded at his work and failed to note the
melange resulting. Marxsen challenges the assumption:

> Aber dass Markus hier ein solches Durcheinander
> verschiedener Meinungen komponiert oder reproduziert
> haben sollte, nur um auch eine Apokalypse zu bieten,
> --das glaube, wer mag.
>
> . . . Richtig Busch . . ." . . . Die vielverbreitete
> Meinung, Mk. 13 bilde ein 'sich stark widersprechendes
> Ganzes' . . . ist ein Vorurteil, das deutlicher Korrektur
> bedarf."[136]

These comments come from a redaction critic who, of course,
believes in the original piecemeal nature of the materials
incorporated by Mark.

The main incongruency seems to consist in the near relationship
of vv. 28-30 and 32. ὅταν ἤδη ὁ κλάδος αὐτῆς ἁπαλὸς γένηται καὶ
ἐκφύῃ τὰ φύλλα. γινώσκετε ὅτι ἐγγὺς τὸ θέρος ἐστίν. . . .περὶ
δὲ τῆς ἡμέρας ἐκείνης ἢ τῆς ὥρας οὐδεὶς οἶδεν. . . .

What has been said regarding the signs of Mark 13 being opposed
to statements of Luke 17 applies here also. Signs which point to

29

a relative period do not negate ignorance of the specific day of Christ's appearance. "The emphasis is not on the immediacy of the End but on its suddenness as in I Thess. 5:12."[137]

Even the parable of vv. 26-30 includes the thought of suddenness.[138] In Palestine, where the spring is short, the transition from winter rains to summer happens abruptly, almost overnight. This concept parallels Luke 17:24-30 where Christ's appearance is compared to a lightning flash, the flood in Noah's day, and the destruction of Sodom. Thus "the signs" point to a period of time during which believers may be aware that Christ could come "at any moment".

Another "inconsistency" of Mark 13 is that Christ's reply seems to be unrelated to the question put to Him by the disciples.[139] The major portion of the chapter relates to the end of the world, while the opening verses speak of the fate of Jerusalem's temple. In a famous comparison, T. W. Manson affirmed that "The ruthless suppression by a great military empire of an insane rebellion in an outlying part of its territory has as much or as little to do with the coming of the Kingdom of God in power as the suppression of the Indian Mutiny."[140] Thus in the Olivet discourse, we have a sudden shift from the local to the universal, from the temporal to the eternal, and from the historical to the supernatural. Such is the problem. What is offered by way of reply?

Firstly, it has already been shown that Christ's reply does concern the temple. There is no way of dissociating v. 14 from the sanctuary.

In Daniel the שׁקוּץ is always linked with the temple. Matthew clearly saw this, and chose a synonym, which throughout the Bible is used for the sanctuary.[141]

Secondly, in Jewish thought the coming of the Messiah was an event which would bring about the establishment of the new temple and the destruction of the old was not the minor event Manson suggests. " . . . already in Tg. on Isa 53:5 (Str-B I, 482) the Messiah builds the house of the sanctuary, cf. also Tg. on Zech. 6:12f. (Str-B I, 94) . . . there is no Jerusalem without the temple."[142] Thus the picture of v. 26 is actually an allusion to the return of the Shekinah glory, and the vindication of the saints at the setting up of a New Jerusalem temple.[143]

Thirdly, this criticism regarding the mingling of the local and the universal, etc. seems to ignore the same familiar practice by the Old Testament prophets. For example, Joel's description of a locust plague upon Judah broadens out into a description of the judgment of the whole world, and Zephaniah's foretelling of a local "day of the Lord" swells into the scene of a universal punishment. Isaiah, too, can swiftly pass from the temporal devastation of the nation to the catastrophic destruction of the face of the earth.[144]

A third "inconsistency", and this time an inconsistency with fact rather than one in mere verbal appearance, is that the discourse makes the End appear imminent; it will engulf that generation, whereas more than forty generations have come and gone since.

But this problem too is of a piece with the entire biblical presentation. Nowhere in the Old or New Testaments is the coming of the Lord characterized as subject to apparently unending delay. That type of expression is explicitly condemned in Mt. 24:48.

Furthermore, there is more than one way of measuring proximity. As far as the New Testament is concerned, the events at the close of the Old Testament era, the death of Christ and the fall of Jerusalem, were the beginning of the End. They were the first act in the drama of the end time, and the last act would be the Parousia. The period of the church age is characterized as "the last time", "the end of the world", "the last hour". The church itself is that generation which will not pass till all be fulfilled. It lives in "lover's time" which is not reckoned by the clock. In Cullmann's famous analogy, the Cross was D-Day, and the Parousia will be V-Day. Certainly the New Testament is agreed in this emphasis. Even in John's Gospel with its strong emphasis on "realized eschatology", the expectation of an ultimate end and the ushering in of a new age remains accepted doctrine.[145] However, despite these suggestions, we believe the real solution to be otherwise, and we reserve its elaboration for part two of this study.[146]

Lastly it should be said that the Bible-writers never distinguish as we do between Historie and Geschichte. For them, the supernatural was ever at work in the natural, and thus there is no real hiatus in a biblical writer's description of history which terminates in a supernatural event. In reviewing the whole, it must be said that we may disagree with the philosophy of the Bible writers, but we can hardly accuse them of inconsistency at this point.

5. The Composition Dates of the Synoptic Gospels

The positions taken on this issue influence to a large degree one's interpretation of Mark 13. Conzelmann, for example, believes the prophecy of v. 2 was made before A.D. 70, but the chapter itself redacted after A.D. 70. N. Walter also places the composition of the Gospel after Jerusalem's fall. This view

31

leads sometimes to subtle theorizing regarding Mark's purpose or meaning, which could not be entertained if the Gospel were dated earlier. Marxsen places the time of writing just prior to the end of the temple, a position indispensable for his thesis.

The majority of scholars assign the period of 65-75 A.D. for Mark, while Luke and Matthew are placed usually in the ninth decade of the era. By far the most striking fact about the dating of the last two Synoptics is that near certainty is made attainable from very slender evidence.

C. F. D. Moule has pointed out that "there is extremely little in the New Testament later than A.D. 70. It has yet to be demonstrated beyond doubt that Matthew's Gospel is later."[147] He points out that Mt. 22:7, which is usually considered a post-eventum reference to the destruction of Jerusalem need not be more than the use of a well-established 'topos' in Rabbinic literature.[148]

The chief reason for the affirming by many of the late date of Luke is his replacing of "the abomination of desolation" by "Jerusalem compassed with armies" in Lk. 21:20. It is assumed that this also is a post-eventum reference, but it is not explained why Matthew, an apparently contemporaneous production, does not use the same clarity of language. Other possibilities, such as envisioned by Harnack and others, exist to explain Luke's different wording. Christ may have used both expressions, and Luke selected that which was simplest for his Gentile readers, or he may merely have paraphrased. On the other hand, the possibility exists that it was Mark and Matthew who paraphrased, giving an apocalyptic note, though this is less likely. If Christ could borrow such expressions as "the kingdom of heaven" and "the Son of Man" from Daniel, there is no reason to deny His use of "the abomination of desolation".

Another reason for the late date ascribed to Luke by some is the assumption that there was a crisis in the early church over the long delay of the Parousia, and that Luke wrote to meet this crisis by providing a historical programme of salvation, including the church era. Such a crisis, it is assumed, took place after A.D. 70, for Luke looks back at the destruction of Jerusalem, and regards it as historical rather than eschatological. However, evidence for the supposed crisis is lacking. Those who have accepted at least part of Schweitzer's Consistent Eschatology such as Martin Werner, Grässer, and Conzelmann, have not provided such.[149]

Other arguments for the late dating of Luke include the assumption that because Luke wrote after many others, his own literary production must have been later. But there could well

have been a spate of literary activity long before A.D. 70. Also
it is often argued that the period between Luke and Matthew was
probably not great, and inasmuch as Matthew belongs to the ninth
decade, so must Luke. This, of course, is arguing in a circle,
and is based on unproven assumptions.

The Synoptic problem, as implied, has bearing on the dating for
all three Gospels. When we enquire as to the nature of other
evidence, we find the data very slight indeed. While the evidence for Mark's priority to most investigators seems overwhelming, and likewise Matthew's and Luke's use of Mark -- when
this has been said, not much more can be added that has definite
bearing on the composition date for Matthew and Luke.

For the dating of Mark, much depends upon the philosophical
assumptions of the investigator as well as upon the objective
problem of finding a suitable Sitz im Leben. If it is taken for
granted that prediction is impossible, or that it is unlikely
that Jesus shared the insight of others who rightly interpreted
signs on the horizon -- then a date this side of the fall of
Jerusalem will consequently be allotted. This position once
assumed then leads to a date in the eighties at earliest for the
other Gospels, because of their dependence upon Mark. On the
other hand, if we refuse to negate the possibility of Christ's
prescience regarding the crisis of A.D. 70, then an earlier date
for Mark may be ascribed. This would harmonize with other
grounds suggested by a large number of exegetes for a date in the
sixties.

In summary, we would say that if truth is discovered by
counting hands, it is certain that Matthew and Luke belong to the
ninth decade of the first century, or later. But if the same
criterion is used for fixing upon the date of Mark then yesterday's "truth" will be no longer such tomorrow, inasmuch as there
is an increasing trend towards the dating of Mark after A.D. 70.
Scholars may need to ponder the words of Moule previously quoted
that "there is extremely little in the New Testament later than
A.D. 70." It will take time to test the validity of J.
O'Callaghan's recent contentions[150] which would date Mark's
Gospel considerably earlier than usually suggested, but whether
his "evidence" from Qumran proves to be rightly interpreted by
him or not, we believe his conclusions regarding the date for the
Gospel at least leans in the right direction.

6. The Specific Purpose, or Purposes, of Mark's Gospel, and of
   Chapter 13 in particular

One's decision on this issue affects all subsequent exegesis of
the Gospel. Marxsen's comments on ch. 13 best illustrate this
fact. He views the Evangelist as urging Jewish Christians to

flee to Galilee from Judea to await the Parousia. Thus for him, Mk. 13:14 is the <u>Angelpunkt</u> on which the whole chapter turns, and possibly the whole book also. If, however we consider the criticisms by Rohde, Knigge, Schweizer,[151] and others to be legitimate, we are led to question many of Marxsen's comments on the Olivet discourse and the entire Gospel.

Martin Kähler's remark that "the Gospels may be called Passion stories with an extended introduction"[152] is often quoted. Certain it is that for each Evangelist the Gospel was in essence a relation of the progress of Jesus to the Cross. Some refinements in terms of purpose are, as indicated above, given significance in the modern discussion. Recent investigations endeavor to answer the questions: What specific needs of the community was this particular work written to satisfy? What is the third <u>Sitz im Leben</u> of these materials? The answers should explain, in part at least, why each Evangelist chose as he did from the traditions at hand, and why he arranged his selections in the finished form available to us.

Is Mark's Gospel intended to be: (1) a reliable account of the ministry, accurate in its chonology and order of events; (2) a patch-work presentation embodying oral materials with artificial connections only; (3) primarily a theological work intended to develop:

a. the Messianic Secret (non-Wrede variety),

b. Pauline theology,

c. a cyclic arrangement whereby the earlier narratives prefigure the later events of the Passion and resurrection,

d. a liturgical scheme, outlining individual pericopes to be read in public worship on certain Sundays of the year,

e. a revelation of Galilee as the favoured land of Jesus,

f. the presentation of Christ as God's agent winning the decisive struggle against evil powers?

The criticism of recent years has not only rejected Wrede's presentation of the Messianic Secret, but it has also refused entire acceptance for any of the above except (a) in a form which contrasts with Wrede, namely Christ's true nature was hidden till the Cross, and only gradually perceived. <u>Mark is neither as "sloppy" or as subtle as some would make him.</u> He certainly does not aim at precision in all matters of chronology or geography,

34

yet the outline is adequate in both senses for reconstructing a sketch of Christ's ministry.[153] As a writer Mark does not reflect the technical literary refinements of modern times. Neither is he without care and purpose in selection and arrangement.

V. Taylor is probably right in saying that Mark reflects the catechesis of the church for which it was written. Certainly it is most significant that the richest concentration of christological and soteriological material is found in the second half of the Gospel. Mark 8:34-38 is the tract's thematic heart. Addressing a church threatened with continuing Gentile persecution,[154] the Gospel shows that there is a cross for every believer as well as for the Master, and it has therefore been described as the "Martyr's Gospel". Probably, we can get no closer to our question regarding the third Sitz-im-Leben than thus to refer to a believing community in an alien and hostile world, needing catechetical instruction and strengthening exhortation.

So much for the purpose of the Gospel as a whole. But why did the Evangelist include his thirteenth chapter? It is the only place in Mark where we find Christ delivering a long speech on a single theme. It is the only lengthy discourse that is recorded by all three of the Synoptics, and all three use it as the climax to that section of the Gospel they were responsible for writing, that is, it comes just before the Passion narrative which already circulated as a separate unity. Mark's tract would have seemed tolerably complete without the Olivet discourse. But, on the other hand, there was no more appropriate time in the ministry of Christ when such instruction could be given.[155]

Nineham agrees with Loisy, Guignebert, Dodd, Lightfoot and Beasley-Murray in recognizing the strategic relief in which the events of Christ's life and death are placed by this interposed address on the return of Him who seemed but another Rabbi. He suggests that this discourse "brings out the infinite significance the Evangelist saw in the events of the ministry."[156] It is only because the ministry of Christ is God's ultimate saving intervention in time that it will be followed by the End and the coming of God's kingdom.

Just as the Gospel as a whole seems to have catechetical purposes, and, in particular, aims at strengthening those who must suffer for Christ's sake, so with this chapter. It gives Christ's own instructions regarding the anticipated end of Jerusalem and the world, but in particular, it displays a theologia crucis rather than a theologia gloria.[157] This would act as an appropriate rebuke to those whose zeal outstripped their good sense as they fervently expected Christ's imminent

appearing but shunned daily duty. And simultaneously the
admonitions would have encouraged the more balanced believers.

R. P. Martin has suggested that this Gospel sets forth "the
paradox of Jesus' earthly life in which suffering and vindication
form a two-beat rhythm" and S. Schulz speaks of the "pattern of
humiliation and exaltation."[158] This pattern is obvious in the
Olivet discourse. While the first two-thirds of Mark 13 speaks
of evil times, of seducers, betrayal, and suffering, the account
is balanced by the picture of the vindicating Lord coming in the
clouds of heaven to gather his oppressed elect. Mark 13:26 would
convey to the early Christians the same consolation as did Dan.
7:13 to the persecuted remnant in Maccabean times.

Various key-words of the chapter reappear in the following
description of the Passion in such a way as to teach that the
disciples' course must be similar to their Lord's, and that there
is no path to glory except via the Cross.

7. The Contextual Setting of Mark 13 - Literary and Chronological

We are here concerned with the relationship between Mk. 13 and
the chapters which precede and follow it.[159]

Of great significance is the fact that the theme of the chapter
-- Judgment -- coincides with the pattern of the preceding events
in Passion Week,[160] as traced not only in Mark, but also the
other Synoptics. Christ's pronouncement of divine visitation
upon Jerusalem at the time of His triumphal entry, the cleansing
of the temple, the cursing of the fig-tree, the utterances of
judgment parables -- vineyard and rejected stone, the marriage of
the King's son, the woes on the Pharisees; all take place as a
series of thunder claps of Judgment. Note particularly the
following verses: Lk. 19:41-44; Mt. 21:12, 19,41-44; 22:7,11-14;
23:32-39, see Mark chapters 11 and 12.

It is obvious that the prediction regarding the destruction of
the temple is perfectly coherent with the preceding pericopes.
Judgment as foretold by words and actions is now crystallized
into an extended discourse on the same topic. The pronouncement:
ἀφίεται ὑμῖν ὁ οἶκος ὑμῶν   is a further comment on Luke 19:
41-44, and itself finds explanation in Mk. 13:1,2,14.

Let us now relate the chapter to the close of the Gospel. R.
H. Lightfoot, Austin Farrer, Grundmann, H. W. Bartsch,[161] and
others have pointed out the correspondence in motifs and terminology between ch. 13 and the succeeding passion chapters. The
most prominent include the following:

παραδίδομαι   three times 13:9,11,12

36

	ten times chs. 14,15
γρηγορέω	Mk. 13 <u>passim</u>. compare 14:34,37
ὥρα	13:32 compare 14:35,41

Thus 13:32-37 acts as a transition to the narrative of the Passion,[162] particularly the section of 14:33-42. In Gethsemane, three of the same four disciples mentioned in 13:3, are given the command to γρηγορέω. The word γρηγορέω occuring in both passages indicates that the Passion began the troubles predicted in chapter 13, thus placing the apostles in Christ's succession on the path to glory via sorrow and crucifixion.

Not only is Mark 13 linked to the preceding and following chapters by the themes of judgment and suffering, but its temple allusions also place it in literary and logical connection with these chapters. <u>Each of the five chapters of Mark covering Passion Week, refer to the temple.</u> See 11:11,15-17; 12:10,33, 41-44; 13:1-4,14; 14:58; 15:38. Mark, writing in the last decade before Jerusalem's fall, is familiar with the concept of the church as the new temple.[163] Even in Qumran the concept of the community as the temple was known. Paul gave expression to the idea repeatedly in his epistles which had circulated widely before Mark's Gospel. And as in Acts 15:14-19 the fallen booth of David's house is said to be raised up by the influx of Gentiles into the church, so the forsaken temple of Israel found its fulfillment in the church as the new temple.

Viewed from this standpoint, Mark 13 warned that the attack to be made shortly on the temple at Jerusalem would be followed by a continuing tribulation for the church-temple, one that would not cease till He came who is the True Tabernacle Himself.[164] The promise of the advent of Christ as the returning Shekinah links the themes of the chapters preceding and following the thirteenth. Judgment is two-sided, and brings not only punishment to the impenitent, but vindication to the suffering remnant.[165] Thus the contextual setting of Mark 13 argues for its value and authenticity.

FOOTNOTES FOR CHAPTER ONE

1. C. H. Dodd, "The Fall of Jerusalem and the Abomination of
Desolation", More New Testament Studies (Manchester, 1968), 70,
comments: "Recent trends in criticism seem to call for a more
radical reconsideration of the question than it has (to my
knowledge) yet received." Despite the passage of twenty-five
years since the statement was first made, this plea for continued
study of the Olivet discourse still has relevance, as the following references indicate. "This passage presents the exegete with
difficulties as great as any in the Gospel." D. E. Nineham, The
Gospel of Saint Mark (London, 1963), 351. (Hereinafter referred
to as Saint Mark). "No one quite knows what the desolating
abomination is." William Barclay, Matthew (Daily Study Bible)
(Edinburgh, ²1958), II, 338. "Une crux interpretationis célèbre."
B. Rigaux, "βδέλυγμα τῆς ἐρημώσεως Mk. 13:14; Mt. 24:15", Bib,
XL (1959), 675. "Dans les Évangiles, il n'est sans doute pas de
passage plus obscur que le discours de Jésus sur la ruine du
temple rapporté par les trois synoptiques." André Feuillet, "Le
discours de Jésus sur la ruine du temple d'après Marc XIII et Luc
Xxi, 5-36", RB, LV (1948), 481. "Mark 13 is the biggest problem
in the Gospel." A. M. Hunter, The Gospel According to St Mark
(London, 1948), 122. " . . . one of the unsolved problems of
New Testament exegesis." Vincent Taylor, "The Apocalyptic
Discourse of Mark XIII", ET, LX (1948), 94.

2. "Dafür lässt sich nun auch die Bedeutungsgeschichte der
Vokabel ἐρήμωσις geltend machen, die ganz durch die LXX (vgl.
Lev 26,34f.; 2 Chr 30,7; 1 Esr 1,55; Ps 72,19; Jer 4,7;7,34;
8,22; 22,5; 32,18; 51,6.22; DanLXX 8,13; 9,18.27; 11,31; 12,11;
DnTh 8,13; 9,2.27; 12,11; 1 Makk 12,11) geprägt ist. Die Vokabel
kommt im NT nur Mk 13,14 Parr vor." R. Pesch, Naherwartungen:
Tradition und Redaktion in Mk 13 (Düsseldorf, 1968), 143.
(Hereinafter referred to as Naherwartungen).

3. G. Schrenk, "ἱερός, τὸ ἱερόν. . . ." TDNT, III, 239. R. H.
Hiers, "Purification of the Temple", JBL, XC (1971), 82-90.

4. Lev. 26:12 (R.S.V. throughout.)

5. Y. Congar, The Mystery of the Temple (London, 1962), 139;
B. Gärtner, The Temple and the Community in Qumran and the New
Testament (Cambridge, 1965), 107,129; R. J. McKelvey, The New
Temple (London, 1969), passim; R. A. Cole, The New Temple
(London, 1961), passim.

6. G. E. Ladd, Jesus and the Kingdom (London, 1966), 305.
(Hereinafter referred to as Jesus).

7. W. Marxsen, J. Lambrecht, F. Flückiger, in particular.

8. Robert W. Funk speaks of the "chaotic state of historical and theological scholarship where apocalyptic is concerned. Premises are rarely shared; no themes, perhaps, open the seams in the historical and theological fabric so readily and so completely." JThCh VI (1969), 13. B. H. Streeter wrote over fifty years ago: "Mark 13 dominates the eschatology of the Second Gospel, and through him that of the two later Gospels . . . . It is the citadel of the extreme eschatological school of interpretation. Hence the question how far it fairly represents the mind of our Lord is crucial." Studies in the Synoptic Problem (Oxford, 1911) 428. (Hereinafter referred to as Synoptic Problem).

9. Ladd, Jesus, xiii. See also Otto Piper, "Principles of New Testament Interpretation", TT, III (1946-47), 197.

10. J. Weiss, "Die drei älteren Evangelien", Die Schriften des Neuen Testaments, ed. J. Weiss (4 vols.; Göttingen, ²1906), I, 195.

11. Ibid., 380.

12. W. Marxsen, Der Evangelist Markus (Göttingen, 1956), 125. (Hereinafter referred to as Markus.)

13. J. Lambrecht, Die Redaktion der Markus-Apokalypse (AB XXVIII) (Rome, 1967), 148. (Hereinafter referred to as Redaktion.)

14. The Gospel according to Mark, (The Regensburg New Testament, II), ed. and trans. Kevin Condon (New York, 1968), 238. (Hereinafter referred to as Mark.)

15. Ernst Haenchen, Der Weg Jesu (Berlin, 1968), 443.

16. A. Suhl, Die Funktion der Alttestamentlichen Zitate und Anspielungen in Markus-evangelium (Gerd Mohn, 1965), 3. (Hereinafter referred to as Alttestamentlichen Zitate.)

17. G. R. Beasley-Murray, A Commentary on Mark Thirteen (London, 1957), 93. (Hereinafter referred to as Mark Thirteen.)

18. "O. Procksch . . . rapproche le 'fils d'homme' de Daniel, qui reçoit 'domination, gloire et règne', de la gloire divine se manifestant dans une nuée (Ez. I,4) 'comme une figure d'homme' (Ez. I, 26) au prophète Ezéchiel sur les bords du fleuve Chobar. P. Volz (Die Eschatologie . . . , p. 189) et W. Eichrodt (Theologie des Alten Testaments, t. 11, Leipzig, 1935, p. 11) sont pareillement en faveur de cette relation littéraire, d'autant plus vraisemblable que la description des assises

judiciaires en Dan. VII, 9-10, avec le trône de feu et les roues de feu, s'inspire elle aussi de la vision inaugurale du fils de Buzi. Pour Isaïe, la gloire divine n'était que la sainteté de Yahweh se manifestant dans la nature et dans l'histoire (Is. VI, 3); avec Ez. 1, 26sq. (cf. III, 12, 23; VIII, 4; IX, 3; X, 4 . . .), la gloire divine commence en quelque sorte à se matérialiser et à prendre 'figure d'homme'; elle s'identifie en somme avec la théophanie que le voyant a contemplée et qui, en terre d'exil, lui rappelle la présence de Dieu dans le sanctuaire de Jérusalem. Avec Daniel nous assistons au dernier stade du développement: chez lui, <u>le Messie 'fils d'homme' se presente comme une sorte d'incarnation de cette forme d'apparition surnaturelle qui s'appelle 'la gloire divine', et en particulier comme une réplique de la manifestation de la gloire de Yahweh dans la nuée du Saint des Saints.</u>" A. Feuillet, "Le discours de Jésus sur la ruine du temple d'après Mc XIII et Lc XXI:5-36", <u>RB</u>, LVI (1949), 70-71.

19. Rev. 21:3. <u>Ibid</u>., 71. " . . . on voit quels liens étroits et profonds unissent l'annonce par Jésus de la ruine du temple et l'annonce de la venue du Fils de l'homme sur les nuées: la seconde fait comme contrepoids à la première; le temple de Jérusalem était le grand signe visible de l'unité du peuple de Dieu (cf. dans le Deuteronome XII, Isq. la loi de l'unité du sanctuaire); au sanctuaire qui disparait, le Christ vient se substituer comme centre invisible de rassemblement d'une nouvelle communauté, la communauté de tous ceux qui croirent en lui." See also Beasley-Murray, <u>Mark Thirteen</u>, 90.

20. B. Rigaux, <u>L'Antéchrist et l'Opposition au Royaume Messianique dans l'Ancien et le Nouveau Testament</u> (Paris, 1932), 243-44. (Hereinafter referred to as <u>L'Antéchrist</u>.)

21. See Dan. 8:13,14; 9:26,27; 11:31; 12:11.

22. Dodd, <u>More New Testament Studies</u>, 69. See also Lars Hartman <u>Prophecy Interpreted</u> (Lund, 1966), 210, 235. (Hereinafter referred to as <u>Prophecy</u>.)

23. <u>Ibid</u>., 221.

24. <u>The Bible, Its Meaning and Supremacy</u> (London, N.Y., Bombay, 1897), 145. See also his <u>History of Interpretation</u> (London, 1886), <u>passim</u>.

25. <u>The Gospel Tradition</u> (Oxford, 1970), 51. See also Robert H. Stein, "The Proper Methodology for Ascertaining a Markan Redaktiongeschichte" (unpublished Ph.D., dissertation, Princeton, 1968), 22-98, and article under the same title in <u>NovT</u> XIII (3, 1971), 181-198. Note 178f. of this present thesis for extracts

from Stein.

26. The Interpretation of the New Testament (London, 1966), 27. (Hereinafter referred to as Interpretation.

27. Ibid., 22.

28. The Quest of the Historical Jesus (London, 1910), 358.

29. The Parousia in the New Testament, Supplements to N.T. vol. XIII (Leiden, 1966), 2. (Hereinafter referred to as Parousia.)

30. "In the age of crisis at the end of the seventeenth century and the beginning of the eighteenth century, forces were set in motion which were destined to result in the triumph of subjectivism in theology. This was an age which laid claim to the whole of reality in the name of reason, but historical reality did not include the Last Judgment. The methods employed led to the rejection of eschatology. Since the modern world is still patterned much after this outlook, the problem of whether the Last Judgment is essential for New Testament theology as proclaimed in the Protestant churches is raised in acute form. The basic question is whether rationalistic and secularistic principles shall be allowed to control biblical exegesis within the Church so that the New Testament eschatology is rejected on the basis of these principles. The entire outlook upon man and the world, and God's relation to both, which forms such an essential part of the idea of the Last Judgment and indeed of the Christian substance itself, were in the late seventeenth century and throughout the eighteenth century formulated with such boldness and completeness that without a frontal attack upon the Last Judgment, it was, nevertheless, rendered inoperative and quite superfluous." James P. Martin, The Last Judgment (Grand Rapids, 1963), 87.

31. D. Strauss, Das Leben Jesu für das deutsche Volk bearbeitet (1864), 236, cited by G. R. Beasley-Murray, "A Century of Eschatological Discussion", ET, LXIV (1953), 313.

32. Die evangelische Geschichte kritisch und philosophisch bearbeitet (1838), 594-5; cited by G. R. Beasley-Murray, "A Century of Eschatological Discussion", 312

33. Jésus-Christ et les croyances messianiques de son Temps (1864), cited by G. R. Beasley-Murray, "The Rise and Fall of the Little Apocalypse", ET, LXIV (1953), 346.

34. Einleitung, 96, cited by G. R. Beasley-Murray, "A Century of Eschatological Discussion", 315.

35. The Synoptic Gospels (London, 1927), 296.

36. Jesus and the Christian Religion, 78, cited by B. W. Bacon, The Gospel of Mark (New Haven, 1925), 63n.

37. His Appearing and His Kingdom, The Christian Hope in the Light of its History (London, 1953), 3.

38. The Gospel of the Kingdom (New York, 1940), 63. (Hereinafter referred to as Gospel.)

39. "Der Ursprung der Apokalypse Markus 13", ThBl, XII, 193-202, cited by G. R. Beasley-Murray, Jesus and the Future (London, 1954), 74. (Hereinafter referred to as Jesus.)

40. Jesus and His Coming (London, 1957), 118-119.

41. Documents of the Primitive Church (New York and London, 1941), 13. (Hereinafter referred to as Documents.)

42. Das Charakterbild Jesu (Wiesbaden, 1964), 183ff., cited by Beasley-Murray, Jesus, 13.

43. Das Evangelium nach Markus (DNTD) (Göttingen, 1947), 168. (Hereinafter referred to as Markus.)

44. The Four Gospels (Dublin, 1967), 322.

45. Saint Mark, 341.

46. Redaktion, 15.

47. Jesus, 216.

48. Real-Encyclopädie Für Protestantische Theologie und Kirche, 3rd ed., XXI, 264.

49. "The Gospel According to Mark", trans. and ed. by Philip Schaff, in Commentary on the Holy Scriptures (Grand Rapids, 41960), VIII, 138.

50. "The Gospel According to Luke", trans. and ed. by Philip Schaff and Charles C. Starbuck, ibid., 321.

51. Nineham, Saint Mark, 356n.: "Have scholars who deny all authenticity to the passage (13:24-27) been influenced at all by the desire to dissociate Jesus from ideas and language strange to modern minds?"

52. C. C. McCown, The Search for the Real Jesus, 18, cited by

Beasley-Murray, Jesus, 1. See Bultmann's "Is Exegesis without Presuppositions Possible?", Encounter XXI (1960), 194-200. And for a further illustration of the theme consider Käsemann's exegesis of Hebrews with the emphasis on gnostic influence so characteristic of Käsemann's own great teacher.

53. That the apocalyptic setting of the gospel is indispensable to the understanding of its essential content. W. Pannenberg, Jesus - God and Man, (E.T., London, 1968), 13,32;217. "I call apocalyptic the mother of Christian theology." E. Käsemann, "On the Topic of Primitive Christian Apocalyptic", JThCh, VI, 133. "The pervasive influence of apocalyptic on Judaism in all the multifaceted variety during this period is a matter of comparatively recent acknowledgment." D. F. Freedman, "The Flowering of Apocalyptic", ibid., 166-67. J. W. Bowman, The Religion of Maturity (Nashville, 1948), 235. "To determine our Lord's attitude towards the subject of apocalyptic is one of the really urgent tasks at the present time confronting Bible scholars."

54. Neill, Interpretation, 195-96.

55. The Message of the Prophets (London, 1968), 271.

56. "The Apocalyptic element in the teaching of Jesus is a very large element, the eschatological, very small. At least one half of all that is recorded is professedly along the lines of Apocalyptic, as the two phrases, 'Son of Man' and 'the Kingdom of God' abundantly show; and the strictly ethical teaching, which is at once a correction of debased ideals and the formulating of the moral law of the Kingdom, is permeated with the thoughts and phrases with which current Apocalyptic had made the minds of the people so familiar", F. W. Worsley, The Apocalypse of Jesus (London, 1912), 24-25.

57. Thus Dodd can refer to "the Apocalyptic Discourse" of Mark 13, and yet point out that "its literary form is not that of an apocalypse . . . " More New Testament Studies, 70, 69. Cf. Ladd: "The apocalyptic type of eschatology found expression in literary forms which were not apocalyptic in character." Jesus, 79. See also H. H. Rowley, The Relevance of Apocalyptic (London, ³1963), 23. (Hereinafter referred to as Relevance.) See also W. Bousset, The New Schaff-Herzog Encyclopaedia, I, 209-210; E. Lohmeyer, RGG (2d ed.), I, col. 402-404; Ladd, "Apocalyptic", Baker's Dictionary of Theology (London, 1960), 52. In his Jesus and the Kingdom, Ladd says: "Most discussions of 'apocalyptic' fail to point out that the word is used to describe two different historical phenomena: a genre of literature, and the particular kind of eschatology embodied in this literature." 73. Hans Dieter Betz urges that "a religio-historical clarification of

the concept and nature of apocalypticism has recently been demanded on several sides. G. Ebeling has requested it in his discussion of Käsemann's thesis. G. von Rad concludes, . . . 'This, however, seems to be clear: our concept of apocalypticism urgently needs a critical revision since its sweeping use as a definition of a literary as well as a theological phenomenon has become a problem.'" "On the Problem of the Religio-Historical Understanding of Apocalypticism", JThCh, VI (1969), 135. See also ibid., 52.

58. Ladd, Jesus, 75.

59. See Ladd, Jesus 75ff; D. S. Russell, The Method and Message of Jewish Apocalyptic (London, 1964), 104-140. (Hereinafter referred to as Apocalyptic.) See Ford, Daniel (SPA), 60ff.

60. It should be stressed that apocalyptic eschatology may exist even where the special literary form is absent.

61. Ladd summarizes: "The apocalyptic eschatology can be understood as a historical development of the prophetic eschatology as the latter is interpreted against the background of the historical evils of the post-Maccabean times. Both prophetic and apocalyptic eschatology can conceive of the establishment of the Kingdom only by an inbreaking of God; both are essentially catastrophic. In both, the Kingdom will be a new and transformed order, redeemed from all corruption and evil. The apocalyptic dualism results from a sharpening of concepts found in the prophets.

"However, apocalyptic eschatology has lost the dynamic concept of God who is redemptively active in history. The apocalyptists, contrary to the prophets, despaired of history, feeling that it was completely dominated by evil. Hope was reposed only in the future. The harsh experiences of the last two centuries B.C. left the apocalyptists pessimistic of any divine visitation in history. God would visit his people to deliver them from evil only at the end of history." Jesus, 97.

62. Torrey, Documents, 14-15.

63. Torrey sees verse 14a as apocalyptic, but also as a later insertion. On this topic Ladd affirms: "The Olivet Discourse is not apocalyptic in form. It makes no use of pseudonymity; it lays no claim to heavenly revelations or visions; nor does it rewrite history in the guise of prophecy. It pictures Jesus taking his stand among his contemporaries and speaking to them about the future as the prophets did. It is distinctly prophetic rather than apocalyptic in form." Jesus, 312.

64. Isa. 24-27; Amos 5:18-20; 8:7-9; 7:4.

65. Vincent Taylor suggests that the "apocalyptic outlook" is foreign to the mind of Jesus (Mark, 516). The same writer (644) speaks of the "glittering apocalyptic robe" needing to be detached from the shoulders of Christ. C. J. Cadoux, F. C. Grant, A. T. Olmstead, Leroy Waterman, J. W. Bowman and others contend that the apocalyptic elements of the gospels are either mere imagery or the result of apostolic misunderstanding. See section 2a. following.

66. For example, F. C. Grant, Gospel; H. B. Sharman, Scn of Man and Kingdom of God (London, 1943); A. T. Olmstead, Jesus in the Light of History (New York, 1942); and to a lesser extent, T. W. Manson, The Teaching of Jesus (Cambridge, 1945), 260-263.

67. Bultmann says: "We need only remember that eschatological expectation in itself is not necessarily associated with the call to repentance and with the preaching of the will of God. It can be combined just as well with wishful fantasies of future glory, with economic ideals and hopes, with thoughts of revenge and pictures of hell. Jewish apocalyptic as well as the history of eschatology elsewhere offers abundant proof of this. It still needs to be explained why such ideas are not found with Jesus and why, on the contrary, with him the demand for obedience goes hand in hand with the proclaiming of the future age." Jesus and the Word, (E.T., London, ²1958), 93-94. But this comment is not to be understood as denying Bultmann's opinion that Jesus was an apocalyptic prophet. Elsewhere he acknowledges Christ's use of apocalyptic terminology, but insists that for us its meaning is existential. See his Theology of the New Testament (2 vols., E.T., London, 1951), I, 23.

68. Yet, as Streeter reminds us, "Jewish Apocalyptic, albeit bizarre to modern eyes, was no ignoble thing", Synoptic Problem, 434.

69. See also C. S. Lewis, Transposition and Other Addresses (London, 1949), 51.

70. J. A. T. Robinson, In the End, God (London, ²1968), 19-21.

71. A. Plummer, St Matthew (London, 1909), 328.

72. A. B. Bruce in his discussion of Mark 13 says: "At this point the παρουσια which, according to the evangelist, was one of the subjects on which the disciples desired information, becomes the theme of discourse. What is said thereon is so perplexing as to tempt a modern expositor to wish it had not been there, or to have recourse to critical expedients to eliminate it from the text. But nothing would be gained by that unless we got rid, at

the same time, of other sayings of kindred character ascribed to
Jesus in the Gospels. And there seems to be no reason to doubt
that some such utterance would form a part of the eschatological
discourse, even if the disciples did not ask instruction on the
subject. The revelation as to the last days of Israel naturally
led up to it, and the best clue to the meaning of the Parusia-
logion may be to regard it as a pendant to that revelation." "The
Synoptic Gospels", in The Expositor's Greek Testament, ed. W.
Robertson Nicoll (4 vols., London, 1897), I, 294. We should also
keep in mind that the essential content of Mk. 13 is present even
in the fourth gospel. " . . . the material in Jn. 14-17 . . .
provides parallels to every verse in Mark 13 . . .", Lloyd Gaston,
No Stone on Another - Studies in the Significance of the Fall of
Jerusalem in the Synoptic Gospels, Supplement to Novum Testamentum
XXIII (Leiden, 1970), 60. (Hereinafter referred to as No Stone on
Another.)

73. "The Apocalyptic Element in the Gospels", The Hibbert Journal
X (1911-1912), 84.

74. Ibid.

75. C. H. Dodd, According to the Scriptures (London, 1952), 109.

76. Synoptic Problem, 425-436.

77. See J. E. Fison, The Christian Hope (London, 1954), 145-195.
Even Streeter, arguing against the "extreme eschatological school"
says: "The argument, however, must not be pushed to the length of
entirely eliminating the apocalyptic element from the authentic
teaching of our Lord . . . it is too great a paradox to maintain
that what was so central in the belief of the primitive church was
not present, at least in germ, in what the Master taught."
Synoptic Problem, 433.

78. Bruce Vawter rightly reminds us: "Jesus could not be called
an apocalyptist in the sense that apocalyptic dominated all his
thinking, just as he could not be called a legalist merely because
he upheld the Law. But apocalyptic had a part in his teaching
even as did historical and realized eschatology. It is part of
the religion of Christianity. Remove it, and the vital New Testament concepts of prophetic witness and sacrifice are removed along
with it. Apocalyptic affirms that this world is under judgment.
Remove it, and the city of man becomes the city of God by its
wishing so, while the transforming word of Christ is reduced to
a 'social gospel'". The Four Gospels (Dublin, 1967), 325. While
other forms of biblical literature affirm that the world is under
judgment, it is the prospect of catastrophic divine intervention
which gives pungency to warnings which otherwise could be easily
shrugged away.

79. But Torrey prefers to call the theory "one of the _curiosa_ of synoptic criticism, _Documents_, 13.

80. _Ibid_., 16.

81. "The Rise and Fall of the Little Apocalypse Theory," 346.

82. _The Earliest Records of Jesus_ (Oxford, 1962), 216.

83. _Interpretation_, 58.

84. _Naherwartungen_, 225.

85. _Prophecy_, 207n.

86. Beasley-Murray, _Jesus_.

87. Suhl, _Alttestamentlichen Zitate_, 3n.,19.

88. "Tempelzerstörung und synoptische Apokalypse", _ZNW_, LVII (1966), 43-45.

89. The editor, Matthew Black, considers the Olivet discourse authentic, but note: "Since 1864 it has been generally agreed that the discourse, the longest attributed to Jesus in this Gospel is composite, and the theory that it is based on a 'little apocalypse' has been widely accepted (see Beasley-Murray, _Jesus and the Future_ (1954); also Taylor, 498f., Grant, IB, vii, 853ff.); but Turner justly remarks 'It is quite impossible to believe that the anticipation of the triumphant return of Christ could have had such firm hold on the first Christian generation, if it had not had deep roots in our Lord's own teaching'. More recently Taylor (636ff.) has urged on the basis of a detailed analysis that 'the Evangelist has combined several groups of sayings, some of which contained apocalyptic elements, and has not simply edited a Jewish -Christian apocalypse' (but cf. Beasley-Murray, 106ff.)." R. McL. Wilson, "Mark", _Peake's Commentary on the Bible_ (London, 1962), 813, (section 709a). "That Jesus at this point delivered an apocalyptic discourse is entirely credible . . . but it should perhaps be noted, with Beasley-Murray, that composition of the discourse as a whole by Mark does not preclude the authenticity of the sayings of which it is composed." _Ibid_., 814, (section 709g). "It is impossible, however to take this chapter and its parallels as the criterion for our Lord's teaching on this topic. To begin with, probably most scholars would rate it a _sententia accepta_ that this 'Little Apocalypse' is a product of the thinking of the Church and not Jesus' teaching at all." J. W. Bowman, "The Life and Teaching of Jesus", _Ibid_., 744, (section 650a). "Jesus did believe in the consummation of the Kingdom at the end of the age, but he taught quite clearly that there would be no precursory

signs of the end . . . " Ibid., (section 650b). " . . . the
modern tendency in regard to Mark 13 is to treat it as a whole
and as an integral part of the entire Gospel (cf. G. R. Beasley-
Murray . . .)." C. S. C. Williams, "The Synoptic Problem",
Ibid., 754, (section 658a).

90. Both Loisy and Holtzmann affirmed that Mark 13:15-16 cannot
belong to a Jewish apocalypse.

91. For example, E. Haenchen, "Wir werden bald sehen, wie
unsicher die ganze Flug-blatt-Hypothese ist." Der Weg Jesu, 438.
"Der nun folgende Abschnitt, V. 14-20, is aüsserst merkwürdig.
Er vor allem hat die Vermutung angeregt, Mk habe hier eine--
jüdische oder christliche--Apokalypse eingearbeitet. Wenn man in
diesem Zusammenhang von dem 'Flugblatt eines Propheten' gesprochen hat, so verrät das einmal eine Forschungsweise, die nur nach
Quellen sucht und, wenn sie welche gefunden zu haben meint, alle
Rätsel gelöst glaubt, und zweitens die naive Übernahme moderner
literarischer Mittel ('Flugblatt!')." Ibid., 443.

92. F. Flückiger, "Der Redaktion der Zukunftsrede in Mark 13",
ThZ, XXVI, (1970), 395-409.

93. Gaston Speculates: "We have surmised that Mark probably
took over the bulk of the discourse vv. 5-37 as sayings of the
risen Christ on the Mount of Olives and composed his introduction
accordingly." No Stone on Another, 54. Gaston confesses elsewhere that his "reconstruction of the history of Mark 13" is
"largely hypothetical". Ibid., 61.

94. See C. F. D. Moule, "The Techniques of New Testament
Research: A Critical Survey", Jesus and Man's Hope, 2 vols. ed.
Donald G. Miller and Y. Hadidian (Pittsburgh, 1970), 29-45;
P. Benoit, "Reflections sur la 'Formgeschichtliche Methode'",
RB, LIII (1946), 451-512; Joachim Rohde, Rediscovering the
Teaching of the Evangelists (London, 1968), passim; Vincent
Taylor, St Mark, 73; H. Riesenfeld, The Gospel Tradition,
passim.

95. Vincent Taylor: " . . . the cry of the unnamed disciple
rings true to the situation of a Galilean disciple visiting the
city." St Mark, 500. And on v. 2, he says: "All the indications point to the primitive character of the Markan form." 501.
Taylor looks upon vv. 3-4 as "not a self-contained narrative,
but an introduction of 5-37, possibly originally to 14-20,
composed by Mark himself on the basis of tradition." Ibid.
" . . . it is not a mere literary setting for 5-37." Ibid., 502.

96. This matter is further discussed under section seven.

97. A. E. J. Rawlinson, Westminster Commentary on Mark (London, 1925), 188.

98. D. Daube, The New Testament and Rabbinic Judaism (London, 1956), 419ff. (Hereinafter referred to as New Testament.)

99. A. Schlatter, Matthew (Stüttgart, 1963), 704.

100. J. Morison, Commentary on Mark (London, 1873), 382f.: "Such a note bene on the part of the evangelist . . . would be an unprecedented intrusion of the narrator's own personality; and it would carry with it something of immodesty, as a kind of presumptuous selection of one from among the other utterances of our Lord, as worthy on the part of a biographer, of very peculiar emphasis, and, on the part of his readers, of very special consideration. Our Lord's counsel is reported by Mt also; and it is analogous, as Wolf remarks, to the oft-repeated 'he that hath ears to hear, let him hear'. Only as there is a reference to a written prophecy, the counsel points to the duty, not of the hearer, but of the reader. It is not unlikely that it is the echo of the counsel of the angel Gabriel to Daniel himself, 'therefore understand the matter and consider the vision.'"

101. Daube, New Testament, 426-431.

102. Mk. 7:19 is frequently adduced as a parenthesis from Mark, and therefore giving credibility to Mark's responsibility for the passage under discussion in Mark 13:14. However, the usual wording for Mk 7:19 found in recent versions constitutes "a paraphrase rather than a translation". "It is just possible that a change has crept in at some point and that in the original Aramaic the meaning was something like: 'all the food being cast out and purged away' (cf. Black, An Aramaic Approach to the Gospels and Acts, 159." Nineham, Saint Mark, 196.

103. Jesus, 59.

104. See B. Rigaux, Les Épitres aux Thessaloniciens (Paris, 1956), 102-106; J. B. Orchard, "Thessalonians and the Synoptic Gospels, Bib, XIX (1938), 19ff., J. P. Brown, "Synoptic Parallels in the Epistles and Form-History", NTS, X (1963-64), 45; Beasley-Murray, Jesus, 232-233.

105. "More than one exegete has taken notice of the verbal coincidences between Paul's Epistles to the Thessalonians and the thirteenth chapter of Mark . . . It might be expected that in these very definite predictions of the future, if anywhere, the apostle would seek to support himself on the words of Jesus himself, and this indeed he claims to have done . . . . He says expressly in v. 15 that he declares this 'by the word of the

Lord', ἐν λόγῳ κυρίου ; and the assurance is found, in the words
of Jesus, in Mk. 13:27,30, from which, with the support of the
current and well-attested eschatological doctrines, every feature
of Paul's declaration can be suredly derived; there is no need
to look further . . ." Torrey, Documents, 36-37.

106. Hartman summarizes the verbal evidence as follows: "Those
parts of the discourse which are instanced at this date by 1 and
2 Ths. or which have parallels therein may be indicated by the
following key-words: 'let no one lead you astray' (13,5), 'I am'
(v. 6), 'be not alarmed' (v. 7), the abomination (v. 14),
troubles (Mt. 24,9; Mk. 13,19), false prophets (v. 22), the
Parousia according to Dn. 7 (v.26), the angels at the Parousia
(Mt. 24,31), the gathering (v. 27), the carelessness of 'the
world' (Mt. 24,37ff., Lk. 21,34), the thief in the night (24,43),
ἀπάντησις (25,6), the sudden arrival (Lk 21,34), and in the
travail-snare (Lk. 21,35)." Prophecy, 205.

107. Our rejection of the "fly-leaf" hypothesis has been with
reference to its usual definition, namely that Mk. 13:5-27, as a
whole or in part, was originally a fictitious presentation,
unrelated factually to dominical logia. It is not only possible
but likely, on the other hand, that collections of authentic
sayings circulated in fly-leaf form, as suggested above. The
most likely of all such collections would have been an abridge-
ment of the Olivet discourse. Contra Burkitt, The History of
Christianity in the Light of Modern Knowledge (London, 1929),
245.

108. Rediscovering the Teaching of Jesus (London, 1967), 45f.

109. F. J. Foakes-Jackson, K. Lake, The Beginnings of Christianity (5 vols., London, 1920-33), II, 115.

110. The Gospel of Luke (London, 1966), 244f., esp. 246.

111. J. A. T. Robinson, Jesus and His Coming (London, 1957),
122-123; A. M. Perry, The Sources of St Luke's Passion Narrative
(Chicago, 1920), 35-38; V. Taylor, Behind the Third Gospel
(Oxford, 1926), 109-125; T. W. Manson, The Sayings of Jesus
(London, 1949), 323-37; Dodd, More New Testament Studies, 74,
82-83. More recent works which contest that Luke was working
with his own source as well as Mark include Lloyd Gaston's No
Stone on Another, and Gerhard Schneider's Verleugnung, Verspot-
tung und Vernör Jesu nach Lukas 22,54-71 (München, 1969).

112. Easton comments on this passage as follows: "When we read
the prediction . . . we realize that we are dealing with a church
in which martyrdoms are practically unknown." Christ in the
Gospels (New York, 1930), 11-12.

113. According to Marshall: "The amount of alteration in the text of Mark required to produce the so-called transformation is so great in comparison with Luke's normal treatment of Mark that it is unlikely to have taken place. Why, we may ask, was Luke so surprisingly conservative in his treatment of most of Mark and so radical in these few cases?" "Tradition and Theology in Luke (Luke 8:5-15)", Tyndale Bulletin, XX (1969), 62. And Caird asserts that "in recent years . . . there has been a growing support for the theory that, where the discourse strikingly diverges from Mark, Luke is drawing on his source L." Saint Luke (Harmondsworth, 1965), 228-29. See Beasley-Murray, Jesus, 226-27; Easton, Christ, 9-13. See C. F. D. Moule, JThSt, XXII (I, 1971), 195. "A good case emerges for believing that Luke was working with a written, self-contained, continuous narrative in addition to Mark's." (Review of Schneider's work mentioned above.)

114. Prophecy, 227n, 233.

115. But see Easton's discussion in Christ in the Gospels, 18-20.

116. Jesus, 227-230.

117. Ladd summarizes thus: "It is evident from a comparative study that the form the discourse has assumed in the three gospels is due to tradition and to the authors." He cites by way of illustration the appearance of Mt. 24:26-28 outside of the Olivet discourse in Luke 17:23-24. See Jesus, 306.

118. Beasley-Murray, Jesus, 212. The undeniable similarities between some of the language of this chapter Mk. 13, and that of well-known apocalypses are due to the influence of the Old Testament upon both.

119. See Rowley, Relevance, 54-137; Russell, Apocalyptic, 271-280; William Barclay, "Great Themes of the New Testament", ET, LXX (1959), 326-330.

120. J. Wellhausen, Comm. Mk. (1909), 100; Lohmeyer, Markus, 285; G. R. Beasley-Murray, "Rise and Fall of the Little Apocalypse Theory", 348f.; Schmid, Markus, 237.

121. St Mark, 135.

122. Ibid.

123. The Teaching of Jesus (Cambridge, 1945), 261-62.

124. Ibid.

125. But see discussions of the parallel in Mk. 14:62 by Beasley
-Murray, Mark Thirteen, 90-91, and J. E. Fison, The Christian
Hope (London, 1954), 192-94.

126. The Synoptic Gospels (2 vols. London, 1909), I, 306.

127. Ibid., 301.

128. Loisy, Synoptiques, II, 438.

129. W. G. Kümmel, Introduction to the New Testament (E.T.,
London, 1966), 188.

130. The Kingdom of God and the Son of Man (E.T., London, 1938),
131.

131. "If Jesus intended nothing further than to reject such
advance calculation, why did he not rest content with denying it?
Why does he add a positive statement of very weighty content,
which he clearly enough introduces as the real point by using the
word 'lo'? This statement is by no means identical with rejection. It is meant to be confirmation; it is meant to give a
fact whose consequence is (a) that the apocalyptic methods of
paratērēsis (observation) are not in place and (b) that there can
be no talk of a Here and a There. Evidently (a) and (b) both
actually result if he is speaking of the kingdom which -- para-
doxically and wonderfully enough -- is already present in its
first dawning. If that were true, then indeed all paratērēsis
would be foolish. And then also all talk of Here or There would
be foolish, for the matter in question was not something relating
to place or space, but something dynamic, in view of whose nature
a Here or There is not applicable. Only as thus understood is
there any meaning in rejecting the Here or There. For in regard
to the future kingdom, Here and There, i.e. local determinations,
did have their place even for Jesus. The future kingdom had a
thoroughly external aspect; it was to come with flaming lightning, with the appearance of the Son of Man, his angels, and the
heavenly tribunal. From heaven yonder it was to descend here to
the earth. From Jerusalem it was to go forth, and to extend
itself all over the world from Zion, in the realm of the twelve
tribes. And even the paratērēsis, as attention to the signs
which indicated his coming and from which his temporal nearness
was to be read, Jesus not only did not reject but he expressly
summoned men to it by referring to the blossoming of the branches
of the fig-tree from which the nearness of summer should be noted:
. . . (Mk. xiii.28f.). That is paratērēisthai, i.e. to pay
attention to signs of every kind regarding the future kingdom."
Ibid., 132f.

132. "What is the import of the passage under consideration? In

any case, something paradoxical and intended to startle. It was
meant to shatter the dogmatism of a finished eschatology and
burst its too narrow limits. Jesus, like his opponents, knew of
the future kingdom, that it would come, that God kept the moment
in reserve, that one had to hold oneself ready for it in constant
watchfulness, that one should be specially attentive as soon as
the indications of its coming appeared, and that one should then
know that it was near. The whole of this referred to the future
kingdom. That was the first pole of his conception of the
kingdom. The second was that the kingdom was already moving and
so already present, in as far as it worked secretly in advance.
Jesus did not reconcile the two poles. He no more adjusted the
antithesis here than the strong inner bi-polarities of his teaching elsewhere. He said that those who exercise force seize the
kingdom of heaven -- and yet he praised the childlike mind which
never acts violently but simply accepts and receives. He promised a heavenly reward for good work and insisted upon the
treasure of good works in heaven -- and yet in the parable of the
workers in the vineyard he rejected all greed for reward. He
related the parable of the growing seed which excluded all human
work -- and yet he demanded resolute personal action. He
appealed to the court of the will and of personal freedom -- and
yet he was a predestinarian. Similarly, in the passage under
discussion, he acts as if there were no future kingdom; every
question that relates to that kingdom he confronts with the
kingdom that 'is in the midst of you'. Perhaps he was at that
moment engaged in controversy and so, deliberately and with
emphatic onesidedness, he brought out the opposite pole. What
he says now only repeats what he had said in his parables of the
kingdom of heaven in the Beelzebub incident." Ibid., 136f.

133. Ibid., 134.

134. Such is probably the meaning of ἐντὸς ὑμῶν. It is not
likely that Christ was telling the carping Pharisees that they
had the kingdom within them. See the discussion in Marshall and
Caird, ad loc.

135. Rowley commenting on Mk. 13 says: "It is surprising with
what regularity apocalyptic writings are divided out among a
variety of authors, and always on the same ground of some inconcinnity of ideas. It seems wiser to recognize that the strictly
logical integration of the elements into a whole is not characteristic of apocalyptic, and is not to be sought there."
Relevance, 162. Although this statement itself shows some
inconcinnity as regards its use of the term "apocalyptic"
Rowley's main point is clear and truly relevant.

136. Willi Marxsen, Markus, 111.

137. W. R. F. Browning, The Gospel According to Saint Luke (London, 1960), 152.

138. Grundmann, Das Evangelium nach Markus, 270.

139. Lloyd Gaston is one of the most recent to make this charge. He says: "Mark's most important contribution to the eschatological discourse, however, one which has misled interpreters down to the present, is provided by the setting of this whole discourse as an answer to a question concerning the destiny of the temple." No Stone on Another, 63.

140. The Teaching of Jesus, 281.

141. τόπῳ ἀγίῳ Mt. 24:15. Cf. Lev. 16:2,3.

142. Shrenk, "ἱερον ", in TDNT, III, 230.

143. See 81.

144. Isa. 24-27. Beasley-Murray's historical study of the "Little Apocalypse" theory is highly significant at this point. He says: "The view that the second discourse was authentic led him (Wendt) to face the question, How does this discourse relate to the query of the disciples in Mk. 13^4? Wendt gave two answers: (1) The trials described provided the disciples with a relative, not specific, sign of the parousia, and so gave a basis for the exhortations to preparedness in vv. 33-37; (2) Jesus had earlier taught that there was a connection between the destruction of the Temple and the judgments of the End. These two answers are plausible, but Wendt overlooked that in giving them he had answered the two major objections to the authenticity of Mk. 13." "Rise and Fall of the 'Little Apocalypse' Theory", 347.

145. See C. Cranfield, "St Mark 13", SJTH, VII (1954), 288.

146. See 68ff.

147. The Birth of the New Testament (London, 1962), 121

148. Ibid. However, Matthew's rewording of the disciples' question in Mk. 13:4 points to a composition beyond this date.

149. Cullmann's criticism of Grässer's work remains pertinent: "Dass die heilgeschichtliche Sicht primär überhaupt nicht als 'Lösung eines Problems' entstanden ist, sondern auf Grund von Geschehnissen, das wird in der heutigen Forschung nicht genügend in Rechnung gestellt. Aus diesem Grunde muss dann die Heilsgeschichte zur "Verlegensheitslösung" werden. Hinter der

heilsgeschichtlichen Einbeziehung der Gegenwart im Urchristentum
steht jedenfalls zunächst einmal nicht die grosse Enttäuschung,
sondern das Geschehen, welcher Art es auch sei, in dem die
Urgemeinde den Beweis der Auferstehung Jesu gesehen hat, d.h.
den Sieg über den Tod und damit die Einleitung des neuen Äons,
stehen ferner auch die Erfahrungen in der Gemeinde, die als
Wirkungen des heiligen Geistes angesehen wurden. So wie hinter
der Naherwartung Jesu nicht Schwärmerei, sondern der Jubel steht:
die Blinden sehen . . . , so hinter der heilsgeschichtlichen
Einbeziehung der Gegenwart nicht verkrampftes Suchen der
Gemeinde nach der Lösung eines "Problems", sondern die Oster-
freude: Christus ist auferstanden! . . . Wir verdanken Conzelmann wertvolle Erkenntnisse, und Grässers Arbeit mag sie in
einigen Punkten tatsächlich erganzen können. Aber sie würden an
Bedeutung gewinnen, wenn sie von jenen fragwürdigen Vorausset-
zungen über die Eschatologie Jesu und auch des Paulus gelöst
würden, und wenn anderseits das Prinzip der "konsequenten
Eschatologie" von Grund auf, und nicht nur hinsichtlich einiger
ihrer Hypothesen revidiert würde." "Parusieverzögerung und
Urchristentum", TLZ, LXXXIII (1958), 12. Also C. F. D. Moule:
"Neither the expectation of a parousia the day after tomorrow or
its postponement sine die is characteristic of N.T. thought,
which concentrates far more on the datum - on the fact that
already the Kingship of Christ has been established, already the
Kingdom of God has been inaugurated, and that the responsibility
of the children of the Kingdom is to act here and now as those
who are charged to bear witness to its reality." The Birth of
the New Testament (London, 1962), 102. Also E. Schweizer: "It
is possible that for a while the expectation of the approaching
parousia suppressed any other questions. But we must say that
this expectation has not exercised any substantial influence on
the earliest summaries of the Church's faith", Lordship and
Discipleship (London, 1960), 22.

150. "Papiros neotestamentarios en la LIII:1 Cueva de Qumran",
Bib LIII (I, 1972), 91-100 Lloyd Gaston agrees with Moule that
little of the New Testament can be dated after A.D. 70. He
suggests that Mark "was written in Rome after Peter's death and
before the fall of Jerusalem, probably towards the end of the
period 64-70 A.D. No Stone on Another, 465. This is nearer the
traditional dating, and not as radical as O'Callaghan's more
recent suggestion.

151. Schweizer denies Marxsen's view that Mark's purpose is to
point specifically to the Parousia, and opts rather for the
traditional view of the Passion as central in "Eschatology in
Mark's Gospel", Neotestamentica et Semitica, ed. E. Earle Ellis
and Max Wilcox (Edinburgh, 1969), 114-117.

152. The So-called Historical Jesus and the Historical, Biblical

Christ (E.T., Philadelphia, 1964), 80n, 11.

153. C. H. Dodd, "The Framework of the Gospel Narrative", ET, XLIII (1932), 396-400.

154. " . . . his [Mark's] gospel was written for the purpose of consoling a persecuted church . . ." Gaston, No Stone on Another 468.

155. Torrey sums the matter up well when he says: "The material which constitutes ch 13, also, could suffer no curtailment. The first response of any hearer of the great announcement would be the question, What have we now to expect? What program did the Messiah leave to his disciples? How are the promises of the God of Israel, given through his prophets, to have their fulfillment? The answer must have been provided immediately, it could not possibly have been delayed. This was a matter of the very first importance, and as such it had, of course, been recognized by those who sent out the written propaganda into the cities and towns of Palestine." Documents, 13.

156. Nineham, Saint Mark, 341.

157. Chas. B. Cousar: "Eschatology and Mark's Theologia Crucis", Interpretation, XXIV (1970), 335. James L. Price, Interpreting the New Testament (New York, 1971), 196-99.

158. "A Gospel in Search of a Life-Setting", ET, LXXX (1969), 361-64. (R. P. Martin cites S. Schulz, Studia Evangelica, II, 144.)

159. "Mark 13 is very relevant indeed to its context." Gaston, No Stone on Another, 478.

160. In his discussion of Mark 13, Gaston shows that Mark saw a parallel between the last days of Jesus and the final experience of believers in Him. He points out, for example, that "there are many indications that Mark saw Jesus' last days in Jerusalem against the background of Zech. 9-14", and that these chapters constitute an apocalypse "about the destiny of Jerusalem at the end of the world." Ibid., 472. This view is analogous to those referred to in the next footnote.

161. R. H. Lightfoot, The Gospel Message of St Mark (London, 1950), 51f.; A. Farrer, A Study in St Mark (Westminster, 1951), 284-286 (hereinafter referred to as St Mark); W. Grundmann, Markus (ThZNT) (Berlin, [5]1971), 259; H. W. Bartsch, "Early Christian Eschatology", NTS, XI (1964-65), 396; Gaston, No Stone on Another, 469, 477f.; Hendrikus Berkhof, Well-Founded Hope (Richmond, 1968), 23-24: " . . . in all synoptic Gospels

statements about the future are summarized right before the Passion story. The themes dealt with are watchfulness, oppression decrease of love, flight, and finally spectacular natural phenomena and the coming of the Son of Man in glory. It is conspicuous that all these themes recur in the following chapters which deal with Christ's suffering, death, and resurrection . . . the meaning is obviously that the future will show--on a larger, and eventually worldwide scale--a repetition of what has happened in the crucifixion and resurrection of Jesus." Cf. Farrer's comment: " . . . the substance of the Last Things and the substance of the Passion are one and the same." St Mark, 285.

162. "When he comes to tell the passion story it will be understood against a certain background, which is essential for a full understanding." Gaston, No Stone on Another, 479. "By making use of the light the eschatological discourse and the passion story throw on each other, Mark is able to suggest without explicit mention the judgment in ch. 13 (= Jesus' death) and the resurrection in ch. 16 (= parousia)." Ibid.

163. See A. Cole, The New Temple; McKelvey, The New Temple; Congar, Mystery; Grässner, Temple, passim for this position. " . . . the image of the temple as the community goes back not only to the Jerusalem church but to Jesus himself . . ." Gaston, No Stone on Another, 243.

164. See 109ff of this volume. Caird, writing on Lk. 21, says: "The L material, read by itself, forms a continuous and homogenous prophecy of a succession of historic events, the persecution of the Church by the Jewish people, the punishment of Jerusalem by God for her refusal of the gospel . . . the true Israel is the Church, and Jerusalem, instead of being able to look forward to ultimate vindication, finds herself classified with the enemies of God." Saint Luke, 228. We do not think that the non-Marcan material here is disparate from the Marcan. What is explicit in L is implicit in Mark. See further discussion in 111ff.

165. C. F. D. Moule, SNTSB, III (1952), 40-53, "From Defendant to Judge--and Deliverer".

CHAPTER TWO

EXEGETICAL SURVEY OF MARK THIRTEEN

59

This "rätselvollen Kapitel"[1] has always constituted an unusual challenge to exegetes. To modern minds, it seems replete with difficulties and apparent inconsistencies. While not all these difficulties are directly exegetical in nature, they have nevertheless influenced commentators in their explanation of the chapter.

Some of the questions which automatically arise are the following:

1. What is the primary theme of this discourse, the destruction of Jerusalem as an imminent historical event, or the end of the world?
2. What is the relationship between the two themes, if indeed, there are two?
3. Are these themes in their existing form the result of the mingling of two separate discourses, or did Christ Himself blend His presentation of these matters?
4. If the fall of Jerusalem is here discussed, and if the end of the world is also considered -- are the events pictured as separated by a large tract of time, or are they regarded as intimately linked?
5. Is the discourse of vv. 5-37 related to its immediate setting, vv. 1-4?[2]
6. Do the versions of Matthew and Luke reflect essentially the same viewpoint as Mark, or has redactional activity adapted the discourse to the needs of a later generation?
7. If the times of distress (vv. 8,14,19) apply to the end of the world, what possible value could consist in flight, and why would the season of the year be a matter for petitionary prayer?
8. On the other hand, if the tribulation referred to is that connected with Jerusalem's fall, why does it hint at universality? If only a seige is under consideration, why is it described as being a time of trouble without parallel before or after?[3] Does the peril that οὐκ ἄν ἐσώθη πᾶσα σαρξ refer only to Jewish flesh?
9. If the elect is a Christian elect,[4] how can they be said to be imperilled in a seige which they are able to avoid by heeding Christ's warning? And if the elect are gathered from the four quarters of the earth, does this indicate that the tribulation was similarly widespread?
10. Why does this chapter both contain signs of the end, and yet also a warning that the end cannot be calculated?
11. How much is included in the ταῦτα of vv. 4,29,30? Does the word mean the same in each instance?
12. Did Jesus teach the the End of the world would come upon His generation? If He has been proved wrong in this instance, are His teachings in other areas worthy of consideration?
13. What is the purpose of the warning of v. 32? Is it saying that even Christ's own pronouncement on the time of the end is subject to the Father's will, or is it affirming that while all things must be accomplished in that generation, the exact time

60

cannot be pin-pointed?

14. If the gospel must first be preached to all nations, is there an element of conditionality present in the apparently absolute statement about οὐ μὴ παρέλθῃ ἡ γενεὰ αὕτη. . .?

15. Did Jesus actually use such a pastiche of O.T. quotations as we find in vv.24-27? Does this bizarre concatenation of events, described in Mark 13, really reproduce the mind of Jesus about the future?

16. Has Jesus taken over "lock, stock, and barrel" the portrayal of the O.T. apocalypse Daniel? Or has He adopted only its form, filling it out with Christian substance? And how is it that He could take Danielic passages regarding the events of almost two centuries previously, and apply them to the future? Wherein did His expectation differ from His contemporaries[5] who were forever reshuffling possible fulfillments of the prophecy of the seventy weeks of Daniel 9, and of the wilful king in 11:36-45? Why does He cite both these passages[6] and with what implications?

17. How are the indications of time throughout this chapter to be regarded? Do they indicate a traceable sequence of events?[7]

18. Why are so many eschatological issues such as the destruction of Antichrist, the resurrection of the dead, the bliss of the redeemed etc. left untreated?

19. Is there an ideological relationship between the two signs most emphasized -- the sign of the βδέλυγμα, and the sign of the ὁ υἱὸς τοῦ ἀνθρώπου?

20. After all, how important to the New Testament is the Parousia? Some of these issues have been dealt with in preceding pages. The rest of this chapter will consider the remainder.

As has been indicated in earlier pages, the difficulties of Mark 13 account for some of the theories regarding its literary origin. If what we have in this chapter is a patchwork including genuine dominical logia mingled with sayings from a Jewish apocalypse or the writing of a Christian prophet, then many difficulties are automatically resolved, inasmuch as literary patchwork usually results in some loss of homogeneity. However, as already shown, it is exceedingly doubtful whether such "escapes" from exegesis are valid.[8]

Some would cut the Gordian knot by rejecting the Parousia doctrine, but, this is, from an academic viewpoint, high-handed and unwarrantable.[9]

With H. H. Rowley, we "find no reason to deny that most of the material of this chapter consists of genuine utterances of Jesus . . . Even the linking together of the fall of Jerusalem and the end of the age may be due to Him . . ."[10] As Schniewind suggests "jedes einzelne Wort hat eine solche Prägung, wie sie nur von der Wirklichkeit 'Jesus' her möglich ist".[11]

This matter of the difficulties of the Olivet discourse occasioning a variety of literary theories regarding its origin is related to the phenomenon of a variety of schools of interpretation being similarly created. The difficulties, and prior philosophical or theological prejudices,[12] account for as many of the varieties of interpretation attending Mark 13, as do the principles of grammatico-historical exegesis.

> To everyone it (Mk. 13) interprets itself according
> to his own existing assumptions. I state my assumptions,
> and my exegesis is ready-made. If I am wrong, it is
> because my assumptions are false.[13]

Perhaps Neville should not so readily ascribe his own inadequacy for objectivity to others, but the cold fact remains that the total lack of unanimity among interpreters of Mark 13 implies some such influencing factor as he suggests.

Among the assumptions which so vitally affect one's exegesis, is that of the literary nature of the discourse. Is it apocalyptic, or is it akin to the prophetic tradition? For example, most of the exegetes in school two, mentioned below, are committed to the Little Apocalypse theory.

A review of the commentaries upon this topic shows that exegetes fall mainly into four different schools.[14] The respective positions on Mark 13 are as follows:

1. Application to the fall of Jerusalem only.

2. Application to the end of the Age only.

3. Application to both events (though understood in the Gospel as distant in fulfillment from each other) on the basis that either Christ or the Evangelist blended the themes.

4. Application to both events, regarding such as promised by Christ to the generation contemporary with Him. This view makes the fall of Jerusalem a part of the predicted end of the Age.

To give descriptive titles to these schools may be helpful, though not precisely accurate, which is true also of our use of the word "school" itself. The first school could be said to represent the typical Roman Catholic position until recently. The second represents the modern Protestant position, particularly that of most German exegetes. The third is often spoken of as the "traditional" view, intimating that it speaks for the majority of commentators over the centuries. It is more difficult to denominate the fourth group. Here odd bed-fellows are

to be found. Rationalists such as Strauss and Renan, some
conservative liberals such as Rowley, and some pure conservatives
such as Beasley-Murray[15] agree that the discourse links the fall
of Jerusalem and the end of the Age as features of the final act
in the drama of human existence.[16]

Let us consider these respective modes of interpreting the
thirteenth chapter of Mark. The first two schools can be considered together, representing as they do the opposite extremes
of the exegetical spectrum. Each depends heavily upon reading
metaphorically an important section of the chapter, and taking
literally that which the opposing school refuses so to construe.

The first school, which applies the chapter to the downfall
of Jerusalem in A.D. 70, is represented by scholars such as Gould
and Swete, and more recently Feuillet and Carrington.

Gould, in giving a critique of other positions and an apologetic for his own, simultaneously reveals the motivation behind
the first school, and to our mind, thereby invalidates it.

> . . . the traditional interpretation, postpones the
> latter part indefinitely, and is still looking for the
> world-catastrophe which its advocates suppose to be
> predicted here. The difficulties in the way of this
> interpretation are grave and insurmountable. It
> ignores the coupling together of the two parts in
> the discourse, as belonging to one great event. Mt.
> v. 29 says that they will follow each other immedi-
> ately. Mk., that they belong to the same general
> period. It passes over also, or attempts to explain
> away, the obvious notes of time. All of the accounts
> wait until they have come to the end of the prophecy,
> including both parts, before they introduce the
> statement of the time of all these events, and the
> statement itself is, that that generation was not to
> pass away till all these things came to pass . . .
>
> The other interpretation, . . . places the time of
> its fulfillment in that generation. That is, they
> involve Jesus himself in the evident error of the
> other N.T. writings and of the Church in the subse-
> quent period . . .
>
> A third interpretation, the one adopted here, holds
> that the event predicted in the second part did take
> place in that generation and in connection with the
> destruction of Jerusalem. The event itself, and the
> signs of it, it interprets according to the analogy
> of prophecy, figuratively . . . The prophecy becomes

thus a prediction of the setting up of the kingdom,
and especially of its definite inauguration as a
universal kingdom, with the removal of the chief
obstacle to that in the destruction of Jerusalem.[17]

Such commentators are saying in effect, "We see the discourse
as a unity. There are no grounds for assuming a great gap
between the events in the first half, and those of the second.
The end of the world did not come in the first century A.D. and
therefore the description which at first glance seems to pertain
to the second advent must actually apply to something else --
something which can be located in Christ's generation." The
exegesis of vv. 24-27[18] thus arrived at may be correct, but the
method of arriving there certainly is not. The exegete's primary
task is not apologetic. Using literary, philological, and
historical tools, he must make up his mind what the words before
him actually mean. It is not his primary task to enquire whether
the meaning is acceptable, or even whether it is consistent with
other facts.

A number of other commentators have difficulty with vv. 24-27
because it does not fit in with their views on eschatology. H.
B. Sharman, L. Waterman, A. T. Olmstead, C. J. Cadoux, E. J.
Goodspeed, W. Manson, F. C. Grant, C. H. Dodd are in this
category.[19]

Again it must be said that the interpretation offered by any
one of these scholars may be correct, but the path to such
conclusions was hardly the right path for an exegete to travel.

The second school of interpreters, which applies the discourse
to the end of the world, faces a problem similar to that of the
first group, but with reference to verses 14-19. Again, we have
the face-value meaning denied. Commentators such as Loisy,
J. Weiss, Rawlinson, Werner, Grässer, Bultmann, Conzelmann,
Branscomb, Lohmeyer, Suhl, Haenchen, Schmid, in short the great
majority of modern commentators, particularly German scholars,
see in vv. 14-20 a description of the Antichrist at the end of
the Age.[20] Again, in some instances at least, the conclusion
has not sprung solely from the text. In numerous cases, denial
of the phenomena of prediction, coupled with belief in Consistent
Eschatology, has had more to do with the exegesis offered than
the Scripture passage itself. Disbelief in prediction may be,
of course, a perfectly valid philosophical position, but what has
that to do with exegesis, i.e. what should that have to do with
exegesis?

Thus, in considering the exegetical stance of the first two
schools, it is apparent that almost everything depends upon the
interpretation given to vv. 24-27 and 14-19. If the former

passage can be regarded in entirety as metaphorical, the view-point of the first school remains unembarrassed. Similarly, if the second passage can be construed as apocalyptic description of a universal rather than a local situation, then the second school is exegetically unhindered. But if neither of these "ifs" can be substantiated -- and it proves impossible to relegate 24-27 to the realm of imagery, or to regard 14-19 as other than a local historical situation -- what then? Then the exegete must choose between positions three and four on the weight of evidence.

Let us look more closely at these key passages. The description of vv. 24-27 is today overwhelmingly taken as applying to the end of the Age and the Parousia. Gould's interpretation[21] has fallen out of favour, and with good reason. The verses stand in strong contrast to the merely terrestrial phenomena of verse 7 forward. The convulsion of the heavens appears to be a fitting accompaniment of the manifestation of the Son of Man to the world which has rejected Him. Vincent Taylor writes, "In the light of 5f. (wars, earthquakes, famines) and 26 (the coming of the Son of Man with clouds), it seems probable that objective phenomena are meant."[22] The "gathering of Israel" is frequently pictured in the Old Testament as an event of the end-time. See Isa. 60:4ff., Micah 4:1-7 etc. There does not seem to have been any plainer language Christ could have used to convey the message of the Son of Man's literal coming than v. 26. We must ask those who apply this verse and its context metaphorically -- just how could Christ have made the point of His return, if words as clear as these are capable of another meaning? We would also enquire whether the New Testament teaching on the resurrection and the Age to come is not evaporated by such exegesis. While it is true that the fall of Jerusalem helped the young church to attain independence, it remains to be doubted whether those Christians persecuted after A.D. 70 considered themselves to be in the Age of glory.

Each and all of the statements preceding and succeeding the picture of the Son of Man coming in the clouds, bears witness to the significance of this central description. The great tribulation, described as occurring just before the convulsion of the heavens, is linked with "the time of the end" in its Old Testament source. See Dan. 12:1-4. Verse 32, by its reference to ἡ ἡμέρα ἐκείνη pin-points the event of the great day of Yahweh so often referred to in the prophets,[23] while the parables of the fig-tree and the master of the house, which bracket the reference to ἡ ἡμέρα ἐκείνη echo the need for alertness in view of its proximity.[24]

The case is similarly overwhelming for the interpretation of vv. 14-19 as local and historical. V. G. Simkhovitch long ago lunged at the heart of the matter when he asked "If it refers to the end of the world, what difference does it make whether that end is to come in the winter or in the summer?"[25]   And C. H. Dodd in similar vein affirmed that the description in these verses fits precisely a condition of besiegement.[26]

Unless these verses have reference to the destruction of Jerusalem and the temple, Christ has not truly replied to the enquiry from His disciples which provoked the discourse. Furthermore, the setting of this passage in Mark's Gospel is particularly important as has been shown earlier. Christ had warned the church leaders of His day that they were shortly to witness the Judgments of God.[27]   The temple had been declared abandoned.[28]   It is then that we have the announcement to the disciples regarding the dissolution of the sacred building.[29] Because Mark has given Christ's prophecy within this context, it is an immediate presumption that the discourse discusses the very issue which raised it, and in the manner of the prophets rather than that of the apocalyptists. Chapters 11 to 15 each refer to the temple, and such an extended description of its fate as 13:14-19 might have been expected.[30]

Neither was the event of A.D. 70 "similar to the suppression of the revolt of an Arab sheik"[31] or akin "to the suppression of the Indian Mutiny".[32]   J. C. Ryle saw the event in better perspective when he wrote:

> Jerusalem and the temple were the heart of the Old
> Jewish dispensation. When they were destroyed the Old
> Mosaic system came to an end. The daily sacrifice,
> the religious feasts, the altar, the holy of holies,
> the priesthood, were all essential parts of revealed
> religion till Christ came, but no longer. When He
> died upon the cross their work was done. They were
> dead, and it only remained that they should be buried.
> But it was not fitting that this thing should be done
> quietly. The ending of a dispensation given with so
> much solemnity at Mt. Sinai might well be expected
> to be marked with peculiar solemnity. The destruction
> of the holy temple where so many old saints had seen
> 'shadows of good things to come' might well be expected
> to form a subject of prophecy.
>
> And so it was . . . the Great High Priest describes
> the end of the dispensation which had been a school-
> master to bring men to Himself.[33]

Not all today would see the significance of Jerusalem and the Temple as Ryle saw it, but his words may well convey the senti- ments of the early church, and of the author of Mark's Gospel. And this being the case, it is not strange that the last discourse of Christ's recorded by the Synoptic writers should allude to the passing of what had been the centre and mainspring of the 'once holy faith'.

Some object that in Mk. 13:14 neither Jerusalem nor the temple are specifically named. But the vital point is that the שׁקוץ in its O.T. contexts (those very contexts to which Mt. 24:15 alludes) is always associated with a desecrating attack on Jerusalem and its temple.[34] Matthew's τόπος ἅγιος is the very expression used over and over in Scripture for the Temple.[35] And Mark's ὅπου οὐ δεῖ with its hint of the desecration of a holy place could refer to one site only, so far as Christ's hearers were concerned.[36]

Old Testament parallels exist for this apparent neglect to specify the fate of the temple in detail. In the prophets, the fate of the temple is inevitably linked with the fate of Jerusalem.[37] See, for example, Jer. 26:6,9, and 7:14,34. Jer. 7:30 shows that it is the presence of abominations in the temple which pollute it, and therefore call for the judgment described in the following verses. But after v. 14 of this chapter, the destruction of the temple is never expressed. The general catastrophe involving the city and the nation is referred to, and by inference the same destruction razed the holy place. The situation is identical in Mark 13, and the lack of specific reference to the temple is no evidence that it is not in view.

The ordinary tools of exegesis applied to vv. 24-27 and 14-19 of Mark 13 negate the viewpoints categorized earlier as belonging to schools one and two.

What should be said of the third view -- namely that the discourse includes both the crisis of A.D. 70 and the greater crisis at the end of the world, yet separates them one from the other?[38]

Not all who see both the end of Jerusalem and the end of the Age in this same chapter, interpret it along identical lines. Lagrange and Rigaux, for example, differ considerably. The former considers the arrangement of Mark 13 to be the work of the Evangelist as he blended two discourses of Christ, one concerning the ruin of the temple, and the other the second advent. Not so Rigaux, who holds that the two perspectives were indissolubly united by Christ in the single presentation. Cranfield's position is similar to Rigaux's. He says: "Neither an exclusively historical nor an exclusively eschatological interpretation is satisfactory, . . . we must allow for a double reference, for a mingling of historical and eschatological."[39]

From a faith standpoint such viewpoints may seem acceptable,

but exegetically they are hardly tolerable. Most of these
commentators, for example, point to the twofold question of Matt.
24:3: Εἰπὲ ἡμῖν, πότε ταῦτα ἔσται, καὶ τί τὸ σημεῖον τῆς σῆς
παρουσίας καὶ συντελείας τοῦ αἰῶνος; . . . But when one takes
into consideration the accounts of the same enquiry found in
Mark and Luke, it is evident that the disciples had in view a
single event only, of which the fall of Jerusalem was a significant part.[40] Note the parallelism in Mark 13:4.

πότε - τί τὸ σημεῖον

ταῦτα - ταῦτα πάντα

ἔσται - μέλλη συντελεῖσθαι

In effect, the question of the disciples is, "When will this
take place, and what will be the sign of it?"

The most obvious difficulty for commentators of this school,
particularly those who view the discourse as separating the two
crises, is finding the precise point of division between the two.
Some select v. 24, but it is obviously tied to the preceding
verse. Others prefer v. 20, despite its obvious link with v. 19.
Still others fix upon v. 21, but only by ignoring τότε in this
same verse, which links the statement to the preceding and
following passages. The majority settle for v. 19 despite the
fact that αἱ ἡμέραι ἐκαῖναι connects the verse to the previous
description.

It must ever be kept in mind that v. 24 which introduces the
Parousia is riveted just as closely to the tribulation heralded
by the coming of the βδέλυγμα against Jerusalem, and without any
hint of a separating chasm of centuries.[41]

The great stumbling-block, however, is v. 30.[42] Ἀμὴν λέγω
ὑμῖν ὅτι οὐ μὴ παρέλθῃ ἡ γενεὰ αὕτη μέχρις οὗ ταῦτα πάντα γένηται.

Lagrange, Busch, and others apply vv. 28-31 to the first crisis,
but surely this must be on a par with the behaviour of one of
Lewis Carroll's characters who practised believing sundry
impossible things every morning before breakfast. Such an
application has been rightly described as the most arbitrary of
exegesis, and a veritable feat of strength.

Various and ingenious are the stratagems, both exegetical and
philosophical, which have been devised to explain away Christ's
"hard saying". The first tack usually adopted is to find a
broader meaning for γενεὰ. But, wherever we read in the New
Testament of γενεὰ[43], it is the contemporaries of Christ who are
signified. See Mt. 11:16; 12:39,41,42,45,23-26, Mk. 8:38,

Luke 11:50f., 17:25. E. Ellis's suggestion[44] is that γενεὰ here has a similar connotation to that found in some Qumran texts, namely, that of an indefinite period sometimes involving a number of literal generations, somewhat akin to the New Testament's usage of such eschatological expressions as ἐσχάτη ὥρα ἐστίν in 1 Jn. 2:18.[45]

This has much to recommend it, but hardly meets the need when the repeated linking of the two crises into one throughout the chapter is considered, and the usual meaning of γενεὰ throughout the Gospels is remembered.

A. L. Moore is one of the most recent scholars to repeat an old expedient with reference to this troublesome verse. He contends that ταῦτα πάντα could apply to the entire discourse of vv. 5-27, but that on the other hand ταῦτα in v. 30 must have an identical reference to the same word in v. 29, where it is clear that only the events prior to the End are in view. He says " . . . if the reference of ταῦτα in v. 29 is taken as being the events preceding the End only, that πάντα of v. 30 can be understood as emphasizing that all the 'signs' of the End (vv. 5-23) are to come upon the contemporary generation."[46]

But this really will not do. It is understandable that ταῦτα in v. 29 can mean the signs listed in vv. 5-23, because v. 29 itself detaches the Parousia from the ταῦτα by saying ὅταν ταῦτα ἴδητε. . .γινώσκετε ὅτι ἐγγύς ἐστιν. But the statement in v. 30 is followed by ὁ οὐρανὸς καὶ ἡ γῆ παρελεύσονται . . .[47] and by v. 32, which on two counts cannot mean just the fall of Jerusalem. One, the expression is far too solemn to be limited to that event, and secondly the expression ἡ ἡμέρα ἐκείνη is a technical term for the End.[48] Besides, how incongruous to teach that all the signs of the imminent event would take place, but the event itself tarry for centuries! The signs surely cease to be signs if this be the case. The position taken by Moore destroys the very purpose of the fig-tree parable.

Moore replies to Beasley-Murray's objection that the addition of πάντα in v. 30 rules out any limitation of the reference to exclude vv. 24-27, but he has not presented or countered the whole of Beasley-Murray's case. The latter points out that Luke omits ταῦτα altogether (21:32), and thus makes πάντα to embrace the whole discourse. Furthermore, Christ evidently regarded the fall of Jerusalem as part of the judgments of the End, and therefore the time of the final tribulation would also witness the final deliverance.[49]

C. H. Dodd, O. Cullmann, C. Cranfield, and others, have set forth appealing philosophical positions to explain the New Testament language regarding the imminence of the advent. Dodd declares that "When the profound realities underlying a situation are depicted in the dramatic form of historical prediction, the certainty and inevitability of the spiritual process involved are expressed in terms of the immediate imminence of the event."[50] 0. Cullmann includes the view of Dodd within his own more comprehensive suggestion: "L'élément essentiel de la proximité du Royaume n'est donc pas la date finale, mais bien la certitude que l'oeuvre expiatrice de Christ sur la croix constitue l'étape décisive dans l'approche du Royaume de Dieu."[51] We cannot but view these statements as more appropriate to abstract theology than to exegesis. They speak truth, but we think they do not speak the whole truth, if applied to Mk. 13.

It is apparent that the post-apostolic age has rarely been able to approach this chapter as did its first readers. Particularly in the modern age, aware of the passage of the centuries, present-day readers instinctively reach out for some resolution of the problem that the plain meaning of these verses (particularly v.30) creates. This reaction, as much emotional, in some cases, as intellectual, does not augur well for the exegesis thus stimulated. One who illustrates the exegetical wrestling involved in the effort to make Mk. 13 consistent with itself and the facts of history is Feuillet, whose own interpretation has been labelled "monstrous" by Kümmel.[52] We will notice a few of his comments, for all in all, we consider that this commentator, without intending to do so, actually strengthens the position of school four.

> Alors en effet on se trouve réduit à cette alternative. Ou bien il faut soutenir que Jésus s'est trompé en faisant coincider dans sa réponse les deux événements, hypothèse non seulement subversive de la foi chrétienne, mais encore critiquement inconciliable avec les passages qui attribuent à Jésus l'idée de fonder une religion nouvelle et une société visible stable, pourvue d'une hiérarchie destinée précisément à faire oeuvre de propagande; inconciliable également avec les paraboles où le royaume est comparé à un grain de sénevé, au levain, au froment qui croît avec l'ivraie, à une vigne confiée d'abord aux Juifs, puis, après leur condamnation, aux Gentils;. . .Ou bien il faut chercher dans le présent discours certains traits qui permettent de distinguisher les deux événements et de montrer que le Christ ne les a pas confondus. Mais cette entreprise des commentateurs paraît être une véritable gageure. . .

> Franchement, si l'on veut soutenir que Jésus, ayant traité ensemble les deux thèmes de la ruine du temple et de la fin du monde, les a cependant parfaitement distingués (1) on ne peut le faire qu'a priori en s'appuyant sur l'impossibilité pour le Christ de se

tromper, car les documents qui nous rapportent son
discours ne permettent de faire aucune discrimination
nette entre ces deux événements. Lagrange le reconnaît
volontiers, et il suppose que les évangélistes, étant
encore de temps à autre sous l'impression de l'espérance
incoercible de la prochaine venue de leur Maître,
auraient plutôt favorisé la pénombre" (L'Évangile
de Jésus-Christ, Paris, p. 478). On hésite a s'arrêter
à une telle hypothèse; on ne pourrait le faire qu'en
désespoir de cause.[53]

Let us briefly consider Feuillet's objections to what we have
categorized as the fourth position. He declares it to be
irreconcilable with passages which attribute to Jesus the
founding of a new religion, and a stable, visible society, whose
task is to propagate the Christian message to the rest of the
world. He also urges that the growth parables, in particular,
indicate that the church would do its work over a long period.
These are popular objections which must be considered.

As regards the first argument, it must be conceded that the
Gospels teach Christ's establishment of the church, and His
training of its pioneers for a task subsequent to His death.
The Twelve were called to 'be with him' and to be 'sent forth'.
It is important to note that prior to the Cross, the only
fulfillment of the vocation of the Twelve was the short preaching
tour recorded in Mk. 6:6ff. But this antedates that phase of
Christ's ministry which was specially devoted to the training
of His disciples. As A. L. Moore has commented, "If Jesus had
not had in mind further, much more extensive preaching by the
disciples, it is difficult to understand why after this short
tour, he should have laid such emphasis on training them."[54]

Having conceded that much to Feuillet, we must next criticize
him for taking for granted that Christ intended the work of the
church to involve centuries. Lagrange similarly affirms that
there are no grounds for believing that the times of the Gentiles
would be shorter than the ages allotted to Judaism.[55] On the
contrary, there is every reason for so believing. Exegetically,
we know of no evidence that so far as Christ's thinking was
concerned, the task allotted to the disciples and the early
church could not have been completed within that generation.[56]

Another objection to the position of the fourth exegetical
school is the concept that Luke has historicized Mark, and made
provision for a time-lag of great length between A.D. 70 and the
end of the Age. This view is almost universal among recent
German scholars. It represents, however, an exaggeration of the
true situation. In Luke 21, Jerusalem's fall is still viewed
eschatologically. While in Mark we have mention of the θλίψις

οἷα οὐ γέγονεν τοιαύτη followed by cosmic signs and then the advent, Luke's presentation, though more detailed in some respects, retains the same pattern. Both I. Howard Marshall and E. E. Ellis agree that Luke is not historicizing Mark.[57]

Lagrange's view (mentioned above) of καιροὶ ἐθνῶν is typical of many commentators. Few of them have read, or at least agreed, with Harnack, who sixty years ago contended that Luke's expression should be interpreted by the parallel passages in the other Synoptics. His own conclusion, expressed in The Date of the Acts and of the Synoptic Gospels, was that the Evangelist could not have contemplated a period exceeding months.[58] Inasmuch as the Lucan reference points back to Dan. 8:13,14 with its assignment of 2300 evening-mornings for the trampling underfoot of the sanctuary at Jerusalem,[59] it cannot be demonstrated that Christ or Luke had centuries in mind. Schmid, and many others, have missed this point, as is shown by their frequent contrasting of Luke 21:24 with the Markan account.[60]

Having considered the real weaknesses of the exegetical positions of the first three schools of interpretation, and the supposed weaknesses of the fourth we are now shut up to the last as the only approach which can successfully withstand detailed investigation. We consider that Strauss and Renan on the one hand, and Beasley-Murray et al. on the other, carry the day in asserting that the Olivet discourse links the fate of Jerusalem with the end of the world, and promises both to the generation listening to Christ. This victory should not be construed as via default. It stands on its own feet, and is shown to be correct by the weight of exegetical evidence. Most of this evidence has been offered by way of refutation of the positions of the interpreters. Vv. 14-20 do refer to a local, historical event, and vv. 24-27 cannot be taken metaphorically, and both are connected with the great tribulation inaugurated by the coming of the βδέλυγμα. Furthermore, both are to be witnessed by the generation listening to Christ, v. 30. In summary, it can be said that the most significant piece of evidence for this fourth view is that it understands Mark 13 just as it stands without the skilful twistings and turnings which are more becoming to blacksmiths than to exegetes.[61]

At this point, in support of the position just espoused, we wish to diverge from the beaten track of critical orthodoxy. We believe that there is additional evidence to be gleaned from Mark 13 on this topic, which is rarely considered from the viewpoint of its bearing on the issue under discussion.

Many exegetes have pointed out that Christ's discourse is a midrash upon Daniel.[62] It has often been shown that, apart from the reference to the Son of Man, for the most part the Olivet

72

discourse by its allusions is re-interpreting Daniel 9:24-27,[63] and its expansion in 11:31 to the end of the book. Jewry in Christ's time regarded these passages as prophecies awaiting complete fulfillment[64] and, judging from Mark 13, Christ was a typical Son of His Age in this respect.

Let it be noted that 9:24-27 is the only passage in Daniel which clearly links the ravaging of the city and temple with the ushering in of the eschatological kingdom, and just such a connection is implied in the Olivet sermon.[65] It is significant that there is no hint in the Danielic passage of any great gap in time between the devastation of the city and the subsequent judgment on the שׁקוץ which accompanies the setting up of the Messianic kingdom.

> Seventy weeks of years are decreed concerning your
> people and your holy city, to finish the transgression,
> to put an end to sin, and to atone for iniquity, to
> bring in everlasting righteousness, to seal both vision
> and prophet, and to anoint a most holy place . . . And
> after the sixty-two weeks, an anointed one shall be
> cut off, and shall have nothing; and the people of the
> prince who is to come shall destroy the city and the
> sanctuary. Its end shall come with a flood, and to
> the end there shall be war: desolations are decreed.
> And he shall make a strong covenant with many for one
> week; and for half of the week he shall cause sacrifice
> and offering to cease; and upon the wing of abominations
> shall come one who makes desolate, until the decreed
> end is poured out on the desolator.
>
> Dan. 9:24-27

Christ assayed no mathematical calculations, but according to Lohmeyer and Lagrange we have in Mark 13:20 an allusion to Dan. 9:24. Far more certain is the fact that the great themes of this passage as a whole are re-applied in the eschatological discourse, and with a similarity of pattern.

The book of Daniel thus anticipated that the final end of sin and the ushering in of everlasting righteousness, plus the anointing of the Messianic temple, would succeed the greatest crisis of the ages -- namely the attack of the שׁקוץ upon Jerusalem, its temple, and its people. Both chapter 9:24-27 and the presentation of 11:31-12:13 picture the Messianic era as being precipitated by the Antichrist's onslaught on "the holy mountain". Thus Mark 13 presents the same sequence of events as the O.T. Apocalypse. As surely as Daniel suggests no great time gap between the attack on the city and the end, so it is with the eschatological discourse.[66]

73

The words of Johannes Weiss merit thoughtful attention:

> . . . schon Jesus selber sich die Zukunft nach der
> Form der jüdischen Endzeit-Erwartungen gedacht habe.
> Wie er sich mit seiner Messias-Vorstellung an die
> Weissagung Daniels angeschlossen hat, so werden auch
> in anderen Zukunftsdingen die Lehren der Apokalyptik
> für ihn massgebend gewesen sein.[67]

Loisy speaks similarly. While we usually disagree with his
fundamental approach, some of his exegetical insights are undeniably valuable. As with Weiss, Loisy holds that the author of the
eschatological discourse has conformed it to the frame-work
traced by Daniel. He stresses the fact that as surely as Daniel
taught only a short time of desolation for Jerusalem before the
glorious appearance of the Messiah, so with the presentation of
Mark 13.[68]

The full force of the present argument only becomes apparent as
we remember Christ's attitude to the Old Testament. Neither He,
nor His contemporaries, thought of the book of Daniel as a pseudonymous production of the 2nd century B.C. Neither He nor they
considered the forecasts in that book regarding the Antichrist
and the Messianic kingdom to have been completely fulfilled.
Therefore, so far as Christ was concerned, if thus "it was
written", then thus "it must be".

On this additional basis, therefore, that Christ's concept of
the future was faithful to that of the Old Testament presentation
in Daniel, we find the fourth school of interpreters more consonant with the facts than any other. This school retains the
strengths of schools one and two, but sheds their weaknesses.
Here again, as is so often the case, the heresies prove "true in
what they affirm, but false in what they deny".

Excursus on Mark 13:30

The conclusion just mentioned not only embarrasses those who
hold to the first three positions. Some like Beasley-Murray, who
are committed to the remaining interpretation, confess that they
find their own conclusion hard to digest. This is not strange.
William Temple, writing to Ronald Knox in 1913 said: "Anyhow
I think our Lord definitely rejected the apocalyptic idea of
Messiahship. And if I thought He expected an immediate catastrophe other than His own Death and Resurrection, I think I
should have to renounce Christianity."[69] A Cambridge Church
Congress held about the same time, was told by the Bishop of
Birmingham that Henry Sidgwick became an agnostic because Christ
foretold things which had not happened. And E. C. Selwyn has
asserted that Mark 13:30 must take a major share of responsibility

for such a collapse of faith.[70] Strauss and Renan found their
exegesis of Mark 13:30 an effective tool in undeceiving
biblicists.

The quandary to which we refer, however, is surely not a
matter for exegesis. It belongs to the realm of apologetics.
True, but has the _exegesis_ of even school four been exhaustive?
It has come up with the truth, but does it have all the truth
on this matter -- i.e. all the _exegetical_ truth?

It is our intention to ask whether the key verse of Mk. 13:30
has yet been fully exegeted. It is agreed that the interpretation given by school four alone takes v. 30 fully into account.
It shows what is the evident meaning of the language employed.
But is no more to be said? Does not exegesis take account not
only of the plain meaning of the words, but of cultural attitudes
and habits which occasionally give Semitic expressions nuances
additional to that which the translated words convey to readers
of other cultures?

It is our suggestion that modern Western readers with their
sometimes fatalistic or predestinarian outlook often take as
absolute, Semitic pronouncements which in their own day would
have been considered as less than absolute. In harmony with a
small but significant group of commentators, we believe that
Mk. 13:30 may be understood as belonging to a similar genre
as Jonah's "Yet forty days and Ninevah shall be overthrown."[71]
Here was the fiat of the Almighty to Nineveh. Hardly could a
prediction be more definite as to what and when. The whole book
of Jonah revolves around it. Yet the forty days passed, and
according to the narrator, Ninevah still pointed its proud towers
to the heavens. Jonah was certainly angry, but he was not
suprised. He seems rather to have anticipated it. "I knew that
thou art a gracious God, and merciful, slow to anger, and abound-
ing in steadfast love, and repentest of evil."[72]

An unusually frank commentator was Hermann Olshausen. It
seemed his habit to acknowledge difficulties, and to confess the
inadequacy of current explanations. Concerning Mk. 13:30 he
wrote: " . . . we do not hesitate to adopt . . . the simple
interpretation -- and the only one consistent with the text --
that Jesus did intend to represent his coming as contemporaneous
with the destruction of Jerusalem, and the over-throw of the
Jewish polity."[73] His editor did not agree with him, and saw
fit to indicate this by a footnote. But the same Olshausen took
pains to introduce his exegetical comments on Matt. 24 by a
preparatory note regarding the contingent nature of prophecy.
His measured statements afford a reasoned philosophy for his
own approach -- a philosophy which he felt was drawn from
Scripture itself.[74]

It is certain that Christ and His contemporaries were well aware of contingent promises recorded by Moses and the Prophets. Had not Yahweh promised to take the captive Israelites direct from Egypt to Canaan -- a distance requiring less than a fortnight's journeying? And had not that same generation wandered outside Canaan for forty years and then failed of entrance?[75]

We submit that the exegesis of Mk. 13:30 is only complete if we allow for the possibility that Christ, as a Hebrew of the Hebrews, may have used an absolute statement with less than an absolute meaning, in harmony with those Scriptures He so implicitly trusted. It is possible that He believed that if the early church proved faithful to its missionary commission, and if the chastened Jewish nation repented, the end would transpire in that same Age.[76] It is this linking of the gospel proclamation to the world with the end of the Age that provides the hint of the contingent element. Such proclamation would be dependent upon the whole-hearted dedication of the church. An uncertain human element is involved.

Excursus on Mark 13:14-24

To our additional comment on Mk. 13:30, another on Mk. 13:14-24 should be added. We have expressed agreement with the local historical nature of the scene that begins with the 14th verse. But again we enquire whether there is any more to be said. It is, for example, possible that Christ foresaw the attack upon Jerusalem as the beginning of a world-wide aggression against the Christian "elect" by the idolatrous Romans? Did He anticipate that the gospel of His kingdom spreading to all the world would inevitably arouse the antagonism of the Empire, precipitating a tribulation on a scale hitherto unknown?

Such a view is not a denial of the fact that Mk. 13:14ff. is local and historical. If, as we have seen, Christ expected the End in His generation, and viewed Jerusalem's fall as part of the eschatological woes, implicit in such a view must have been the spread of the Palestinian tribulation to all quarters of the world. One must not be so busy rebutting the application that sees only the end of the world in Mark 13 as to miss the point that the universal destruction is indeed portrayed, not to the exclusion of Jerusalem's fate but as its continuation. And, in effect, this is precisely that Luke's version says. Verse 24 plainly sets forth the destiny of Israel's capital.
καὶ πεσοῦνται στόματι μαχαίρης καὶ αἰχμαλωτισθήσονται εἰς τὰ ἔθνη πάντα, καὶ Ἰεπουσαλὴμ ἔσται πατουμένη ὑπὸ ἐθνῶν, ἄχρι οὗ πληρωθῶσιν καιροὶ ἐθνῶν. But there is no way of separating these words from those which follow and which distinctly refer to universal signs including: σημεῖα ἐν ἡλίῳ καὶ σελήνῃ καὶ ἄστροις

76

καὶ ἐπι τῆς γῆς συνοχη ἐθνῶν ἐν ἀπορία ἤχους θαλάσσης καὶ σάλου, ἀποψυχόντων ἀνθώπων ἀπὸ φόβου καὶ προσδοκίας τῶν ἐπερχομένων αἱ γὰρ δυνάμεις τῶν οὐρανῶν σαλευθήσονται, καὶ τότε ὄφονται τὸν υἱὸν τοῦ ἀνθρώπου ἐρχόμενον ἐν νεφέλῃ μετὰ δυνάμεως καὶ δόξης πολλῆς.

In this passage we are distinctly told of distress of __nations__. The συνοχη appears to embrace the whole world, for the canvas of Luke's word painting takes in all creation. The scope of this tribulation, which is undeniably linked with Jerusalem's siege, is universal. The thought that Israel's trouble spreads to all nations could not be more clearly and strongly affirmed than it is in this passage.

If Mk. 13:14ff. describes a period of tribulation beginning at Jerusalem, but quickly extending to the known world, some contextual difficulties are automatically resolved. Verses 19-26 have always constituted a major problem of exegesis precisely because of its two-fold connection with the fate of Jerusalem and that of the entire world. ἔσονται γὰρ αἱ ἡμέραι ἐκεῖναι θλῖψις, οἷα οὐ γέγονεν τοιαύτη ἀπ' ἀρχῆς κτισεως, ἥν ἔκτισεν ὁ θεὸς ἕως τοῦ νῦν καὶ οὐ μὴ γένηται. καὶ εἰ μὴ ἐκολόβωσεν κύριος τὰς ἡμέρας, οὐκ ἄν ἐσώθη πᾶσα σάρξ. ἀλλὰ διὰ τοὺς ἐκλεκτοὺς οὓς ἐξελέξατο ἐκολόβωσεν τὰς ἡμέρας. καὶ τότε ἐάν τις ὑμῖν εἴπῃ, "Ἴδε ὧδε ὁ χριστός. "Ἴδε ἐκεῖ, μὴ πιστεύετε ἐγερθήσονται δὲ ψευδόχριστοι καὶ ψευδοπροφῆται καὶ ποιήσουσιν σημεῖα καὶ τέρατα πρὸς τὸ ἀποπλανᾶν, εἰ δυνατόν, τοὺς ἐκλεκτούς. ὑμεῖς δὲ βλέπετε προείρηκα ὑμῖν πάντα. Ἀλλα ἐν ἐκείναις ταῖς ἡμέραις μετὰ τὴν θλῖψιν ἐκείνην ὁ ἥλιος σκοτισθήσεται, καὶ ἡ σελήνη οὐ δώσει τὸ φέγγος αὐτῆς, καὶ οἱ ἀστέρες ἔσονται ἐκ τοῦ οὐρανοῦ πίπτοντες, καὶ αἱ δυνάμεις αἱ ἐν τοῖς οὐρανοῖς σαλευθήσονται. καὶ τότε ὄφονται τὸν υἱον τοῦ ἀνθρώπου ἐρχόμενον ἐν νεφέλαις μετὰ δυνάμεως πολλῆς καὶ δόξης.

Vincent Taylor's comment echoes the opinion of many[77] when he declares that the assertion in v. 19 "is much too emphatic for a siege." He continues:

> . . . it is clear that the thought of 19 is eschatologi-
> cal. This is undoubtedly true of 20. Here the idea
> found in many apocalyptic writings, that in His mercy
> and for the sake of the elect God has shortened the
> period of tribulation for mankind . . . is strongly
> expressed. Cf. Dan. xii. 7, 1 Enoch lxxx. 2, 4 Ezra
> iv. 26 . . .[78]

Rigaux's suggestion[79] that " . . . Jérusalem et la Judée sont le centre des événements de la fin . . . les transes finales mettront toutes les existences en danger," would solve some serious contextual problems regarding the ἐκλεκτοί. The weakest part of the exposition of that group which stresses the local nature of vv. 14-23 is the exposition of the ἐκλεκτοί. Some see them as Jews in the siege who may ultimately become Christians. Others consider that the ἐκλεκτοί are the Christians who, though not involved in the siege, are praying for those who are, and that therefore, because of their prayers the days of siege will be shortened. Such expositions as these do not harmonize with the text. Verse 20 clearly intimates that the ἐκλεκτοί are also involved in suffering in this tribulation, and it is the same company who will shortly be gathered from the four winds -- therefore the tribulation must also be in the same four quarters. Thus we have here more than vengeance τῷ λαῷ τούτῳ - Jews. Here is trouble involving the saints.[80]

In essence, it can be said that if the elect are world-wide, then the tribulation which threatens them must likewise be general. It is obvious that the early verses of the discourse deal with world-wide events. ἡγεμόνες καὶ βασιλεῖς and their territories are involved.[81] Following his comments on this section of the text, Schweizer says: "V 13 might have led us to expect that the discussion would continue to be about the end . . ."[82], and Meyer on the early verses and v. 15 in Mt. 24 affirms that "The predictions before us respecting the Messianic woes become more threatening till just at this point they reach a climax."[83] Rigaux says again "La catastrophe mondiale commence par atteindre la Judée et se déclanche ensuite sur tout le monde."[84] This declaration is consistent with the conjunction we find in Luke 21:24,25 -- Israel's sorrows, then the sorrows of all nations.

It is almost certain that Christ had in mind the whole picture of the last part of Daniel 11 and all of Daniel 12.[85] The Olivet discourse refers to both chapters, and it is fundamentally wrong to treat the reference to the βδέλυγμα as though Christ's reference was only to a single facet of the Danielic picture. Inasmuch as Christ quotes also from the verses preceding Daniel 12:1, as well as the verses following, the exegete also should take that whole section of the Old Testament apocalypse into account. The final verses of Daniel 11 picture an anti-God power spreading over the world in "the time of the end", which period culminates in a time of trouble "such as never has been" for the "holy people". This distress is relieved only by the standing up of the great Prince who is the protector over these same holy ones. Daniel 12:7, which refers back to 12:1, makes it clear, in addition to the evidence of the earlier context, that it is the believers who are menaced by the Antichrist in this final trial.

We believe that Lambrecht rightly represents the passage in

Mark when he writes:

> Der Greuel steht im Tempel zu Jerusalem; Judäa
> muss flüchten; auch hier sollte man den Horizont noch
> weiter sehen: die Katastrophe hat Weltausmass. Dies
> stimmt mit der ausserordentlichen Grösse -- und
> Einmaligkeit in der Zeit! -- Überein.[86]

Such an interpretation, at least, recognizes the close liaison
between 13:14ff. and the end of all things.[87] Lambrecht also
affirms that the description in v. 27 assumes the catastrophe of
vv. 14-20.[88]

The Relationship between τὸ βδέλυγμα and ὁ υἱὸς τοῦ ἀνθρώπου

It has long been recognized that Mark 13 revolves around two
chief signs -- the sign requested by the disciples whereby they
might know that the end was near, and the sign accompanying the
end itself. But it has not always been seen that the second sign
is the response to the first -- ὁ υἱὸς τοῦ ἀνθρώπου is heaven's
reply to the βδέλυγμα.[89]

Feuillet comments on the close and deep connection between the
announcement of the destruction of the temple and the announcement of the coming of the Son of Man. He also declares that the
second makes a counterbalance of the first. As the temple of
Jerusalem was the great visible sign of the unity of the people
of God prior to the Cross, so Christ Himself replaces it as the
centre of the reassembling of the new community.[90] The same
writer also points out that the same relationship is to be found
in the proclamation made before the Sanhedrin. Again the promise
of the coming of the Son of Man in the clouds is given in the
perspective of the ruin of the temple. The High Priest had asked
"Are you the Christ?" -- a question which means "Is it true, as
they have accused, that you claim to give us a new temple?"[91]

Loisy[92] makes the same connection between the two signs. He
asserts that the two facts are correlative, the first introducing
and provoking the second, and the second making amends for the
scandal of the first.

The שׁקוץ in its Old Testament contexts is forever menacing
the saints and trampling them, and their place of worship underfoot. Its shameful activities cry aloud for redress, and for
vindication of the helpless, suffering remnant. Similarly, the
Son of Man, in its Old Testament context, represents the justification and exaltation of the oppressed ones, and the destruction
for the oppressor. These same meanings are retained in the
eschatological discourse of the New Testament.

To sense the full appropriateness of the expression ὁ υἱὸς τοῦ ἀνθρώπου in the context of Mark 13, it is necessary to briefly review the significance of the expression elsewhere.

The greater number of the Son of Man passages fall into two categories: (a) those descriptive of humiliation and suffering; (b) those descriptive of vindication and exaltation.[93] For example, Mk. 8:31 exemplifies (a) καὶ ἤρξατο διδάσκειν αὐτοὺς ὅτι δεῖ τὸν υἱὸν τοῦ ἀνθρώπου πολλὰ παθεῖν, καὶ ἀποδοκιμασθῆναι . . .καὶ ἀποκτανθῆναι. . . .And Mark 14:62 examplifies (b). . . ὄψεσθε τὸν υἱὸν τοῦ ἀνθρώπου ἐκ δεξιῶν καθήμενον τῆς δυνάμεως καὶ ἐρχόμενον μετὰ τῶν νεφελῶν τοῦ οὐρανοῦ. There are scholars who deny the authenticity of either one of the two groups, or of Christ's use of both. Inasmuch as the evidence does not compel unanimity among scholars, such wholesale emasculation of the text may be traceable to the procrustean bed of prior suppositions, even if the conclusions of each group are correct in certain instances. While it is still not yet beyond dispute, there seems good reason for believing that Christ was the first, at least in those Jewish circles represented by His disciples, to link the two concepts of Messiah and the Son of Man.[92] But He did more. He linked both concepts with a third -- that of "the suffering Servant".[93] Textual study shows that Daniel's writings were dependent to some extent, not only on Jeremiah and Ezekiel, but also on Deutero-Isaiah. Both bodies of literature make reference to the wise (Dan. 12:3; Isa. 52:13), who make the many righteous (Dan. 11:33,35; Isa. 53:3f.). Daniel's Son of Man (7:13,26), representing the faithful remnant of Israel, endures suffering in a similar way to the Servant described in Isaiah. The Qumran covenanters were among the first to make this connection. Even Morna Hooker, who disagrees with the earlier mentioned position of Jeremias, T. W. Manson, V. Taylor, et al., considers that Daniel 7 is a vital part of those Scriptures wherein it was written that the Son of Man must suffer many things.[96]

Thus the term כבר אנש in Daniel 7 embodies concepts of suffering and subsequent vindication. It is thus emblematic of the theme of the entire book. In the Gospels the same two-fold meaning is associated with the bulk of the Son of Man sayings, and this is particularly true of its usage in Mark 13:26.[97]

While it is the case that the arrival of the Son of Man in Mark 13 is connected, as in Daniel, with the theme of present suffering and future vindication, this is not so with the use of the Son of Man figure in 1 Enoch and 2 Esdras. These sources stress vindictiveness rather than vindication. The emphasis is upon the judgment of the wicked, a theme only lightly touched upon in the Olivet discourse.[98]

Thus the presence of ὁ υἱὸς τοῦ ἀνθρώπου is not only consonant
with its Mark 13 context, but remarkably appropriate. It helps
to unify the chapter, and lends support to the thesis that both
it and its context are authentic. It is highly doubtful that a
melange of material, partly authentic and partly not so, could
present a picture so consistent with the entire Biblical picture
of the Son of Man.

More still needs to be said about the relationship between the
sign of the persecuting βδέλυγμα and the vindicating υἱος τοῦ
ἀνθρώπου. The first sign augurs the destruction of the temple,
while the second heralds the establishment of the everlasting
temple -- the community of the saints established when the
covenant promise of Lev. 26:12 is at last fulfilled and Yahweh
comes to dwell with His people forever.

Many writers have pointed out that Dan. 9:24, especially למשה
קדש קדשים   , and Eze. chs. 40-48 led the Jews to anticipate
a Messianic temple contemporaneous with the age when transgression would be finished, and everlasting righteousness be ushered
in. Joachim Jeremias has spoken of "the age-old conception that
a new reign commences with a newly-consecrated temple: Mk. 13:2
must be placed alongside Mk. 14:58, Acts 6:14."[99]

>   The Temple will be destroyed, but after the destruction
>   of the Temple the parousia of Jesus will take place and
>   the building of the heavenly temple, the glorified
>   community.[100]

The New Testament incorporates the sanctuary symbolism in
connection with the glorified church gathered by the Son of Man
(Rev. 21:3,22), and it is to this that Mark 13:26 points. He
who comes in the clouds with great glory is Himself the
which is to be with men, and dwell with them. Concerning the
city of God, John wrote: ἡ πόλις οὐ χρείαν ἔχει τοῦ ἡλίου . . .
ὁ λύχνος αὐτῆς τὸ ἀρνίον.

All this corresponds to the hope expressed in Daniel.
Feuillet, Congar, Gärtner and others have written at length on
this point.[101] In summary, Mk. 13:26-27 points to the fulfillment of Dan. 9:24 when sin is to be ended, and everlasting
righteousness established. Part of the imagery of this latter
verse has to do with the anointing of a new temple, which in
New Testament thought is applied to the community of glorified
saints gathered by Him who is their Shekinah.[102] Mk. 13:26 is
thus an admirable counterpart to the 14th verse of the same
chapter which describes the desecration and destruction of the
Old temple by the Antichrist.

Nature of the Discourse: Prediction or Paraclesis? Or Both?

The discussion so far has endeavoured to reach a conclusion
regarding the perspective of the Olivet discourse. We have seen
that of the four major interpretations, only that which views the
destruction of Jerusalem as part of the eschatological drama
meets the tests of exegesis. Next we might well enquire as to
the nature of Christ's revelation. Is He chiefly concerned with
conveying precise information about the future, or with offering
pastoral admonition?

To ask the question is practically to answer it. It has been a
matter of frequent remark how different Mark 13 is to typical
Jewish apocalyptic matter.[103] In many respects the sermon is
both surprising and disappointing. There is no horoscope for
mankind, no lurid description of the bliss of the saved, or the
terrors of the lost. But what is present from beginning to end
is the note of warning, the admonition to be right rather than
merely to know or profess the right. The first and last words of
Christ are βλέπετε, and His imperatives throughout amount to
nineteen. It is evident that His prophecy has primarily a moral
purpose, as was the case also with most Old Testament predictions.

Having said that Christ's primary purpose was pastoral and
admonitory, should Busch be followed in holding that there is no
true succession of events delineated? We feel Kümmel is more
accurate at this point. The various terms of chronological
significance throughout Mark 13 cannot be ignored. Some of them
definitely imply a sequence of events. Furthermore, this
sequence, for the most part, is preserved in the threefold
Synoptic record. The pattern looks somewhat like the following:
religious agitation and persecution; increasing confusion on
national and international planes, accompanied by terrestrial
signs such as earthquakes; world-wide proclamation of the gospel;
increasing religious intolerance; apostasy; onslaught on
Jerusalem; the great tribulation with its accompanying intensified deceptions; cosmic signs climaxed by the revelation of
Christ to gather His elect.

While the notes of time[104] which are scattered through the
discourse cannot be ignored, we do not feel that there is any
marked emphasis by Christ on chronological precision. For the
most part, this address falls neatly into a threefold time
division: preliminaries to the tribulation, the tribulation
itself, deliverance of the elect by Christ from the tribulation.
The advent of the βδέλυγμα betokens the beginning of the θλῖψις,
but prior to that fearful coming, lesser signs will be observed.
Any closer chronological delineation than this is liable to
affect distortion, but any laxer or hazier presentation is likewise unfaithful to the evidence.

In this exegetical summary we have made no attempt to study microscopically any minute portions of the eschatological discourse. A survey of commentaries indicates that already too many exegetes have failed to see the wood for the trees. Later chapters, however, will give close attention to Mk. 13:14, its various components, and its significance for the discourse as a whole.

FOOTNOTES ON CHAPTER TWO

1. Haenchen, Der Weg Jesu, 434n.

2. "Isolated from its setting, it makes complete sense -- better
sense, in fact than in its present position. For the introductory words refer to the destruction of the temple, whereas the
discourse itself says nothing about this but deals with the End
of the Age and the coming of the Son of Man." B. H. Branscomb,
The Gospel of Mark, (MNTC)(London, 1937), 231. "Seit alter Zeit
sind die Meinungen geteilt, ob . . . dann die Rede überhaupt eine
Antwort auf die gestellte Frage enthält. Eine Antwort auf die
Frage nach dem Zeitpunkt der Zerstörung des Tempels wird aber in
der ganzen Rede überhaupt nicht gegeben, da man sie auch in V.
28-30 nicht finden kann. In V. 14 wird man sie deshalb nicht
sehen dürfen, weil hier nicht von der Zerstörung des Tempels,
sondern nur von seiner Entweihung gesprochen wird. Diese
Beobachtung, dass die Rede auf die Frage der Jünger gar nicht'
eingeht, ist für ihre Beurteilung im ganzen wichtig. Aber auf
die erste, allein dem Zusammenhang mit V. 1f entsprechende Frage
folgt noch eine zweite, die sich nicht mehr auf die Tempelzerstörung beziehen kann, sondern nur auf das 'Weltende'.
Sowohl die Worte 'dies alles' als auch das feierliche 'vollendet
werden' beweisen dies. Die richtige Erklärung dieses Sachverhalts
wird nicht die sein, dass die Jünger als fromme Juden sich den
Untergang des Tempels nur mit dem Ende 'dieses Äons' zusammen
denken konnten, sondern die, dass hier der Evangelist V. 5-27,
also den eschatologischen Hauptteil der Rede vorbereitet. Daraus
folgt aber, dass dieser von Haus aus nicht mit der Jüngerfrage
verbunden war." J. Schmid, Markus, 238. "The connexion is . . .
awkwardly made, for the discourse itself contains no explicit
reference to the Temple, though it is probable that a mysterious
future profanation of the Holy Place may be part of the meaning
of the veiled allusion in verse 14. The scope of the discourse
is in any case much wider than the question ascribed to the four
disciples in verse 4 would suggest if interpreted strictly by
reference to verse 2, and it is probable that the repeated phrase
these things in verse 4 should in fact be interpreted rather in
the light of what follows than of what has preceded . . . "
A. E. J. Rawlinson, The Gospel According to St Mark (Westminster
Commentaries)(London, 1949), 179. See also A. Loisy, Les
Évangiles synoptiques, II, 395; E. Schweizer, The Good News
According to Mark (E.T., London, 1971), 262; Nineham, Saint Mark,
343. Contra Carrington et al. " . . . it is all in line with the
question of the disciples to which the Little Apocalypse is an
answer." Mark, 279. A. Feuillet, " . . . or il est incontestable
que, comme l'a souligné Lagrange, le verset 14 de Marc . . . se
donne comme la réponse à la question posée par les disciples au
verset 4 . . . " "Le discours de Jésus sur la ruine du temple

d'après Marc XIII et Luc XXI,5-36", RB, LV (1948), 495. See also
Plummer, Gould, Swete, Cranfield, Beasley-Murray (Mark Thirteen)
ad loc. The position of Lagrange is not identical with that of
the group last mentioned, and should be carefully noted. "Le
début du discours ne répond pas directement à la question: . . .
(Victor). De plus, les vv. 5b et 6 semblent faire double emploi
avec le v. 21 (Wellh., Klost., Loisy). Mais il n'y aurait
répétition inutile que dans la hypothèse fausse de Loisy etc. où
un seul sujet serait traité qui ne serait pas la ruine du Temple.
La répétition, qui est incontestable, marque le parallélisme
entre les deux parties du discours, ayant chacune un objet
différent; chaque période a ses faux Messies. Le Christ ne
répond pas directement parce qu'il traite un double thème à propos
d'une question." Évangile selon Saint Marc (Paris, 1929), 335.
W. G. Kümmel differs from all the preceding but is, perhaps,
closest to Beasley-Murray. "Mark unquestionably understood this
destruction of the temple as a part of the final happenings, since
the inquiry about their date (13.4) πότε ταῦτα ἔσται undoubtedly
refers back to the destruction of the temple." Promise and
Fulfillment, (E.T., London, 1957), 99, 100. If the first cited
commentators (Branscomb et al.) are correct, we cannot but wonder
at Mark's dullness and clumsiness, that he should not have seen
the incongruity of his redactions. Would he have re-read his
work?

3. "This assertion is much too emphatic for a siege; it is clear
that the thought of 19 is eschatological. This is undoubtedly
true of 20." Vincent Taylor, St Mark, 514.

4. "By 'the Elect' . . . the members of the Christian community
are meant." Ibid.

5. The Qumran community, for example.

6. See 151ff.

7. "Now Busch is undoubtedly wrong when he says that the
Evangelist had no intention of describing a succession in time of
eschatological happenings." Kümmel, Promise, 97. But Busch has
many supporters. See Beasley-Murray, Jesus, 214-15.

8. See 11-59, and compare the following: "The largest block of
eschatological teaching to be found in the Gospels is that which
we find in Mark 13 and its parallels in Luke and Matthew. It was
at one time fashionable among scholars to regard it as highly
unauthentic in its present form, and even to postulate an
original Jewish 'little apocalypse' which had been worked over
by later editors within the Christian community. The resultant
compilation might be held to contain embedded in it a certain
number of authentic logia, but it could not as a whole command

the respect of those who set out to reconstruct the beliefs of
the historical Jesus. The steps by which such a conclusion was
reached were fragile enough, and the 'fly-sheet' hypothesis is
interesting chiefly as an illustration of how preconceptions
about the historical Jesus could lead to the rejection of
inconvenient evidence." G. Neville, The Advent Hope (London,
1961), 45. A. L. Moore gives a useful summary which we append
without his detailed footnotes: "The main arguments against
authenticity are as follows:
   i. That the discourse is out of character with Jesus' teaching
elsewhere. But the contents of the chapter can, in fact be
paralleled considerably. Further, the discourse form is not
necessarily a sign that the contents are unauthentic.
   ii. That it is internally inconsistent, v. 32 and the emphasis
on a sudden End being (it is said) out of keeping with the idea
of preceding 'signs'. But signs encouraging watchfulness and
expectancy are capable of being held in tension with the idea of
suddenness.
   iii. That the apparent privacy of the teaching is a mark of
secondariness. Against this, however, we must notice how suitable
private instruction is in the case of material of an apocalyptic
character (if not an 'apocalypse'): other sayings appear to have
been spoken in private, and in this particular case one might well
expect some caution and privacy -- 'Apart from other considerations, it would have been indiscreet for Jesus and his followers
to discuss in the open the anticipated ruin of the temple, involving as it did that of the city and nation also'.
   iv. That Mk. 13,14 (Mtt. 24,15) reveals secondariness. But
this verse, if not authentic to Jesus is intelligible as a Markan
editorial device, or dark hint, without supposing that Mark is
referring to a written source.
   v. That the discourse fits better the early church situation;
but only on a priori views of cleavage between Jesus and the
early church's understanding could this be an argument against
authenticity. There therefore seems good reason for the judgement
'that 13:5-37 does give us substantially our Lord's teaching', to
which a number of scholars incline." Parousia, 178-79.

9. Discussing the question whether the Resurrection and the
Coming of the Son of Man should be identified, A. M. Hunter says:
"Attractive prima facie as this view may seem, it has two serious
weaknesses:
      (1) It fails to do justice to all the Gospel evidence;
      (2) It fails to account for the early Christians' hope of
the Parousia,
      The only satisfactory solution, therefore, is the traditional
one, that our Lord predicted not only a coming in history--of
which the Resurrection and the advent of the Spirit were the
reality--but a coming in glory at the consummation of the Kingdom."
The Work and Words of Jesus (London, 1950), 110. " . . . a

86

Christian faith without its Advent Hope is as much a bowdlerized edition of the Apostolic Gospel as one in which the Son of Man is not risen from the dead." Matthew Black, "The Son of Man in the Teachings of Jesus", ET, LX (1948), 36. " . . . the rejection of this hope is a mutilation of the message of the New Testament." H. H. Rowley, The Faith of Israel (London, 1956) 200n.

10. Rowley, Relevance, 147. See also Cullmann, The Early Church (E. T., London, 1956), 160.

11. Das Evangelium nach Markus (DNTD) (Göttingen,⁶1952), I, 168.

12. Bo Reicke in his review of Beasley-Murray's Jesus and the Future alludes to these: "Solange man in einer Welt lebte, die immer besser zu werden schien, hat die eschatologische Perspektive nicht sehr verlockend gewirkt. Man versuchte deshalb, Jesus von jeder eschatologischen Belastung dadurch zu befreien, dass man nach Möglichkeit die apokalyptischen und eschatologischen Aussagen als Reste jüdischen Denkens betrachtete oder der späteren Kirche zuschrieb. Dabei wurde Mark 13 ein besonders dankbares Gebiet literarkritischer Operationen, weil hier zwei Motive vorliegen, die scheinbar nicht richtig zueinander passen wollen. Erstens spricht nämlich Jesus von der Zerstörung des Tempels, zweitens von der Parusie des Menschensohnes. Und diese Ereignisse würden nach ihm gleich aufeinander folgen. Nun ist aber Jerusalem einige Jahrzehnte nach Jesu Tod zerstört worden, während der Tag des Menschensohnes nach fast zweitausend Jahren noch ausbleibt. Um den Meister von einem schweren Irrtum zu retten, hat man also verschiedentlich erstrebt, Jesus jene Aussage abzusprechen." ThZ, XI (1955), 128.

13. G. Neville, The Advent Hope, Introduction.

14. For a discussion of other positions, see Beasley-Murray, Jesus, 141-166.

15. Beasley-Murray gave himself this appellation when writing for the Baptist Quarterly many years ago. See "A Conservative thinks again about Daniel", XII (1948), 341.

16. Others who held this position more than a century ago include Fritzsche, Fleck, Schulz, de Wette, and Olshausen. Lagrange categorized three of these schools as follows: "Depuis l'antiquité, le sujet en a été compris de manières tres différentes. D'après Victor, Apollinaire et Théodore de Mopsueste l'ont entendu de la fin du monde, Titus de Bosra et Chrysostome de la ruine de Jérusalem. Parmi les modernes, Maldonat pense que, les disciples ayant interrogé à la fois sur la ruine du Temple et sur la fin du monde, le Christ a répondu

87

lui aussi <u>confuse</u>: . . . Le Christ aurait donc conçu sa réponse
de façon a laisser les apôtres dans leur erreur sur le lien entre
la fin du Temple et la fin du monde, erreur qui devait leur être
salutaire en augmentant leur énergie. S'il y a, comme le
prouvent le dissentiment des Pères sur le sujet du discours et
la confusion constatée par Maldonat, un certain embarras dans le
discours n'est-il pas plus prudent d'en chercher la cause dans
la composition des évangélistes synoptiques que dans une
intention positive de Jésus?" Lagrange paves the way for his
own exposition by alluding to exegetes who reject the authenticity of Mark 13. His outline thus gives a useful summary of the
state of the question nearly fifty years ago. "Les critiques
libéraux, auxquels s'est joint M. Loisy, mettent le discours en
opposition avec la prophétie sur la destruction du Temple. Ils
ne lui attribuent à peu près aucune authenticité. Voici par
exemple l'analyse de Wellh.: Une apocalypse juive, comprenant
7.8-12; 14-22; 24-27; le reste est d'origine chrétienne,
notamment 28-37. Klosterm. admet en outre des paroles de Jésus
notamment 30.31.32, sûrement authentiques. Loisy dit l'apocalypse
juive (6 (ou 7)-8; 14-20; 24-31) complétée par des discours déjà
écrits. D'une façon générale tout le discours serait en opposition avec la pensée de Jésus, lequel a toujours réprésenté la fin
comme imminente et subite, donc sans aucun autre signe prélimin-
aire que sa propre prédication. Environ quarante ou cinquante ans
après la Passion, voyant que la fin n'était pas venue, on se
serait imaginé que c'était parce qu'il restait à voir passer
certains prodromes, et l'on aurait composé ce discours en
combinant une apocalypse juive avec certaines données acquises à
la tradition. Dans le courant de son exégèse, Loisy est très
préoccupé de tout expliquer sans allusion à la ruine de Jérusalem
en l'an 70, ce qui l'entraîne à quelques contradictions . . .
L'explication que nous donnerons montrera que, s'il y avait en
effet une confusion dans l'esprit des disciples, l'intention de
Jésus fut précisément de distinguisher la ruine du Temple de la
consommation finale en leur dictant une attitude différent en vue
des deux événements." <u>Marc</u>, 334-335. In more recent times,
Josef Schmid has given us a similar classification brought up to
date. See <u>Markus</u>, 235.

17. E. P. Gould, <u>The Gospel according to St Mark</u> (ICC) (Edinburgh
1896), 240-241.

18. For a defence of the authenticity of these verses, in answer
to Glasson, J. A. T. Robinson, and N. Perrin <u>et al</u>., see Beasley-
Murray, <u>Jesus</u>, 246-250; Neville, <u>The Advent Hope</u>, 48,49; and
A. L. Moore, <u>Parousia</u>, 186,187. Particularly pertinent is the
following section from Moore: " . . . there is much to be said
in favour of the authenticity of sayings which are a pastiche of
quotations or allusions (cf. e.g. Mk. 4,32 - Dan. 4,12; 21,
Ezek. 17,23; 31,6), and this applies to Son of Man sayings too,

for the grounds on which the authenticity of Mk. 8,38 par. (cf.
I Enoch 61,8; 10. 62,2) and Mk. 13,26 (cf. Is. 13,10; Zech. 12,
10f., Dan. 7,13f.) is challenged are inadequate. It is important
to notice that of all the Son of Man sayings in the Gospels it is
precisely those which speak of his future glory which contain
Old Testament (or Pseudepigrapha) references. But it is precisely
in this sphere that we would expect such references or allusions.
Where the present situation of the Son of Man is spoken of, there
is no necessity to call in traditional imagery; but how else
ought one to speak of heaven, of glory, of the End, but in traditional imagery?"

19. These scholars follow E. Meyer in attributing the verses to
the early church, or interpret them as a symbolic expression of
spiritual realities. In more recent years, C. H. Dodd, however,
has allowed for a cataclysmic ending of the Age. See his Coming
of Christ (Cambridge, 1952), 26f.

20. It needs to be repeated that if the chapter is considered
(as some of the preceding do consider) to contain a Little Apocalypse, such an interpretation automatically results. If however
the chapter is viewed as authentic, and more akin to the prophets
in style, a very different exposition may result. See 13-19.

21. Not that this mode of exegeting 24-27 began with Gould. One
of the most powerful expressions of it came twenty years previous-
ly with J. S. Russell's The Parousia, A Critical Enquiry into the
New Testament Doctrine of Our Lord's Second Coming (London, 1878).
Alexander Brown, The Great Day of the Lord (London, 1890); D.
Lamont, Christ and the World of Thought (Edinburgh, 1934); and
A. Nairne, The Epistle of Priesthood (Edinburgh, [2]1915) expound
this same approach. See, for example, Nairne 207.

22. St Mark, 518. Cf. J. Schmid, Markus, 245: "Unmöglich ist
es, zusammen mit V. 14-23 auch V. 24-27 zeitgeschichtlich zu
verstehen und hier mit Berufung auf die atl Propheten, die mit
ähnlichen Bildern (vgl. zu V. 24 f) auch rein lokale Strafgerichte
schildern, das Gericht über Jerusalem und das Judentum beschrieben
zu finden und die Sammlung der Auserwählten auf die Gründung der
Kirche zu deuten. Die hier geschilderte kosmische Katastrophe
und das Erscheinen des Menschensohns müssen ebenso realistisch
verstanden werden wie die irdischen Katastrophen und Drangsale
in V. 7f. Versteht man dagegen V. 14-23 eschatologisch, so fügen
sich V. 24-27 ausgezeichnet daran an." Over a hundred years ago,
Olshausen commented, "It is beyond all doubt, that the following
description neither relates to an invisible advent of Christ, nor
can be understood in any metaphorical sense whatever. For
although ἔρχεσθαι and ἥκειν(come), alone might be so understood
(comp. the observations on Matth. xxiv. 1), no passage can be
adduced in which the complete phrase, ἔρχεται ὁ υἱὸς τοῦ

ἀνθρώπου ἐν νεφέλαις μετὰ δυνάμεως the Son of Man cometh in the clouds of heaven with power and glory, can with any probability be thus understood. (Comp. Matth. xxvi. 64; Mark xiv. 62; 1 Thess. iv. 16,17; 2 Peter iii. 10; Rev. xix. 11; Dan. vii. 13,14) Let anyone, with an unprejudiced mind, place himself within the sphere of ideas familiar to the hearers of Jesus, and he will entertain no doubt that the clouds, in which he promises to appear are literally clouds of light . . . According to constant custom, deeply founded in the nature of man, all appearances of God are surrounded with light, in the Old Testament as well as in the New; there is no imagination whatever, individual or national, that can conceive of the Deity under any other image than that of light." And on Matthew 24,29, he remarks, "According to the scope of the whole -- and the succeeding verses (30-31) do not leave a doubt on this subject -- the signs (σημεῖα) in the sun, moon, and stars, cannot be interpreted allegorically, as representing political or ecclesiastical relations and their dissolution; for political disturbances have already been spoken of, ver. 7." Matthew (Commentary on the New Testament) (E.T., New York, 1957), 250, 247. (Emphasis his.)

23. We think that A. L. Moore has the edge on Beasley-Murray when he says: "Since there is no compelling reason to under- stand 'that day or that hour' as precise temporal terms, it is natural to take them, following the Old Testament background as references to the Last Judgement and the Parousia. Beasley- Murray's case would be helped if the demonstrative adjective were missing: indeed, his argument allows it to lapse when he says, 'If at the present time one were asked, "Have you any idea when war will break out in Europe?" and the reply were given, "I do not know the day or hour". . .'-- whereas the point is that 'that day' carries Old Testament overtones which 'the day' in modern usage does not." Parousia, 99,100.

24. Hendriksen's comment upon the parallel passage in Matthew is significant at least for indicating how a later Gospel writer understood Mark. He enquires: "Does He merely mean to say that no one knows when Jerusalem will be destroyed? Does that sound like a convincing explanation of v. 36 in the light of the sublime paragraph just quoted? In v. 37 . . . Is the destruction of the face of the earth by means of the Flood a type merely of Jerusalem's fall, or is it a type of 'the passing away of heaven and earth' to which reference is made in v. 35? Not only the immediate context, but also 2 Peter 3:5-7 furnishes the answer . . . Our Lord continues His discourse in ch. 25 . . . If the lofty language of 24:29-31 refers to nothing more momentous and final than Jerusalem's destruction in the year A.D. 70 then by the same process of reasoning the very similar words of 25:31-46 must be given this restricted interpretation. Observe the

parallel: in both cases the Son of man appears in great glory, and the people ('his elect' -- 'all nations') are gathered before Him. But 25:46 proves without possibility of successful contradiction that the end of the age has been reached . . . 'And these shall go away into everlasting punishment: but the righteous into life eternal.'" Lectures on the Last Things (Grand Rapids, Michigan, 1951), 24.

25. Cited by Beasley-Murray, Jesus, 199.

26. The Parables of the Kingdom (London, ²1961), 51.

27. Mk. 12 and Mt. 23.

28. Mt. 23:38.

29. This pronouncement is obviously genuine according to Vincent Taylor and many others. See Taylor's St Mark, 500-501.

30. "Wie bereits gesagt, weist der Kontext in Mk 13 mit der Strukturparallele Vv. 7-8 und dem unmittelbar auf V. 14 folgenden Aussagen auf Kriegsereignisse. Die Auslegung von Vv. 7-8 ergab, dass der Evangelist das Thema Krieg besonders hervorkehrt, den Krieg zugleich im Zusammenhang mit der in der Einleitung vorhergesagten Tempelzerstörung (Vv. 2.4) sieht. Mit ὅπου οὐ δεῖ ist nun auch in V. 14 vom Tempel die Rede. Der Kontext legt also nahe, dass hier mit der danielischen Chiffre auf die Zerstörung des Tempels abgezielt ist." Pesch, Naherwartungen, 142. "Die befohlene Flucht V. 14c-16 und die θλῖψις-Schilderung V. 17-20 lassen unvermeidlich an einen unbarmherzigen, schonungslosen Krieg denken. Mehr noch! Oben wurde gezeigt, wie der ὅταν- Vordersatz bezogen ist auf das Zeichen von V. 4; nun ist unleugbar, dass V. 4 selbst auf die Tempelverwüstung von V. 2 anspielt. Daraus folgt, dass V. 14 sich mit V. 2 berührt; beide haben übrigens den Tempel im Auge. Die angekündigte Verwüstung V. 2 macht es äusserst wahrscheinlich, dass ἐρήμωσις Mk. 13,14, abgesehen von dem, was der richtige Sinn bei Dn oder 1 Makk ist, bedeutet: die Verwüstung oder der leere, trostlose Zustand, der die Folge davon ist." Lambrecht, Redaktion, 151. "Les versets 15 à 18, qui insistent sur la nécessité d'une fuite immédiate et rapide, préparent le verset 19: 'Car ces jours-là seront des jours de tribulation . . .' Bref la fuite s'impose, parce qu'une catastrophe sans précédent est imminente. Cf. K. Weiss, Exegetisches zur Irrtumlosigkeit . . .., 79. Plus haut déjà, on a souligné l'unité interne de toute la péricope qui va des versets 14 à 23. On ne doit donc pas séparer le verset 19 de ce qui précède et en faire le début d'une nouvelle prophétie sur la fin du monde. Pour justifier cette dernière position, le P. Lagrange et beaucoup d'autres allèguent que dans Mc. XIII, 14-18 on a un péril localisé, dû à une armée et auquel il sera possible d'échapper par la fuite, tandis que Mc. XIII, 19-20 décrit une

catastrophe mondiale, qui vient de l'omnipotence divine et frappe tous les hommes: alors évidemment la fuite serait un non sens. On peut n'être pas convaincu par cet argument." A. Feuillet, "Le discours de Jésus sur la ruine du temple d'après Marc XIII et Luc XXI, 5-36", RB, LV (1948), 481.

31. Schweizer, The Good News, 274.

32. T. W. Manson, Teaching, 281.

33. St Matthew (London, 1856), 317.

34. Dan. 9:26,27; 11:31; 12:11.

35. Lev. 16:2; Acts 6:13 etc.

36. Schweizer affirms, "undoubtedly the phrase 'where he should not be' refers to the temple, since the entire passage presupposes a Jewish situation." The Good News, 272. "Da das βδέλυγμα bei Dn sich zweifellos im Tempel befindet, ist es ratsam, auch in der unbestimmten Formel Mk 13,14 eine Anspielung auf den Tempel zu sehen: dadurch wird das βδέλυγμα eigentlich erst ein profanierender Greuel." Lambrecht, Redaktion, 152.

37. M. Hooker, The Son of Man in Mark (London, 1967), 153.

38. Scholars who have taken this view include W. Beyschlag, F. Godet, E. F. K. Müller, A. B. Bruce, B. Rigaux, C. Cranfield, G. E. Ladd.

39. Saint Mark, 402.

40. Matthew probably distinguished the two events because, at the time he wrote, the first had already transpired.

41. Compare the comments of Schmid and Lagrange, particularly the shift adopted by the latter when he declares the γὰρ of v. 21 of Mt. 24 to be only a form. We think that Lagrange at this point is unfaithful with regard to the facts. His position concerning γὰρ has no foundation. "Diejenige Deutung, die in V. 14 bis 23 das Ende Jerusalems vorausgesagt findet, muss hier einen ungemein schroffen Übergang annehmen, da unter völliger Ignorierung jeglicher Perspecktive Ereignisse einer nahen und solche einer mehr oder weniger fernen Zukunft unmittelbar aufeinander folgen. Denn wenn auch wenigstens bei Markus (siehe dagegen Mt 24,29 'alsbald nach der Drangsal jener Tage . . .') der zeitliche Zwischenraum zwischen V. 14-23 und V. 24-27 unbestimmt gelassen wird, so lässt sich doch der Eindruck nicht verwischen, dass der Evangelist ihn nur als gering angesehen hat." Markus, 245. "Chrysostome et Jérôme que nous suivons dans

leur application des discours à la ruine de Jérusalem et à la fin du monde, ne placent delibèrement le commencement du second thème qu'au v. 23. Ce qui est très fort pour ce sens, c'est le γὰρ au debut de cette péricope, dans Mt. comme dans Mc., qui semble relier étroitement ce debut à ce qui précède. C'est précisement la difficulté de tout le discours. Mais nous pensons qu'il y a ici une soudure plûtot qu'un lien organique qui conduirait à n'admettre qu'un seul thème. Deux raisons: a) l'analogie de Dan. XII, suivant XI,45; après la consummation du persécuteur, il y a de nouveau une tribulation; ce sont deux horizons distincts, sans aucune indication d'intervalle; b) le parallélisme des deux discours ou du moins des deux thèmes, qui doivent commencer tous deux par la détresse (cf. RB. 1906, p. 395). Le γὰρ doit donc être une liaison de pure forme, sans portée pour les idées." <u>Saint Matthieu</u>, 462-63.

42. Schweizer, <u>The Good News</u>, 281, is representative of those who accept the plain meaning of the text when he says: "Certainly 'all these things' must include the parousia of the Son of Man." Cf. Lohmeyer. "In dem Zeitraum dieser jetzt lebenden Generation wird alles dieses geschehen; Geschlechter über Geschlechter sind vorübergegangen, dieses Geschlecht vergeht nicht mehr, sondern sieht dieses alles geschehen." <u>Markus</u>, 281. Beasley-Murray, <u>Mark Thirteen</u>, 99f.

43. And particularly ἡ γενεὰ αὕτη.

44. <u>Luke</u>, 246.

45. See also Heb. 9:26.

46. <u>Parousia</u>, 132.

47. We are aware that many commentators restrict the meaning of this expression to merely a guarantee of the permanence of Christ's words as in Mt. 5:18, but we consider that its appropriateness in its present context is too felicitous for that view. Furthermore, it is a question whether in Mt. 5:18 only a guarantee, rather than a forecast, is intended.

48. Lohmeyer, <u>Markus</u>, 283.

49. <u>Jesus</u>, 261. Others who understand v. 30 as including the Parousia include Allen, <u>Mark,ad loc.</u>; Kümmel, <u>Promise</u>, 61; Klostermann, Markus <u>Evangelium</u>, 154; Gould, <u>Mark</u>, 253; Taylor, <u>St Mark</u>, 521.

50. <u>Parables</u>, 71.

51. <u>Le Retour du Christ</u> (Paris, 1945), 27. Cranfield's position

is similar to the foregoing. "The clue to the meaning of the nearness of the End is the realization of the essential unity of God's Saving Acts in Christ--the realization that the Events of the Incarnation, Crucifixion, Resurrection, Ascension, and Parousia are in a real sense one Event. The foreshortening, by which the Old Testament sees as one divine intervention in the future that which from the viewpoint of the New Testament writers is both past and future, is not only a visual illusion; for the distance actually brings out an essential unity, which is not so apparent from a position in between the Ascension and the Parousia. "St Mark Thirteen", SJTH, VII (1954), 288.

52. Promise, 97n.

53. Feuillet, "Le discours de Jesus sur la ruine du temple d'après Marc XIII et Luc XXI, 5-36", RB, LV (1948), 486-489.

54. Parousia, 97-98.

55. Évangile selon Saint Luc (Paris, [2]1921), 529.

56. As regards the growth parables, Easton has commented: "We should naturally not overstress time elements in a parable, but we have at least the duty to note that there is no parable of Jesus' that compares the development of the present kingdom to the growth of an oak tree from an acorn; grain and mustard seed grow up in a few weeks, while leaven works overnight." Christ, 163. And Bultmann refers to a similar parable, accompanied by its interpretation, found in the Epistle of Clement: "O you fools, consider a plant, a grapevine for example. First it sheds the old leaves, then the young shoots sprout, then leaves, then flowers, then the green grapes, finally the ripe grapes appear. You see how quickly the fruit is ripe. Even so quickly and suddenly will God's final judgement come, as the Scripture testifies: He will come quickly and will not tarry, suddenly the Lord will come to His temple, the Holy One for whom you wait." I Clem. 23.4-5 cited by Bultmann, Jesus and the Word, 34. Beasley-Murray quotes also the following from Haupt approvingly: "Everything said about the parousia and the events that precede it continually moves in the second person plural, hence the presupposition is that those addressed would live to see it; further, not in one single place is the possibility reckoned with that they all would die beforehand." Jesus, 184.

57. Marshall, Luke: Historian and Theologian (London, 1970), 135; Ellis, The Gospel of Luke (Century Bible n.s.)(London, 1966), 244ff.

58. 121.

59. Compare wording of Lk. 21:24 and Dan. 8:13 regarding the "treading underfoot" of Jerusalem. See also comments of Beasley-Murray, _Jesus_, 203-204. It should be kept in mind that Dan. 8:13 is saying the same thing as Dan. 7:25, but using different imagery, and it is this imagery of Dan. 8 which Luke adopts. Easton comments on "the times of the Gentiles" of Lk. 21:24: "The saying is based on such passages as Dan. 8:13f., 12:7,11f . . ." _The Gospel According to St Luke_ (Edinburgh, 1926), 312. Beasley-Murray agrees. _Jesus_, 247. Likewise Marshall, _Luke_, 135n.

60. e.g. Schmid, _Markus_, 245.

61. Lloyd Gaston suggests a valid argument for the fourth school which frequently passes unnoticed. He says: "' . . . seeing the Son of Man' is a conception very closely allied to the death of martyrs. In context, however, Mk 9:1 speaks to the situation not of the martyrs themselves but of those facing martyrdom, and it holds out for them the promise of consolation.
    "Mk 13:30 is similar. If 'this generation' is going to undergo all the tribulation which Mark 13 entails, and it is to be recalled that this chapter was formulated for people who had already experienced tribulation, then fairness demands that this generation also experience the promised vindication. If the promise of the parousia is to have any relevance at all for those addressed, then it must be promised for their lifetime. That the suffering of Israel should be greatest just before the end is not just some apocalyptic theologoumenon called Messianic woes; the point is that the suffering was already there and it was the suffering which called forth the expectation of the speedy coming of the end, and not the other way around. Experience of persecution is a disease characterized by apocalyptic fever, and the nearness of the expected end is directly proportional to the severity of the persecution. This acceleration of the end because of suffering is very well expressed in Mk 13:20, 'If the Lord had not shortened the days no one would be saved (= escape a martyr's death); but for the sake of the elect whom he chose he shortened the days.'" _No Stone on Another_, 453-54.

62. F. F. Bruce, _Biblical Exegesis in the Qumran Texts_ (London, 1960), 88; C. H. Dodd, _More New Testament Studies_, 69; Farrer, _St Matthew and St Mark_, 16; L. Hartman, _Prophecy_, 145, 235.

63. As Daniel reinterpreted the seventy years of Jeremiah 29.

64. Lloyd Gaston declares that the widespread interpretation in Judaism that "the 490 years of Daniel 9 were just coming to an end" casts light on the Parousia emphasis in Mark 13. See _No Stone on Another_, 468. Also Ford, _Daniel_ (SPA), 200.

65. Cf. Mark 13:2; and Luke 19:41-44.

66. See also chapter three.

67. Markus, 193

68. The following quotations are representative references from commentators on the relationship between Mark 13 and 9:24-27 of Daniel. "Suivant le cadre tracé par Daniel, dans la prophétie des semaines, il faisait plutôt entendre qu'il y aurait pour Jérusalem un temps relativement court de désolation, profanation religieuse et calamités de toutes sortes, qui se terminerait par l'apparition glorieuse du Messie. Ces jours seraient abrégés, parce que, sans cela, 'tout chair', c'est-à-dire tous les hommes, et non seulement tous les Juifs, périraient, et que Dieu ne veut pas livrer à la mort tous les élus. Ceux-ci ont dû fuir au moment où a paru 'l'abomination'; mais la Judée ne sera pas seule à souffrir, et le monde entier sera en proie aux douleurs du grand avènement." Les Évangiles synoptiques (Ceffonds, 1908), II, 424. "We have no doubt . . . that . . . expositors in general are right in assuming, on the one hand, that our Lord's direct reference is to the great fontal predication in chapter ix. 24-27, and in assuming, on the other, that in the expression which he quotes, as well as in his own mind, there was a reference to something that was to happen in connection with the destruction of Jerusalem by the Romans." Morison, Matthew's Memoirs of Christ, 507-508. (Emphasis ours.) "The Greek phrase . . . comes from the Septuagint, or Greek, version of Dan 9:27 . . . By the time of our Gospel, the original reference of the passage had been lost sight of, and it was merely a mysterious prophecy which yet was to be fulfilled." Branscomb, Mark, 237. " . . . the meaning of the prophecy was not regarded as having been exhausted by its contemporary fulfillment, and the mysterious phrase about the abomination of desolation . . . was regarded as a prophetic word still destined to find fulfillment in the future." Rawlinson, Mark, 187. ". . . in Mark the Little Apocalypse takes up those tragic events through which Israel must pass, and especially the destruction of the temple. . . it uses a Danielic vocabulary, and follows the Danielic pattern. The words 'come to an end' or 'fulfillment' have a Danielic sound." Carrington, Mark 272. "The word (for 'end') which is used in this chapter of Mark is telos, which has the meaning of aim, purpose, objective and fulfillment, as well as finality. . . . We find it in Daniel ix, where it seems to imply the finale or outcome of the present historical afflictions in Israel, including, for instance, the capture of the city and the cessation of the daily sacrifice, which is itself an 'end'. . . . In this context it assumes the meaning of the final fulfillment of the prophecies under consideration, whatever this may be." Ibid., 275. "A direct reference is now made to Daniel, and the lector is bidden to use his intelligence: 'When ye see the abomination of desolation standing where it ought not -- let him that readeth

96

understand.' The reference is to the phrase in Daniel ix:27. . . .
it is clear to us at once what is being announced in the Little
Apocalypse; it is a second agent of desecration and desolation
of a comparable character." Ibid., 278. "Daniel does contemplate the destruction of the city and temple, as the intelligent
lector would find if he turned to Daniel ix:26." Ibid., 279.
". . . Daniel, in a mysterious passage, speaks of a Prince-
Messiah (who may be the high priest of his day), and a verse
later says that 'the Messiah will be cut off'. This chapter of
Daniel contributed one or two important concepts or expressions
to the tradition in Mark:
Dan ix. 26,27:   the Messiah cut off (Mark viii.31, ix.31, x.33)?
                 the sanctuary destroyed (Mark xiii.2, xiv. 58,
                 xv. 29).
                 war or wars (Mark xiii.7).
                 the end (Mark xiii.7,13).
                 the abomination of desolation (Mark xiii.14).
Now Jesus certainly accepted the title of Messiah in xiv.62, and
combined it with the symbolism of the Son of Man of Daniel vii.23,
who comes with the clouds of heaven and receives the Kingdom from
God; but it looks as if he also took into account the death of
the Prince-Messiah in Daniel ix.26,27, since he made use of those
verses in his apocalyptic; it would seem that he saw in them an
image of the tragic times through which Israel was to pass during
that evil generation; the Messiah cut off, wars and rumours of
wars, the temple destroyed, and the abomination of desolation
standing where it ought not." Ibid., 183. "Setzen wir voraus,
dass die geprägte Wendung τὸ βδέλυγμα τῆς ἐρημώσεως Dan 12,11
entnommen sei, so konnte der Evangelist, der sie mit dem
Vorlagetext übernahm, durchaus an die Zerstörung des Tempels
denken. In Dan 12,11 ist zwar unmittelbar nur von der Entweihung
des Tempels die Rede, der Ausdruck in Dan 12,11 bezieht sich aber
wie auch Dan 11,31 auf Dan 9,26f. zurück, wo von dem die Rede ist,
der die Stadt verwüstet. Vielleicht soll der Leser gerade auf
diesen Zusammenhang achten, der sich von Mk 13,2 her bereits
nahelegt. In Dan 9,26f. ist die Vernichtung von Stadt und Tempel
angesagt, und Dan 11,31; 12,11 sind nur - literakritisch
vielleicht sogar sekundäre - Bezugnahmen auf diesen Spruch. Der
Ausdruck τὸ βδέλυγμα τῆς ἐρημώσεως kann also nicht nur an eine
Entweihung des Tempels, sondern ebensogut an Krieg und Zerstörung
von Stadt und Tempel erinnern. Da die Tempelzerstörung in Mk 13,
2 so deutlich geweissagt ist, da diese Vorhersage den Anlass zur
Jüngerfrage und damit zur ganzen nachfolgenden Rede bietet, muss
το βδέλυγμα τῆς ἐρημώσεως zwangsläufig im Licht von 13,2
verstanden werden. Der Evangelist spricht in Mk 13,14 von der
Zerstörung des Tempels." Pesch, Naherwartungen, 142-43. (Pesch
cites K. Staab, J. Huby, C. Perrot and others to similar effect.
See his footnotes ad loc.) "The more vividly Jesus Himself
foresaw the coming ruin . . . the fuller, moreover, the acquain-
tance which the disciples must have had with the prophecy in

97

Dan ix. . . so much the more intelligible is this introductory
passage. . ." Meyer, Commentary on New Testament, The Gospel of
Matthew (E.T., N.Y., 6Ī884), 406. "The main passage here
referred to by the Lord is the remarkable prophecy, Dan. 9:26-27,
which we find more definitely expressed, Dan xi. 31; xii.11."
Olshausen, Matthew, 236.

69. Iremonger, William Temple, cited by A. L. Moore, Parousia,
93.

70. See Beasley-Murray, Jesus, ix.

71. At this point, a reader may be tempted to cry "Another
apologetic!" We submit that for our purposes in the exegesis of
Mark, the extent of the Kenosis is not an issue. We merely beg
leave to enquire whether the Jews viewed predictive statements
in the same absolute fashion as members of the modern Occident.
It is absolutely certain that Christ viewed the time of His
return as somewhat contingent. See Mk. 13:10 and Matt. 24:14.

72. Jonah was familiar with the principles expressed in later
days by Jeremiah and Ezekiel: "If at any time I declare concerning a nation or a kingdom, that I will pluck up and break down
and destroy it, and if that nation, concerning which I have
spoken, turns from its evil, I will repent of the evil that I
intended to do to it. And if at any time I declare concerning
a nation or a kingdom that I will build and plant it, and if it
does evil in my sight, not listening to my voice, then I will
repent of the good which I had intended to do to it." Jer. 18:7-
10. "Yet you say, 'The way of the Lord is not just.' Hear now,
O house of Israel: Is my way not just? Is it not your ways that
are not just? When a righteous man turns away from his righteousness and commits iniquity, he shall die for it; for the
iniquity which he has committed he shall die. Again, when a
wicked man turns away from the wickedness he has committed and
does what is lawful and right, he shall save his life." Eze. 18:
25-27. Another O.T. example is that of Isaiah's words to
Hezekiah, "Thus says the Lord: Set your house in order; for you
shall die, you shall not recover." Isa. 38:1. Hezekiah did not
die. He did recover, and lived another fifteen years. The New
Testament also yields us several examples of this principle.
Consider the following case: "As they had been long without
food, Paul then came forward among them and said, 'Men, you
should have listened to me, and should not have set sail from
Crete and incurred this injury and loss. I now bid you take
heart; for there will be no loss of life among you, but only
of the ship. For this very night there stood by me an angel of
the God to whom I belong and whom I worship, and he said, 'Do
not be afraid, Paul; you must stand before Caesar; and lo, God

has granted you all those who sail with you.' So take heart,
men, for I have faith in God that it will be exactly as I have
been told. But we shall have to run on some island.' When the
fourteenth night had come, as we were drifting across the sea of
Adria, about midnight the sailors suspected that they were
nearing land. So they sounded and found twenty fathoms; a little
farther on they sounded again and found fifteen fathoms. And
fearing that we might run on the rocks, they let out four anchors
from the stern, and prayed for day to come. And as the sailors
were seeking to escape from the ship, and had lowered the boat
into the sea, under pretense of laying out anchors from the bow,
Paul said, 'Unless these men stay in the ship, you cannot be
saved.'" Acts 27:21-31. The point in this story, of course, is
that Paul did not act as though the divine prediction was an
absolute pronouncement. He seemed rather to believe that the
reckless wickedness of a dozen men could change the divine
purpose toward the remaining three score. We have another
example in Acts 21:10-14: "While we were staying for some days,
a prophet named Agabus came down from Judea. And coming to us
he took Paul's girdle and bound his own feet and hands, and said,
'Thus says the Holy Spirit, "So shall the Jews at Jerusalem bind
the man who owns this girdle and deliver him into the hands of
the Gentiles."' When we heard this, we and the people there
begged him not to go up to Jerusalem. Then Paul answered, 'What
are you doing, weeping and breaking my heart? For I am ready not
only to be imprisoned but even to die at Jerusalem for the name
of the Lord Jesus.' And when he would not be persuaded, we
ceased and said, 'The will of the Lord be done.'" In this
instance, Paul's Christian friends did not regard the prophecy
as of inevitable fulfillment. Instead they treated it as a
kindly warning whereby the disaster might be averted. This is
the Christian and Jewish view of prophecy, in contrast to that
of the oriental fatalists. The parable of the unmerciful servant
in Matthew 18 has often occasioned difficulty. How could the
master of the house (representing God, see v. 35), forgive his
slave the debt of ten thousand talents and yet later change his
mind toward him? But no problem exists, as we take the preceding
examples into account. The biblical view of prophecy is that a
forecast is not necessarily a prediction to be fulfilled at all
hazards. Rather a prediction of disaster is a hint in order
that proper steps might be taken to avert the evil. Similarly
a prediction of blessing is an encouragement, that there might
be perseverance in a right course. This view of the conditional
nature of prophecy was not devised to meet the problem of Mk. 13:
30. It has long been held and applied to many sections of the
Scripture. Some modern exegetes have seen its relevance for the
present issue. Possibly C. F. D. Moule had this in mind when he
commented on Mk. 13:30 as follows: ". . . he might have been
absolutely right if he had said what verses 30-31 say; for
there is a sense in which great prophets see so clearly and

expect so eagerly. . . what might happen if only men responded
. . ." The Gospel According to Mark (Cambridge, 1965), 103. See
particularly the discussion in Gaston's No Stone on Another,
426f.; and J. Hempel's Die Mehrdeutigkeit der Geschichte als
Problem der prophetischen Theologie (Göttingen, 1936), 41. R. A.
Knox speaks similarly: "By a rather free interpretation of the
language used you can just maintain that our Lord spoke only
about the destruction of Jerusalem, and tacitly refused information about the Second Coming. By supposing that the Evangelists
here, as elsewhere, include one or two sayings which really
belonged to a different context, you can save the accuracy of the
prediction, but at the same time you rob it of all certainty. Is
it possible to preserve the unity of the passage, and at the same
time to interpret its phrases in their natural sense? Only on
the supposition that this was a conditional prophecy (cf. Jonah
3:4 and 10) and that the condition of it, namely the conversion
of the Jews remained and still remains unfulfilled (cf. Rom. 11:
22 and notes on 2 Thess 2:6). In this way we can see the picture
as a continuous whole, and at the same time understand why the
fulfillment of it has only been partial." A New Testament
Commentary, (vols., London, 1952), I, 56. G. B. Caird has
something to say along the same lines: "Jesus clearly indicated
that in its final manifestation the Day was known only to God,
not because God had fixed a date which he guarded as a close
secret, but because the coming of the Day was contingent upon the
full realization of the purposes of God. . ." The Apostolic Age
(London, 1958), 189. "The Jew was able to take in his stride
paradoxes which have perplexed Gentiles ancient and modern.
Where we should make a guarded statement, the Semitic mind
prefers to throw together two extreme statements and allow the
one to qualify the other. The prophets repeatedly declare God's
irrevocable judgement on human sin, and almost in the same breath
call on men to repent before it is too late." Ibid., 192. Caird
also quotes from J. Paterson: "Many things were foretold precisely that they might not come to pass." Ibid. In this connexion, the words of A. L. Moore are also worth consideration. He
says: "Only the motif of grace withholds that which properly
belongs to the complex of eschatological events which ended with
the Ascension and Exaltation." Parousia, 206.

73. Matthew, 222.

74. We append a specimen of his remarks: "Another circumstance,
by which the distinct declarations of the Lord, respecting the
near approach of his advent, are completely removed from the
province of error, is the conflict between freedom and necessity,
which appears peculiarly prominent in this passage. On the one
hand, the time of fulfillment is represented as fixed in the
counsels of God (Dan xi.36; Acts 1.7); on the other, the time
seems uncertain, and open to be deferred or hastened by the

faithfulness or unfaithfulness of men (Habak. ii.3; 2 Pet. iii)
. . . . Accordingly, when the Redeemer promises the near approach
of his coming, this announcement is to be taken with the restric-
tion (to be understood in connexion with all predictions and
judgments), 'All this will come to pass, unless men avert the
wrath of God by sincere repentance.' None of the predictions of
Divine judgments are bare historical proclamations of that which
will take place; they are alarms calling men to repentance--of
which it may be said that they announce something, in order that
that which they announce may not come to pass." Ibid., 225-26.
Compare the more recent discussion by Gunther Härder in "Das
eschatologische Geschichtsbild der sogenannten kleinen Apokalypse
Markus 13", TV, IV (Berlin, 1952), 71-107. "Man sollte die
Naherwartung Jesu in ihrer Echtheit stehen lassen. Im Augenblick
ihrer Verkündigung war sie wahr, d.h. gültige Verkündigung des
Willens Gottes, seiner Drohung und Verheissung. Die Entwicklung
in der Urchristenheit und ihr Niederschlag im NT zeigt, dass
Gottes Wort sich nicht zum Besitz des Menschen machen lässt, als
könne er es zum Mittel seiner endzeitlichen Berechnung machen.
Es ist dem Menschen nicht gegeben, um sich zu sichern. Wer es
dennoch versucht, es auf diese Art zu verstehen und sich
anzueignen, muss erfahren, dass Gott frei ist, seinen Willen
und sein Wort jederzeit zu ändern, wie es nicht grossartiger als
in Jeremia 18 ausgedrückt werden kann. Gott kann sein Vorsatz
gereuen. Mit dem Kommen Jesu war das Ende in der Tat ganz nahe
herbeigekommen. Wer die Geschichte der Christenheit bis zum
heutigen Tage mit Aufmerksamkeit betrachtet, wird verstehen,
weshalb es Gott gereute, dieses Ende kommen zu lassen."
Olshausen uses practically identical words to Paterson as
quoted by Caird. He then proceeds gently to stricture those who,
to his mind, misinterpret the Olivet discourse through failing to
recognize the contingent nature of prophecy. "The overlooking
of these points accounts for the fact, that many expositors, with
a good intention, but contrary to the simple meaning of words,
would make a forced separation between events yet future, and
that which is described as near--viz., the destruction of
Jerusalem. Such a separation can never be substantiated from
the mere language, and since the whole teaching of Scripture
is in harmony with our passage, nothing remains but to justify
this form of Scriptural representation upon higher grounds, in
the manner which we have attempted." Matthew, 226.
Another writer of an earlier day has written thoughtfully upon
this topic, and it is not necessary to agree throughout with his
theology in order to see a viewpoint which was possibly akin to
that of New Testament believers and Christ Himself. Fairbairn
sets forth the basic principles of his case somewhat similarly to
Olshausen and then adds: "Thus, to refer to the predictions. . .
respecting the second advent of the Lord--there can be no doubt,
that (however definitely fixed in the counsels of Heaven) certain
things among men are represented as tending, on the one side to

hinder, on the other to forward its approach. Our Lord, in one
of his parables (Luke xviii.1-8), speaks as if it hung on the
steadfast faith and persevering prayer of his elect people. St
Peter uses still stronger language; he exhorts believers to a
hopeful, godly and consistent life, that they might hasten on
the day of the Lord's coming, (for such is the plain import of
his words, . . . 2 Pet. iii.12). And St Paul not only speaks of
a grand development of apostacy (sic) necessarily preceding the
arrival of that day, but of certain things, which he does not
further characterize, hindering this development, and by implication retarding the personal appearance of the Lord, which in the
chain of providences was to be subsequent to the other." The
Interpretation of Prophecy (Edinburgh, 1956), 64-65. Fairbairn
then spells out his belief for the reason of the delay of the
Parousia. ". . . for the church being then in the full spring-
tide of its life and blessing, burning with holy zeal for the
proper fulfillment of its mission, it might well seem, as if that
mission were hastening to its accomplishment, and all things were
becoming ready for the final harvest of the world. Yet, it must
have been impossible for any one to read with care some of the
parables of our Lord, or even what was written by St Paul of the
great apostacy (sic) . . . without coming to the conviction, that
there was still an implied alternative; namely, that if the
church of Christ should degenerate in her course, if she should
begin to slumber in the work given her to do, still more, if she
should become adulterated by the carnal spirit, and the corrupt
practices of the world, then the shadows of the evening should
need to be lengthened out, and. . . the Lord should have to
protract the day of His appearing." Ibid., 65. Fairbairn gives
several examples from Scripture in support of his thesis. He
reminds us, for example, that Christ promised the Twelve
(including Judas!) that they would one day sit upon twelve
thrones, judging the twelve tribes of Israel -- a statement
apparently as absolute as Mk. 13:30.

75. See Numbers 14:34 margin.

76. There is nothing strange in part of Christ's prophecy being
fulfilled, and the other part unfulfilled. This is true in other
cases of Hebrew prediction. See Matt. 19:28, for another example
from Christ Himself.

77. E.g. Nineham, Saint Mark, 355; Dodd, More N.T. Studies, 80.
Mk. 13:19-27 echoes Isa. chs. 24-27 at several points, and
Daniel's sources for the "time of trouble" may include this
passage (as well as Jer. 30:7), one which obviously is wider in
application than the destruction of Jerusalem. For Daniel's use
of Isaiah, see Gaston, No Stone on Another, 376-382, and E.
Bickermann, Der Gott der Makkabäer (Berlin, 1937), 172.

78. <u>Mark</u>, 514.

79. <u>L'Antéchrist</u>, 243.

80. On these difficulties Olshausen remarks: "True, the siege
might have lasted longer, and the ruin might have been such that
not a single person should have escaped; but how can it be said
that this was prevented for the sake of the elect, does not
appear. For the Christians fled to Pella. . . . Schott, indeed,
thinks (p. 57) that we are not to understand by the elect the
Christians, but such Jews as were about to go over to the Church
of Christ. But the reference of the elect, ver. 24 and 31, to
the members of the church, renders this hypothesis quite untenable. This passage also evidently has its final reference to the
advent of the Lord, preceded by the birth-pangs of the Messiah;
these will fall at once upon believers and unbelievers--upon the
former to perfect, upon the latter to punish them; but for the
sake of believers the merciful One will shorten them. . . ."
<u>Matthew</u>, 243. Discussing Mt. 24:23-26 he adds: "The reference
of the 'elect' in this passage to any others than the apostles
and believing members of the church, is utterly untenable, for
the whole is addressed directly to the apostles themselves.
Hence the words can only be taken as meaning "so as to lead
astray, if possible, <u>you</u> and <u>all</u> the elect". . . it is only thus
that the force of the admonition can be felt." <u>Ibid</u>.

81. Mk. 13:9

82. <u>Mark</u>, 272.

83. <u>Meyer's</u> Commentary on the New Testament, <u>St Matthew</u> (E.T.,
Edinburgh, [5]1879) II, 136.

84. <u>L'Antéchrist</u>, 243n.

85. See chapter three.

86. <u>Redaktion</u>, 168.
  Haenchen makes some interesting comments on Mk. 13:14. We
have not found quite their like elsewhere in commentaries old or
new. While he follows most of his countrymen in passing by the
local application, his suggestions as to what may have been in
the mind of Mark as he wrote this passage are worthy of consideration. We quote from him without endorsing his view in entirety.
"Mk hat ja sein Evangelium nicht für jüdaische Leser geschrieben.
Warum gibt er dann hier den Christen in Judäa Anweisungen?. . . .
  Endlich: wozu bringt Mk diese Nachricht, die für seine Leser
doch keine Bedeutung haben konnte? Soll man annehmen, er schreibe
mechanisch etwas ab, das er vorfindet, einschliesslich der
Bemerkung: 'Der Leser merke auf!'? Wir müssen doch voraussetzen,

dass Mk in alledem einen für seine Leser höchst wichtigen Sinn
gefunden hat, und dieser Sinn muss etwas Aktuelles sein.
Besonders ungereimt wäre die Vermutung, dass Mk die Aufforderung,
der Leser solle verstehen, übernommen hätte, ohne dass er selbst
musste, [sic] worum es geht. An diesem Umstand scheitert mit
tödlicher Sicherheit die Vermutung, Mk habe eben ein Geheimnis
weiter tradiert. . . .

"Wir behaupten: Mk verwendet hier Mittel, die uns schon aus
anderen Stellen im N.T. bekannt sind.

"Beginnen wir mit dem Einfachsten. Jedem Leser des N.T. ist
es bekannt, dass manche ntl. Verfasser für 'Rom' den Namen
'Babylon' eingesetzt haben. Das ist ganz sicher der Fall in
Offb 14,8; 16,19; 17,5; 18,2.10.21. Wahrscheinlich verhält es
sich ebenso auch 1. Petr 5,13. Bei den Stellen der Offb ist der
Grund für diese Umschreibung leicht zu erraten: es wäre
lebensgefährlich gewesen, hätten die Christen hier offen von
Roms Untergang geschrieben. Damit eröffnet sich uns eine
Möglichkeit: eine umschreibende, verhüllende, geheimnisvoll
dem Uneingeweihten unverständliche Ausdruckweise kann dadurch
veranlasst sein, dass die ('unverschlüsselte') Mitteilung höchst
gefährlich ist und Verfasser und Leser bzw. die Gemeinde, in der
eine solche Schrift verbreitet wird, durch die 'Verschlüsselung'
vor dieser Gefahr bewahrt werden sollen.

"Ein anderes Beispiel für die gleiche Sache ist die Art, wie
Apk 13,17 f. der Name des 'Tiers' nur als ein Zahlenwert
angegeben wird -- etwa 'Kaiser Nero(n)' zu sagen wäre allzu
riskant gewesen. . . ."

"Wenn wir nach der Analogie dieser Beispiele aus der Offb
urteilen dürfen, könnte auch in Mk 13 diese Redeform gewählt
sein, weil die Aussage im Klartext gefährlich ist, d.h. sich
gegen Rom richtet.

"Der Text verwendet offensichtlich Wendungen aus dem Buch
Daniel. Dort war 9,27 davon die Rede, dass auf das Heilige
(den Altar) der Greuel der Verwüstungen kommen werde, dass der
Greuel der Verwüstung 1290 bzw. nach der LXX 1335 Tage bestehen
werde, und es war zugleich gesagt, dass die Rede versiegelt sein
solle bis zum Zeitpunkt des Endes (12,11.4). Ferner hiess es:
'und die Zeit wird eine Trübsal sein, eine Trübsal, wie sie
nicht dagewesen ist, seit ein Volk existiert' (12,1).

"Wir wissen heute: Das Buch Daniel ist in Wirklichkeit zur
Zeit des syrischen Königs Antiochus Epiphanes verfasst worden,
um die Juden zum Ausbarren in der Verfolgung zu ermuntern. Wir
können ziemlich genau den Zeitpunkt angeben, wo es geschrieben
ist. Denn von diesem Punkt an (Dan 11,40) verstösst die
angebliche Weissagung gegen die historische Wirklichkeit, während
sie für die vorhergehende Zeit zutrifft -- dort war sie ja nur
scheinbar Weissagung, in Wahrheit aber Rückschau auf vergangene
Ereignisse. Das Buch muss noch vor dem Tod des Antiochus
Epiphanes im Jahr 164 v. Chr. geschrieben sein, aber nach 167 v.
Chr. All das wussten die christlichen Leser des Buches Daniel

aber nicht. Für sie war diese geheimnisvolle Weissagung in den
Vorgängen unter Antiochus Epiphanes noch nicht erfüllt. Sie
ahnten auch nicht, dass die Schilderungen des 1. Makkabäerbuches
über die Verfolgung durch Antiochus und den jüdischen Aufstand
in Wirklichkeit denselben Vorgang beschreiben, wie das Ende des
Buches Daniel. Dagegen konnte die Schilderung im 1 Makk wohl
dazu dienen zu zeigen, wie eine solche Verfolgung und Verführung
ins Werk gesetzt werden konnte.

"Wenn wir nun an unserer Mk-Stelle Wendungen aus Daniel
erscheinen sehen, dürfen wir vermuten, dass sie für den Verfasser
einen konkreten, aktuellen Sinn besassen: was der Prophet Daniel
geschaut hatte, das war jetzt -- oder bald -- im Begriff, sich zu
erfüllen. Aber in welcher Weise?

"Einen gewissen anhalt kann uns die Offb geben. Sie spricht
13,12 davon, dass das 'zweite Tier' die Bewohner der Erde dazu
bringt, dem (ersten) Tier ein Bild zu machen, 'und es wurde ihm
gegeben dem Bild des Tieres Lebensgeist zu verleihen so dass das
Bild des Tieres sogar redete und bewirkte, dass alle getötet
wurden, die das Bild des Tieres nicht anbeteten'. Hier wird
offensichtlich erwartet, dass der Kaiserkult im Römerreich mit
Gewalt durchgesetzt werden wird und jeder getötet wird, der ihn
verweigert. In 13,17 f. bringt die Offb eine ähnliche Erwartung
zum Ausdruck: Wer nicht das Zeichen des Tieres auf Stirn oder
Hand trägt, darf weder kaufen noch verkaufen -- hier wird der
Kaiserkult also mit den Mitteln des wirtschaftlichen Boykotts
erzwungen.

"Nun kommt es nicht darauf an, ob der römische Staat damals
tatsächlich derartige Pläne erwogen hat. Entscheidend ist, dass
jene Christen, für welche die Offb geschrieben wurde, ihm
tatsächlich etwas derartiges zugetraut haben, wie es die Offb
beschreibt. Damit haben wir das Recht, nun auch -- versuchsweise
-- in Mk 13 eine ähnliche Erwartung vorauszusetzen: Rom wird mit
Gewalt die Anbetung des Kaisers zu erzwingen versuchen -- was
sollen die Christen dann tun?

. . . . Sobald der 'Tag x' anbricht, wo man alle Christen zur
Anbetung des Kaisers zwingen will, soll jeder Christ so schnell
wie möglich fliehen, fort aus dem Ort, wo er wohnt. Denn ist
erst einmal die Bevölkerung vor dem Altar versammelt, so bleibt
nur noch die Wahl zwischen Verleugnung des Christus und dem Tod.
Freilich ist auch diese rasche Flucht -- sie muss so rasch
erfolgen, damit man die Christen nicht noch im letzten Augenblick
ergreift -- nicht einfach und nicht ohne Gefahr: sie wird für
die schwangeren und säugenden Frauen furchtbar sein, zumal wenn
sie in der schlechten Jahreszeit, bei Sturm und Regen, angetreten
werden müsste. Wir wissen heute nach den Erfahrungen der
Flüchtlingstrecks nur zu gut, wie eine solche Flucht aussehen
kann.

"V. 19 berührt sich so eng mit Dan 12,1, dass deutlich wird:
mit diesem Geschehen wird sich für Mk die danielische Weissagung
erfüllen. V. 20 beschreibt indirekt das Furchtbare dieser

Verfolgungszeit: wenn Gott nicht -- seinen Erwählten zuliebe --
die (Zahl der) Tage verkürzt hätte, würde niemand gerettet werden
-- auch keiner der Erwählten! . . . .

"Wenn man sich vor Augen stellt, dass die Christen in solchem
Falle von einer Minute zur andern, ohne alle Vorbereitung
flüchten müssen, im Gebirge oder in der Einöde den Unbilden der
Witterung ausgesetzt, womöglich von Häschern des heidnischen
Staates gejagt, dann ist die Überzeugung des Mk, dass sie das
nicht aushalten könnten, keineswegs phantastisch, sondern
durchaus realistisch. Und Vorbereitungen kann man nicht treffen,
weil der 'Tag x' der Verfolgung eben nicht bekannt ist, sondern
völlig unbestimmt!

"Auch wer in dem Abschnitt V. 14-20 einen älteren Text zu
finden meint, muss darum die soeben vorgetragene Deutung nicht
ablehnen. Selbst wenn ein dem Evangelisten vorliegender Text
wirklich nur von dem gesprochen hätte, was sich so ausgelegt
haben, wie wir dargelegt haben, und nur so wäre er für die Leser
des Mk bedeutungsvoll gewesen." Der Weg Jesu, 444-448.

87. Lloyd Gaston writes as follows on Mark's understanding of
13:14. ". . .Vs. 14 which he has interpreted not just of the
great tribulation at the fall of Jerusalem but of a manifestation
of the Antichrist. When we consider the use made of Daniel in
Vs. 14, it is an interpretation which lies near at hand." No
Stone on Another, 63.

88. ". . . es ist eine Wiederaufnahme von 13,20.22. Der ganze
Satz setzt überdies die 13,14-20 beschriebene Katastrophe
(=Flucht, Vertreibung) voraus. Während es 13,20 ausdrücklich
hiess, dass der Herr (=Gott, Vater) die ἐκλεκτοί retten wird,
werden sie nun die Auserwählten des Menschensohns (αὐτοῦ)
genannt." Redaktion, 185. cf. A. Menzies, The Earliest Gospel
(London, 1901), 240. "At the time of his coming there are
Christians in every part of the world. . . . They constitute a
new Diaspora." And Suhl, Alttestamentlichen Zitate, 11-12.

89. "Jesus gives two signs: the ensign of the hostile army will
signalize the destruction of the city, the ensign of the Son of
Man will herald the redemption of his people. The σημεῖον of the
Son of Man most probably signifies the Shekinah glory with which
he comes, a fitting counterpart to the impious שׁקּוּץ of the
Romans." Beasley-Murray, Mark Thirteen, 93. (See also Farrer,
St Mark, 361.) "The discourse took its rise from a prediction
of the destruction of the temple. That event of necessity forms
the crowning point of the judgment of the old Israel. The
explication of the prophecy, accordingly, reaches its climax
in a description of the Son of Man gathering the members of his
new community into the consummated Kingdom." Mark Thirteen, 90.

90. "Le Discours de Jésus sur la ruine du temple d'après Marc

XIII et Luc XXI, 5-36", RB, LVI (1949), 71-73. See also "Le Fils de l'Homme de Daniel et la tradition biblique", RB, LX (1953), 198.

91. Ibid. (1949), 73.

92. Les Évangiles synoptiques, II, 435.

93. For discussion of the authenticity and grouping of these sayings see A. M. Hunter, The Work and Words of Jesus (London, 1950), 84-87; N. Perrin, The Kingdom of God in the Teachings of Jesus (London, 1963), 102-107; O. Cullmann, Christology of the New Testament (E.T., London, 1959), 137-92; H. E. Tödt, Der Menschensohn in der synoptischen Überlieferung (Gütersloh, 1959); The Son of Man in the Synoptic Tradition (E.T., London, 21965); A. J. B. Higgins, Jesus and the Son of Man (London, 1964); "Son of Man-Forschung since 'The Teaching of Jesus'", New Testament Essays, ed. A. J. B. Higgins (Manchester, 1959), 119-35; E. Sjöberg, Der verborgene Menschensohn in den Evangelien (Lund, 1955); E. Schweizer, "Der Menschensohn", ZNW, L (1959), 185-209; S. G. Mowinckel, He that Cometh (Oxford, 1956); P. Vielhauer "Gottesreich und Menschensohn in der Verkündigung Jesu", Festschrift für Gunther Dehn ed. W. Schniemelcher (Neukirchen Kries Moers, 1957), 51-79; M. Hooker, Jesus and the Servant (London, 1959), M. Hooker, The Son of Man in Mark (London, 1967); C. Colpe, "ὁ υἱὸς τοῦ ἀνθρώπου" TWNT, VIII, 403-81; F. Borsch, "Son of Man", AnglThR, XLV (1963), 174-190.

94. Cullmann, Christology of the New Testament.

95. Wm. Manson, Jesus the Messiah (London, 1943), 173 f.; T. W. Manson, Teaching, 227ff.

96. The Son of Man in Mark, 30.

97. "Although chapter 13 begins with the theme of judgment upon Israel, it is equally concerned with the fate of the disciples; its' theme in fact, is very largely the trouble which is in store for those who are not ashamed of Jesus and who do not deny him. Before the time of judgment and condemnation for the enemies of Jesus, there is a period when they will be in a position to judge and condemn his followers; the disciples must be prepared for persecution before the final vindication. The whole of chapter 13 is thus an elaboration of the theme found in 8:34-38: those who wish to follow Christ must expect to follow the same path of suffering, for they will be hated by all because of his name; but those who are ashamed of Jesus and who do not endure to the end, will not be saved. It is against this background we must understand the climax of the chapter in vv. 24-27. . .

its relevance to the general theme of the chapter is clear: the
revelation of the Son of man is synonymous with judgment: for
all who have rejected Jesus this means disaster: for those who
have been faithful it means vindication." The Son of Man in Mark,
156.

98. Ibid., 158.

99. Beasley-Murray, Jesus, 202.

100. Jesus als Weltvollender, 39-40. Cited by Beasley-Murray,
Ibid. Cf. R. Hummel, Die Auseinandersetzung zwischen Kirche und
Judentum im Matthäusevangelium (München, 1963), 93; Schniewind,
Markus, 175; R. J. McKelvey, The New Temple, passim.

101. The following quotations are representative of their work.
". . . le sanctuaire occupe une place prépondérante dans la pensée
de Daniel. . . . toutes les autres visions font une place au
temple dans leurs perspectives eschatologiques. . . . après quoi
il sera "justifié". . . ce qui corresponde au règne du Fils de
l'homme. . . .
     L'onction de Dan. IX,24, qui peut être une allusion à celle
prescrite pour le tabernacle. . . doit s'entendre figurativement,
croyons-nous, de l'établissement du règne messianique. . . .
     "Qu'est-ce à dire, sinon que les trois oracles de VII, 13-14;
VIII,14 et IX,24 se complètent mutuellement et contribuent à
exprimer la même realité? La sanctuaire tout spirituel que Dieu
oint (IX,24) est assuré de la présence divine grâce à la venue
avec les nuées du Fils de l'homme (VII,13-14), et c'est de cette
manière que Dieu venge (VIII,14) le temple matériel profané par
Antiochus." Feuillet, "Le Fils de l'homme de Daniel et la
tradition biblique", RB, LX (1953), 196-198. "Daniel was already
contrasting with the Temple, profaned and even destroyed. . . a
spiritual sanctuary formed by the believers over whom the Son of
man reigns." Congar, Temple, 159. (See also list of sources
given by M. Hooker, The Son of Man in Mark, 165.) "1QS viii (is)
an important text for the study of temple symbolism. Here, too,
we find clear associations with the concept of 'the new temple'
and the new fellowship with God.
     "As in Targum Jonathan liii, where an exposition of the Ebed
theme is combined with the idea of the return of God's Shekinah
to the temple, so we find in Daniel a combination of 'the saints
of the most High' and the idea of the 'new temple' which is to be
established in the last days. On the subject of the evil to come
it is said that one of the 'horns' of the 'he-goat' shall. . . .
defile the temple. . . But the good to come also stands related
to the temple; atonement shall be made for the evils of the
people and eternal righteousness shall be established, 'to seal
both vision and prophet, and to anoint a most holy place'.
. . . This vision of the future has sometimes been interpreted in

spiritual categories, the implication being that 'the saints'
make up a new temple, a spiritual temple. It is the kingdom of
'the saints' which is called an anointed sanctuary upon which
rests the presence of God (7:13,14). . . .it is important to
note that the concept of the 'anointed sanctuary' is connected
with the ideas of the Son of Man and the 'saints of the most
High'. Brownlee, The Servant of the Lord, pp. 13f. considers
this to be an interpretation of the Ebed as the 'saints', and
writes that 'the collective interpretation of the Servant of
the Lord would seem to embrace Jerusalem and its temple as well
as the 'prince' and his people.'" Gärtner, Temple, 129, 130.

102. R.A. Stewart, "Shekinah", The New Bible Dictionary
(London, 1962), 1174-75, says, "The glory of God -- kabod in the
Hebrew Bible, doxa in LXX and New Testament -- is another name
for the Shekinah. . . . it may be specially associated with the
tent of meeting. . .or with the Temple. . . It is present in a
special way in the heavenly temple (Rev xv.8) and in the
heavenly city (Rev. xxi.23)."
      "Why is Christ 'greater than the Temple'? There can be only
one all-embracing answer. It is because God's presence is more
manifest in Him than the Temple. On Him, not on the Temple,
now rests the Shekinah. . . .The Lord Himself is the true
Temple." Alan Cole, The New Temple, 12. "So neither the
teaching about the New Temple 'not made with hands', nor the
abolition and destruction of the old material Temple. . .are
accidents or after-thoughts to Christianity. They are of its
esse, inevitable corollaries of its central message." Ibid., 55.

103. E.g. Lohmeyer, Torrey, Beasley-Murray.

104. E.g. τότε, ὅταν, εὐθέως, ἐν ἐκείναις ταῖς ἡμέραις,

CHAPTER THREE

RELATIONSHIP OF DANIEL TO THE OLIVET DISCOURSE

Almost every discussion of the β.τ.έ. pays some attention to that Old Testament book[1] where the phrase first occurs, and occurs repeatedly. The question usually asked is: "What did the writer of Daniel mean by the שׁקוץ ?[2] Having settled that question by a review of the circumstances calling forth the book and a confirmatory glance at 1 Macc. 1:54 etc., attention is shifted back to the Synoptic Gospels.

To do this, however, is to move much too quickly. It is to forget that the β.τ.έ. in Mark 13 is only one part of a Danielic complex "peshered" by the Olivet discourse. The β.τ.έ. does not stand alone, even in Mark 13. Linked to it are the ὁ υἱὸς τοῦ ἀνθρώπου, ἡ θλῖψις   and ἡ βασιλεία[3]-- key-notes of the ancient apocalypse. The relationship with Daniel is more intimate yet. Other expressions from the eschatological address are also found to be allusions to Daniel. The references to τέλος; μέλλῃ ταῦτα συντελεῖσθαι πάντα; ἱερόν; δεῖ γενέσθαι; ὁ δὲ ὑπομείνας εἰς τέλος, οὗτος σωθήσεται; ὁ ἀναγινώσκων νοείτω . . . .   are some items on this list.

Thus the close relationship between Mark 13 and Daniel cannot be too much stressed.[4] It has all too often been given only passing notice, and that not always sympathetically.[5] The truthfulness of Farrer's crisp summary cannot be denied. "It is the prophecy of Daniel", he says, "which gives its decisive shape to Christ's prediction on the Mount of Olives."[6]

According to P. Schegg,[7] the Jews called the Book of Daniel משׁמם השׁקוץ   in the same way that they called Genesis בראשׁית We have not been able to find proof for this, though the suggestion is not improbable. Schegg's contention is significant chiefly for showing that the שׁקוץ is the appropriate emblem of the tragedy and trials which produced the book.

It is more than interesting that Christ, in His reference to the book of Daniel, did not place His finger upon some isolated and easily detached phrase, but chose rather to emphasize passages from the very heart of the Old Testament apocalypse. This is true of both His declaration at the commencement of His ministry, "The time is fulfilled, and the kingdom of God is at hand",[8] and His words in the Olivet discourse. Christ's selection from Daniel of the concepts of the Kingdom, the Son of Man, the abomination of desolation, and the tribulation involving Jerusalem's being trodden underfoot, was far from idle. Rather, He thereby encompassed all the main motifs of that book which more than any other was influencing the religious milieu of the times.

Because all these expressions are related as different aspects of the same picture it is impossible to understand the signif-

icance of any one of them without consideration of the over-all
significance of the Danielic pattern which Christ reproduces and
amplifies. Let us say it again -- because the βδέλυγμα is only
one part of the pattern Christ is retracing, it should never be
studied on its own. The entire plan must be surveyed, the chain
must be felt link by link. And this is the purpose of the
present chapter. Such a survey, among other things, should
point out the basic theme of Daniel, the place of the שׁקּוץ
the relationship between the כבר אנשׁ and the שׁקּוץ and the
קדשׁ and the שׁקּוץ. Reminders on these matters should aid
exegesis of the New Testament midrash, and Mark 13:14 in
particular.

But first, some comment upon the unity of Daniel is in order.
Spinoza, in the seventeenth century, suggested that the last
five chapters of the book had a separate author. Sir Isaac
Newton, a century later, expressed his opinion that the chapters
containing the visions of the prophet were indeed the work of
Daniel, but that the narratives were the product of another hand.
In the nineteenth century Bertholdt maintained that nine writers
had been responsible for the book. However, not long after,
Bleek made what appeared to his contemporaries such a satisfactory demonstration of the unity of Daniel that contrary
opinions fell out of favor. For the rest of the nineteenth
century most critical scholars held to the belief of a single
author. Just prior to the dawn of the twentieth century the
tide turned again and many have been the subsequent attempts
to show the divided authorship of the book. As H.H. Rowley
has pointed out "the effective answers to many of the arguments
can be found in the case for others of these divisive views."[9]

The observation of Moses Stuart well expresses the conviction
of most defenders of the unity of the book of Daniel.

> It seems to me impossible for any one at all skilled
> in discerning the characteristics of writing, to read
> the book through attentively in the original, without
> an overwhelming conviction that the whole proceeded
> from one pen and one mind.[10]

We believe that this unity will be demonstrated by the
following review of the message the writer of Daniel sought to
convey. What Farrer said regarding the authenticity of Mark 13
applies to some extent to the unity of Daniel. It is established
if it can be shown that it "results from the imaginative process
which produced the whole book", and that each of the chapters
"builds on what precedes and is built into what follows" as "the
very stuff of the author's mind."[11]

Certain key words or phrases in the book stand out, either

because of their repetition, or because of their uniqueness of terminology or situation. Among those significant because of repetition are the words מלך and מלכו. These words appear over 190 times. It is the latter which is particularly pertinent[12], appearing several times more often than the equivalent word in all the prophets put together. Daniel's theme, then, certainly has to do with the kingdom of God. Each of the visions climaxes in such a portrayal, and Nebuchadnezzar's dream as well. Note the following:

> And in the days of those kings the God of heaven will set up a kingdom which shall never be destroyed, nor shall its sovereignty be left to another people. It shall break in pieces all these kingdoms and bring them to an end, and it shall stand for ever.[13]

> And the kingdom and the dominion and the greatness of the kingdoms under the whole heaven shall be given to the people of the saints of the Most High; their kingdom shall be an everlasting kingdom, and all dominions shall serve and obey them.[14]

> And many of those who sleep in the dust of the earth shall awake, some to everlasting life, and some to shame and everlasting contempt. And those who are wise shall shine like the brightness of the firmament; and those who turn many to righteousness, like the stars for ever and ever.[15]

All the other elements of Daniel, such as the שקוץ and the כבר אנש also appertain to this primary theme of the kingdom of God. In most cases they betoken its immediate antecedents or attendant circumstances.

In the second group of key expressions, those which are unique in terminology or by way of climactic placing, are כבר אוש and נצדק קדש. The former appears in the climax of a graphic representation of the sad record of the centuries for Judaism. Israel's "underdog" experience as the object of spite for all the nations who crossed and recrossed her borders is set forth in the seventh chapter -- the most important chapter of the book according to many commentators. The worst aggressor is pictured as a proud and malevolent little horn. ". . . this horn made war with the saints, and prevailed over them. . ."

> . . . he shall be different from the former ones, and shall put down three kings.
> He shall speak words against the Most High, and shall wear out the saints of the Most High, and shall think to change the times and the law; and they shall be given into his hand. . .[16]

114

But now occurs a dramatic reversal:

> I looked then because of the sound of the great words
> which the horn was speaking. And as I looked, the beast
> was slain, and its body destroyed and given over to be
> burned with fire.
> . . . I saw in the night visions,
> and behold, with the clouds of heaven
>   there came one like a son of man,
> and he came to the Ancient of Days
>   and was presented before him.
> And to Him was given dominion
>   and glory and kingdom,
> that all people, nations, and languages
>   should serve him;
> his dominion is an everlasting dominion,
>   which shall not pass away,
> and his kingdom one
>   that shall not be destroyed.[17]

Thus are presented two opposing figures, central to the
teaching of the book. The כבר אנש is heaven's counter to the
little horn which elsewhere is called השקוץ משמם or הפשע שמם.
The little horn appears again in the imagery of the succeeding
chapter,[18] but this time the redress is imaged by the expression
נצדק קדש. As the two little horns parallel each other, so the
vindication of the sanctuary parallels the coming of the Son of
Man. Thus נצדק קדש joins the other expressions as expressive of
the main motif of Daniel.

We have by no means exhausted the key terms of Daniel,[19] but
these are sufficient to indicate the theme of the book and the
objective of the writer.[20] Let us now spell out the latter more
closely.

The writer of Daniel speaks as though he lived in the
sixth century B.C.[21] His viewpoint is that of a Jewish patriot
who has witnessed the collapse of the Theocracy and the victory
of the idolatrous Gentiles. The ark of the covenant, the
center of the nation's polity, had gone, and the Shekinah, and
Urim and Thummin, besides the kingly rule of the descendents of
David.

The burning of the temple was an overwhelming catastrophe for
Israel. "Its destruction was an inevitable symbol of judgment
and the severance of the relationship between Yahweh and His
people."[22] The Spirit of prophecy also was silent, no longer
was there any vision. As Calvin has said concerning the last
centuries of Israel's history before the coming of Christ:
". . .if ever there were times of distress, such as might tempt

men to imagine that God was asleep in heaven, and had become
forgetful of the human race, it was certainly then, when the
revolutions that took place were so frequent and so various."[23]
It was an age that cried out for a Theodicy, and this the writer
of Daniel offers.

Wrong was on the throne, and right upon the scaffold. What
was Yahweh doing? Was He sleeping or ajourneying while His
people suffered from fire and sword? Why were the Gentiles,[24]
who were idolaters, suffered to triumph over the pious worshippers of the true God? In the heart of the book occurs the
cry: "For how long. . . the transgression that makes desolate
. . .?"[25] How long would wickedness triumph? How long would
Israel be without her daily sacrifice and priesthood? How
long before the longed-for messianic kingdom would be
inaugurated, and Israel take her place at the head of the
nations?

This cry, of course, is not unique to the book of Daniel. It
occurs repeatedly throughout the later Scriptures. It belongs
to the days of Israel's dispersion, and echoes through psalms
and prophets. It is the implied wail of Jeremiah's
Lamentations.[26]

The intervention sought in each instance is divine vindication and restoration. For example, after the utterance of the
cry in Ps. 35 we read:

> Bestir thyself, and awake for my right,
>   for my cause, my God and my Lord!
> Vindicate me, O Lord. . . .
> Let those who desire my vindication
>   shout for joy and be glad. . .[27]

And in Zechariah 1, the reply to the angel's "How long. . .?" is
that "the Lord answered gracious and comforting words to
the angel" and we are told the content of these words:

> Cry out, Thus says the Lord of hosts: I am exceedingly
> jealous for Jerusalem and for Zion. And I am very angry
> with the nations that are at ease; for while I was
> angry but a little they furthered the disaster. Therefore
> thus says the Lord, I have returned to Jerusalem with
> compassion; my house shall be built in it, says the
> Lord of hosts, and the measuring line shall be stretched
> out over Jerusalem. Cry again, Thus says the Lord of
> hosts: My cities shall again overflow with prosperity,
> and the Lord will again comfort Zion and again choose
> Jerusalem.[28]

The question and answer in Daniel are similar in nature to the foregoing instances. The reply is a promise of vindication and restoration. "And he said to him, For two thousand and three hundred evenings and mornings; then the sanctuary shall be restored to its rightful state."[29] Most commentators hold that this reply gives the best indication to the time of composition of the book. The daily sacrifice has been taken away, and its restoration is yet future. But the verse is significant for more than that. It shows the central message of the book. The word of promise in 8:14 is נצדק. Only once does it occur in this form in the Old Testament. With right do some translate it as "vindicated". Daniel is the book of judgment, of vindication. The very title means "God is my Judge", and passage after passage climaxing the visions, promises that Yahweh will judge His people and their enemies, vindicating the former and destroying the latter. Commentator after commentator employs this word "vindication" -- the keynote of all apocalyptic -- in commenting upon the message of the book.[30] Furthermore, this vindication is to come ἄνωθεν. It is no merely human help. The best the Maccabean heroes could do was but a faint shadow of what Yahweh offered His saints.[31]

The promise of the restoration of the sanctuary was a promise of the Messianic kingdom.[32] The temple was a microcosm of the kingdom of God. There were the emblems of His government and covenant. Skillfully the writer has interwoven repeated references to the sanctuary as background to the promises of the establishment of Yahweh's kingdom of glory. These references occur in both the narrative and the prophetic sections of the book. The sanctuary with its abiding Shekinah indicated Yahweh's will to dwell with His people. The writer of Daniel pledges that the shadow is soon to give place to the substance. A new sanctuary is to be anointed as transgression is finished, sin atoned for, and everlasting righteousness brought in. New Testament writers interpret the promise as applying to God's own tabernacling with His people in the παλιγγενεσία [33]

To see the parallelism between the coming of the Son of Man, the vindicating of the sanctuary, and the arrival of the kingdom of God, one needs only to compare Daniel chapters seven and eight.

DANIEL 7	DANIEL 8
Persecuting powers symbolized by beasts.	Persecuting powers symbolized by beasts.
Climactic aggression by little horn.	Climactic aggression by little horn.
Judgment and coming of the	The vindication of the sanc-

117

DANIEL 7	DANIEL 8
Son of Man. (Judgment is given for the saints and they receive the kingdom. The same judgment takes away the dominion of the little horn and it is destroyed.)	tuary. (The little horn is broken without human hand. The vision reaches to the time of the end.)

Some have debated whether the little horn is identical in the two chapters. As Rowley has pointed out, the real case for the identification "does not rest on the similarity of the terms, but on the indications of the character and deeds of the person each stands for."[34] Note the following comparisons.

DANIEL 7	DANIEL 8
Seemed greater than its fellows, v.20.	Grew exceedingly great, v.9.
Speaks words against the Most High, v. 25.	Magnifies himself, v. 25.
Thinks to change the times and the law, v. 25.	Took away the continual burnt offering, v. 11.
Triumphant for "a time, two times, and half a time". v.25.	Triumphant for "two thousand three hundred evenings and mornings". v. 14.
He . . .shall wear out the saints, v. 25	He shall destroy many, v. 25.
His dominion shall be taken away, v. 26.	He shall be broken, v. 25.

In both instances the little horn represents the last persecutor of history. In both instances its overwhelming triumph precipitates its own destruction. In both cases, its warfare is against the cult of Yahweh in particular. In one case it is given a name הפשע שמם which links it with the השקוץ משמם of the later chapters and the β.τ.έ. of the Synoptic Gospels. "The phrase 'abomination of desolation' or the like, is found in 8:13; 9:27; 11:31; 12:11, where the reference is doubtless the same, binding the chapters together once more in their point of climax."[35] Jeffery, in discussing the first of these verses, affirms similarly.

This comparison between chapters seven and eight is an excellent example of the unity of the book. One pen portrayed the same concepts in both chapters. Furthermore, these same concepts are the very stuff out of which all the later chapters are composed. The pattern clearly traced is that of a Gentile oppressor whose idolatry displaces the worship of Yahweh, and whose physical might destroys the worshippers of the temple -- and all this on the eve of the ushering in of the messianic

kingdom. Thus there is no separating the שׁקוץ from the אנש
כבר or the קדשׁ. The three are intimately related. This is
significant for any adequate interpretation of the Olivet
discourse where again the βδέλυγμα and ὁ υἱος τοῦ ἀνθρώπου
and the ἱερόν are central.

Let us look more closely still at the relationship between
אנש כבר and צדק קדשׁ. The former is perhaps the most well-
known metaphor of Daniel's book. All commentators recognize
it as signifying the vindication of the oppressed saints. Even
in the gospels "this vindication-theme attaches to it more
readily than any distinctively redemptive associations."[36]

Thus כבר אנש is the counterpart of the little horn, the
divine response to the שׁקוץ. The figure represents the
reversal of Antichrist's work. The saints, who have been made as
refuse, now become kings. To them is given the dominion,
a dominion reminiscent of Adam's in the beginning. The powers
of rebellious chaos become subject to them. This giving of the
kingdom to the saints at the Judgment is the equivalent of the
vindication of the sanctuary and the making an end of sins and
the ushering in of everlasting righteousness (8:14; 9:24).[37]

The demonstrated relationship between Judgment and
Vindication is important. To the Jewish mind, judgment showed
not so much who was righteous but who was "in the right".[38]

Morna Hooker also stresses this concept. After pointing out
the repeated linking of the ideas of Yahweh's kingship and his
judgment she says:

> The sequence of thought is logical, since God's
> decisive action must be at once the re-establishment of
> his kingship and the manifestation of his righteousness,
> which punishes the wicked and rewards the humble. Daniel's
> vision is a pictorial representation of an idea which
> pervades the psalter, whether it is expressed there in
> historical, cultic or eschatological terms.[39]

However, Daniel's vision is more. It not only is a pictorial
representation of a concept which pervades the psalms, it
pervades the whole of Scripture. Moule's article just quoted
does much to demonstrate that. The pattern implicit in Daniel
7 and 8 regarding the vindication of the oppressed saints by
the judgment of God is presented in rather similar terms
elsewhere in the prophets, the Gospels, and the book of
Revelation. Examples are Zechariah 3, Luke 18:1-8, and Rev.
6:9-11. We would draw particular attention to the second of
these passages, as not only being an instance of divine vindication but being also a case where the expression ὁ υἱος τοῦ

ἀνθρώπου is found in appropriate connection:

The parable of Luke 18 represents the elect as an oppressed
widow who pleads for vindication against her adversary. Christ
finishes the story by saying:

> Hear what the unrighteous judge says. And will not
> God vindicate his elect, who cry to him day and night?
> Will he delay long over them? I tell you he will
> vindicate them speedily. Nevertheless, when the Son
> of Man comes, will he find faith on earth?[40]

Matthew Black rightly points out that the reference to the
Son of Man in this context is very illuminating. There have
been many willing to discount the phrase in this place as a
redactional supplement for its connection with the parable is
not immediately obvious. But what we have here actually is
"all the essential features of the old Biblical Son of man
apocalyptic." Black concludes that "the old Biblical Son of man
apocalyptic has not, therefore, been foisted upon the teachings
of Jesus by later tradition; it represents the substance of
His teaching about the coming Judgment."[41]

Thus the unity of thought apparent in Daniel 7 and
Daniel 8 with its parallel presentations of the kingdom being
given to the Son of Man, and the sanctuary being vindicated,
is a unity reflected in both Testaments. It reflects what
C.H. Dodd calls "a single 'plot'", even the "twofold rhythm of
the pattern of history" finding "characteristic expression in
terms of death and resurrection."[42]

Much has been said here about the theme of vindication in
the book of Daniel. This theme unifies the various sections
of the book, the visions and the narratives. Its emblem is
כבר אנש but its actual statement is found in 8:14. Here is
the one place where the actual term for vindication appears.[43]
We wish to underline the fact that this verse which strikes the
key-note of the book by its reference to vindication is also
the climactic point of the symbolism of the book. Commentators
have been far from unanimous as to where a natural division in
this book occurs. For example, is chapter seven to be seen
as belonging to the first section of the book or the second?
What has not been noticed is that in Daniel 8:14 we have a
distinct literary dividing point, for this verse terminates
the usage of visionary symbols requiring interpretation.[44]
Hereafter, all is explanation.[45] We repeat, Dan. 8:14 is the
climax of the symbolic "forecasts" of the book. The next
verse says Daniel sought to "understand" this vision. Then he
hears a voice saying, "Gabriel, make this man understand the
vision." The words of the angel are "understand, O son of man
. . . ." After this threefold reference to the need for

120

understanding we have an explanation given of the symbols of
chapter 8, except for the climax of that presentation, namely
v. 14. Daniel is not told all that is involved in the
restoration of the sanctuary. He is told about the kings of
Media and Persia, the king of Greece and the four divisions of
that empire. The significance of the little horn is given, but
the only reference to "the evenings and the mornings" is that
it is true, and that it should be sealed up. At this point
Daniel confesses that he was appalled by the vision and that he
did not understand it. The rest of the book is devoted to
explaining in greater detail the vision of chapter 8 (which
itself is an enlargement of the vision of chapter 7),
particularly its climax regarding the restoration or vindication
of the sanctuary.

Both Jeffery and Porteous see in the last verse of Daniel 8
a literary device to draw attention to the importance of the
revelation found therein. Porteous declares "Daniel's
inability to understand the interpretation is a little odd. It
is little more than a device on the part of the author to prepare
the way for the highly detailed interpretation of chapter 11."[46]

We think Porteous is not entirely correct in this statement.
The interpretation of Daniel 8:14 is not reserved for chapter
11 alone. It is presented briefly in Dan. 9:24-27. Thus
chapter 9 expressly mentions both the angel interpreter and the
vision of the preceding chapter -- "the man Gabriel, whom I had
seen in the vision at the first. . . ."[47] And Gabriel's first
words are related to the previous references to "understanding"
that we have already referred to. "I have now come out to
give you wisdom and understanding. . . therefore consider the
word and understand the vision."[48] The words which immediately
follow are related to time (as 8:14) and give to נצדק קדש
an exposition applying it to the messianic kingdom. ". . . to
finish the transgression, to put an end to sin, and to atone
for iniquity, to bring in everlasting righteousness, to seal
both vision and prophet, and to anoint a most holy place" --
that, says the angel in effect, is the vindication of the
sanctuary. In such a way does the seer receive the understanding
he sought.

In summary, after his inability to understand in chapter eight,
Daniel is represented as turning to the prophecies of Jeremiah
regarding Jerusalem and the sanctuary. He prays that Yahweh
will cause His face to shine upon the sanctuary which is
desolate but which the vision of chapter eight promised would
be restored. And now with Gabriel's return he learns that
the sanctuary is to be anointed with the advent of the long-
awaited kingdom.

Feuillet, Buhl, <u>et al</u>. are undoubtedly correct in seeing
that the three passages of Dan. 7:13,14; 8:14; 9:24 parallel
each other and apply to the messianic kingdom.[49] The parallel
can be further illustrated by viewing the visions of eight and
nine side by side as follows:

<table>
<tr><td><u>DANIEL 8</u></td><td><u>DANIEL 9</u></td></tr>
<tr><td>"Gabriel, make this man <u>under-
stand the vision</u>." v. 16.</td><td><u>Gabriel</u>, whom I had seen in
<u>the vision</u> at the first. . . .
and he said. . ."I have now
come out to give you. . .
<u>understanding</u>. . . . I have
come to tell it to you. . .
therefore consider the word
and <u>understand the vision</u>."
vv. 21-23.</td></tr>
<tr><td>. . . the place of his sanctuary
was overthrown. v. 11.</td><td>". . . shall destroy. . .
the sanctuary. v. 26.</td></tr>
<tr><td>. . . through transgression
. . . v. 12.</td><td>". . . to finish the transgre-
ssion. . . ." v. 24.</td></tr>
<tr><td>". . . the transgression that
makes desolate. . . ." v. 13.</td><td>". . . upon the wing of
abominations shall come one
who makes desolate. . . ."
v. 27.</td></tr>
<tr><td>". . . then the sanctuary shall
be restored to its rightful
estate." v. 14.</td><td>". . . to atone for iniquity,
to bring in everlasting
righteousness. . . and to
anoint a most holy place."
v. 24.</td></tr>
<tr><td>. . . the Prince of the host
. . . v. 11.</td><td>". . . an anointed one, a
prince. . ." v. 25.</td></tr>
<tr><td>". . . a king of bold count-
enance. . ." v. 23.</td><td>". . . the prince who is to
come. . . ." v. 26.</td></tr>
<tr><td>". . . the vision is for the
time of <u>the end</u>." v. 17.</td><td>". . . to <u>the end</u>. . . ."
v. 26.</td></tr>
<tr><td>". . . the appointed time of
the end." v. 19.</td><td>". . . until the decreed end
. . . ." v. 27.</td></tr>
<tr><td>". . . destroy mighty men and the
people of the saints." v. 24.</td><td>". . . shall destroy the city
and the sanctuary. . . ."
v. 26.</td></tr>
</table>

DANIEL 8	DANIEL 9
. . . the continual burnt offering. . . taken away. . . ." v. 11.	". . . offering and sacrifice to cease." v. 27.
". . . by no human hand, he shall be broken." v. 25.	". . . the decreed end is poured out on the desolator." v. 27.
". . . the giving over of the sanctuary and host to be trampled under foot. . . for two thousand and three hundred evenings and mornings . . ." vv. 13-14.	". . . to the end there shall be war: desolations are decreed." v. 26.
". . . shall even rise up against the Prince of princes. . . ." v. 25.	". . . an anointed one shall be cut off. . . . v. 26.

The significance of these parallels will be rapidly appreciated if summaries are compared.

DANIEL 8	DANIEL 9
He shall even rise up against the Prince of princes. . . and the place of his sanctuary was overthrown. . . giving over of the sanctuary and host to be trampled under foot. . . "For two thousand and three hundred evenings and mornings; then the sanctuary shall be restored to its rightful state."	". . . an anointed one shall be cut off. . . and the people of the prince who is to come shall destroy the city and the sanctuary. . . and to the end there shall be war: desolations are decreed." "To finish the transgression, to put an end to sin, and to atone for iniquity, and to bring in everlasting righteousness. . . and to anoint a most holy place."

Not only does Dan. 9:24-27 purport to explain the vision of chapter 8,[50] but so also does the final outline of events found in chapters 10-12. This closing section is similar in literary form to chapter 9. Whereas chapters 2, 7 and 8 present a series of symbols followed by explanation, this is no longer the case in chapters 9-12. After 8:14, symbolism requiring interpretation ceases, and everything is now of the nature of explanation itself. This is in harmony with the division previously commented upon, whereby the stress on beasts, horns, etc. is succeeded by straightforward commentary. Having already noticed the parallels between chapters 7 and 8, and 8 and 9, we now set forth a comparison between 8 and 10-12.

DANIEL 8	DANIEL 10-12
. . . I was at the river Ulai. v. 2.	. . . I was standing on the bank of the great river. . . . v. 4. (ch. 10)
. . . I raised my eyes and saw, and behold. . . . v. 3.	I lifted up my eyes and looked, and behold. . . . v. 5. (ch. 10)
. . . he did as he pleased. . . . v. 4.	". . . a mighty king shall . . . do according to his will." v. 3. (ch. 11)
. . . magnified himself. v. 4.	". . . he shall. . . magnify himself. . . . v. 36.
. . . but when he was strong, the great horn was broken, and instead of it there came up four conspicuous horns toward the four winds of heaven. v. 8.	"And when he has arisen, his kingdom shall be broken and divided toward the four winds of heaven. . . ." v. 4.
Out of one of them came forth a little horn, which grew exceedingly great. . . . v. 9.	". . . he shall become strong with a small people. v. 23.
. . . toward the glorious land. v. 9.	". . . the glorious land. . ." v. 16. See also vv. 41,45.
. . . the continual burnt offering was taken away. . . v. 11.	". . . shall take away the continual burnt offering . . . ." v. 31. Cf. also 12: 11.
". . . and the place of his sanctuary was overthrown. v. 11	". . . and profane the temple. . . ." v. 31.
". . . how long is the vision . . .?" v. 13.	". . . How long shall it be till the end of these wonders?" 12:6.
". . . the transgression that makes desolate. . . ." v. 13.	". . . the abomination that makes desolate." 11:31.

And I heard a man's voice between the banks of the Ulai. . . . v. 16.	The man clothed in linen, who was above the waters. . . and I heard him. . . 12:7.
". . . the vision is for the time of the end." v. 17. Cf. v. 19.	". . . until the time of the end. . . ." 11:35. Cf. 11:40 and 12:4.
As he was speaking to me, I fell into a deep sleep with my face to the ground; but he touched me and set me on my feet. v. 18.	Then I heard the sound of his words; and when I heard the sound of his words, I fell on my face in a deep sleep with my face to the ground. And behold, a hand touched me and set me trembling on my hands and knees. 10:9,10.
". . . the latter end of the indignation. . . ." v. 19.	". . . till the indignation is accomplished." 11:36.
". . . the vision. . . is true. . ." v. 26.	. . . the word was true. . . . 10:1.
". . . seal up the vision, for it pertains to many days hence." v. 26.	". . . shut up the words, and seal the book, until the time of the end." 12: 4. "For the vision is for days yet to come." 10:14.
". . . he shall be broken." v. 25.	". . . he shall come to his end. . ." 11:45.
And he said to him, "For two thousand and three hundred evenings and mornings; then the sanctuary shall be restored to its rightful state." v. 14.	. . . your people shall be delivered. . . . And those who are wise shall shine like the brightness of the firmament. . . for ever and ever." vv. 1-3. See also 12-13, which makes reference to "the end of the days".

Thus does the last section of Daniel enlarge the picture of the ultimate divine vindication. It is to include not only the destruction of the terrible שׁקוץ but a timely deliverance for the living saints, and rewards for them and the resurrected dead. Glorification in the kingdom of God and the possession of an eternal inheritance or "lot", as personified by the promise to Daniel, is held out before the wise. The latter are said to be those who understand and thereby make many righteous.

To this point we have discussed the evidence for the unity
of theme in the book as found in the visions. Something should
be said about the evidence on the same matter to be derived from
the narratives. In essence, the narratives convey the same
message as the visions -- the message of vindication for the
faithful and destruction for the wicked.[51]

The work of the author of Daniel is much more profound than is
sometimes recognized. He was a scribe of no mean literary
skill.[52] Once the unity permeating the visions of the book is
recognized there is nothing strange in recognizing also that
the same writer impregnated his stories with identical motifs.
Once this is granted, whether we share Fairbairn's theological
positions or not, it is no effort to recognize the essential
truth in his remarks on the narrative portion of Daniel. We
are sure some commentators on the book have gone much too far
in what they have ascribed to the writer as his didactic
intentions, but others decidely err the other way. Bentzen has
suggested that behind the story of Daniel in the lion's den
we ought to recognize the story of the descent of a hero into
the Underworld to confront demons (symbolized by the lions).
We doubt if this conclusion is necessary, but find more sense
in Bentzen's other suggestion that stories such as are found
in chapters 6 and 3 are an "embodying of sentences" (cf. Psa.
57:4-6; 91:13). Porteous says that "The words of Psa. 57:5 and
7 ('I lie in the midst of lions that greedily devour the sons
of men; . . . they dug a pit in my way, but they have fallen
into it themselves') might almost have suggested the story of
chapter 6 to an inventive story-teller."[53]

Morna Hooker has underlined the relevance of the narrative
of ch. 4. The story of the king who became as a beast casts
light on the imagery of ch. 7. She suggests that it is a
profitable line of enquiry to examine those passages in Daniel
"where human characteristics are attributed to figures which in
other respects are to be classified as 'beasts'".[54]

It is not by coincidence that the author introduces his book
by a description of a northern invader marching upon Jerusalem
to ravage its temple and worshippers.[55] Here is a skilful
literary artistry. The theme of the treading underfoot of the
sanctuary and the host, and the suspension of the daily sacrifice
begins here.[56] It is to reach its high-point in Antichrist,
but in this feature as others the activities of Antichrist are
foreshadowed first by the narratives. Belshazzar drinks wine from
the sacred vessels taken from the sanctuary, and it is then that
the mysterious finger etches a message of judgment upon the
banquet-room wall. So later, when Antichrist reaches the height
of iniquity, invading even the holy places of Yahweh, then
judgment will fall.

> . . . the fact that the world-power has deified itself
> and has attacked the true religion, setting up its own
> image in God's sanctuary, is the proof that sin has passed
> its permitted limit.[57]

Thus the narratives point the moral ahead of the visionary
representation. In chs. 3 and 6 those who persecute the saints
and enforce idolatrous worship are themselves humiliated and
compelled to acknowledge the true God. Thereby the author
foreshadows his later descriptions of Antichrist's coming to
his end, broken without human hand, consumed and destroyed.

Discussing the chief characters of the narratives Rowley
says:

> In each case the particular thing for which the kings
> are held up to obloquy is something which has its
> counterpart in Antiochus, while the particular thing for
> which the pious Jews are held up to honour is something
> which pious Jews in the days of Antiochus might with
> peculiar appropriateness be encouraged to imitate.[58]

All the key characteristics of Antichrist, pride, blasphemy,
idolatry, and oppression are represented in the stories.
Nebuchadnezzar boasts of his prowess and is humbled to the
position of the beasts of the field. He enforces worship of
an idol [59] and is confronted with a messenger from the Most
High God. Belshazzar blasphemes the God of heaven by profaning
the holy temple vessels and praising his idols, but then it
is written that he has been weighed in the balances of judgment
and been found wanting, and that his kingdom is divided and given
to others.

As for the matter of oppression, we find here an illustration
of how the writer artfully repeats identical concepts in both
sections of his work[60] in order to point out the desired moral.
The Jews who refuse to bow down to Nebuchadnezzar's image are
told that no god can "deliver" them. They reply: "O
Nebuchadnezzar, we have no need to answer you in this matter. If
it be so, our God whom we serve is able to deliver us. . . and
he will deliver us. . . ." Then there is a note particularly
appropriate for the Maccabean martyrs. "But if not i.e. if
Yahweh chooses not to deliver . . . we will not serve your
gods. . ." Again in chapter 6 we find the same key-word
emphasized. The threatened Daniel is encouraged by Darius "May
your God, whom you serve continually, deliver you!" But later,
approaching the den, he laments "O Daniel. . . has your God. . .
been able to deliver you from the lions?" Then in the royal
proclamation it is declared concerning Yahweh that "He delivers
and rescues. . . he who has saved Daniel. . . ." The wording is

similar to Nebuchadnezzar's decree when he too affirmed that
"there is no other god who is able to <u>deliver</u> in this way."

So much for the use of this idea of deliverance in the
narratives. Let us now compare Dan. 12:1. Keeping in mind that
the previous verses picture an onslaught by the king of the
north upon the glorious holy mountain, an onslaught attended
by "great fury" and the intense desire to "exterminate and
utterly destroy many", how appropriate is the climax then
presented!

> At that time shall arise Michael, the great prince who
> has charge of your people. And there shall be a time of
> trouble, such as never has been since there was a nation
> till that time; but at that time your people shall be
> <u>delivered</u>. . .

Those who had read the narratives could not but say to
themselves: "When iniquity reaches its limit, and the saints
are faced with death, then God will intervene, destroying the
wicked and delivering the righteous -- just as He delivered the
three in the days of Nebuchadnezzar, and delivered Daniel in the
days of Darius."

While it could be that Farrer's fertile imagination sometimes
tempts him to excess, it could be that he is not too wide of
the mark when he affirms that Daniel in the den of lions was
"a sign of the whole divine dispensation."[61] The issue is not
whether Daniel had been "worn out" by the lions, but whether
he had been persecuted and oppressed, cast down, and then
delivered and vindicated.[62] The author's presentation of just
such a career for his hero is but one aspect of the literary
skill which has tailored all his materials to fit his chosen
theme.

We have stressed the importance of the expression נצדק קדש[3]
as indicating the theme of vindication which permeates both the
narratives and the visions. The word נצדק is worthy of a closer
examination. While words of the צדק[64] group occur over five
hundred times in the Old Testament, the Niph'al use in Dan. 8:14
is unique.

The verb צדק "to be just, righteous" occurs 41 times, while
the adjective צדיק , occurring 208 times, is usually translated
by either "just" or "righteous". The feminine noun צדקה ,
similar in meaning to צדק often gives more emphasis to an active
deed of righteousness as in Isa. 64:6. This word appears 155
times in the Old Testament.

It is obvious that the basic meaning underlying צדק is

simply to be "just" or "right". A study of the root in
cognate languages supports this conclusion. However, there are
important nuances of meaning which should be taken into account.
Some of these may be of particular importance with reference
to נצדק   in our text.

Certainly צדק   has a clear forensic sense. See 2 Sam. 15:4;
1 Kings 8:32; 2 Chron. 6:23; Ex. 23:7; Ps. 82:3; Deut. 25:1.
Of the 117 occurrences of the masculine noun צדק, 67 of these
(over 50 per cent) are used in some connection with jurisprudence
Occasionally it is used as directly synonymous with judgment.
Similarly, 45 instances out of the 155 occurrences of the
feminine noun show that the root is used in connection with
jurisprudence.

Another related concept to those of righteousness and
judgment is that of salvation. The word righteousness as
descriptive of a judge denoted not merely impartiality but a
positive energy on the side of the right. Eight times the
noun righteousness is used synonymously with "salvation". See
Isa. 56:1. Particularly in Judges, Deutero-Isaiah, and in the
Psalms do the words of this group approximate to the meanings
"save", "saving", and "salvation".

This brief review indicates that the root term used in Dan.
8:14 is extraordinarily rich in meaning.[65] נצדק   implies a
judicial and soteriological process of judging, acquitting, and
restoring. It harmonizes with the meaning of the name of the
book, the judgment scene in ch. 7, the significance of the אנש
כבר and the overall motif of vindication in the narratives
and visions.

Important concepts for the exegesis of Daniel emerge from
the preceding analysis. Firstly, the theme of the book is
everywhere apparent -- the vindication of Yahweh, His worshippers
His temple, and His truth. Secondly, the place of the שקוץ
is similarly clear-cut. The שקוץ represents the final threat
to the pious remnant, the inaugurator of the greatest
tribulation of all time. It is the final devastator of the
divine worship, and the most dreadful temptation to apostasy
Israel has ever known. Its importance in the book is shown
by the disproportionate treatment it receives in each of the
visions.[66] Thirdly, the relationship between the שקוץ and the
קדש must be observed. They are ever linked. This is vital for
interpreting ὅπου οὐ δεῖ in Mk. 13:14 and ἐν τόπῳ ἀγίῳ
in Mt. 24:15. Lastly, it is the שקוץ which is the precipitating
factor of the great tribulation, and therefore the forerunner
of the kingdom of God.

All these factors present in Daniel are to be found also in

the Olivet discourse, and in each case the presentation is true
to the original Old Testament picture in form, though it adds
to the substance. Especially is this true of the theme of
vindication.[67] The coming of the Son of Man is the answer to
the שׁקוּץ and the great oppression of the saints. The morning
of deliverance succeeds the midnight of the tribulation
initiated by the שׁקוּץ. During this midnight many will be
offended and iniquity will abound. False Christs and false
prophets will work their deceiving miracles, and those who have
not received a love of the truth will succumb. Scarcely can
even the elect survive. But out of the darkness light will
shine. The sign of ὁ υἱος τοῦ ἀνθρώπου will replace the sign
of το βδέλυγμα, and the persecuting tribes of the Gentiles
will mourn while the faithful lift up their heads and rejoice.
Such is the picture painted by Christ in His eschatological
discourse, and it is almost with a shock that we discover it
is the picture first sketched by "Daniel the prophet".[68]

Excursus on the Usage of Daniel by the Olivet Discourse

Markan passages compared with parallels in Daniel.

MARK 13	DANIEL
". . . when these things are all to be accomplished?" v. 4.	". . . all these things would be accomplished." 12:7.
". . . wars and rumours of wars." v. 7.	". . . tidings. . . shall alarm him, and he shall go forth with great fury to destroy. . . ." Dan. 11:44. See also 9:26.
". . . this must take place . . . ." v. 7.	". . . what will be. . . ." 2:28.
". . . you will be hated by all for my name's sake. But he who endures to the end will be saved." v. 13.	". . . they shall fall by sword and flame, by captivity and plunder, for some days . . . . to refine and cleanse them and to make them white, until the time of the end . . . ." 11:33,35. ". . . your people shall be delivered. . . ." 12:1.
". . . the desolating sacrilege set up where it ought not be . . . ." v. 14.	". . . the transgression that makes desolate. . . ." 8:13. ". . . upon the wing of abominations shall come one

who makes desolate. . . ."
9:27. ". . . the abomination
that makes desolate." 11:31.
". . . the abomination that
makes desolate. . . ." 12:11.

". . . let him that readeth
understand. . . ." v. 14.

Daniel uses the thought of
understanding over a score of
times. See particularly
8:15,16,17; 9:2,22,23; 10:1;
11:33; 12:8.

". . . such tribulation as has
not been from the beginning of
the creation which God created
until now. . . ." v. 19.

"And there shall be a time
of trouble, such as never has
been since there was a nation
. . . ." 12:1.

". . . if the Lord had not shortened the days. . . ." v. 20.

"Seventy weeks of years are
decreed concerning your
people. . . ."[71] 9:24.

"False Christs and false prophets
will arise and show signs and
wonders. . . ." v. 22.

"He shall give no heed to the
gods of his fathers." 11:37.[72]

". . . the Son of man coming
in clouds with great power and
glory." v. 26.

". . . behold, with the
clouds of heaven there came
one like a son of man. . . .
And to him was given dominion
and glory and kingdom,. . . ."
7:13.

1. "The influence of the prophecy of Daniel has always been unique, even to modern times," Torrey, Documents, 33. "No one can understand the attitude of medieval Christians, especially in the West, unless they realize how important this book was to the ordinary Christian." K. & S. Lake, Introduction to the New Testament (London, 1938), 182. For specific examples of the influence of Daniel in the N.T., see C. H. Dodd, According to the Scriptures, 67-70.

2. The complete phrase is השקוץ משמם.

3. ἡ βασιλεία is present by implication in Mk. 13, and in fact in Mt. 24:14 and Lu. 21:31.

4. See Hartman, Prophecy, 145-77. 5. E.g. C.H. Weisse, G. Hölscher.

6. A Study in St. Mark (London, 1951), 136.

7. Evangelium nach Matthäus, III, 248, cited by van Dodewaard, "De gruwel der verwoesting", St. Cath., XX (1944), 128.

8. In view of the plethora of material written on the Kingdom of God in the New Testament, it is a marvel that scholars have not bestowed proportionate attention on the same topic as set forth in Daniel -- the Old Testament source of Christ's teaching on the matter. One classic treatment, however, is found in Lagrange's Le Judaisme avant Jésus Christ (Et. bibl.)(Paris, 1931) 62-69.

9. The Servant of the Lord (Oxford, [2]1965), 260. The same writer gives a fine summary of his own viewpoint when he says: ". . .the links of style and outlook, which are so clearly acknowledged that the theories of glossing have been so extensively resorted to, are added to the community of error, the case for the unity of authorship is a strong one. The stock argument against it is just that touch of looseness and inconcinnity which is really the strongest argument for it. Community of error can be accounted for by borrowing; but a quality of mind, or mental habit, is not so easily borrowed. Hence the fact that this is found in the oft-severed parts of the book is of the first significance. Not less so is the difficulty of finding any clear division, since the threefold test of language, form, and presumptive authorship yields different results, while chapter 7 will continue to embarrass the dissectors by its refusal to be assigned to either half alone. "The onus of proof lies upon those who would dissect a work. There, however, nothing that can be seriously called proof of

compositeness has been produced. On the other hand, evidence for the unity of the work that in its totality amounts to a demonstration is available." Ibid., 280. R. H. Pfeiffer says, ". . . there is no compelling reason to ascribe the two parts of the book to different authors." Introduction to the Old Testament (London, 1952), 764. See also Lagrange, Jüdaisme, 63. This author stresses the unity of theme manifest in all parts of the book of Daniel.

10. Cited by Rowley, The Servant of the Lord, 273. Montgomery, Eissfeldt, Ginsberg, Baumgartner, and others have set forth the various conflicting views regarding the origin of Daniel based on the fact of the change in both the language and prophetic calculations as well as the theory of selections from a Daniel cycle, but Rowley's words still apply -- "the effective answer to many of the arguments can be found in the case for others of these devisive views." The requirements of logic disqualify , the majority of theories automatically. The niche will not hold too many hypothetical statues at the same time. Occam's razor may be needed and possibly the view contending for a single author (even if using traditional material) is the most profitable application of it. See the following: J. A. Montgomery, The Book of Daniel (ICC)(Edinburgh, 1927); H. L. Ginsberg, Studies in Daniel (New York, 1948); O. Eissfeldt, Einleitung in das Alte Testament (Tübingen, ³1963); particularly, W. Baumgartner, "Ein Viertejahrhundert Daniel-forschung", ThRs (NF), XI (1939), 59-83, 125-144, 201-228.

11. St Mark, 261. None of these references should be under stood as denying that the author of Daniel used already-existing accounts. "These legends, with their manifest didactic purpose, were originally addressed to the Jews of the Persian diaspora." Gerhard von Rad, The Message of the Prophets (London, 1968), 276.

12. Concerning מלכות von Rad says, "Prior to Daniel the religious world made little use of it." But in Daniel there is "a much more precise delineation of the kingdom of God". TDNT, I, 570. See also John Bright's discussion of the kingdom theme in Daniel. The Kingdom of God (New York, 1953), 182-186. His immediate conjunction of Christ's teaching on the subject with Daniel's is not only a matter of chronology.

13. Dan. 2:44.

14. Dan. 7:27.

15. Dan. 12:2,3. "The visions and their interpretations all culminate in the final establishment of the Kingdom of God", H. H. Rowley, "Daniel", Dictionary of the Bible, ed. F. C.

Grant and H. H. Rowley (Cambridge, [2]1963), 200. Cf. Lagrange, Judaïsme, 68.

16. Dan. 7:24-25.

17. Dan. 7:9-14.

18. Dan. 8:9-13.

19. "Time of the end", and its equivalent "latter days", are also prominent.

20. According to Lagrange, the sanctuary of Dan. 9:24 is a "symbole du règne de Dieu". Judaïsme, 69. He, as Dodd and others finds in the visions of Daniel the origin of the kingdom teachings by Christ and Paul. Dodd stresses ch. 7 as the primary source, but Lagrange gives as much emphasis to Dan. 9:24-27. See Gaston's remarks on the equivalence of the temple and the kingdom. No Stone on Another, 230, 243.

21. The New Testament takes for granted that setting for the book, (Mt. 24:15), as did the Christian church till the nineteenth century. See the author's commentary on Daniel (Southern Publishing Association, Nashville, 1978) for discussion of the dating of Daniel.

22. M. Hooker, The Son of Man in Mark, 151.

23. Calvin, Daniel (reprinted from Calvin Translation Society edition of 1852-3, London, 1966), 80.

24. "We cannot regard Nebuchadnezzar and Belshazzar, still less Darius the Mede, simply as portraits of Antiochus Epiphanes. The author is contending, not against Antiochus personally, but against the heathenism of which Antiochus was the champion." A. A. Bevan, A Short Commentary on the Book of Daniel (Cambridge, 1892), 24.

25. Dan. 8:13. See Gaston, No Stone on Another, 378.

26. Typical occurrences are Ps. 74 (particularly v.10); 79 (particularly v.5); 89:3-4,38-46; 94:1-3; Zech. 1:12. Apart from these communal laments are found personal supplications in similar vein, such as in Ps. 6:2-3; 13:1-2; 35:17, and Hab. 1: 2-4.

27. Ps. 35:23-24, 27.

28. Zech. 1:14-27.

29. Dan. 8:14.

30. E.g. E. Heaton, Daniel, Torch Bible Commentaries (London, 1967), 35, 195, 197, 212. Cf. R.H. Pfeiffer, Introduction to the O.T. (London, 1952), 781.

31. As Welch has written: ". . . the prophet nowhere shows any sympathy with the party which led the Maccabean rising. Indeed, it is more natural to hold that, while he expects the deliverance to come solely by the intervention of God, . . . he is distinctly opposed to the ideals which animated the revolt." Visions of the End (London, 1922), 132. It is however possible that the phrase "a little help" is the writer's estimate of the work of the Maccabean patriots. See 11:34. "His hope for the end has a scope and a character which no rebellion, however motivated by religion, could ever claim." Ibid., 50.

32. Buhl, "Daniel", The New Schaff-Herzog Encyclopaedia of Religious Knowledge, III, 349.

33. A. Jeffery, "Daniel", IB, VI, 497. Lloyd Gaston says, "It is significant that there is in Daniel no mention of a hoped-for rebuilding or rededication of the temple. In Daniel 2 a great stone 'not made with hands' shatters the fourth kingdom and becomes a 'kingdom which shall never be destroyed' (2:44). In 7:14,27 it is again a kingdom which is given to the people of the saints of the Most High, when the fourth kingdom is destroyed. Accordingly it may very well be that we should interpret 9:24 'to anoint a holy of holies' in accordance with the usage of the Dead Sea Scrolls, to refer to a community." No Stone on Another, 118.

34. Darius the Mede and the Four World Empires in the Book of Daniel (Cardiff, 1935), 126.

35. H. H. Rowley, A Companion to the Bible, ed. T. W. Manson (Edinburgh, 1939), 73-74.

36. C. F. D. Moule, "From Defendant to Judge-and-Deliverer", SNTSB, III (1952), 40. Concerning Daniel's usage of the term Hooker comments: "The saints who are now crushed on earth are already recognized in heaven as those to whom the dominion belongs, and stand even now before the throne of the Most High. The appearance and enthronement of the Son of Man are thus seen to be integral parts of the whole book of Daniel, for the author's conviction that God will intervene on behalf of his saints, and that he will end their sufferings and give them the kingdom, is here given its most dramatic expression." The Son of Man in Mark, 29. Cf. Lagrange, Judaïsme, 69, ". . . dès le

135

moment où le grand ennemi de Dieu sera frappé, Dieu va commencer son oeuvre, son règne est dans la perspective prochaine. . . ."; Gaston, No Stone on Another, 449.

37. Feuillet has rightly stressed the parallel nature of these three passages. ". . . les trois oracles de vii,13-14; viii,14 et ix,24 se complètent mutuellement et contribuent à exprimer la même réalité? Le sanctuaire tout spirituel que Dieu oint (ix,24) est assuré de la présence divine grâce à la venue avec les nuées du Fils de l'homme (vii,13-14), et c'est de cette manière que Dieu venge (vii,14) le temple matériel profané par Antiochus." "Le Fils de l'homme de Daniel et la tradition biblique", RB, LX (1953), 197-98. (Cf. Jeffery's comment on Dan. 9:24, IB, VI, 497;) ". . . the sanctuary of Dn 8:14 and 9:24 should be interpeted figuratively in terms of the holy community." Gaston, No Stone on Another, 175.

38. W. R. Smith, The Prophets of Israel (Edinburgh, 1882), 71f. "The ideas of right and wrong among the Hebrews are forensic ideas; that is, the Hebrew always thinks of the right and the wrong as if they were to be settled before a judge. Righteousness is to the Hebrew not so much a moral quality as a legal status. The word 'righteous' (saddîq) means simply 'in the right', and the word 'wicked' (rasha‘) means 'in the wrong'." Cf. David Hill, Greek Words and Hebrew Meanings (Cambridge, 1967), 89n; Gaston, No Stone on Another, 380.

39. The Son of Man in Mark, 23.

40. Luke 18:8.

41. "The Son of Man in the Teaching of Jesus", 37.

42. According to the Scriptures, 102,129.

43. ". . . Dan. 8:14 should probably be interpreted along these lines: 'the holy place shall be put right, restored to what it should be'. Here the LXX translator appears to have interpreted according to the general sense required by the context, since that meaning could not be elicited from δικαιωθήσεται which would have been the normal rendering of the Hebrew." David Hill, Greek Words and Hebrew Meanings (Cambridge, 1967), 84n. Dan. 7:22 reflects the same concept of vindication.

44. "It is sometimes argued that vv. 13 and 14 are interpolated, but it should be noticed that they stand or fall with v. 26 which refers back to them." N. Porteous, Daniel, 127. Cf. 129, Ibid.

45. ". . . in the third vision the imagery is laid aside. . .
The fourth vision, the last and longest of them all, drops the
symbolism entirely. . ." S. B. Frost, Old Testament Apocalyptic
(London, 1952), 183. On Daniel 8:14, in particular, Frost says:
". . . he was not prophesying when the re-dedication as such was
going to take place, but . . . the eschaton. . . ." Ibid., 199.

46. Daniel (London, 1965), 130.

47. Dan. 9:21.

48. Dan. 9:23.

49. See also Gaston, No Stone on Another, 175, 243, 380-381.

50. Even the shortened 'week' of the 2300 evening-mornings may
be implicit in the allusions to the war upon the sanctuary and
the host in the 70th week, just as the vindication of the same
verse refers not to "the re-dedication as such. . . but the
eschaton. . . -- the eschaton described in 9:24-27." Frost,
Old Testament Apocalyptic, 199.

51. Says Bevan: "In every one of these stories we see the
righteous rewarded or the wicked signally punished, as the case
may be. On the one hand, Daniel and his three friends, the
servants of the True God, though apparently helpless in the
midst of the heathen, triumph over all opposition, while on the
other hand the mightiest Gentile potentates are confounded and
humbled to the dust." Daniel, 22-23. Rowley says that "point
can be found for every story of the first half of the book in the
setting of the Maccabean age to which the latter part is
assigned." The Servant of the Lord, 276. Cf. Jeffery, IB VI,
346. Heaton goes further still by asserting that "chs. 8-12 seem
to be in large measure dependent on the first section and are
probably best regarded as a commentary on it. . ." Daniel, 50.
Cf. A. Jeffery: ". . . a great many little things link the two
parts together as a unity." Ibid., 346. This is a bold statement
and at first glance not very far removed from the position
taken by conservative interpreters of the last century.
Typical of that group was Patrick Fairbairn who wrote as follows:
"Daniel's history, too, was in the closest manner connected with
his prophecy. The one may fitly be regarded as a type of the
other, and on that account, probably, occupies so large a place
in his book. The grand aim of the revelations imparted to him,
was to unfold the progress of the kingdom of God from deep
depression, and through manifold struggles, to the supreme
place of honour and glory, and the process is already imaged
in the marvellous rise of Daniel himself from the conditions of
a Hebrew exile to the place of highest power and influence at
the court of Babylon." The Interpretation of Prophecy, 35.

52. An illustration of this skill is found in the prayer of ch. 9 which interweaves most of the key expressions later embodied in the message of Gabriel in vv. 24-27. Note references to sin, transgression, iniquity, Jerusalem, sanctuary, desolation, righteousness, etc. Thus even in this chapter, the narrative helps interpret the vision.

53. <u>Daniel</u>, 87.

54. <u>The Son of Man in Mark</u>, 15. (See also Rowley's emphasis that the ignoble nature of the Gentile kingdoms was expressed by the symbolism of the beasts. <u>The Faith of Israel</u>, 194.) "Thus in Dan. 7 itself we find that the first beast 'was lifted up from the ground and made to stand upon two feet like a man; and the mind of a man was given to it' (v.4). Exactly the same idea is to be found in the account in Dan. 4 of Nebuchadnezzar's dream and its sequel. In spite of the added confusion of the tree metaphor the contrast is clear: Nebuchadnezzar's mind is changed from a man's to a beast's; he lives with the animals in the fields and behaves like them, until his reason is restored. . . . What the context does suggest. . . is that the change from a man's mind to a beast's typifies Nebuchadnezzar's loss of reason. . . . But it is the interpretation which the author gives to this change that supplies the clue to its importance. For it is made clear that the reasons for Nebuchadnezzar's downfall and disgrace were his self-glorifica- tion and pride in his own achievement (v. 30). . . .According to chapter 4, it is when Nebuchadnezzar forgets that his kingdom and glory are God-given that he loses his dominion, not only over men, but over birds and beasts as well, and is reduced to the level of the beasts.
   "<u>The same emphasis on self-magnification is found in the later visions of Daniel.</u> Thus in chapter 8 we read repeatedly of the animals and their horns that they magnified themselves. Similarly, chapter 11. . . As for the beasts in chapter 7, it is self-evident that they. . . are in rebellion against God and have seized power for themselves. This connection between man's rebellious self-sufficiency and animal life is found also in the Psalms. . . . Ps. 73:21f. . . 49:21. . . ." <u>Ibid.</u>, 15-16. (Emphasis ours.) Cf. A. Farrer, <u>St Matthew and St Mark</u> (London, 1954), 17.

55. Dan. 1:1-2. See Rowley, "The Bilingual Problem of Daniel", <u>ZAW</u>, L, (1930), 258, on the relevance of Dan. 1.

56. Even the reference to the desolate sanctuary in a prayer recorded as having been offered in the sixth century B.C. "is probably an allusion to 'the abomination of desolation'. . . ." Porteous, <u>Daniel</u>, 138-39.

57. Welch, Visions, 103.

58. Servant, 279.

59. Cheyne, in explicating the significance of the שְׁקוּץ affirms that his interpretation of the vision harmonizes with the didactic narrative of Daniel 3. "Abomination of Desolation", EB, I, 21ff. See also Bentzen's comment on the connection between Dan. 7 and the preceding narratives. Introduction to the Old Testament (E.T., Copenhagen, 1952), 195.

60. O. Eissfeldt, The Old Testament (E.T., Oxford, ³1965), 527: "In both halves of his book the compiler is assuring. . . his contemporaries of consolation. . . ."

61. St Matthew and St Mark, 17. Eissfeldt says: ". . . the author wished to persuade those who were suffering with him of the certainty that everything which they had to bear was not the result of blind chance, but had been predetermined by God long ago", The Old Testament, 528.

62. This is made perfectly clear by the moral attached to the story. 6:26-28.

63. J. A. Montgomery, The Book of Daniel, 343 says: "The verb in 'the sanctuary shall be cleansed' is an interesting but perfectly proper use of צדק . . . ." A. Bentzen stresses that Dan. 8 links backwards with ch. 7., and forwards with chs. 9-12, The Old Testament, 198.

64. See Hill, Greek Words and Hebrew Meanings, 82-98.

65. "In the first place, the righteousness of the judge and of the king has a bias towards 'assistance' or 'deliverance'. Secondly, when the root is used in connection with a plaintiff, it bears the meaning 'in the right'. . . ." David Hill, Greek Words and Hebrew Meanings, 93.

66. As Bevan says: ". . . in these visions very little is said about the first three Gentile Empires, while the history of the Fourth is described at great length, and with increasing minuteness as we approach the time of 'the king' whose crimes are so vividly set before us." Daniel, 23.

67. M. Hooker, The Son of Man in Mark, 156; Gaston, No Stone on Another, 449.

68. Cf. Torrey, Documents, 32.

69. Lohmeyer and Lagrange et al. make this association of texts.

70. See Hartman, _Prophecy_, 155. This book is exhaustive in its
treatment of allusions to Daniel in Mk. 13 and Mt. 24. With
Hartman's conclusions these of Karl Heim should also be considered. He declares: ". . . at least in its main features Jesus
accepts the vision of the future of the world given by Daniel.
For he solemnly adopts the principal part in the final act of
the cosmic drama seen in the book of Daniel. . . . the
'Kingdom of heaven' also, which He announced in His first call
to repentance, is the eternal Empire that according to Daniel
is to follow the terrestrial empires. For the import of this
solemn declaration by Jesus it is immaterial whether the author
of Daniel lived about 600 B.C. under Jehoiakim in the Babylonian
exile, as he says himself, or whether the book was written in
the first half of the 2nd century B.C. . . ." _Jesus, the
World's Perfector_ (E.T., London, 1959), 142.

CHAPTER FOUR

EXEGESIS OF MK. 13:14

Having surveyed preliminary issues which have bearing on the
Olivet discourse and its allusion to the βδέλυγμα τῆς ἐρημώσεως,
it is now our purpose to attend more closely to the basic
textual reference itself, namely Mk. 13:14. ὅταν δὲ ἴδητε τὸ
βδέλυγμα τῆσ ἐρημώσεως ἐστηκότα ὅπου οὐ δεῖ, ὁ ἀναγινώσκων νοείτω,
τότε οἱ ἐν τῇ Ἰουδαίᾳ φευγέτωσαν εἰς τὰ ὄρη. . . .

These words constitute a renowned crux interpretationis, and
have been subjected at times to as much exegetical scrutiny and
as wide a range of opinion as Galatians 3:20 and Revelation 13:18.
"Deze woorden van Jesus hebben ten allen tijde de menschen
gefascineerd", says van Dodewaard.[1] Certainly, they are central
to the eschatological address, even pivotal.[2] They point to a
crisis[3]for the disciples, Judaism, and the world. The event in
question, whatever it is, signalizes the commencement of the time
of trouble such as never was, and it is impossible to read the
chapter with candour and not see that it teaches that in the days
of the βδέλυγμα τῆσ ἐρημώσεως and the tribulation it
precipitates, the Son of Man would be revealed in the clouds to
gather His threatened elect.[4] ". . . fast jedes Wort macht
Schwierigkeiten."[5] The verse seethes with obscurity, or is it
that the phraseology is purposely chosen in order to accomplish
its purpose of riveting attention? The grammatical anomaly
found in ἐστηκότα, the vagueness of ὅπου οὐ δεῖ , the admonition
νοείτω , and what Vincent Taylor refers to as "the general
atmosphere of reserve which marks the passage"[6] -- all betoken,
not only mystery, but importance.

In this discussion, the ground traversed in chapters one to
three will not be retraced. The prejudices which have long led
to the neglect or perversion of this verse were there reviewed,
and also the variety of interpretations given to the eschatological discourse as a whole. We now propose to find, not only
what the early church of the first century saw in this enigmatic
pronouncement, but what the original Speaker and/or writer
intended.

Mk. 13:14 -- Textual Criticism

The weight of textual evidence attests the passage as set out
above. This has been made the basis for all recent translations.
Certainly τὸ ῥηθὲν ὑπὸ Δανιὴλ τοῦ προφήτου of the Textus
Receptus has no right in this verse, and the fact has long been
recognized. It originated through assimilation to Matthew's text,
but is now omitted by all modern editions of the Greek text. It
is easy to see how this addition could have been interpolated,
but not so easy to explain its absence from B, D, etc., if it is
genuine. This is not to assert definitely that the clause had no
part in the original discourse. The context makes it possible

142

that Christ uttered these last words also, but there is no way of demonstrating that they are not an interpretative addition by the later Evangelist.[7]

Beasley-Murray has set forth a case for emendation of Mk. 13:14 but it seems to us the least probable of all that scholar's suggestions. He has proposed that originally the text may have run ὅταν δὲ ἴδητε τὸ σημεῖον τοῦ βδελύγματος φεύγετε εἰς τὸ ὄρος . . . . Beasley-Murray points out that ἑστὸς ἐν τόπῳ ἁγίῳ is omitted in Matthew by Syr. sin., and that both Merx and Streeter affirm the omission to be correct. Further, in Mt. 24: 15, the Greek text behind Syr. sin did not have ἐρημώσεως. Then, if we agree with those who believe ὁ ἀναγινώσκων νοείτω to be an addition to the original logion and that οἱ ἐν τῇ Ἰουδαίᾳ φευγέτωσαν has possibly displaced φεύγετε , the text is shorn still further, leaving but the single line suggested above.[8]

There is, of course, weight in all these points, but not sufficient weight to offset the manuscript testimony for Mk. 13: 14 in its accepted form. Beasley-Murray's judgment is to be agreed with when he affirms that "it is admittedly hazardous to set the Syriac tradition over against the mass of textual evidence. . . ."[9] For one thing, whether ὁ ἀναγινώσκων νοείτω came from Jesus originally cannot be disproved. Many scholars have claimed a dominical origin for the expression.[10] Furthermore, it appears that Beasley-Murray labours to relieve this text of any dependence upon Dan. 9:27; 11:31, or 12:11. He says that "there is no necessity to identify the βδέλυγμα with the שמם שקוץ of Daniel."[11] But, in answer, we would suggest that in view of the manner in which Mk. 13 elsewhere reflects Daniel, and, in particular, those visions of the book regarding the fate of the sanctuary, this dissociation would not only be an advantage but would result in the throwing away of a positive interpretive key. The Old Testament apocalypse pictures the Son of Man as supplanting the Antichrist when the latter reaches the zenith of its impiety.[12] Thus the kingdom of God follows fast on the heels of the שקוץ שמם according to Daniel's repeated testimony. The situation is identical in Mk. 13. We find it difficult to understand why Dr. Beasley-Murray, so critically acute, seems to have missed the intimate connection between the Olivet discourse and the temple visions of Daniel where the שקוץ שמם figures so conspicuously.

Luke 21:20-21 must be taken into account in the search for the primitive text. It reads: Ὅταν δὲ ἴδητε κυκλουμένην ὑπὸ στρατοπέδων Ἰερουσαλήμ, τότε γνῶτε ὅτι ἤγγικεω ἡ ἐρήμωσις αὐτῆς, τότε οἱ ἐν τῇ Ἰουδαίᾳ φευγέτωσαν εἰς τὰ ὄρη, καὶ οἱ ἐν μέσῳ, αὐτῆς ἐκχωρείτωσαν, καὶ οἱ ἐν ταῖς χώραις μὴ εἰσερχέσθωσαν εἰς αὐτήν. . . .

That this passage relates to the same subject as Mk. 13:14 is apparent not only from its presence in the same discourse, but also from linguistic parallels. We have the words ὅταν δὲ ἴδητε in the first clause, the word ἐρήμωσις in the second, and the words which follow, τότε οἱ ἐν τῇ Ἰουδαίᾳ φευγετωσαν εἰς τὰ ὄρη, parallel Matthew and Mark, and must have the same meaning. It is not necessary to agree with the many commentators who assert that what we have here is a Lucan paraphrase for the benefit of Gentile readers.[13] The original words of Christ could have been somewhat as follows:

> Whenever you behold Jerusalem encompassed with armies, then know that its desolation is near; whenever you behold the abomination of desolation --that spoken of by Daniel the prophet, standing in the holy place, where it ought not, let him that readeth understand, then let them which are in Judea flee to the mountains; and let them which are in the midst of it depart out.[14]

Neither is there any necessity to believe the frequently made assumption that Luke was writing after the event. True, Dodd himself believes this assumption to be "fairly certain", but on his own arguments against Lucan editing a strong case can be made for denying any compulsion to assign this Gospel to a date post A.D. 70. If the wording employed by Luke is drawn from familiar Old Testament passages, it could have been used by both Christ and Luke before their renewed fulfilment. Others who made no claim to supernatural prescience and who were contemporary with Christ hailed the coming destruction of the city and temple.[15]

If the suggested reconstruction offered above is a likely one, then the main problem of interpretation for Mk. 13:14 is automatically resolved. If the reconstruction is viewed as unlikely we are still confronted with the fact that a contemporary of Mark understood the βδέλυγμα τῆς ἐρημώσεως as applying to the Roman armies in A.D. 70. However, this observation is more pertinent to the section which follows.

Certainly Mk. 13:14 as it stands in modern Greek texts has every claim to confidence.[16] The original wording when spoken may have been more, and it is not likely that it was less.

Mk. 13:14 -- Exegesis

A brief review of the context of this verse is in order. It occurs in the heart of a chapter which itself is the central chapter of five climactic ones in the Gospel, each of which refers to the temple. Chapter thirteen succeeds the implied threat of the parable of the vineyard whereby it was foretold that the "owner of the vineyard" would "come and destroy the

144

tenants, and give the vineyard to others."[17] The same chapter
which records this threat also paints in lurid colours the
hypocrisy of the religious leaders of Israel, <u>particularly as
it was manifested in holy places</u>. They were guilty of seeking
the best seats in the synagogues, and of making long prayers and
pretentious offerings despite their pride, oppression of the
needy, etc. Their conduct evoked warning and woes from the
One claiming to be Lord of the temple. All this in the chapter
preceding the Olivet discourse was itself a continuation of what
is found in chapter 11, where the temple is cleansed and the
fig-tree symbol of the judgment-bound nation is described
graphically. There we read of the fig-tree, and of course, of
Israel, "May no one ever eat fruit from you again."[18] So much
for the literary context.[19]

Thus Mk. 13:14 occurs in a passage which, in both its literary
and historical contexts, is climactic. Even the pictured
geographical setting, the view of the rejected temple and city
from the opposite hill, is pertinent to the significance of the
discourse. The latter is presented as flowing naturally from the
immediately preceding events. After the disciples have heard
Christ's woes and His prediction that the temple would be left
desolate and its hypocritical worshippers be denied a view of
Him till they acknowledged the returning Messiah -- it is then
that the fate of the temple is further discussed. And v.14
of Mk. 13 not only occurs in a passage which is thus climactic,
it is itself a <u>crescendo</u>, as Lambrecht has shown.[20] The same
ὅταν which begins v.14 occurs also in vv. 7,11. In the latter
two cases the word is associated with prohibitions: μὴ θροεῖσθε;
μὴ προμεριμνᾶτε. But here in v.14 we have a positive instruction
φευγέτωσαν. Similarly ἰδεῖν is more than ἀκούειν and lastly τότε
comes climactically in v.14 alone. It is not found in vv.7,11.
It signifies the time for action, long awaited. These facts
indicate that v.14 is indeed the answer to the specific request
of the disciples for a sign of the coming destruction of the
temple and the end of the age. It is clear that the mysterious
βδέλυγμα τῆς ἐρημώσεως must be something very specific, for
it constitutes a signal, and a signal of no mean importance.
Thousands await it. Upon its recognition depend the lives of
multitudes. C.C. Torrey's arguments for the necessity of the
sign being obvious are entirely sound. He says:

> The sign, unlike all the others in the chapter, was one
> to be acted upon immediately. On what impulse do companies
> of men "flee to the mountains" in wild haste, leaving even
> their outer garments behind? Not because of some obscure,
> mystifying phrase, nor because of any happening which may
> or may not be portentous.[21]

In harmony with this reasoning is the presence of the article

with βδέλυγμα in contrast to the anarthrous state of the signs
in verses 7 and 8. Whatever the βδέλυγμα τῆς ἐρημώσεως   is,
its significance must be apparent to those who anticipate its
coming. It is no mere abstraction, or idealistic portrayal. It
is concrete, menacing, and stirring. Time is of the essence, for
nothing is to be taken from the houses. Lives are endangered.
It is no longer safe to stay in the city or to seek it as a place
of refuge. "Seek rather the shelter of the hill country," is
Christ's admonition. Loisy and others have found it hard to
reconcile such extravagant warnings with a mere event of
profanation.[22] Their question should not have been "Why this
atmosphere of panic?" but, "Is more than a profane act alluded
to?"

Dodd represents another group of commentators when he affirms
that the context precisely fits the situation of a city about
to be besieged. He says:

> Verses 17-18 are naturally and no doubt rightly understood
> as referring to the sufferings of the civilian population
> in a country overrun by the enemy. . . . Verses 15-16, in
> this context, refer to the necessity of <u>instant</u> flight
> when the quick-marching Roman armies are advancing.[23]

We have looked so far at the crescendo nature of v.14 as
indicated by ἴδητε and φευγέτωσαν. The evidence for this is
intensified by the δὲ. It must be given its full adversative
force. A note of contrast is thereby sounded. Christ has
admonished the disciples that neither false Christs, nor wars,
and rumours of wars, or even persecutions are the main sign to
be awaited. Having so said He now utters His ὅταν δὲ or its
Aramaic equivalent. In effect, He says, "but here now is the
real thing, the crucial event".[24] This ὅταν δὲ begins a section
which closes as it began, with another sign, that of the
appearance of the Son of Man coming in clouds with great power
and glory. <u>These two signs constitute the heart of the chapter,
and one answers to the other</u>.

The time references in v.14 have light cast upon them by the
reference to τέλος in the preceding verse of that chapter, and
also in v.14 of Mt. 24. In Mark the meaning of the term is open
to dispute, though Dalman has asserted that it is the equivalent
of the Hebrew קֵץ in Dan. 12:13, and Schniewind regards it as
an idiom for the last day. Inasmuch as the chapter as a whole
regards the advent and the crisis at Jerusalem taking place
in the same generation there is little need to distinguish
between the two possible meanings for τέλος.[25]

> Der Begriff des Endes umfasst hier Beides: das Ende der
> Menschen und Völker am Tage des Zornes Gottes wie das Ende

des Frommen, der seine Standhaftigseit bis in den Tod des
Märtyrers besiegelt.[26]

There can be no disputing, however, regarding the meaning of
τέλος in Mt. 24:14. Here it is obviously eschatological. This
conjunction of τέλος with the reference to the βδέλυγμα τῆς
ἐρημώσεως is another indication that Mk. 13:14 is climactic,
pointing to the final act of the drama.

When Erasmus attacked Luther's teachings on the bondage of the
human will, the German reformer asserted that Erasmus, scorning
secondaries, had reached for his throat. Similarly, this
expression to which we have at last come is the "throat" of the
Olivet discourse. Exegesis of the whole chapter revolves
around the exegesis of this phrase. If it is found to signify
an event in history, certain eschatological interpretations
lapse, though not all. The meaning attributed to the coming of
the Son of Man is, with some interpreters, dependent upon
their prior understanding of the phrase here under discussion.
Definition of the great tribulation mentioned in the context
is likewise conditioned, though with great agility some
commentators have done their best to achieve the impossible.
Redaction techniques can be used to solve some of the incongru-
ities demanded by a priori positions of interpreters, but
their legitimacy is very much open to question. Too often the
surgeon's knife seems to follow the predilection of the surgeon
rather than the location of the disease.[27] The vexed issue of
οὐ μη παρέλθη ἡ γενεα αὕτη is yet another example of a vital
interpretation being dependent upon the prior exegesis of the
βδέλυγμα τῆς ἐρημώσεως.

Our first step must be to consider the original setting of
this Old Testament expression. Almost all commentators except
Beasley-Murray recognize it as being a reference to the
equivalent expression found in Daniel.[28] Matthew indeed says so,
and there is no compelling reason to deny the textual
authenticity of the comment.

Part of our task to understand the original Danielic expression must be a prior analysis of the components of the phrase,[29]
without denying a unique usage in Daniel and Mark. We begin with
the initial Greek term, βδέλυγμα. There is no mystery in the
meaning of βδέλυγμα as ordinarily used in Scripture. It comes
from βδέω to make foul, or βδελύσσω to stink. As with the
O.T. parallel שקץ, it particularly applies to idols or items
associated with idolatrous worship.[30] ἐρημώσεως, while used by
the LXX translators for the שמם of Dan. 9:27; 11:31; 12:11
(desolate or appall) does not have its equivocal meaning. Its

reference is purely to desolation.[31]

In view of the coupling of the concepts of βδέλυγμα and ἐρημώσεως in Mk. 13:14, it is of interest and possibly of great significance to note that there are several O.T. chapters (such as Jer. 4, 7, 44, and Eze. 5-7), which also link these concepts, using either the words studied above, or their synonyms. Charles Perrot and Béda Rigaux have both stressed this point in their respective articles on the eschatological discourse.[32]

Examples of divine threats of <u>desolation</u> as a result of Israel's abominations have been pointed out by Perrot and Rigaux.[33] The conjunction is important, providing an atmosphere or ideological environment whereby the later phrase may be better understood.

The study of such chapters indicates certain matters of significance for our consideration of Mk. 13:14. Firstly, the abominations spoken of are, as might be expected, linked with idolatry and profanation of the sanctuary. Secondly, because Israel herself has thus violated the sanctuary it is declared that God will permit others to come and profane the holy place (Ezekiel 7:20-23, etc.) Their abominations will bring the abominations of the Gentiles. Because they have repelled the presence of God by their idolatry and spiritual harlotry, the once holy land will become forsaken and desolate by man as well as by God. And lastly, the intention of God's judgments is reformatory. "Then you will know that I am the Lord." ". . . they will be loathsome in their own sight for the evils which they have committed." The judgments are meant to bring Israel to her senses. In Mark 13, all these factors apply, except that the abominations of Israel causing the divine judgments are no longer those of <u>outward</u> idolatry, and Mark does not anticipate any national repentance.[34] Once more the sanctuary is considered as defiled because of the lack of sanctity among the people, and they will see the abominations of the invading Gentiles as a result of their own abominations. The land and sanctuary will be desolated because they have already desolated them of the divine presence.

So much for the component parts of the phrase used in Mk. 13: 14 and typical instances of their usage in the Old and New Testaments. It is now our intention to study the actual phrase itself as it is found in its O.T. source. While the terms שׁקוץ and שׁמם are found in close association before Daniel as has just been shown, it is in this later book that they are first coupled. In a sense, the book could well be entitled "The Abomination of Desolation," for such is a major theme within it. From the first chapter to the last, this O.T.

apocalypse deals with the apparent triumph of proud, idolatrous, desolating powers, and the ultimate vindication by Yahweh of the little remnant which refuses to conform to false worship.

The following table sets out the instances where the phrase occurs, and the closely parallel case in Dan. 8:13. The variant readings in the Theodotion and Septuagint translations are indicated.

	Hebrew	Theodotion	LXX
9:27	שקוצים משמם	βδελυγμα τῶν ἐρημώσεων	βδέλυγμα τῶν ἐρημώσεων
11:31	השקוץ משמם	βδέλυγμα ἠφανισμένοω	βδέλυγμα ἐρημώσεως
12:11	שקוץ שמם	βδέλυγμα ἐρημώσεως	το βδέλυγμα τῆς ἐρημώσεως
8:13	הפשע שמם	ἡ ἀμαρτία ἐρημώσεως	ἡ ἀμαρτία ἐρημώσεως

It is readily apparent that there are grammatical anomalies in the three references to the שקוץ שקם and in the allied expression of 8:13. In 8:13 and 11:31 we have the substantive with the article and the participle without it. In 9:27 we have a plural noun with a singular participle. These all read as oddities. If 11:31 has the meaning of "the abomination of a devastator" we would expect the construct state, and the article would not be present. Only 12:11 is present in a form which is grammatically correct.

Obvious questions arise as one studies the Hebrew passages. What interpretation is to be given to שמם ? Does it mean "to alarm, to agitate", as might be expected if the context concerns profanation, or does it mean "to desolate" as the Greek translations suggest? What is the function of שקוצים in 9:27? Is it a genitive linked with wing, or a subject?

What is the function of משומם in 11:31? Is it a genitive form or a participle? A similar question arises with reference to 9:27 and 12:11. Should the plural שקוצים of 9:27 be emended to the singular (compare 11:31 and 12:11)? But the Greek translations indicate that the first translators construed the expression as plural in significance.

Suggestions have not been lacking to solve the irregularities. Dittography could be responsible for the plural form in 9:27 and thus it could be reconciled to the other usages of the term and to its singular poel participle. If a preformative mem has dropped out of 12:11 and 8:13 the forms concerned could be taken as poel participles. Neither שמם nor משמם in these contexts can really signify "desolation" or "desolated" or "appalled", but משמם could mean "desolating" or "appalling". However, any student who has read Montgomery's commentary on Daniel will, if tempted to adjust the text, feel the shadow of his warning regarding light-hearted emendations which at the best are only plausible.[35] And if one feels inclined to place weight on the Greek translation he should remember Charles' comment on the LXX at this point, that it is "an impossible rendering", and Wellhausen's that it is "completely misleading".[36] These comments, of course, are based not only on the possible translations of the Hebrew שמם, but on the context. which speaks of profanation rather than desolation. Or thus it seemed to Charles and Wellhausen, though some other commentators find both meanings present.[37]

The string of grammatical abnormalities in these occurrences in Dan. 8-12 point to a specific cause. Daube has pointed to the rabbinical habit of attaching great significance to any expression in the original which hints at mystery and importance by its irregularity of form. "It is hardly too rash to suggest that hashshiqqus meshomem, with its extraordinary article, must very early have been taken as a deliberate reference to something or somebody special."[38] He adds:

> What emerges as probable is that behind Mark's Greek stands this passage from Daniel, with the article in Midrashic fashion interpreted as singling out a particular individual--the Antichrist, a heathen god, the Emperor or his statue, or whoever else it might be.[39]

Nestle's significant article of 1883 has influenced practically all subsequent commentators as the unusual phrases in Daniel have been considered.[40] His findings quickly recommended themselves inasmuch as it was clear from Ex. 23:13 that the Hebrews avoided using the titles of heathen deities, and furthermore it was recognized that the prophetical writings of the O.T. as well as many of the Jewish apocalypses are full of puns.[41] When Nestle declares that his view still does not fully explain the grammatical problems, we understand him to mean that the specific irregularities are not thereby explained, although the general situation causing them could now be understood. Daube's conclusions complement Nestle's in this matter.[42]

Nestle raises the question as to whether a statue of Zeus was set up as well as a pagan altar. Almost certainly the answer is 'yes'.[43] While many commentators have applied

Daniel's references to an altar only, it should be kept in mind that the most common use of שִׁקּוּץ in the O.T. is for an idol. C.C. Torrey documents his position that an image was employed, by referring to Joseph ben Gorion's ("Josippon") History of the Jews, and Bevan's allusions to the practice of Antiochus in other cities.44 Beasley-Murray reminds us that "Since in any case altars and idols in heathenism went together, it is likely that Antiochus had both an image of Zeus Olympius and a heathen altar erected on the great altar of the Jewish temple.45 H.H. Rowley adds that the association between שׁמם and madness is another indication that the eccentric Antiochus is in the view of the author of Daniel.46 All of which is significant as indicating that the real abomination was not merely some tangible object in the sanctuary, but the invading heathen and their prince. In the original phrase, Baal is referred to -- the heathen God, his votaries and his worship.47 Antiochus Epiphanes was the visible representation of it all. "Nestle rejoignait ainsi Grimm et Gesenius en voyant dans la réalité designée un individu."48

After commenting on Nestle's article, Rigaux proceeds:

> Mais il y a plus. Le terme שׁמם revient dans 9,27d et là, il n'y a pas de doute qu'il désigne le dévastateur: "jusqu'au terme designé pour le dévastateur". Il est naturel de reporter sur 9,27c le sens clair de 9,27d et nous concluons que l'expression hébraïque conduit vers l'idée d'un être personnel qui est à l'origine de l'abomination de Daniel.49

Rigaux suggests that the translators of the Hebrew were influenced by Jeremiah's many references to the desolation God would accomplish in the land. Thus the renderings of the passages under discussion by Theodotion and the LXX which influenced the translators of 1 Maccabees and the author of Mark. While granting a relationship between שׁמם in 9:27c and שׁומם in 9:27d, and understanding the latter as applying to a personal devastator, he does, of course, not commit himself to the acceptance of the translations of Theodoret or the LXX. However, Jeffery, in his commentary, declares that שׁמם in 9:17 is intended to be reminiscent of שׁמם 9:27, and S.B. Frost reminds us that "desolate" rather than "appall" "was the current interpretation ca. 135, when 1 Maccabees was written" and that this "tradition. . . on the side of 'desolation'. . . should be respected."50

Let us next enquire as to which of the Danielic passages does Mk. 13:14 refer. There are some who contend that Christ must have had His eye specifically on Dan. 12:11, or at least on this verse and 11:31, but not on Dan. 9:27. G. Ch. Aalders, for example, writes as follows:

Resultaat van de vergelijking der Hebreeuwse en LXX-
teksten leert dus, dat er alle waarschijnlijkheid voor
pleit, dat de verwijzing van de Heiland naar Daniël niet
op 9:27 doelt, maar alleen de beide andere plaatsen op
het oog moet hebben: het Hebr. שקוצים sowel als het
Gr. τῶν ἐρημώσεων bieden daar alle grond voor. Nu wil
men door wijziging van de tekst, verandering van het
meervoud שקוצים in het enkelvoud שקוץ, Dan 9:27
met de beide andere plaatsen meer in overeenstemming
brengen (men zie Baumgartners tekstkritische noot in
Kittel, Biblia Hebraica[3]) en zodoende eveneens voor
de verwijzing in Matth. 24:15 in aanmerking doen komen,
maar het is het meest verantwoord de Hebr. tekst
onveranderd te laten. Daar komt bovendien nog bij dat het
woord שקוצים   als nomen rectum verbonden is aan het
voorafgaande כנף in statu constructo, zodat hier
sprake is von "een vleugel van gruwelen". Dat heeft
eveneens weer aanleiding gegeven tot conjuncturale
tekst-emendaties, waarvan een zeer bekende afkomstig is
van onze landgenoot J.W. van Lennep en overgenomen door
de vroegere Oud-Testamenticus van Leiden, Abr. Kuenen
(in zijn Historisch-critisch onderzoek naar het ontstaan
en de verzameling van de boeken des Ouden Verbonds,
(Tweede deel, Leiden 1889, bl. 472) en die door de
Engelse commentator van Daniël, A.A. Bevan, gequalificeerd
wordt als "an emendation which appears wellnigh certain"
(A Short Commentary on the Book of Daniel, Cambridge,
1892, blz. 160), nl. om in plaats van כנף te lezen כנו;
de zin wordt dan: "in plaats daarvan" (te weten het
in het voorafgaande genoemde "slachtoffer en spijsoffer").
Juist zulk verder gaand gepeuter aan de tekst versterkt
echter ten zeerste de noodzaak om deze onveranderd te laten;
als we aannemen, gelijk in het Hebreeuws zo vaak
geschiedt, dat de copula dient te worden verondersteld,
krijgen we de vertaling, zoals die in de Nieuwe
Vertaling Ned. Bijbelgenootschap gegeven wordt: "en op een
vleugel van gruwelen zal een verwoester komen" (zo ook
de Amerikaanse Revised Standard Version: "upon the wing
of abominations shall come one who makes desolate"), vgl.
ook nieuwere commentaren als die van Behrmann, Driver,
Nötscher en Bentzen. En daarmee wordt het volkomen
duidelijk dat het over iets anders gaat dan "de
gruwel der verwoesting" van Matth. 24:15.[51]

We agree with Aalders that it is best to leave the Hebrew text
unaltered. He is not alone in the world of scholarship as
regards that position, as his references show. It is probably
true in this case as in others of apparent incongruity that

the text may have been transmitted with special care.[52] However, Aalders' contention that 9:27 is about something other than the βδέλυγμα τῆς ἐρημώσεως of Mt. 24:15 is unfounded. Aalders seems to apply Dan. 9:27 to events entirely outside of the Maccabean era, and this position is quite contrary to that of most exegetes of Daniel. It ignores the obvious parallels between chs. 7,8,9,11-12. Aalders is correct in suggesting that Mk. 13:14 and Mt. 24:15 are linguistically closer to 11:31 and 12:11, than to 9:27. The emphasis should lie particularly on 12:11 from a philological standpoint, but philology is not enough. The parallel concepts of the various chapters, as well as the similarity of language, demonstrates that all the instances referring to the abomination or abominations apply to the same set of events.[53]

Aalders' position is the very opposite of Rigaux's. The latter contends that:

> il est évident que, dans Daniel, 12,11 est secondaire. Cette péricope ne se comprend que par référence à 9,27. En effet, Dan 12,11-12 écrit: "A compter du moment que sera aboli le sacrifice perpétuel et posée l'abomination de la désolation, mille deux-cents quatre-vingt-dix jours. Heureux celui qui tiendra et qui atteindra mille trois-cents cinq jours". Ces versets se trouvent au terme d'un développement qui ne les appelle pas. De plus, le comput exposé ne s'harmonise pas avec celui de 8,14 qui est primitif et qui porte "mille cent cinquante jours". Il y a donc trace évidente d'addition au texte primitif, addition antérieure à la traduction des LXX. Si nous voyons bien, malgré la parenté plus grande avec les mots de 12,11, le texte synoptique vise le passage rapporté dans 9,27 qui constitue la clef des developpements subséquents.[54]

Undoubtedly Rigaux is correct in seeing 9:27 as underlying 12:11, and therefore Mk. 13:14. Van Dodewaard, Lagrange et al. join Rigaux in seeing 9:27 as the source of Christ's reference. Says van Dodewaard, "Nu kan men wel met zekerheid zeggen, dat Dan. 9,27 hier bedoeld moet zijn".[55] But his reason is not as reliable as his conclusion. He continues, ". . .want Dan. 11,31 handelt volgens alle exegeten over den tijd van Antiochus Epiphanes (vgl. 1 Macc. 1,49-64; II Macc. 6,2-9) en was ten tijde van Christus reeds lang vervuld, terwijl hetzelfde geldt voor Dan. 12,11.[56] While it is true that most exegetes view 11:31 and 12:11 as descriptive of Maccabean times, as has already been said it should be recognized by van Dodewaard, Aalders, E.J. Young, and others that the same is true of 9:27.

Van Dodewaard refers to Schanz who affirmed that it cannot be determined with certainty which text Christ pointed to, and also to Schegg who held that the expression in the Gospels is not an exact citation but a general appeal to a well-known formula summarizing Daniel's prophetic presentation. Van Dodewaard, of course, disagrees with both viewpoints. Despite our already expressed agreement with Rigaux that 9:27 underlies Mk. 13:14, there is much to be said for the likelihood of Christ's reference being a summary statement as well. This is not to contradict oneself, but only to say that the reference to Dan. 9:27 would automatically create attention to the parallel passages, and that this too was within Christ's purpose.

Lambrecht points out that the casual correspondence in the use of the article by Mark and by the Septuagint of 12:11 can scarcely be any indication in this matter, inasmuch as no one knows which translation Mark had at his disposal.[57] Besides, it is clear that Mark also cited from elsewhere in Daniel than chapters 11 and 12.[58] Furthermore all three Daniel passages refer to the same profaning act of Antichrist, and it is unlikely that 1 Macc. 1:54,59; 6:7 trace back to only one of the original references. Lambrecht concludes his case as follows:

> All diese Gründe zusammen machen es wahrscheinlich, dass Markus nur anspielte, d.h. einen aus Dn. bekannten Ausdruck übernahm, ohne dabei eine bestimmte Stelle (wohl vielleicht die konkrete Geschichte von Antiochus) im Auge zu haben.[59]

Hartman has a similar position:

> If we accept the thesis that to the interpreter the Dn pericopes could constitute a group of texts in which the units illustrated each other, the difficulty of deciding whether it is Dn 9:27 or 11:31, or even 12:11 which is quoted disappears.[60]

As intimated above, there is much to be said for the conclusion of Lambrecht and Hartman. Nevertheless, the truth they express is not the entire truth, for as Rigaux has pointed out, it is obvious that 11:31 and 12:11 are secondary references, dependent upon the prior usage of 9:27. Even more significant, however, is the fact that Christ is referring to the βδέλυγμα τῆς ἐρημώσεως in connection with the destruction of Jerusalem, and the only case in Daniel where the שקוץ שמם is specifically linked with the destruction of the holy city is in Dan.9. Lambrecht's criticisms of Rigaux do not take either of these facts into account. We conclude that Christ encompasses all the allusions of Daniel in his reference, but that He thinks particularly on 9:27. We would go even further than Rigaux by contending that, in Luke's thinking, Christ also had Dan. 8:13-14 in view. This is indicated by Luke 21:24 which quotes from that passage. Hendriksen has shown that Dan. 8 is the foundational reference on which all later Antichrist passages in Daniel and the New Testament are based.[61] One fact which should never be forgotten is that the Mk. 13:14 allusion to Daniel is not isolated. In the same chapter are other significant quotations from the same book, including references to passages on either side of Daniel 9.[62] Thus Christ has not used a minute fragment from a mosaic but the mosaic itself, and added thereto his own adornments.

At this point we should pause to recall the reason for the mention of the βδέλυγμα τῆς ἐρημώσεως in the eschatological discourse. The question. "what does this particular phrase mean?" can only be rightly answered after many prior questions, including the primary enquiry, "Why was this discourse given at this time?" The answer should suggest some hint at least as to the possible meaning of any section of the address, and of the βδέλυγμα τῆς ἐρημώσεως in particular. We have covered this ground before in some detail,[63] so only a cursory review with some added material is necessary at this time. We wish particularly to show that Christ's words would not have been novel to his hearers. Rather, they were reminiscent of history and prediction familiar to every Jew. His very terminology echoed hallowed words of esteemed prophets, not Daniel alone, but Jeremiah, Ezekiel, Micah, and Zephaniah, as well as psalmists and historians.

Just before the eschatological sermon from Olivet, Christ had warned His countrymen that judgment was coming upon them in a measure transcending anything known before. The guilt of all the false worshippers from the days of Cain would fall upon the heads of the present generation. Their "house", their pride and joy, would no longer be recognized by Yahweh. On the day of His triumphal entry He had wept over the city declaring that enemies would come, cast up a bank, hem in the inhabitants, and then ravage the city not leaving one stone upon another.[64]

Every Jewish hearer hearing such things could not but be reminded of previous judgments upon the nation, particularly those linked with damage to the temple. The destruction of the sixth century, and the profanation of the second, would be pre-eminent in their thinking. Their scriptures contained many warnings as to the inevitable fate of the city and temple once Yahweh departed from His people because of their transgression. Some of these warnings had already been fulfilled, but others had yet to be.[65]

One threat especially had been often repeated by loyal Jews who knew of its past fulfilment, and feared that it would yet be fulfilled again.

> . . .if you turn aside from following me. . .and
> do not keep my commandments and my statutes which I have
> set before you. . .then I will cut off Israel from the
> land which I have given them; and the house which I have
> consecrated for my name I will cast out of my sight; and
> Israel will become a proverb and a byword among all
> peoples. And this house will become a heap of ruins. . .[66]

Thus Christ's shocking announcement to those who showed Him
the grandeur of the temple was not shocking in the sense that
such a thing had never been heard of. It shocked, because it
meant that the most dire prognostications of the later
prophets were on the verge of fulfilment. And as for the phrase
-- βδέλυγμα τῆς ἐρημώσεως -- its elements were household items
to all loyal sons of the Torah. We will consider briefly a few
Old Testament pronouncements which would be recalled by Christ's
hearers -- pronouncements separate from the most well-known
embodiment of Christ's words in Daniel.

Ezekiel 7 is but one of several chapters which sound notes of
warning similar to the eschatological discourse. It is the
climax to the first series of Ezekiel's messages. Frequent
repetitions in the chapter give great force to its denunciations.
Key words include "end", "punish", "doom", "abominations",
"profane", "desolation". "Abomination" or cognates is found
four times (as often as in the previous two chapters combined,
and as frequent as in the chapter which follows). Yahweh
complains that because of the "abominable images" the sanctuary
shall be profaned. "I will turn my face from them, that they
may profane my precious place; robbers shall enter and profane
it, and make it a desolation."[67] The word "destruction" stands
out in the chapter, though it is not prominent elsewhere in the
book. In the tenth chapter, the Shekinah departs from the
temple as the prelude to its profanation and destruction.
Judgment is to be so severe that to the prophet it seems that
a full end is to be made of Israel.[68] This same section of
Ezekiel refers to the judgments of war, famine, and pestilence,
which are also mentioned in the Olivet discourse. These are
linked with the ultimate desolation which results from the
abominations of the people.[69]

Not only Ezekiel and Jeremiah,[70] but several of the Psalms
and the entire book of Lamentations mirror the dreadful scenes
of Yahweh's desolation of the temple and city. Because of
Israel's abominations which they have sown to the wind, they
reap a whirlwind of the same.[71]

Coupled with these references to the desolation of the

sanctuary because of abominations is the plaintive plea for restoration and vindication. The cry, "How long, O Lord?" continually ascends.

In Psa. 80, for example, the prayer, "Restore us, O God. . . ." is found in vv. 3,7 and 19 while the same concept is expressed repeatedly in other terms in the same psalm. Similarly in Lamentations, the climax of appeal is found at the close, "Restore us to thyself, O Lord, that we may be restored!"[72]

Not only would the disciples have recalled such passages as these as they listened to their Lord's words of doom, but they would also be reminded of the warnings of a later devastation found in the post-exilic prophets.[73] Furthermore, there were many in Israel who believed that Antiochus Epiphanes had not completely fulfilled the visions of Dan. 8, 9, 11 and 12. That book had promised the advent of the kingdom of God after the profanation of the sanctuary by the wilful king. But certainly the kingdom had not come with the rededicated sanctuary of 165 B.C. Therefore, they reasoned, the woes under Antiochus must have been pre-figurative of worse woes to come.[74]

In these last pages we have suggested that those Jews who heard Christ's words regarding the βδέλυγμα τῆς ἐρημώσεως would have thought of more than a mere profanation. The word ἐρημώσεως to Mark's readers, was a common term of the LXX and meant what it said. It is not likely that Christ's hearers, or those who later read the Gospel account, thought of the paronomasia being employed by the writer of Daniel. Thus we follow such exegetes as Vincent Taylor, Jeffery, Carrington, Kevan, Pesch and Lambrecht, et al.

> Es ist sicher, dass der griechische Übersetzer von Dn mit der Wiedergabe des שׁמם -Stamms durch ἐρήμωσις oder ἀφανίζειν   den Verwüstungsaspekt, der deutlich z.B. Dn 9,26 (שׁחת) und 11,44 (צשׂ) vorhanden ist, verstärkt.[75]

The purpose of these last pages has been to show that Christ's discourse, and v.14 in particular, in many respects rang the changes of an old refrain, even the warning dirge of the prophets, characterized by the minor key of doom. Any exegesis which fails to take this fact into account must also fail in its purpose.

The central issue of our study, the significance of the βδέλυγμα τῆς ἐρημώσεως   must now be brought into clearer focus. What did Christ intend to convey by this arresting expression? Answers have been many and varied from the very

first. Beasley-Murray tells us that in the last century the
situation has been the same. ". . .the interpretations of the
βδέλυγμα prevailing at the present time were all suggested in
the earliest stages of the critical discussion."[76] He, himself,
gives the best review of interpretations of this matter that
we have seen.[77]

The various applications given to the βδέλυγμα τῆς ἐρημώσεως
will now be listed and evaluated.

1. The statue of Titus erected on the side of the desolated
Temple.

This was a commonly-held view in Patristic times.[78] However,
it is very questionable whether such an event ever occurred. It
seems more likely that the tradition owes its origin to the
memory of the standards of the Romans being erected in the
temple area by order of Titus. Thus the reality behind this
recollection is discussed under 6.

In interpreting the βδέλυγμα τῆς ἐρημώσεως   it should be
kept in mind that because the word βδέλυγμα translates the
familiar Old Testament term for an idol is not sufficient
ground for affirming that an image of any kind is now intended.
In many passages of the O.T. שקץ and its cognates apply to
impure things associated with idolatry rather than to idols
themselves,[79] and even more important is the fact that in some
of the Prophets and in Proverbs and elsewhere, "abomination" is
often the equivalent of ἀνομία   as shown by the LXX.

2. Statues erected by Pilate and Hadrian.

According to Jerome, Pilate placed in the temple an image of
the emperor, and Hadrian erected an equestrian statue of the
Capitoline Jupiter on the site of the demolished temple.
Probably this speculation also, as the above instance, is a
misunderstanding. Some time after A.D. 26 Pilate brought the
standards of the cohorts into the temple, and these standards,
of course, bore medallions of the emperor, but whether he ever
did more than this is uncertain. While many of the Church
Fathers hold this idea of a defiling statue, none seem able to
denote with certainty which statue is meant. Therefore ". . .
heeft ieder zijn eigen hypothese".[80]

Deze sententie heeft voor, dat zij op het spraakgebruik
steunt, maar zij heeft de feiten tegen zich. Niets is er
met zekerheid over het plaatsen van een beeld in den
tempel bekend. Dat Pilatus een beeld in den tempel
liet plaatsen is uit de historie verder niet op te maken.[81]

Thus these speculations, like the first, seem based on hazy
recollection and cannot be taken seriously. While Baur
championed the Hadrian hypothesis and used it to date the
eschatological passage and the Gospels containing it, hardly
the most extravagant of critics today would follow him in this.
Furthermore, the abomination, according to Jesus, precedes
the destruction of the city and is the signal for flight. The
supposed acts of Titus and Hadrian follow the city's fall,
while Pilate's had to take place before he ceased to be
procurator in A.D. 36, and certainly, nothing he did
precipitated any general flight.

3. The Atrocities of the Zealots.

In the nineteenth century, as with Josephus in the first,
a favorite interpretation of the βδέλυγμα τῆς ἐρημώσεως
was to regard it as an allusion to the desecrating deeds of the
Zealots during the siege of Jerusalem. This viewpoint was held
by Elsner, Hug, Stier, Alford, Wordsworth, Bevan, Fulford, Nast,
Pfleiderer, Weiffenbach, Keim, and Pünjer. Most of the older
English Bible dictionaries, such as Smith's and Hastings', set
forth this view.

The evidence presented was threefold. (1) 2 Thess. 2 was
understood as contemplating a Jewish apostasy. (2) The word
used in Daniel is properly used, not of idolatry in the abstract
but of idolatry or false worship incorporated into Jewish circles.
1 Kings 11:5; 2 Kings 23:13; Eze. 5:11. (3) Among the Jews
there existed a tradition to the effect that their holy city
would be destroyed if Jewish hands polluted the temple. Josephus
is usually cited to this effect.[82]

The German writers mentioned above did not hold to the dominical origin of Mk. 13:14, but viewed the latter as written about
the time of the fall of the temple, when such traditions
flourished. The English writers usually regard the statement as
a predictive logion from Christ.

Occasionally today the same view regarding the Zealots is
espoused. Van Dodewaard includes it in a broader interpretation.[83]

We do not regard van Dodewaard's position as sound, but will
content ourselves for the present with criticizing the Zealot
position as usually taken. Regarding the three-fold cord of
evidence it can be said that (1) Certainly not all exegetes
today would insist that 2 Thess. 2 is speaking of a Jewish
apostasy. Such an interpretation is not obvious from the text
itself. (2) It is not true to say that שקוץ is used chiefly
for false worship among the Jews. Even 1 Kings 11:5 and

2 Kings 23:13 apply the term to the idols of other nations. That
is to say, these idols were already abominations in an objective
sense before Solomon incorporated their worship into Judaism.
(3) Traditions are so various and so contradictory that the
statements from Josephus can be given but little weight in
interpreting Christ's statement.

Furthermore, most exegetes today would say that those who hold
the Zealot position ignore the fact that the term שקוץ שמם
is used in Daniel with obvious reference to בעל שצין the
Lord of Heaven, as worshipped by Antiochus, and that therefore
Mk. 13:14 alludes to something analogous. The despicable deeds
of the Zealots were hardly a matter of any kind of worship
whatever, and therefore could not be intended by Mk. 13:14.[84]

4. Caligula's attempted Profanation.

A more popular view in the 20th century has been the understanding that Mk. 13:14 is an allusion to Caligula's attempted
profanation. Spitta suggested that the text was written in
apprehension of the fulfilment of Caligula's profane ambition.
Pfeiderer abandoned his initial view, and suggested that
Caligula's threat inspired the statement as now found in Mark
and Matthew. He believed that the events of 39-40 A.D. created
the fear that another emperor would succeed where Caligula had
failed. This exegesis was adopted by Holtzmann, Schmiedel,
Menzies, and J. Weiss.[85]

C.C. Torrey believed that Lu. 21:20 was an original oracle
about Jerusalem's downfall but that Mk. 13:14 and Mt. 24:14
incorporated a variant as a result of the Caligula scare.[86]

Many have followed Torrey's example.[87] B.W. Bacon particularly made a quite elaborate case out of the Caligula possibility -- a case referred to by Beasley-Murray as "very ingenious,
very intricate, and very improbable".[88]

For reasons traced in our first chapter we find Beasley-
Murray's appraisal of Bacon's case both apt and accurate.

5. The Antichrist as the βδέλυγμα τῆς ἐρημώσεως.

Certainly the most popular interpretations are those which
yet remain for discussion -- the abomination seen as the
Antichrist,[89] and the view of its fulfilment in the Roman armies
with their idolatrous ensigns. Let us first think upon the Antichrist position.

Almost all Continental scholars are committed to this view, and
similarly a large number of exegetes in this country and America.

The construction ad sensum in the masculine participle ἐστηκότα linked to the neuter βδέλυγμα and the obvious parallel found in 2 Thess. 2:6-7, constitute the major reasons for this consensus. An additional reason is found in the prevailing belief in N.T. times that the Danielic pictures of Antiochus Epiphanes were yet to have a greater fulfilment. Thus Jerome (himself influenced by 2 Thess. 2) commented on Dan. 11:36 as follows:

> From this place onwards the Jews think that Antichrist is spoken of. . . .a king shall arise who shall do according to his own will, and lift himself up against all that is called God, and speak great things against the God of gods, so that he shall sit in the Temple of God and make himself god, and his will be performed, until the wrath of God be fulfilled: for in him shall the end be. Which we, too, understand of Antichrist.[90]

The almost universal expectation among the early church Fathers that the fall of the Roman empire would usher in the Antichrist is a valuable testimony "inasmuch as some of them seem not merely to be offering an exegesis of particular texts of Scripture, but recording a primitive tradition coeval with the New Testament."[91]

Naturally, those who see in Mk. 13:5ff. an incorporated "Little Apocalypse" are agreed that its author pointed to Antichrist by his mystical reference. This also is a recognition that writers of later apocalypses frequently utilized figures from the earliest specimen of all such literature.

On this position regarding the Antichrist, Beasley-Murray asserts that "the supports with which the interpretation is buttressed are uncommonly weak" but continues later by saying that:

> On the other hand, it would be possible to align the βδέλυγμα with the Antichrist doctrine if, with Althaus, it be recognized that in the N.T. this doctrine is fluid, possessing a variety of forms and above all has what he terms 'immediate actuality' . . . .That is, the concept of a power at work against God is applied to forces operative in the contemporary situation. . . .[92]

We think that Beasley-Murray's contention that the supports for the Antichrist interpretation are uncommonly weak grows out of his failure to see in the βδέλυγμα τῆς ἐρημώσεως a definite allusion to the similar references in Daniel. Undoubtedly the strongest evidence for the Antichrist position is that Mark 13 reproduces the eschatological pattern of Daniel wherein the abomination plays a prominent part in the desecrating and desolating of the temple of God, as well as the menacing of the saints in the last days prior to the establishment of the eternal kingdom.[93] Mark 13 places flesh on some portions of the predictive skeleton of Daniel, rather than basically detracting from that original outline. Thus v.14 places the abomination at the commencement of that great tribulation which terminates in the deliverance by the Son of Man, and this is in complete harmony with the visions of Dan. chs. 7,8,9,11-12. In each of these latter passages we witness the attack upon the holy by the impious king, which onslaught precipitates the vindicating intervention of heaven. When these facts are kept in mind, it is apparent that the buttresses for the Antichrist view are uncommonly strong. Despite this criticism, the exegetical good sense of the follow-up statement by Beasley-Murray must be gratefully acknowledged, and it should be pointed out that Lagrange and Vincent Taylor are among those who take a similar position.

Not least to be numbered among those who apparently viewed Mk. 13:14 as applying to the Antichrist are the apostles Paul and John.[94] As has been already shown,[95] 1 and 2 Thessalonians draw heavily upon the eschatological discourse recorded in Mk. 13, and it is just as clear that the writer of the last canonical apocalypse likewise drew from that source for his verbal pictures in chs. 11, 13, and 17.[96]

Christ's View of Antichrist

Of course, to say that Christ in Mk. 13:14 has the Antichrist in mind is, in a sense, somewhat premature, inasmuch as there is no evidence that the term was even known in His day.[97] It is not to be found in the scriptures which then existed, and in the New Testament its first appearance is in the epistles of John. Even Paul does not use the word in 2 Thess. 2. On the other hand when the title does occur for the first time, the matter is not discussed as a novelty. Evidently the concept was old, even if the term were new. ". . .you have heard that antichrist is coming. . . ." says John.[98] Apparently the early Christians received abundant instruction in eschatology, and the theme of Antichrist was part of that instruction. 2 Thess. 2 confirms this impression. Paul also reminds his converts that they already know about the man of lawlessness who is to come. He says: "Do you not remember that when I was still with you, I told you this?"[99] And "this" was all within a brief period of weeks apparently.[100] Obviously, the matter was considered important.

Thus years before the Gospel of Mark was written, the Antichrist concept was a familiar one to the Christian church. Caligula's threat had added fuel to the eschatological fire. It

is probably impossible now for us to conjure up in imagination
the intensity of excitement which must have prevailed in Jewish
and Christian communities as the word spread of the mad
Emperor's intended blasphemy. The coming event would inevitably
have been interpreted as a sign of the end, and as a fulfilment
of Daniel's and Christ's predictions. In later years both Mark
and Paul would have looked upon the Emperor's attempt as a
pattern of the horror soon to be accomplished, precipitating the
Lord's return. The Antichrist doctrine before A.D. 50 was
regarded as part of that faith committed to the saints by
Christ Himself.

Christ's own views on eschatology sprang, in part at least,
from the book of Daniel, as we have seen. It was here that
repeatedly a power was mentioned as arising near the end of time
to pollute the holy things and devastate the holy ones. The
blasphemies and aggression associated with the Syrian king are
applied by Christ in this discourse to a power soon to attack
Jerusalem and precipitate a time of tribulation, not only for
the Jews as a nation, but for all Christians everywhere. As
Swete[101] and others have noted, Rome takes the place of Syria.

In this sense we believe the βδέλυγμα τῆς ἐρημώσεως of the
Olivet discourse is Antichrist, but an Antichrist whose
work takes place in history despite the fact that its culminating
savagery is accompanied by the supernatural "fireworks", or
miraculous signs, attending the end of the age. Christ's
presentation of the end consists of a complex of events. The
finale is attenuated.[102] Thus it is likely that the βδέλυγμα
τῆς ἐρημώσεως is a comprehensive term applying first to the
armies of Rome, but including later manifestations of Antichrist.[103]

Even in Daniel itself, the work of the evil prince is seen to
have at least two phases. The initial attack upon the holy city
would begin a series of desolations which were to continue
until the end.[104] Later, the sacrifice and the oblation would
be caused to cease for 3½ years, and the temple would become
filled with abominations, as though to its pinnacle itself.[105]
Then would follow the desolation of the desolator.[106] Daniel
11 is clearer still. Vs. 28 speaks of him whose heart would
be set against the holy covenant after a great victory against
the king of Egypt. This prince would "work his will" before
returning to his own land. But after a later attack upon
Egypt, this time unsuccessful, he would again "take action
against the holy covenant". The continual burnt offering would
be taken away and the abomination that makes desolate the temple
would be set up.[107] But neither is this the end. After many
days, there would be another attack upon the king of the south[108]
and an ultimate onslaught upon the holy mount. This time,
however, the attack would bring the tyrant himself to the end

decreed for him by the watching heavens. As Belshazzar witnessed with terror the message of judgment on the walls after his act of impiety in profaning the temple vessels, so would the last impious king receive his doom in consequence of not only violating the holy things, but anathematizing the holy ones.[109] And it is especially this final overwhelming flood of persecution with which "the time of trouble such as never was" is coupled.[110]

Christ has certainly not spelled out the details of such a programme for the end He anticipated. Yet it is obvious that He viewed the times of Antiochus as prefigurative of what lay ahead. Furthermore, He has taken elements from the several presentations of Daniel to express His convictions, citing from Dan. 7, 8, 9, 11, and 12.[111]

Some of C.C. Torrey's remarks are interesting in this particular. He accuses Colani, the founder of the "little apocalypse" theory, and his successors, of failing to note that the Gospels take into account the Old Testament programme of the End. Then he proceeds to set forth his understanding of that programme.

> First of all (according to the Prophets), a hostile army is to capture and devastate Jerusalem. Half of the inhabitants will be carried away into captivity, and yet it will continue to be a Jewish city (Zech. 14:2). Thereupon will follow a season of wars, of famine and pestilence, of unexampled tribulation, of sore persecution (Dan. 12:1), which will continue for "a time, times, and a half" (Dan. 12:7). This interval is to be especially a time of missionary activity. The truth must be proclaimed first to the Jews; then to the Gentiles in every land, in preparation for the scenes described in Is. 45:14, 49:22 f., 60:3-14, 66:19 ff., and in other similar passages, when the "saved" of all the peoples of the earth join the Israelites in worship of the One God. Finally, the hostile nations will unite their forces, to make an end of Jerusalem and the religion of Israel. Their onslaught will be preceded by warning portents in the heavens and on earth, Joel 2:30 f, 3:4. . . The heavenly hosts will encounter them in "The Valley of Jehoshaphat." The Messiah will come in the clouds of heaven (Dan. 7:13 f.) and at the right hand of Yahweh (Is. 41:12 f., 45:1, Hab. 3:13, Ps. 110:5) will see the destruction of the last enemies of Israel.[112]

Not all would agree with Torrey's précis of the Old Testament picture of the End, but it is certainly at least close to the pattern traced in the New Testament itself. For example, the author of the Apocalypse speaks of the holy city as being attacked, and then trodden down for 3½ years during which the

164

church witnesses to the gospel of Christ before the nations.[113] The finishing of that testimony is succeeded by a final attack from the beast out of the abyss, a beast which had formerly attacked and then retired for a season.[114]

In the following statement, Torrey again distinguishes between the initial and ultimate attacks made by the opposers of Yahweh.

> In the time of the fourth beast, of course understood by the Jews of the first century as the Roman empire, the great world-catastrophe was to come. Along with the obscure predictions which occupy all the latter part of the book (Daniel) this much is said plainly: the last king of the last empire oppressing Israel will bring an army against Jerusalem (9:26 f., 11:31); he will set up the Abomination of Desolation in the holy place. . ."he will exalt himself". . . .At last, "he will plant his royal tents between the sea and the glorious holy mountain" . . ."but he shall come to his end, and none shall help him". . . .
> Who was the enemy who was destined "to come to his end" in the manner described? Certainly no one thus far known to history; must it not be the Roman emperor. . . ? The city must indeed be taken and devastated. . . .
> . . .following the capture of the city and the death of the impious Gentile monarch, "there will be a time of trouble. . . ." The world powers in their last throes will do terrible things. . . .[115]

Note how Torrey distinguishes between the coming of the army against Jerusalem as referred to in Dan. 9:26f., 11:31, and the further attack of the blaspheming tyrant "at last". Torrey seems to distinguish the final attempt of the tyrant from that of the world powers in their last throes, but in view of other passages such as Zech. 12 and 14, and particularly Eze. 38-39 and Joel 3, it is doubtful whether such a separation is necessary. One should also keep in mind the oscillation in Hebrew thought between the corporate and the individual. It is likely that the writer of Daniel has drawn from Ezekiel's picture, as well as from Isaiah 10, where invading powers from the north were sketched, and embodied them in his own presentation of the king of the north. And all these lineaments had been scrutinized and meditated upon by that Mind which had distilled from the prophets the characterization of Himself as the suffering Servant, and the Son of Man who would be vindicated at the end-time before Israel's foes and His own people.

In summary, the evidence indicates that Christ saw in the activity of Antiochus Epiphanes, the little horn of Dan. 7 and 8, the prince of Dan. 9:26-27, and the wilful king of 11:36f., a shadow of the final opposition to Jerusalem and the church. The term βδέλυγμα τῆς ἐρημώσεως reminiscent of the Syrian tyrant, was an adequate emblem of the powers which would profane and devastate the holy places and the holy people, beginning with Rome's besieging armies. The masculine ἑστηκότα was sufficient indication that no mere "thing" was intended by this βδέλυγμα τῆς ἐρημώσεως. The threat was to come from sources which were personal and unique.

Apparently Christ expected Rome's attack upon Jerusalem to be succeeded by growing antagonism between the empire and the missionary-minded church, and resultant conflict between agencies on earth (including first the Emperor), claiming reverence and adoration with those who called for acknowledgement of Christ as King of kings.[116] If Jewry itself joined the proselytizing venture, the work would be cut short in righteousness[117] with converts from all nations flocking to the church.[118] The conflict would culminate in supernatural manifestations, signs and wonders soliciting to false worship, with their author, or authors, working through the state and anathematizing the non-conformists.[119] This final conflict would issue in deliverance for the menaced saints by the coming of the Son of Man, the nemesis of the βδέλυγμα τῆς ἐρημώσεως. All this already lay before Christ in outline in the prophets. What we have left of the eschatological discourse is possibly only a pale relic of His original animation of this outline.[120]

6. The βδέλυγμα τῆς ἐρημώσεως as the invading Roman Armies[121]

There can be no denying the historical setting of the phrase in question, and the graphic picture of war-time conditions therein sketched.[122] But this is entirely compatible with position 5 just discussed,[123] for it is the action of Antichrist in history which is contemplated, though the later verses proceed to present history's supernatural terminus.[124]

What we have in Mk. 13 is an excellent example of that fidelity to the context of the original Old Testament allusion upon which Dodd and others have commented. The eschatological discourse draws from the Old Testament descriptions of invasions of the Holy Land by Assyria, Babylon, and Syria. These invasions had come because of transgression, i.e. as a result of Israel's own defection from Yahweh. Israel's own abominations caused the influx of the abominations of the heathen.[125] This is the import of Jer. 7; Eze. 5-7; Dan. 8-9, as well as Mk. 13:1-4,14,19. The real origin of the βδέλυγμα τῆς ἐρημώσεως concept is to be traced to history rather than prophecy. The writer of Daniel begins his book by describing the desolating invasion of Babylon upon Jerusalem. A proud, idolatrous, and persecuting power makes war on the holy land, the holy people, and the temple. The symbol of the theocracy is destroyed, desolated, and the daily sacrifice taken away. The ensuing chapters repeat the same theme over and over. Idolatry, persecution, blasphemy and pride are seen to characterize Israel's enemies and these attributes are allowed by Yahweh to have full exercise as a scourge to His people who have cherished abominations. The prayer recorded in Daniel 9 says specifically the same thing as such passages as Jer. 7, Eze. 5-7, namely that Israel's own faults had brought her desolations. As Jeffery has pointed out, this particular term שמם in 9:17 is purposely used in order to make an association in thought with the coming שקץ שמם.[126]

In Christ's day there already existed the understanding that "a great and desolating war" would "herald the coming of the kingdom and that it (would) be directed against Jerusalem and its temple."[127] This idea, says Rowley, "was doubtless derived from the Gog passages of the book of Ezekiel and from the book of Daniel."[128] And it is this concept which Christ adopts. He says in effect, "What the idolatrous Babylonians and Syrians did in ages past is to be repeated by another heathen power. The emperor of Rome will set on foot a similar fateful sequence of events as did Nebuchadnezzar and Antiochus IV of old."

Let us look again at the expression βδέλυγμα τῆς ἐρημώσεως. Usually commentators woodenly appropriate the limited meaning given this expression in 1 Macc. 1:54, but as Gould, Swete, A.B. Bruce, et al. have insisted, there is no need to restrict Christ's use of a term to the limited connotation existing hitherto. The latter is usually included but also transcended.[129] Profanation is anticipated by Christ, but much more besides. Even in O.T. usage the equivalent of βδέλυγμα could mean much more than merely an idol. The extended meaning given to the expression שקץ in Proverbs and elsewhere are a hint of Christ's own meaning in this place. Thus a heathen army with idolatrous ensigns invading Yahweh's land and temple could be a βδέλυγμα indeed. Loisy, et al. have seen the difficulty that ensues when βδέλυγμα τῆς ἐρημώσεως is understood merely as concerning a profanation.[130] Why should men flee for their lives to the mountains just because of an event in the temple? Why should there be so much haste as to leave behind one's clothes because of a misplaced altar?

At this stage we should attend more closely to the term ἐρημώσεως. We believe Vincent Taylor is entirely correct when he says ". . .if ἐρημώσεως is taken over with the phrase from

167

.Dan., it is possible that it is welcomed because it suggests more than the profanation of the Temple."[131] There is no need to look upon the βδέλυγμα τῆς ἐρημώσεως phrase as a mere tautology such as is suggested by the translation "the appalling horror". While most scholars have heeded the meaning of the Hebrew original as elucidated by Nestle, there seems an increasing tendency on the part of some to grant ἐρημώσεως its full weight in this context of war and devastation. Pesch gives this matter much emphasis. He says, "Der Kontext legt also nahe, dass hier mit der danielischen Chiffre auf die Zerstörung des Tempels abgezielt ist."[132] He points out that the passages of Dan. 11:31 and 12:11 both refer back to Dan. 9:26f., which describes the devastation of the city, and not alone its profanation.[133] This interpretation harmonizes with the clear announcement in Mk. 13:2 of the approaching destruction, and also with v.4 where the disciples enquire after a sign of the imminent fall of the city. Pesch also argues that the use of ἐρημώσεως emphasizes the active sense of ἐρημώσεως "es geht um eine zerstörende Person oder Macht, den römischen Feldherrn oder sein Heer, jedenfalls um die Aktivität 'd'un dévastateur personnel'."[134]

Even in the O.T. picture, devastation as well as profanation, is certainly intended. The suggestion of Foerster and others that a profanation desolates inasmuch as it empties the violated shrine of true worshippers is only a part of the story Daniel tells. Obviously, no idol could physically wreak havoc, but as Rowley, Torrey, et al. have shown, it is Antiochus who is in view here, and not merely an altar or idol, and he through his soldiers did perpetrate actual physical violence upon people and buildings. When Apollonius entered Jerusalem by guile he massacred its inhabitants, burnt its houses, and demolished its walls. Heaton comments, "Having broken up their city and their homes, Antiochus took the logical step of trying to destroy the Jews' faith."[135] The impact of the words שמף, שחת, שלך, שמד as used by Daniel regarding the work of the שקוץ שמם should not be dissipated by settling for a purely metaphorical application.[136]

Thus we find difficulty in accepting the common view as expressed by Beasley-Murray in his comments upon Mk. 13:14. He says, ". . .it is clear that the expression has by itself no thought of the temple's destruction but purely of its desecration."[137] We do not think it is clear, and for the very reason adduced by that author himself.[138] Thus, even if Nestle's understanding is taken as not only true but the whole truth, on the grounds of Beasley-Murray's reasoning above, we are entitled to look for a broader significance still when the phrase from Daniel is used by Christ. However, as has already been said, we think that Frost, Carrington, Jeffery, Pesch, et al. are right when they give to שמם its own literal meaning,

without denying the pun intended also by the phrase of which it
is a part. This viewpoint gives weight to both profanation and
devastation, and certainly the Roman invasion brought both.[139]
This understanding, and this understanding alone,[140] rings true
to the demands of the literary, philological, and historical
evidence of Mk. 13. While an abundance of material exists to
illuminate this sixth interpretation further, we doubt if our
repetition of mere descriptive data is required.

ἑστηκότα From the time that Mark's Gospel first appeared, this
word has stood out to many readers as a warning beacon. Almost
all have read it as a masculine accusative singular, rather
than as a neuter accusative plural. The fact that Mark
elsewhere lapses into similar usage has not discouraged the
conviction that in this instance the contravention of grammar
implies something, or rather someone, special.

Those who like Lenski and Volkmar affirm that ἑστηκότα is
a neuter plural find its fulfilment in defiling objects such as
bones, or corpses, or the multiplicity of idolatrous Roman
banners. The interpretation which favours the fulfilment
by the Zealots naturally inclines to this reading of the term.
On the other hand, those who see ἑστηκότα as a masculine form
almost always view the Antichrist as being intended.[141]

Daube reminds us that it is not enough to speak of the
construction as being ad sensum.[142] Usually Mark, as with all
other writers, followed the rules of grammar and not of sense.
Why the deviation this time? Probably Daube's further observations are the most pertinent on this subject that can be
found. He reminds us that Mark's device followed the habit of
Rabbinical expounders of Scripture whereby they were ever ready
to draw special conclusions from any grammatical anomaly
present in the sacred manuscripts.[143] As has already been
noticed, each instance of the usage of the original phrase
in Daniel (except 12:11) is marked by a deviation from correct
grammar. Thus, almost certainly, scribally-minded Jews, long
before Mark's day, had scented a mystery. Mark follows the
tradition, imitating Daniel[144] by his deviation from correct
form. And if some find this difficult to accept, the likelihood
still remains that Mark was enlightening his readers as best
he could as to the true nature of the βδέλυγμα τῆς ἐρημώσεως.
He may thus have condensed into less than a word what Christ
may have spelled out at length to the initiated. ". . .this
much may be considered as certain, that the kind of construction
ad sensum to be met with in this passage sprang from, and was
intended for, a milieu thinking in Rabbinic terms and reading
through Rabbinic spectacles."[145]

ὅπου οὐ δεῖ This is hardly the phraseology one employs when desirous of communicating with precision an exact location. What does Mark mean? or what did Christ mean, if these were His words? Matthew also uses an expression which, although slightly more specific, remains somewhat nebulous -- τόπῳ ἁγίῳ.

The possibilities include the following:

1. Some key holy place such as the temple,
2. Jerusalem itself, but including the temple, of course,
3. The land of Palestine.

The main clue to Mark's meaning is to be found in the Old Testament's location of the שקוץ שמם. It is always linked to the sanctuary.[146] But Daniel also speaks of the infamous king represented by the שקוץ שמם as planting the tabernacles of his palace στήσει, cf. ἑστηκότα "between the sea and the glorious holy mountain."[147] And this "stand" is described as inaugurating "a time of trouble, such as never has been".[148] So, from Daniel we find that at least two of the above possibilities could be in focus in Mk. 13:14. An invading army, with its military tents about the holy mount wherein lay the temple, certainly would stand ἐν τόπῳ ὅπου οὐ δεῖ. In Old Testament times Jews were wont to refer to the whole land as holy.[149]

If Christ has enlarged the meaning of the βδέλυγμα τῆς ἐρημώσεως then it is similarly likely that His reference as to the location of the abomination could include the Jerusalem temple-site and the surrounding land.

On the other hand if Mark has paraphrased Christ at this point the reason is no doubt that offered by Vincent Taylor. ". . . in Rome, during a time of persecution, when Christians were crucified and burnt. . .more precise language was politically dangerous."[150] Taylor proceeds to add that possibly both βδέλυγμα τῆς ἐρημώσεως and ἑστηκότα were used to replace an original reference to armies surrounding Jerusalem and menacing the temple.[151] It cannot be denied that this is a possibility, but the evidence for it is far from compulsive. We prefer the reconstruction offered on p.141.

ὁ ἀναγινώσκων νοείτω This passage has already been discussed in some detail.[152] We believe it possible that Christ and not Mark uttered the words, thereby using a key concept of Daniel itself. The word בין or related terms occurs 27 times in the ancient apocalypse, and its occurrences swell to a crescendo in connection with the references to the שקוץ שמם The vision of Daniel 8 is called by the writer "the vision concerning. . . the transgression that makes desolate", and for this vision he sought understanding. Note the recurring emphasis on this.

170

When I, Daniel, had seen the vision, I sought to
understand it. . . . And I heard a man's voice. . .
"Gabriel, make this man understand the vision.". . . .
he said to me, "Understand, O son of man, that the
vision is for the time of the end."[153]

. . . but I was appalled by the vision and did not
understand it.[154]

. . . O Daniel, I have now come out to give you wisdom
and understanding. . . consider the word and understand
the vision.[155]

And he understood the word and had understanding of the
vision.[156]

. . . from the first day that you set your mind to
understand. . . .[157]

. . . And those among the people who are wise shall
make many understand.[158]

. . . none of the wicked shall understand; but those
who are wise shall understand.[159]

The last four and a half chapters of Daniel are avowedly
given so that Daniel and the "wise" might understand the vision
concerning the power which defiles the sanctuary. Thus with
Rigaux, "nous n'hésitons pas à nous ranger parmi les exégètes
qui entendent:ὁ ἀναγινώσκων νοείτω de Mc 13,14 comme une
invitation à bien comprendre, non pas le texte de Marc ou de
la source, maid le livre qui contient la formule βδέλυγμα τῆς
ἐρημώσεως   le livre de Daniel.[160]

τότε οἱ ἐν τῇ 'Ιουδαίᾳ φευγέτωσαν εἰς τα ὄρη

The warning is not only to those within the city. The
dwellers of the countryside are warned against the usual
practice of fleeing to the capital for refuge. As to which
"mountains", this has ever been a matter for debate. Does
Christ refer to the mountains of Moab, or the hills of Judea,
or is it merely the employment of a well-known apocalyptic motif?
We do not think it can be just the last-named, though it may
well be included. The context is too "down-to-earth" to make
this exhortation merely poetic and visionary. When Schniewind
avers that ". . . das Fluchtmotiv selbst gehört zur Erwartung
der letzten Dinge, und man darf nicht an irgendein
geschichtliches Ereignis denken",[161] we must answer with
Marxsen, "Warum nicht? Das müssen doch keine Widersprüche
sein! Man muss die Geschichte des Markus anvisieren, der in

171

einer Zeit lebt, in der alte Ankündigungen sich zu erfüllen
beginnen."162 On the basis of what has already been argued in
preceding pages about the nature of the discourse as a whole,
Schniewind's contention is not apposite. The eschatological
discourse in entirety is both historical and eschatological.
Haenchen's comment upon this flight is much nearer the mark.163
Luke 1:39 with its reference to ἡ ὀρεινή is probably the best
guide to interpreting τὰ ὄρη   Compare also Neh 8:14.164

τότε does not always have a significant temporal meaning
in Mark, but in this case being linked as a consequence to ὅταν
such a meaning is intended. The appearance of the βδέλυγμα τῆς
ἐρημώσεως   is the awaited signal. Drop all, stay not, flee
-- all this is comprehended in the present use of τότε
Subsequent usages of τότε in the following verses are worthy of
study, as they too express the thought of crisis and climax.
"And then if any one says to you, 'Look, here is the Christ!. . .
do not believe it."165 "And then they will see the Son of man
coming in clouds with great power and glory. And then he will
send out the angels, and gather his elect from the four winds,
from the ends of the earth to the ends of heaven."166

Thus from the first τότε to the last in this discourse we
are hurried urgently from one climax to another with intensifying
momentum. Reading the discourse from this aspect reminds one
of listening to the Hallelujah chorus. The appearance of the
βδέλυγμα τῆς ἐρημώσεως,   the subsequent miraculous
manifestations during the tribulation, the true epiphany, and
the rapture, are all marked by τότε but these successive
events all belong to the one act, the final act. Thus is the
βδέλυγμα τῆς ἐρημώσεως   the terrifying harbinger of the End.

Excursus on the Meaning of βδέλυγμα and ἐρημώσεως

In the LXX βδέλυγμα is used chiefly to translate a). תועבה
b). שקץ c). שקוץ (More rarely, βδέλυγμα is used by the LXX
to translate פגול.) The complete N.T. list of its appearances
is as follows: Lu. 16:15; Rev. 17:4-5; 21:27; Mt. 24:15;
Mk. 13:14. The term is found in the passive in Rev. 21:8
and once it occurs in the middle voice, Rom. 2:22.

AG states that the literal meaning of βδέλυγμα is "(1) anything that must not be brought before God because it arouses
his wrath. . . .(2) As in the Old Testament. . . . of everything
connected with idolatry."

In TDNT we read that:

. . . in the legal parts of the Bible the reference may
be to things which are cultically (-aesthetically?)

172

"unclean", "repugnant", or "abhorrent", and especially to certain pagan things which are particularly abominable to the God of the O.T. Thus idols themselves. . . may be called βδελύγματα. This usage is found in the writing prophets. . . but in them there is an extension which makes βδέλυγμα parallel to ἀνομία . . . . In the Wisdom literature this development leads to the point where the opposition to paganism disappears and the word simply denotes God's hostility to evil. . . .[167]

As regards usage in the LXX the same work continues:

The word group βδελυκ- in the LXX is a. a regular translation of the word group תַּעַב (92 times). There are 6 exceptions in Jer., Ezr., Chr., Ez. and Prv. In Ez. the word group תעב occurs 44 times, and 30 times βδελυκ- is not used; ἀνομέω and derivatives are used in 24 of these. On 8 occasions out of 21 תעב is not rendered βδελυκ- in Prv., ἀκάθαρτος, ἀκαθαρσία are used 5 times. Again, b. βδελυκ-; is used relatively infrequently for certain Heb. terms for idols, along with other attempted renderings such as εἴδωλον γλυπτόν, χειροποίητον, μάταιον, δαιμόνιον, ἔνθυμα, ἐπιτήδευμα. c. It is used quite often for the word group שׁקץ (9 times in Lv., 20 in the prophets incl. Da., elsewhere only 3 times), along with such renderings as προσοχθίζειν, προσόχθισμα.

The LXX continued the extension of the term begun in the prophets, and helped to liberate it from natural and aesthetic connections (--598), partly by equating it with ethical concepts like ἀνομία (for תּוֹעֵבָה 599), and partly by pouring into it the purely ethical content acquired by תּוֹעֵבָה especially in Prv. (-- 598), and thus giving it a completely new orientation. This is particu- larly plain in Sir. 15:13, where the LXX has πᾶν βδέλυγμα for the double term ועה ותעבה. As an expression of the dualistic antithesis between the will of God and that of man, βδέλυγμα can also denote the repugnance of the ungodly to the will of God (Prv. 29:27; Sir. 1:25; 13:20).[168]

BDB has little to add to the above for our purposes, but typical instances of the employment of שׁקץ and תועבה or cognates are the following:

שׁקוץ   See 1 Kings 11:5; Nah. 3:6; 2 Kings 23:24; Eze. 20:7-8.

שׁקץ   See Lev. 11:11,43; 20:25; Deut. 7:26; Ps.22:24.

שקץ   See Lev. 11:10,12;   Isa. 66:17.

תועבה   See Gen. 46:33-34;   Deut. 14:3;   1 Kings 14:24;
           2 Kings 16:3; 2 Kings 23:13.

It should be noted that the last verse is an excellent example
of the synonymous nature of תועבה   and שקץ. Both words are
found in the verse and are used of false gods in an identical
sense.

ἐρημώσεως

   Feminine, genitive, singular of ἐρήμωσις from ἐρημόω.
ἐρημώσεως cannot be defined quite as simply as שמם   when
viewed in the setting of Mk. 13:14. Firstly, it is not the
case that this word perfectly represents the Hebrew שמם for
the latter is equivocal in meaning, while the former is not.
Secondly, as Nestle pointed out nearly a century ago, the
usage in Daniel of the term reflected in Mk. 13:14 is a case of
paronomasia. Let us, however, first consider the significance
of the Greek ἐρημώσεως in isolation from its O.T. "equivalent".
ἐρημόω signifies "to lay waste, make desolate, bring to ruin",
and the complete list of New Testament occurrences is as
follows: Mt. 12:25; Lu. 11:17; Rev. 17:16; 18:17,19.
ἐρήμωσις occurs only in the βδέλυγμα τῆς ἐρημώσεως   passages,
and their parallel in Lu. 21:20, but ἔρημος (desert) is of
more frequent usage.

TDNT summarizes as follows:

   The adj. ἔρημος (usually τόπος in the NT) and the subst
   ἡ ἔρημος usually refer to "abandonment", whether of a
   person (πατρὸς ἔρημαι Soph. Oed. Col., 1717: ἔρημα κλαίω
   Eur. Suppl., 775; cf. Gl. 4:27: ἡ ἔρημος "the abandoned
   wife"), or a cause (ἐσθὴς ἔρημος ἐοῦσα ὅπλων   Hdt., IX,
   63), or a locality. The latter does not have to be a
   desert. It is a place "without inhabitants", "empty",
   e.g., an "abandoned city" or a "thinly populated district"
   (Hdt., IV,17f.; VI,23; VIII,65: κώμη ἔρημος διὰ τὸ πλείω
   χρόνον μὴ βεβρέχθαι;   p. Lille, I, 26,3 (3rd cent. B.C.),
   cf. Mt. 23:38 vl.: Lk. 13:35; Ac. 1:20). It can naturally
   mean "waste" in the strict sense, e.g., an unprofitable
   "waste of stone or sand" (e.g. Hdt., III,102: κατὰ γὰρ
   τοῦτό ἐστιν ἐρημίη διὰ τὴν ψάμμον), and it can thus
   be used for a "lonely" heath (e.g. Lk. 15:4, where the
   shepherd leaves the 99 sheep ἐν τῇ ἐρήμῳ).[169]

   5. That a city or country is ἔρημος or ἠρημωμένη
   ("devastated") is the natural result of the destructive
   attack of enemies (Mt. 12:25: ἐρημοῦται --   ἐρήμωσις).

174

It may also be, as in many prophetic saying of the OT
(Is. 6:11; Lam. 5:18; Ez. 6:6 etc), the consequence of the
divine wrath (Mt. 23:38 vl. and par.: Rev. 17:16).[170]

ἐρήμωσις; -εως is commonly used in the LXX for שׁמם.[171]
Typical examples, apart from the phrase in Daniel are Lev.
26:34,35; Ps. 72 (73):19; 2 Chron. 30:7; 36:21; Jer. 4:7.
To the Hebrew word we now turn.

BDB, as with all lexicons, shows the ambivalent meaning of
שׁמם which seems to emanate from the metaphorical use of the
primary meaning "to stun" or "to make silent".

Typical usages in the O.T. of שׁמם or cognate forms include
the following:

שׁמם	to be laid waste, desolated. See Eze. 33:28; 35:15.
שׁוממוה	Plur. f. places laid waste, ruins. See Isa. 61:4; Dan. 9:18,26.
שׁמם	to be astonished. See 1 Kings 9:8; Jer. 18:16
שׁומם	Part. laid waste. See Lam. 1:4,13,16; 3:11; 2 Sam. 13:20.
נשׁם	Niphal. to be astonished; to be laid waste. See Jer. 4:9; 12:11.

The same twofold meaning is found in all other forms of the
verb, and further examples are unnecessary. The instances in
Daniel, for the most part, have been left for later discussion.

FOOTNOTES FOR CHAPTER FOUR

1. "De gruwel der verwoesting", St Cath, XX (1944), 125.

2. Marxsen, Markus, 125.

3. Weiss, Die Schriften des Neuen Testaments, I, 195.

4. See discussion on 68-76.

5. Lambrecht, Redaktion, 145. Cf. Nineham's "This passage presents the exegete with difficulties as great as any in the Gospel", Saint Mark, 351. Rigaux admits, "On hésite à reprendre une étude du problème qui a déja reçu tant d'interprétations divergentes". "βδέλυγμα τῆς ἐρνμώσεως (Mc 13,14; Mt. 24,15)", 675.

6. St Mark, 511.

7. Compare Mt. 2:5,15,17,23. But see Rigaux, "βδελυγμα. . ." 682.

8. Jesus, 255.

9. Mark Thirteen, 71. The reason for the divergence in the Syriac tradition has been suggested by van Dodewaard. ". . .de Pesitta als van den Cod. Sinaiticus welke beide immers een uitgesproken tendez tot paraphraseeren vertoonen." "De gruwel der verwoesting", 127. He cites Cornely-Merk, Introd. in S.S. Libri Compendium, Parisiis 1934, 200; and A. Vaccari, Institutiones Biblicae I,3. Romae 1937, 249.278.

10. See 20-21.

11. Jesus, 255.

12. C.H. Giblin says: "Though the precise structural arrangement in Mt-Mk is not the same, the figure occurs in these authors at a climactic moment. . . . the climactic moment of the apparent triumph of the unholy. . . . followed immediately by the appearance of the Lord who is the Rebel's nemesis. . . ." The Threat to Faith (AB XXXI)(Rome, 1967), 74.

13. Dodd's well-known remarks are apposite. "The fact is that the whole significant vocabulary of both Lucan passages belongs to the language of the Septuagint and is for the most part characteristic of the prophetical books; and what is still more to the point, several of these terms

tend to recur alike in prophecies of the doom of Jerusalem
and in historical accounts of its capture by Nebuchadnezzar
in 586 B.C." More New Testament Studies, 75. ". . . not
only are the two Lucan oracles composed entirely from the
language of the Old Testament, but the conception of the
coming disaster which the author has in mind is a gen-
eralized picture of the fall of Jerusalem as imaginatively
presented by the prophets. So far as any historical event
has coloured the picture, it is not Titus' capture of
Jerusalem in A.D. 70, but Nebuchadnezzar's capture in
586 B.C. There is no single trait of the forecast which
cannot be documented directly out of the Old Testament."
Ibid., 79. "There appears therefore to be no sufficient
reason for supposing that Luke xxi.20 is a mere 'editing'
of Mark xiii.14." Ibid., 74.

14. Cf. F. Blass, Philology of the Gospels (London, 1898), 46.

15. Says Raymond E. Brown, "Jesus was not alone among his
contemporaries in this premonition. There is a Jewish
tradition (TalBab, Gittim 56 a; Midrash Rabbah on Lam.
1,5; that Rabbi Zadok began fasting about A.D. 30 to
forestall the destruction of Jerusalem. Ca. A.D. 62
Jesus bar Ananias warned of the impending destruction of the
Temple (Josephus, War VI.6,3; 300ff.)." Jesus, God and
Man (London, 1968), 69. However, we recognize that the
modern dating for Luke-Acts is based particularly upon the
catholicity of outlook and the apparently advanced views
on church organization found there.

16. Robert G. Bratcher and Eugene A. Nida, A Translator's
Handbook on the Gospel of Mark (Leiden, 1961), 405.

17. Mk. 12:9.

18. Mk. 11:14.

19. If we compare the records of all three synoptics, and John's
Gospel, the context in terms of events is even more complete
According to Matthew, Christ was not content with merely
predicting "greater condemnation" for the scribes and
Pharisees, but addressed to them a chain of eight woes as a
result of their rejection of Him who claimed to be "the
Way, the Truth, and the Life." At this time the plot to
eradicate Christ is consummated. According to Matthew,
Christ described the coming persecution which would not
only engulf Himself but also the "prophets and wise men
and scribes" He would send. As a result, divine judgment
would fall. ". . . that upon you may come all the
righteous blood shed on earth, from the blood of innocent

Abel, to the blood of Zechariah. . . whom you murdered
between the sanctuary and the altar." Mt. 23:35. And
all this was to come upon that present generation. They
are told, "your house is forsaken and desolate." Mt.
23:38.

It is at this point that Matthew inserts the
eschatological discourse. Luke's presentation is similar.
He also warns that the rejected stone will crush the
builders who have rejected it, and forecasts condemnation
for Israel's leaders. Lu. 20:17-18.

20. Redaktion, 148.

21. Documents, 30.

22. Synoptiques, 422. Loisy says there is nothing to indicate
the necessity for sudden flight, and adds a whimsical
note regarding the difficulty for one on the roof-top to
take off into the air. See T.W. Manson's resolution of
the problem in The Sayings of Jesus (London, 1949), 329-330,
a resolution which we do not consider to be necessary or
accurate. See 167-169 of this thesis.

23. More New Testament Studies, 80.

24. See Allen, Gould, et al., ad loc.

25. Beasley-Murray, Mark Thirteen, 52-53.

26. Markus, 274.

27. See the discussion in Robert H. Stein's unpublished doctoral
dissertation: "The Proper Methodology for Ascertaining a
Markan Redaktiongeschichte" (Princeton, 1968), 22-98.
Note the following, particularly: "It is now recognized
that greater care must be taken in judging the authenticity
or unauthenticity of a work on the basis of vocabulary,
because frequently we do not possess sufficient biblical
material to establish a sufficient statistical foundation.

"It is also doubtful that we can assume that the
writers of the New Testament always wrote logically and in
order, so that a 'disarrangement' of the text may be due to
an interruption in the writing of a particular work
as well as a foreign insertion. Some critics have also
erred by assuming that every historical allusion must be
a priori a vaticinium ex eventu. When a critic argues in
this manner, he should be aware that his rationalistic
presuppositions have ruled out the possibility of true
prophecy. When a critic, for instance, claims that Jesus
never prophesied concerning the destruction of Jerusalem,
it is not his scientific investigations of the material that

178

has determined this but his presuppositions." 22.

"Whereas form criticism can help reveal the editorial redaction of the Evangelists, it can not conclude that this redaction is unhistorical. It may well be that an Evangelist like Mark possessed certain information which enabled him to tie together the various pericopae." 56.

"Recently an attempt has been made to attribute some of this creative power of the community to the prophets of the early church. . . .This attempt to attribute to this group the creative power to produce some of the Gospel tradition is no more convincing than Dibelius's attempt to attribute the shaping and formation of the Novellen to the Story Tellers in the church. . . . Käsemann obtains his examples of the eschatological judgment pronouncements of these New Testament prophets from the Apostle Paul. Yet the Apostle clearly distinguishes between the tradition of Jesus' words and his own thoughts and words. (cf. 1 Cor. 7: 8,10,12, & 25 where this distinction is most clear.)" 34-35.

"Schmidt's conclusions concerning the historical and geographical value of the Marcan seams err in being too extreme." 39.

"Various theological presuppositions have also played an important and even determinative role upon the form critical investigation of many of the form critics. Since, as both Dibelius and Bultmann have pointed out, form criticism must argue in a circle, one's presuppositions are extremely important and often determinative in the analysis of the Gospel tradition." 41.

Stein particularly stresses the part that presuppositions inevitably play in the work of form and redaction critics. Among these presuppositions he mentions the view that there was a simple development in the early church from "a highly imminent eschatological expectation to a placing of the parousia into the more distant future." Stein labels this view as "highly improbable". 41. Another presupposition that he mentions is "an anti-supernatural premise", which is the result not of exegesis but of certain preconceived beliefs about the physical nature of the universe.

28. E.g. W.C. Allen; B.H. Branscomb; C.E.B. Cranfield; A.B. Bruce; E.P. Gould; H.J. Holtzmann; E. Klostermann; M.-J. Lagrange; E. Lohmeyer; A. Loisy; D.E. Nineham; A.E.J. Rawlinson; H.B. Swete; J. Weiss; B. Weiss. These all refer to the שקוץ שמם of Daniel, appearing in various forms in 8:13; 9:27; 11:31; 12:11.

29. ". . . the words include complex concepts which are not clearly defined, either in their immediate forms or in the larger context." Bratcher & Nida, Handbook, 406.

30. See excursus at close of chapter.

31. See excursus at close of chapter.

32. Charles Perrot, "Essai Sur Le Discours Eschatologique",
    Recherches de Science Rel., XLVII (1959), 481-514;
    B. Rigaux, "βδέλυγμα . . .", 677; See excursus for
    references.

33. Jer. 4:1,7,20,23,27; 7:10,30,34; 44:6,22; Eze. 5:9,11,14;
    6:4,9,11,14; 7:4,8,9,20,22-23. Lev. 26 should also be
    compared with these chapters.

34. Burkill, Mysterious Revelation, 117-142.

35. Daniel, 377. An endorsement of Kamphausen's comment.

36. Cited by Beasley-Murray, Mark Thirteen, 54.

37. S.B. Frost, "Abomination that makes Desolate", IBD, I, 13-
    14; Pesch, Naherwartungen, 142-143; Carrington, Mark,
    278; Jeffery, "Daniel", IB, VI, 490-491; Gaston, No Stone
    on Another, 118. Charles does, however, acknowledge the
    literal meaning of שמם in 9:26, and refers the reader to
    1 Macc. 1:39; 3:45; 4:38, and his own note on Dan. 8:11.
    Thus while Charles says that the translators of the Sept.
    failed to see the grim jest in 9:27, it is possible that
    they saw other implications, and that therefore their
    rendering is not entirely alien from the intention of the
    Hebrew. See above, particularly Pesch. See also 151, 167-
    169.

38. The New Testament and Rabbinic Judaism, 420.

39. New Testament, 420.

40. This article is small enough and important enough to
    reproduce in full. "Dass unter dem βδέλυγμα ἐρημώσεως
    der dem olympischen Zeus geweihte Altar zu verstehen sei,
    den Antiochus Epiphanes im Tempel zu Jerusalem aufstellen
    liess, darf als ausgemacht gelten; ob auch eine Statue
    des Zeus dabei war, ist noch fraglich. Wie erklärt sich
    aber die so seltsame Bezeichnung im Buch Daniel? Nun
    ganz einfach: שקוץ שמם ist nichts anderes als בעל שמם
    Baal-samen, d.h. Zeus. Ich war sehr überrascht, nachdem mir
    diese Vermuthung aufgestossen war, eben an der biblischen
    Stelle, die von diesem Thun des Antiochus berichtet, II.
    Makk. 6,2, in der syrischen Bibel ζευς wirklich durch
    בעלשמין wiedergegeben zu finden, gleichsam zur Bestätigung
    dieser Gleichsetzung. Nicht als ob im Daniel nun wirklich

שַׁמֵּם oder שַׁמֵּם zu vokalisieren wäre; die massorethische Punktation ist vielmehr absichtliche Verketzerung und als solche beizubehalten; aber gegen Bär wird wenigstens an allen Stellen die defecte Schreibung von שמם vorzuziehen sein. Damit ist freilich die grammatikalisch auffallende Form הַשִׁקּוּץ מְשֹׁמֵם (11,31 ohne Wiederholung des Artikels) und die noch auffallendere שִׁקּוּצִים מְשֹׁמֵם (9,27 Plural mit Singular) nicht besser erklärt als bisher, unter solchen Umständen aber am Ende nicht mehr so verwunderlich. Ich bemerke noch, dass neben dem häufigen aramäischen בַּעַל שְׁמִין (mit Nun) auch בַּעַל שׁמם (mit (Mem) inschriftlich bezeugt ist." E. Nestle, ZAW, IV (1884), 248.

41. R.H. Charles, A Critical and Exegetical Commentary on the Book of Daniel, (Oxford, 1929), 308. For illustrations of Ex. 23:13 see Hos. 9:10; Jer. 3:24; 11:13; 2 Sam, 2:8 (cf. 1 Chron. 7:33). Micah 1:10-16 is an excellent example of assonance and word-play.

42. New Testament, 418-422.

43. Significant for the purposes of this study as indicating that the Jews upon reading or hearing of the βδέλυγμα τῆς ἐρημώσεως would think not only of a profaning altar, but of the person imaged there who was responsible for the desecration and other horrors including martyrdom, the sacking of the city, and the destruction of the temple walls.

44. Documents, 26-27. See also Charles, Daniel, 308, citing Taanith IV.6.

45. Mark Thirteen, 55.

46. The Servant of the Lord, 249.

47. Torrey, Documents, 28.

48. Rigaux, "βδέλυγμα . . .", 676.

49. "βδέλυγμα . . . .", 676.

50. "Abomination of Desolation", 13-14.

51. "De gruwel. . . .", 2.

52. Montgomery, Daniel, 377.

53. We think R.H. Charles is wrong in denying the parallel between Dan. 8:14 and 9:27 etc., Daniel, 209. Most other scholars disagree with him. See Driver, et al., ad loc.

54. "βδέλυγμα . . . .", 678-79. See also Ford, Daniel, 200.

55. "De gruwel. . .", 128. See also Ford, Daniel, 206ff.

56. Ibid.

57. Redaktion, 149.

58. E.g. Mk. 4:32, cf. Dan. 4:10-12; Mk. 13:26; cf. Dan. 7:13.

59. Redaktion, 149.

60. Prophecy, 162.

61. I & II Thessalonians (Baker Bible Commentary)(Grand Rapids, 1955), 176. (Dan. 7 does not link Antichrist with the temple.)

62. Mark 13:26,19.

63. See 35-37.

64. Lu. 19:41-44.

65. E.g. Zech. 14:2.

66. 1 Kings 9:6-8.

67. Eze. 7:22-23.

68. Eze. 9:8.

69. Eze. 5:9-17. The following chapter repeats the threat of desolation. See 6:4,11,14.

70. Jer. 7:32-34, etc.

71. Ps. 74:1-7; 79:1-7; Lam. 1:4-5,8-10,16; 2:7,20; 5:18.

72. Lam. 5:21.

73. E.g. Zech. 14:2.

74. See 160ff.

75. Redaktion, 150.

76. Mark Thirteen, 59.

77. Ibid., 59-72.

78. E.g. Theophylact, Euthymius, Zigabena, Chrysostom. But see discussion by R. McL. Wilson, "Mark", (Peake, Revised edn.), 814.

79. BDB. See Nahum 3:6; Zech. 9:7; Lev. 11:10,12,13,20; Isa. 66:17.

80. Van Dodewaard, "De gruwel. . . .", 132.

81. Ibid.

82. War of the Jews, IV.iii.12; IV.vi.3; VI.ii.I.

83. "De eerste ἐρήμωσις uit den tekst van Lucas is dus a.h.w. een teeken van de tweede ἐρήμωσις, waarover Mt. en Mc. sprecken. Lucas gebruikt dan ook den vageren term ἤγγικεν welken hif ook voor het naderen van het rijk Gods gebruikte. Al is dit een perfectum, toch duidt het niet aan, dat de bedoelde zaak reeds geheel aanwezig is. Zooals men van de lente kan zeggen: zij is er of zij is aan het komen, omdat er verschillende graden in zijn, zoo kan men dat ook zeggen, aldus J. Weiss), van het rijk Gods. Voegen wij eraan toe: en van de ἐρήμωσις hier. Wanneer juist is wat Prat opmerkt, dat de term ἤγγικεν ἡ βασιλεία τοῦ θεοῦ meer het naderende rijk aanduidt dan de nadering van het rijk), kunnen wij dat met evenveel recht hier van de ἐρήμωσις zeggen. Ἐρήμωσις is een complex van feiten en gebeurtenissen, "non stat in indivisibili" om het eens met een ouden term te zeggen.
"De woorden βδέλυγμα τῆς ἐρημώσεως moet men dus niet alleen tot de gruweldaden der Zeloten beperken, zij omvatten een complex, dat en het Romeinsche lege onder Cestius Callus en de vlucht der menschen uit Jerusalem en, de gruwelen der Zeloten insluit. Toen het βδέλυγμα τῆς ἐρημώσεως zijn toppunt bereikte, bevond het zich in den tempel en toen was ook de ἐρήμωσις compleet. Lucas gebruikte dus het werkwoord ἐρημοῦν meer in zijn letterlijken zin van: eenzaam, leeg maken, terwijl Mt. en. Mc. den overdrachtelijken zin van: profaneeren gebruikten." "De gruwel. . .", 135. Note that for van Dodewaard, the mystical phrase is not to be limited to the Zealots, though it includes them. His suggestion is that the term embraces a complex of several events. We agree that more than one entity is embraced by the βδέλυγμα τῆς ἐρημώσεως but the elements must parallel each other. This criterion excludes, therefore, the zealots as extraneous.

84.   "This view should now be abandoned as incompatible with the evidence." Beasley-Murray, Mark Thirteen, 62.

85. Ibid., 64.

86. He says: "In no words of the Master was Messianic authority
more impressively shown than in the last great discourse,
in which he revealed to his nearest disciples what they
were privileged to know concerning the near future.
Reasons have already been given for believing that this
discourse must have been among the first of the writings
that were sent forth. As to the impending clash with the
Romans, followed by the capture of the city (according to
O.T. prophecy), nothing more definite could at that time
have been said than this: 'When you see Jerusalem
surrounded by armies.' Luke, who for all the latter part of
his Gospel made use of a document differing in many respects
from those which were employed by the other Synoptists,
gives precisely this original form of words. Mark,
followed by Matthew, inserted a more definite 'sign,'
the erection of the statue of Caligula on the altar in
the temple. Should not the fulfilment of Daniel's
prophecy be mentioned?" Documents, 35.

87. T.W. Manson, C.J. Cadoux, et al.

88. Mark Thirteen, 65-66. Bacon affirmed: ". . . .the crisis
of the year 40 drew out from Christian 'prophets' a form of
eschatology based on the predictions of Daniel concerning
the desecration of the temple, and . . . the Church became
committed to this eschatology as a 'word of the Lord'. . . .
Mutually independent or not, and however related or
unrelated to the Johannine, the Pauline and the Synoptic
'prophecies' must both go back to the attempt of Caius [sic]
Neither can be accounted for as a 'word of the Lord' in
any other sense than as the Revelation of John may be so
called." The Gospel of Mark: Its Composition and Date
(New Haven, 1925), 91-92.

89. Klostermann, Das Markusevangelium, 151; Loisy, Synoptiques,
ii, 420; Lohmeyer, Markus, 276; A.H. McNeile, The Gospel
According to Matthew (London, 1915), 348; Branscomb, Mark,
237; Schniewind, Markus, 171f.; Foerster, TDNT., I, 598ff.

90. Cited by A.J. Mason, "Thessalonians", Ellicott's Commentary,
(8 vols., Grand Rapids, 1959), VIII, 168.

91. Ibid., 170.

92. Mark Thirteen, 68-69.

93. See Rigaux, L'Antéchrist, 238-249; W.C. Allen, The Gospel
According to Saint Mark (London, 1915), 159.

94. Or whichever "John" wrote Revelation.

95. See 21ff.

96. "The Apocalypse is moulded by that great discourse of our
Lord upon 'the last things' which has been preserved for us
in the first three Gospels. Matt. 24; Mark 13; Luke 21.
. . . .The parallelism between the two is to a certain extent
acknowledged by all enquirers, and is indeed so obvious that
it can hardly escape the notice of even the ordinary
reader." W. Milligan, Lectures on the Apocalypse (London,
1892), 42-43. This statement is particularly relevant to
the Seven Seals, but to a lesser extent applies to the
rest of the Apocalypse also.

97. On the whole topic of Antichrist, see H. Gunkel,
Schöpfung und Chaos in Urzeit und Endzeit (Göttingen, 1895);
W. Bousset, The Antichrist Legend (E.T., London, 1896);
B. Rigaux, L'Antéchrist et l'opposition au royaume
messianique dans l'Ancien et le Nouveau Testament (Paris,
1932); D.S. Russell, The Method and Message of Jewish
Apocalyptic (London, 1964); L.E. Froom, The Prophetic
Faith of Our Fathers (4 vols., Washington, 1950-54).

98. 1 John 2:18.

99. 2 Thess. 2:5.

100. Acts 17:2.

101. St Mark, 286.

102. Rigaux, L'Antéchrist, 246-247.

103. Ibid., 245,246. Cf. van Dodewaard, "De gruwel. . . .", 135
but see 183.

104. Dan. 9:26.

105. Understanding כנף as pinnacle, with many commentators. See
Mt. 4:5 and LXX which uses ἱερόν in 9:27.

106. Dan. 9:27.

107. Dan. 11:28-31.

108. Dan. 11:40-45.

109. Dan. 11:44.חרם. Cf. R.H. Charles' "stringent statute"
9:27, Daniel, 248.

185

110. Regrettably, the connexion between 11:45 and 12:1 has often been ignored.

111. Dan. 7:13 and Mk. 13:26; Dan. 8:13 and Lu. 21:24; Dan. 9: 27 and Mk. 13:14; Dan. 11:31 and Mk. 13:14; and possibly Dan. 11:45 and Mt. 24:15 ἐν τόπῳ ἀγίῳ Dan. 12:1 and Mk. 13: 19.

112. Documents, 18-19.

113. This is an allusion to Mk. 13:10. Allen comments on the latter, and his words are pertinent to the Rev. 11 picture also. "As understood by the hearers, the preaching of the good news to all the Gentiles need not imply any long lapse of time." Mark, 158.

114. Rev. 11:1-8.

115. Documents, 32.

116. Mt. 10:18; 24:9; Mk. 13:9,10.

117. Rom. 11:25-26; 9:28.

118. Isa. chs. 54 and 60.

119. Mk. 13:19-22. Cf. Rev. 13 and 16:13,14. The Apostles allude to certain eschatological teachings which they had taught from the beginning, and which therefore must have originated with Christ. The Pauline and Johannine beliefs referred to above probably sprang from the same source. See 1 John 2:18 and 2 Thess. 2:5 and the chapter in this volume on 2 Thess. 2.

120. The view set forth in this section regarding Christ's understanding of the crisis in the days of Antiochus IV as typical of a greater crisis to come, is found in many commentaries. Rigaux, for example, says: "La fin est marquée, pour Daniel, par l'activité impie et sacrilège du roi païen. Le temple de Dieu et son autel sont souillés. Une fois que cet élément fut entré dans la tradition apocalyptique, il y resta ancré. Dans la tradition chrétienne, le temple ne doit pas seulement être détruit. L'impiété d'Antiochus se retrouvera dans les événements de la fin. L'abomination du devastateur aura une réplique dans l'eschatologie." "βδέλυγμα . . . .", 682. In his classical study on the Antichrist, Rigaux earlier wrote as follows: "En rattachant l'histoire à l'eschatologie, en reconnaissant, dans l'iniquité croissante du tyran syrien, l'annonce de la fin des temps, Daniel ne

révèle-t-il pas, par delà l'histoire d'Antiochus, sa
croyance à la présence, au temps eschatologique, d'un
surcroît d'iniquité et d'une persécution religieuse
formidable? Au même titre que les anciens prophètes,
Daniel doit être regardé comme ayant prophétisé au sens
littéral, l'opposition eschatologique au royaume de Dieu.
Il faut même dire qu'il l'a fait avec plus de netteté dans
le contours et le fonds. Si aucun verset de sa revelation
ne s'applique immédiatement à l'Antéchrist, c'est bien
lui cependant qu'il entrevoyait, comme c'était la
figure idéale du Roi-Messie que les chantres de la royauté
apercevaient dans la pénombre de l'avenir à travers les
images hyperboliques par lesquelles ils exaltaient un roi
de leur époque." L'Antéchrist, 173. G. Ch. Aalders
comments: "Wat er verder in kan liggen is een hernieuwde
verwulling van wat reeds tot vervulling gekomen is." "De
gruwel. . . .", 5. This conclusion to what Aalders calls
"the most difficult question" follows his consideration of
Mt. 2:15,18. He suggests that as the flight of the Christ
child into Egypt and the slaughter at Bethlehem were seen
as new fulfilments of ancient prophecies, so in the
present instance of Mt. 24:15; Mk. 13:14.
Aalders believes that the Olivet discourse discusses two
themes, the destruction of Jerusalem and the end of the
age. His understanding of this matter is the traditional
one, and has been discussed on 65ff. of this dissertation.
Thus he looks upon the Roman invasion as a shadow of the
final onslaught of Antichrist, whereas the present study
takes the position that the Roman invasion was a manifestation of Antichrist, though a manifestation which was to
swell into greater dimensions, eventually enshrining
supernatural events. See Ford, D., Daniel (S.P.A. Nashville).
See also van Dodewaard's "De gruwel. . . .", 131, which
sets forth a position identical with Aalders', in this
respect. In the study of this question, the words of
Johannes Weiss should be ever kept in mind: ". . . schon
Jesus selber sich die Zukunft nach der Form der jüdischen
Endzeit-Erwahrtungen gedacht habe." Die Schriften des
Neues Testaments, I, 195. Weiss reasons that "Wie er sich
mit seiner Messias-Vorstellung an die Weissagung Daniels
angeschlossen hat, so werden auch in anderer Zukunfts-
dingen die Lehren der Apokalyptik für ihn massgebend
gewesen sein." Ibid. The chapter in this volume on the
relationship between the Olivet discourse and the book of
Daniel supports these comments of Weiss.

121. Those exegetes who take this position include the following:
Beasley-Murray, Mark Thirteen, 56-57; Gould, Mark, 246;
Swete, Mark, 286; Vincent Taylor, Mark, 511-512;
W.C. Allen, Matthew, 256; N. Geldenhuys, Luke, 532;

A. Plummer, Luke, 481ff., T. Zahn, Lucas, 649; W. Manson, Luke, 283f.

122. This position has been argued in earlier pages. See 65ff.

123. See Beasley-Murray, Mark Thirteen, 69.

124. Dodd, More New Testament Studies, 80.

125. Both the βδέλυγμα τῆς ἐρημώεσεως of Mk. 13:14 and the ἄνθρωπος τῆς ἀνομίας of 2 Thess. 2:3ff. are presented as punishments permitted by God because of the rejection of His truth. Thus the N.T. picture is identical with the Old which so frequently threatens foreign invaders of Israel as a divine judgment.

126. "Daniel", ad loc.

127. Rowley, Relevance, 76. Cf. Porteous, Daniel, 143. Comment on Dan. 9:26. "The war which the writer anticipates is no doubt conceived of by him as the final eschatological struggle between good and evil (cf. Eze. 38 and 39; Rev. 16:16; and The War of the Sons of Light and the Sons of Darkness)."

128. Rowley, Relevance, 76.

129. "The common extension of meaning given to O.T. passages in the N.T. forbids an insistence that our Lord's use of the expression must be identical with that in the Danielic passages. . ." Beasley-Murray, Mark Thirteen, 55. Cf. Bruce, "Matthew", 292.

130. Synoptiques, II, 422.

131. St Mark, 511.

132. Naherwartungen, 142.

133. Although his work is outdated in some respects, Hengstenberg's comments on the linguistic issues of Dan. 9:26-27 are worthy of study. See Vol. 3 of his Christology of the Old Testament (E.T., London, 1858), 157-163.

134. Ibid., 143.

135. Daniel, 77.

136. Von Rad reminds us that in Daniel ". . .the statements made

about the future are simply exegesis of older words of
scripture. Thus in Dan. 9:26 in the prophecy of Antiochus
Epiphanes, the term שטף occurs. This is certainly not a
random choice, but goes back to Isa. 10:22; for the
very next verse to that (Is. x.23) is used in the same
passage in Daniel, the only difference being that the
'decreed end'. . .is now made to refer to the Seleucid king
(Dan. ix.27). . . ." Old Testament Theology, II, 314.
Certainly the word שטף in Isa. 10:22-23 refers to a
destruction which will come as an overwhelming flood. In
Dan. 9:26 the term applies to the city, though the
following verse describes the fate of the desolator.
Therefore it is not strange that Jews of the first century
saw in Dan. 9:26 something more than merely the partial
desolations accomplished by the soldiers of Antiochus.
The comments of Gaston are more faithful to the actual
wording of Daniel than the usual notes by commentators.
He says: "The 'abomination' in Daniel seems much worse
than that of I Mac. 1:54, and it may be that he expected
the temple to be completely destroyed. The massoretic
text of 9:26 is probably corrupt, but as it stands it
says that 'the people of the prince who is to come will
destroy the city and the sanctuary.' This seems to say that
the temple will be completely destroyed, either by
Antiochus or possibly by the Messiah. We must beware of
reading Daniel too much in the light of what actually
happened according to I Maccabees." No Stone on Another,
18. See also Ford, Daniel, 200.

137. Mark Thirteen, 55.

138. See footnote 38, p. 167f.

139. Branscomb criticises Moffatt's "appalling Horror" transla-
      tion because it "renders only one of two ideas in the
      Greek phrase". He says that due weight should be given to
      the concept of destruction, as well as that of desecration.
      Mark, 237. Kevan says similarly in his article on the
      βδέλυγμα τῆς ἐρημώσεως   in Baker's Dictionary of
      Theology, 17. Carrington affirms that the Greek term
      ἐρημώσεως "can only mean devastation". Mark, 278.
      This is too strong, inasmuch as a desecration can desolate
      by emptying a shrine of worshippers. But Klostermann avers
      that the word marks the work of the βδέλυγμα as devasta-
      tion. W. Grundmann agrees. "Dieser Greuel ist eine
      wirksame Macht, denn er wirkt Verödung und Verwüstung",
      Markus, 266. B. Weiss, cited by Pesch, Naherwartungen, 143,
      says in his Marcan commentary, 422: "ἐρήμωσις führt
      mit Notwendigkeit auf die Vorstellung des das Land
      verwüstenden heidnischen Heeres, das als Collectivum

gedacht ist".

140. We have not listed as options any recent positions on Mk. 13:14, such as those of Austin Farrer (A Study of St Mark), and G. Cotter ("Abomination of Desolation", CJT III (1957), 159-164). While both of these have been published for over fifteen years, they have not awakened scholarly interest or assent. Both seem to pattern after Origen's methods of exegesis. Farrer's contention that the abomination of desolation was seen in the garden betrayal, set up in the spiritual temple of Christ's followers, and some of Cotter's remarks on the symbolic meaning of ἔρημος transcend the speculations in TDNT which James Barr has strictured so roundly. (Kittel's own article on ἔρημος has some likeness to Cotter's, as it sets forth the "theological" significance of the desert.) We think that Farrer and Cotter would each see elements to commend in the other's position, but such a circle of approval is rather too small. Subsequent commentaries on Mark have not made reference to these allegorical interpretations.

141. E.g. Branscomb, Loisy, McNeile, Lohmeyer, Klostermann, Nineham, Rigaux, ad loc. Cf. Vincent Taylor, Mark, 511. Taylor differs with some of the preceding in understanding the passage as pointing to "a manifestation of Anti-Christ in expected historical events."

142. New Testament, 418.

143. Ibid., 418ff.

144. Bacon would have us believe that it is "practically certain that the Markan form of the apocalypse has been affected by the Pauline." Mark, 129. Thus Bacon sees the significance of ἑστηκότα but wrongly accounts for it. H.A.A. Kennedy's remarks apply. "The curious position has been assumed (e.g. by Bousset), that Matt. xxiv. is to be explained by 2 Thess. ii. (see The Antichrist Legend, 23). This is surely one of the paradoxes of New Testament criticism." St Paul's Conceptions of the Last Things (London, 1904), 56n. See the discussion in Rigaux's Les Épitres Aux Thessaloniciens (Paris, 1956), 95-105. If one account reflects the other, it is far more likely that the fuller account is the original.

145. Daube, New Testament, 422. Carrington refers to the Antichrist interpretation based on ἑστηκότα. He calls it "a curious theory", and says that it is based on the fact that "the word translated 'standing' has a masculine form in Matthew [sic]; and that is all it has to recommend it."

Mark, 279-80. He further declares that "The history and
usage of the words makes such a theory impossible, and so
does the text of Mark, which goes on to envisage war
conditions." Ibid. We confess to finding this criticism
itself somewhat curious, and not only the Matthean reference.
As already shown, the particular usage of the שקוץ שמם
phrase in Daniel strongly supports the Antichrist position,
and so likewise does all that has been said above regarding
ἑστηκότα. Possibly what has also been said here about
Antichrist's action in history would make this position
more tenable to Carrington, and the interpretation of
ἑστηκότα associated with it. As in 9:1, the word implies
existence rather than "standing" as such.

146. Dan. 8:13-14; 9:26-27; 11:31; 12:11.

147. Dan. 11:45. Theodotion has πήξει implying the erection
of tents where the invader takes his stand, but the older
LXX has στήσει.

148. Dan. 12:1.

149. 2 Macc. 2:18; 1:7; 3:1.

150. Mark, 512.

151. Ibid.

152. See 20f. and cf. Allen, Matthew, ad loc. Regarding the
supposed parenthesis of the evangelist, Philip Schaff
has written: "It must be admitted that in the first three
Gospels there occurs no similar case of a subjective
insertion calling attention to any event or discourse."
(editorial note on Mt. 24:15, in John P. Lange's "Matthew",
Lange's Commentary, VIII, 425.)
The immediate objection to what Schaff says consists of
Mk. 7:19 and the supposed parenthesis "Thus he declared
all foods clean". We consider it unlikely that the RSV
interpretation (for the words are not actually a translation) is correct in this instance. It is improbable that
Christ Who upheld the Torah so strongly would have made
such a pronouncement. See D. Nineham, Saint Mark, 191-92,
196. Matthew Black is almost certainly correct when
he suggests that in the original Aramaic the meaning approx-
imated 'all the food being cast out and purged away'. An
Aramaic Approach to the Gospels and Acts, 159. Thus
Schaff may be entirely correct, and if so the usual position
regarding the passage under discussion is somewhat
undermined. See also J. Morison, Mark, ad loc. On the
other hand, most modern commentators influenced by the

Greek as it stands, see the phrase as a Markan or scribal addition.

153. Dan. 8:15-17.

154. Dan. 8:27.

155. Dan. 9:23.

156. Dan. 10:1.

157. Dan. 10:12.

158. Dan. 11:33.

159. Dan. 12:10.

160. "βδέλυγμα . . . .", 682.

161. Markus, 174.

162. Markus, 124n.

163. Jesu, 444-448.

164. See discussion in Beasley-Murray, Mark Thirteen, 58.

165. Mk. 13:21.

166. Mk. 13:26-27.

167. Foerster, "βδελυσσμαι . . . .", TDNT, I, 598.

168. Ibid., 599.

169. Kittel, "ἔρημος. . . .", TDNT, II, 657.

170. Ibid., 659.

171. Used in the canonical books eighteen times, of which twelve are translations of שׁמם or cognates.

CHAPTER FIVE

RELATIONSHIP BETWEEN II THESS. 2 AND THE

βδέλυγμα τῆς ἐρημώσεως

From the time of 1 Maccabees till the writing of Mark, the phrase βδέλυγμα τῆς ἐρημώσεως. is unknown to literature. But the concept associated with the term, that of an eschatological opponent of God modelled on the lines of Antiochus Epiphanes, was well-known. It echoes throughout Jewish apocalyptic from the writing of Daniel onwards.[1]

As regards the New Testament, the Synoptics all speak of the sign of the end when the holy city is imperilled, and the great tribulation launched. Two use the phrase central to our thesis, and the third refers to the armies of the invader. But prior to the writing of the Gospels, echoes of Christ's eschatological discourse are to be found in the two letters to the Thessalonian Christians, and among these echoes are some concerning the βδέλυγμα It is in these, the earliest epistles,[2] that the first reference to the Danielic picture of the Antichrist is found. Just as βδέλυγμα τῆς ἐρημώσεως is unknown to literature from the time that 1 Maccabees was written, so the expression ὁ ἄνθρωπος τῆς ἀνομίας when it appeared, was a unique term in literature. Thus our present interest in the Thessalonian epistles, especially the central chapter of the second letter.

What Mark 13 is to that Gospel, and the eschatological discourse to the Synoptics as a whole, so is 2 Thess. 2 to the Pauline corpus. In each case we are confronted with an atypical emphasis, apparently esoteric. "To give a full account of the interpretation of 2 Thess ii.1-12 would be almost the same thing as to write a history of Christendom."[3] As some plants are best known for their thorns, so this passage is renowned because of its difficulties. As the Slough of Despond was noted for its swallowing up of whole cartloads of good instructions, without benefitting thereby, so this passage of Scripture appears to have engulfed a multitude of exegetical tomes without having been rendered entirely luminous. It has been described as "probably the most obscure and difficult passage in the whole of the Pauline correspondence".[4] From the days of Augustine many commentators have evinced an extraordinary humility when confronted with the task of exegeting this famous chapter. Even Rigaux's[5] monumental work on Thessalonians contains a well-known confession of bafflement. At this point, one sees some truth in the couplet:

> Commentators each dark passage shun,
> And hold their farthing candle to the sun.

But if 2 Thess. 2 is an acknowledged part of the biblical sun, it seems to be a part blighted with spots. Its puzzling incomplete allusions were sufficient, doubtless, for those to whom it was first written, but hardly so for subsequent readers. Thus one can own to a sense of frustration when studying the chapter,

a sensation which is heightened by a review of its commentators.
As Farrar rightly said regarding the whole body of opinion on
this pericope: ". . .that vast limbo of exploded exegesis--
the vastest and the dreariest that human imagination has
conceived."[6] And all this despite the fact that another can
say: "There is scarcely a more matter-of-fact prediction in the
Bible." "His [Paul's] language . . .is very positive and
definite. . . .his description of the personality of Antichrist
is vividly distinct; and he asserts the connexion between his
appearance and Christ's return from heaven with an explicitness
that leaves no room for doubt as to his meaning."[7]

Farrar's criticism would tempt one to believe that here is an
instance where the principles of grammatico-historico exegesis
have failed miserably. As in the similar case of Mk. 13:14,
there is no consensus of interpretation.[8] It is quite certain
that if any single group of exegetes is correct in its position,
then the majority (meaning all others) must be wrong. Perhaps
other factors besides the acknowledged canons of interpretation
are at work here, as has been suggested earlier.[9] Contributory
to the chaos of views is the face-value of Paul's Antichrist.
The thought of a supernaturally endowed villain oozing celestial
fireworks from the tips of his fingers and toes, has had little
attraction for either the nineteenth or twentieth century mind.
But it needs to be said again, that such an ideological repulsion
has nothing to do with the task of the exegete. The issue is
"What did Paul mean? What did he believe?" Not "What can the
exegete believe on the same subject?"

The key words of the pericope are ἀποστασία, ὁ ἄνθρωπος τῆς
ἀνομίας, ναός, ὁ υἱὸς τῆς ἀπωλείας.Any interpretation of 2 Thess.
2 worthy of respect must grapple with these, and suggest some
explanations which give congruence to the whole. Before
attempting this task, however, a little should be said on certain
introductory matters of importance.

Authenticity of 2 Thess.

The authenticity of the letter is not of <u>absolute</u> importance
to us, because it is obvious that the letter <u>reveals</u> a personal
ideology which, if not Paul's, is at least modelled upon his.
Therefore, we do not feel it incumbent upon us to minutely
analyze arguments, the issue of which has been agreed upon by
the majority of modern commentators. The authenticity of
2 Thessalonians has often been called into question, but it is
defended by virtually all recent N.T. scholars.[10]

The main argument brought against the authentiticy of this
epistle has ever been its supposed contradiction to 1 Thess.
in the matters of eschatology. Holtzmann was one of the main

scholars to urge that the picture of 2 Thess. 2:1-12 is clearly other than that of 1 Thess. 4:13 to 5:11. This criticism is certainly outdated. W.G. Kümmel, Beasley-Murray, and many others have shown that the suddenness of the Advent is not incompatible with preceding signs. ". . .both conceptions -- the end comes suddenly, and it is historically prepared for -- go together and are viewed together in the apocalypticism of Judaism and primitive Christianity."[11]

The style of this second letter is viewed as restrained and formal in contrast to that of the first. One might answer -- "And so. . .?" What would it prove? A mercurial temperament like Paul's was not bound down to expressing itself in a fixed style. The apostle's task differs in this epistle from the task of the first. A different purpose presupposes a different style. Letters of love and letters of law are notoriously divergent. Paul's are neither solely, but we ever find admonition intermingled with expressions of affection, and the proportions depend upon the situation.

Certainly there are similarities of language and of general structure between the letters. These suggest literary dependence of some kind or other. But it has been rightly argued that it is more likely that Paul would follow some of his own literary habits than that another would laboriously seek to copy him.[12] Furthermore, it is most unlikely that a forger would create the difficulties that the lack of clarity in the second chapter inevitably arouse.[13]

We need reminding that if there were no First Thessalonians, there would probably have been no question regarding the authenticity of Second Thessalonians, and it is just as reasonable to question the genuineness of the first letter on the basis of its contrast to the second, as vice versa. But the traditional picture rings true. First Thessalonians is just such a letter as such a person as Paul would probably write for the first time to a church he had early raised up, and Second Thessalonians does imply that its writer had previously corresponded with the same group of believers.

To quote another, "on the whole, the difficulties in the way of accepting the letter are less difficult than those which are raised by the attempt to account for it as pseudonymous writing of a later period."[14]

Authenticity -- Historical Setting

The customary summary of the background of 2 Thess. suggests that the letter was called forth as a result of a misunderstanding of the apostle's remarks in his first letter regarding the

approaching Parousia. Therefore Paul's aim is now to correct
this misunderstanding of some who believed that the day of the
Lord was already present, and to this end he reminds them of
his earlier teaching about the lawless precursor of Christ's
return.

In recent times C.H. Giblin has challenged this orthodox
view.[15] He has contended that the main aim of 2 Thess. 2 is
directly pastoral, and that references to matters eschatological
grow out of an implied rebuke of charismatic practices of
doubtful character among the Thessalonian believers. There is,
of course, truth in Giblin's contention that Paul's aim is
directly pastoral. This is true also of Christ's discourse, as
we have seen. But the unique features of Giblin's case seem
to have but shadowy support. We do not think that he has
established his positions regarding pseudo-prophetic behaviour
in this infant Christian community. His whole thesis depends
on (1) his philological arguments, and (2) his understanding
of οἱ ἄτακτοι.   Neither of these have recommended themselves to
reviewers,[16] but the basic reason for rejection lies in the fact
that the letters to the Thessalonians just do not contain the
required evidence that the charismatic blight Giblin contemplates
actually dominated the Thessalonian scene, or that it was to
this phenomenon that Paul referred by his use of τὸ κατέχον,

Literary Context of 2 Thess. 2

The very first words of this chapter[17] show that the ensuing
passage is the heart of the letter, and embodies Paul's main
purpose in writing. Paul alludes to the fact that some had been
shaken and excited by the belief that the day of Christ had
begun, and that soon they must behold the Lord Himself. Then
Paul proceeds to argue against such a misunderstanding by
clarifying the eschatological picture. He does so by reference
to what he had earlier taught his Thessalonian converts. But
this is not accomplished by a mere summary allusion. Rather, it
seems that the apostle is glad to spell out again some features
of the coming crisis which he anticipated as the prelude to the
fulfillment of "the blessed hope".

The following chapter begins with a "Finally, brethren. . .",
intimating that his main purpose in writing had been discharged.
Thus the opening words of chapters two and three of 2 Thess.
clearly reveal Paul's eschatological discussion as the conceptual,
as well as the literary, centre of the epistle.

Textual Criticism

There are no major problems in the Greek text of 2 Thess.
According to F.W. Beare "there are only three readings of more

than technical interest which call for consideration."[18] None of
these particularly affect the exegetical problem.

We have chosen to follow ὁ ἄνθρωπος τῆς ἀνομίας   as the
reading for 2:13, not because the case for it is conclusive,
but because it harmonizes best with the context, and because
thus adopted it does not vary much in significance from the
alternative.

Relationship between 1 and 2 Thessalonians and the Eschatological Discourse

The similarities between the Thessalonian epistles and the
Olivet discourse have often occasioned remark.[19] These
similarities extend not only to parallel concepts but also to
verbal expressions. Thus Zahn affirms that the eschatological
presentation of 2 Thess. 2 is historically incomprehensible
without postulating an impetus from Christ such as Mk. 13.[20]
And. H.A.A. Kennedy, commenting on the same Pauline passage says:
"It is no exaggeration to say that Matt. xxiv is the most
instructive commentary on the Chapter before us."[21] J.B. Orchard
expresses the same conviction as Kennedy, and believes that the
epistles to the Thessalonians "are fairly bristling with verbal
coincidences and reminiscences of the eschatological discourse."[22]
More than nine pages are devoted by Rigaux to the setting forth
of these "coincidences and reminiscences", and an analysis of
them.[23]

Just a few of the outstanding parallels are now indicated:

2 Thess. 2:1,2: Now concerning the coming of our Lord
Jesus Christ and our assembling to meet him, we beg you,
brethren, not to be quickly shaken in mind or excited,. . .

Mk. 13:27,7: And then he will send out the angels, and
gather his elect from the four winds, from the ends of the
earth to the ends of heaven.

. . . do not be alarmed. . . .

(ἐπισυναγωγή is used in a unique sense in the first
passage, and all commentators recognize here a reference
to Christ's saying as recorded in the second passage.
θροεῖσθαι is also a unique term, apart from the Olivet
discourse being found only in this Thessalonian text.)

2 Thess. 2:3: Let no one deceive you in any way. . . .

Mk. 13:5: And Jesus began to say to them, "Take heed that
no one leads you astray. . . ."

2 Thess. 2:3,4: Let no one deceive you in any way; for that day will not come, unless the rebellion comes first, and the man of lawlessness is revealed, the son of perdition, who opposes and exalts himself against every so-called god or object of worship, so that he takes his seat in the temple of God, proclaiming himself to be God.

Mk. 13:14: "But when you see the desolating sacrilege set up where it ought not be. . . ."

2 Thess. 2:9: The coming of the lawless one by the activity of Satan will be with all power and with pretended signs and wonders. . . .

Mk. 13:22: "False Christs and false prophets will arise and show signs and wonders, to lead astray, if possible, the elect."

These parallels are representative only, and could be multiplied. If one works in reverse and begins with Mk. 13, the following elements find their counterpart in 2 Thess. The warning against deception (v.5), the claim to Divinity (v.6), the warning against needless fear (v.7), the abomination (v.14), trial (v.19), false prophets (v.22), the advent (v.26), the gathering (v. 27).[24]

Orchard stresses that the comparison between the Synoptic accounts and the Pauline shows that the same Greek words are used in the same sense and in similar contexts. Furthermore, some of these are extremely rare expressions, as has been indicated. He argues that when different authors are found using "the same rare words and the same common words in the same contexts", "it is necessary to admit. . .some kind of literary dependence".[25] We think this conclusion is a non sequitur.[26] The phenomena certainly point to an original source from which both the ideas and words have sprung, but that source need not necessarily be literary. Almost certainly, the source in question is that of the oral tradition which circulated in the early church.[27] Christ's words regarding the last things made a deep impression on his contemporaries, and were often repeated. Written accounts also probably existed, such as Mk. 13 which may first have circulated at the time of the Caligula crisis.

Paul speaks of his use of traditions in his missionary work. What he passed on to others he claimed to have himself received.[28] Thus his letters frequently contain reminders of what he has already taught those to whom he writes. Well-established traditions in the Christian community, traditions going back to Christ and the apostles, frequently find their elaboration in

199

the letters of the New Testament.[29]

<u>Relationship between the βδέλυγμα τῆς ἐρημώσεως and</u>
<u>ὁ ἄνθρωπος τῆς ἀνομίας[30]</u>

At this point, we are concerned with the relationship between
the βδέλυγμα τῆς ἐρημώσεως and its apparent parallel in
2 Thess. 2. The similarities are as follows:

The βδέλυγμα τῆς ἐρημώσεως appears in a discourse which
has as its theme the end of the age and the Parousia of Christ.

It is associated with a time of lawlessness and apostasy, of
false claims supported by miracles, and a time of special
testing for the elect through supernatural manifestations just
prior to the return of the Lord.

The βδέλυγμα τῆς ἐρημώσεως is to be manifested in "the holy
place" where "it ought not to be". It constitutes a key sign
of the impending end, and comes as a judgment upon those
who have rejected the gospel.

Judging by its O.T. counterpart, the βδέλυγμα τῆς ἐρημώσεως
consists of a power that is proud, blasphemous, and outrageously
ambitious, arrogating to itself the position of deity.[31] Its
supremacy is short-lived, and its success is the signal for its
doom. It "comes to its end" with time itself, as a prelude to
the setting up of the kingdom of God.

Turning now to 2 Thess.:

The ἄνθρωπος τῆς ἀνομίας appears in a pericope devoted to
a discussion of the end of the Age and the Parousia of Christ.

He is represented as being lawlessness incarnate, and
epitomizes apostasy. His manifestation takes place at the end of
time, and is associated with false claims supported by signs
and wonders.

He takes his seat in the temple of God.

This culminating apostasy is the certain sign that the day of
the Lord has dawned, and the ἄνθρωπος τῆς ἀνομίας like the
βδέλυγμα τῆς ἐρημώσεως is a judgment upon those who have
rejected the gospel.

The ἄνθρωπος τῆς ἀνομίας displays himself as God,
manifesting a proud, blasphemous attitude against all other
objects of reverential regard.

His supremacy is short-lived, for his manifestation is quickly followed by the coming of Christ and subsequent doom.

Both the Olivet discourse and the Thessalonian epistle draw heavily from Daniel for their presentation, and this helps to explain why the same things are represented of each power. When it is remembered that this series of parallels between one part of the eschatological discourse and 2 Thess. 2 is but a fragment of the overall parallelism, the case for equating the βδέλυγμα τῆς ἐρημώσεως with ὁ ἄνθρωπος τῆς ἀνομίας is almost overwhelmingly complete. Thus the denials of some scholars such as Carrington are incomprehensible.[32] We believe it is beyond successful refutation that, the βδέλυγμα τῆς ἐρημώσεως standing in the holy place, and the ἄνθρωπος τῆς ἀνομίας sitting in the temple of God, on one level of interpretation at least, point to the same phenomenon. For this reason, some exegesis of 2 Thess. 2 is necessary in order that whatever is implicit in the parallel might find further elucidation.

The key-terms of the pericope will now be considered. Despite the inadequacy of available explanations, in view of the unsuccessful nature of recent innovations in this regard, there will be no attempt at extreme originality. Nevertheless, as regards the κατέχων some suggestions have been hazarded which embody well-known positions, but this time in a Gestalt which we have not seen elsewhere. If the latter has any worth, each element grows in separate significance, and the whole in luminosity.[33]

ἡ ἀποστασία

Is this to be understood as a Jewish apostasy, a Christian dereliction, or as descriptive of a world in revolt against its Maker? Possibly the most significant piece of evidence available for the formulation of a conclusion is that Paul does not set about to give any special explanation, but proceeds on the basis that all he continues to say is pertinent to his initial reference. In the verses that follow, the apostasy is not given any independent part. Rather, it is the characteristics and behaviour of the lawless one which occupy the picture.[34] Therefore, one should not attempt to distinguish the apostasy sharply from the revelation of the great rebel. The latter is mentioned in the same breath as the former. His being revealed (ἀποκαλυφθῇ) parallels to some extent the fact that the apostasy comes (ἔλθῃ).

The word itself always signifies religious revolt, so far as the Scriptures are concerned.[35] This is true of both Testaments. The classical usage referring to political defection is absent from the Bible. However, the present reference is an excellent example of the principle that a word must be given significance according to its setting, and not only according to etymology, or common usage. The setting here is undoubtedly that of a culminating, world-wide rebellion of mankind against God. Paul is not thinking primarily of Jewish apostasy. That event had already happened and the apostle prefers to speak of their misplaced zeal than to use the present term.[36] He yet had hopes for many of his race. Neither does Paul proceed to reflect upon Christian apostasy, although such could be included in his view as a contributory or minor feature. At the time at which he wrote there was little indication of any large-scale Christian defection, and in these present letters he congratulates the Thessalonians on their fidelity. But what we do find in this passage is a description of the maturing of evil, and its final blossoming so as to fill the world stage. Satan's climactic effort to defeat God by seducing the majority of the race by signs and wonders is dramatically sketched. The result is to be a separation of all men into two groups, those perishing, and those being saved. Finally comes the reference to judgment, ἵνα κριθῶσιν πάντες . . . . Thus ἡ ἀποστασία in this context denotes, "a wide-spread and violent defiance of the authority of God."[37] This rebellion is to be fostered by miraculous signs authenticating error, resulting in false worship and idolatry.

A key factor in interpreting the apostasy is the description given of the lawless one. His characteristic is also the characteristic of the apostasy which he epitomizes. Ἀνομία includes transgression of divine precepts, but it is fundamentally rebellion against God. Its primary meaning is not the legal sense, but rather "an active personal hostility more malicious than the transgression of a norm of action."[38] Furthermore this term has cosmic scope as the classic Qumran text cited by Rigaux testifies.[39] Thus the basic nature of the apostasy finds its key in the nature of the great rebel here described.

Another important key to interpreting this apostasy is the contrast afforded it in the context by the mystery of lawlessness which ἤδη ἐνεργεῖται. Paul here implies that prior to the final crisis evil is at work in hidden form.[40] This is not to say that it does not ever become flagrant, but rather that in general it is characterized by subtlety and underhand activity. However, that which at present is veiled is soon to be manifested openly. With the man of lawlessness will come a violent upsurge of unrighteousness. No longer will it be cloaked or restrained.[41]

Most of what Paul has to say, or has already said in person, to the Thessalonians has its seed form in some λόγος κυρίου.

The eschatological discourse had forecast the time when lawlessness would be multiplied.[42] This event would be associated with
the working of false prophets.[43] Neither did this picture have
its origin with Christ. The Old Testament apocalypse, Daniel,
and pseudepigraphical writings, testified to the same. According
to the former, a king of bold countenance would arise at a time
when "the transgressors" would have "reached their full measure".[44]
Apocryphal writings, produced just before and just after the
beginning of the Christian era, amplify Daniel's allusions to
apostasy.[45] Ethiopic Enoch pictures world-wide anarchy and
distress as characterizing the time of the end. The earth is to
be filled with blood, the heavenly orbs will be worshipped and
the Creator abandoned. Sin, injustice, blasphemy, violence in
all its forms, apostasy and transgression will abound.[46] In IV
Esdras the portrayal is similar. The inhabitants of the earth
are to be seized with a great panic, truth will be hidden and the
earth deprived of faith. Then "iniquity will increase above that
which you see now, and that which you have understood for a long
time."[47]

Long before Daniel and the later pseudepigraphical writings,
however, the concept of a final rebellion is to be found in the
prophets. Gog and his hosts, even all nations, would make war
on God by attacking His people Israel.[48] Later New Testament
statements point to the same belief. At Armageddon the nations
of the earth have their rendezvous with God. They are pictured
as gathered to make war on the Warrior who rides forth from
heaven.[49] And even beyond this point, after the millennium the
same scene reoccurs with Satan in the van leading Gog's rebel
armies against the holy city.[50]

It is no wonder, then, that we find the article with
ἀποστασία. The event of which Paul speaks is familiar to the
Thessalonians, both because of his own instruction, and because
Jews and Gentiles alike already possessed legends of just such a
climax to history.

The preceding discussion of the ἡ ἀποστασία has relevance
for all that follows. If this understanding is a correct one, we
are already partly on the way towards discovering the identity of
ὁ ἄνθρωπος τῆς ἀνομίας, the nature of the ναός as well as the
significance of τὸ κατέχον. These terms represent elements
in the unified presentation of the apostle's picture. The
accuracy of each definition finds part of its testing in the
relevance of that definition to the related ones. Therefore, we
close with a summary of what has preceded, intending thereby an
introduction to what follows.

By ἡ ἀποστασία Paul points to an eschatological rebellion
anticipated by the early Christians. It comprehends a world-wide

revolt against God, His gospel, and His law. It marks the rejection of Christian preaching, and the acceptance instead of another gospel, even "the lie" offered by the man of lawlessness. This embracing of a false gospel leads to a false worship of a pseudo-God. Instead of the fruit of the Spirit, the authenticating signs of the new gospel will be miraculous wonders performed with "all power". The key terms of this passage such as ἀνομία, ἀποκαλυφθήσεται, ἀπωλείας point to the nature, time, and issue of the rebellion. At its heart is the man of lawlessness who enshrines in himself the self-idolatry, blasphemy, and hostility of the apostasy. His deceptions bring mankind to the test, separating the sheep from the goats, and pave the way for the Judgment.[51] The rebellion will be short-lived, for the height of blasphemy brings the true Christ, Whose very presence suffices to annul all opposition, and to destroy the Pretender. This presentation by Paul finds further illustration to the last apocalypse, where, according to most exegetes, the final rebellion finds its most detailed, though symbolic, description.

ὁ ἄνθρωπος τῆς ἀνομίας

Paul now characterizes a well-known figure. Four times he uses the article in four descriptive phrases. ὁ ἄνθρωπος τῆς ἀνομίας, ὁ υἱὸς τῆς 'ἀπωλείας, ὁ ἀντικείμενος κ.τ.λ., ὁ ἄνομος. The ἄνθρωπος τῆς ἀνομίας and ὁ υἱὸς τῆς ἀπωλείας are Semitic in character, and not used by Paul elsewhere. Two of the four expressions are equivalent, ὁ υἱος τῆς ἀπωλείας and ὁ ἄνομος and they, as well as the other two, connote rebellion, anarchy and ruin. As Satan himself is the original rebel and destroyer, so this final representative of his is an opposer or adversary, and is not only himself destined for destruction but lures οἱ ἀπολλύμενοι to the same fate. As with Lucifer of old, this being also desires to "sit on the mount of assembly" making himself "like the Most High", but he will be brought down "to the depths of the Pit."[52] His session in the temple of God is succeeded by his dissolution at Christ's Parousia. Thus, in remarkably small compass Paul has sketched one in the likeness of the Prince of evil. It is difficult to conceive how any literary artist purposing to represent a coming one as patterning after Satan could have improved the picture.

The literary marvel is magnified as we recognize that there is also another likeness incorporated into the same portrait. This figure not only resembles Diabolus but also Prince Emmanuel. He is a parody of Christ, with an unveiling, a parousia, a fixed appointed time, possessing power to work signs and wonders, and claiming worship. Either Paul anticipates John, or John copies Paul, but the Antichrist is sketched by both as a counterfeit of the true Messiah.[53]

204

This matter of parody, or counterfeit, is probably implicit
in the initial term used by Paul. The phrase ὁ ἄνθρωπος τῆς
ἀνομίας is a literary parallel to the expression "the man of God"
The Septuagint uses ἄνθρωπος τοῦ θεοῦ over sixty times as a
technical term designating a prophet. The term ἀνήρ is never
used with a defining genitive to express the thought of prophet,
and ἄνθρωπος elsewhere is only used rarely with the genitive.
Thus, as Giblin says, "we wonder whether a NT author like Paul,
who was certainly perfectly familiar with the LXX, could have
used ἄνθρωπος + genitive (with the article) without having
in mind the notion: 'Man of God'."[54] Therefore what we have in
2 Thess. 2 is an allusion to one who copies God's Man, but who
is in fact, the very opposite. Rigaux speaks similarly to
Giblin when he suggests that "L'Antéchrist paulinien fait figure
de prophète, d'instaurateur d'une religion, par prédication
et miracles."[55]

The phenomena referred to give us our best clues relative to
the time, nature and work of this Antichrist. If he is a counterfeit of Christ, like Him he must be a single individual. If he
is to be unveiled by a parousia in glory, and is then obliterated
by the coming of the real Christ, his time of manifestation is
limited to the last of the last days. "Ce signe n'est pas
un signe, qui une fois produit pourra ne pas avoir pour suite
la venue du Seigneur, car cette parousie de l'Antéchrist est
presentée comme directement en rapport avec la parousie de
Jésus."[56]

Thus, in the setting of 2 Thess. 2, Antichrist is an individual
to be manifested at the end of time.[56a] His parousia is a sign that
the end has come. Therefore, any interpretation which applies
this passage to an individual of past history, or to a succession
of such, misses the mark. Similarly, it must be affirmed that
all modern interpretations which make the apostle's words to
signify generic evil or some such can hardly be said to be
exegetical in the true sense of that word. The views thereby
expressed may themselves be accurate, but they do not set forth
the natural significance of Paul's statements. Rather they
represent concessions to our own 20th century Weltanschauung.[57]
Let us rather seek in this study to find Paul's own concept, and
to that end we will now enquire regardng his sources.

Most of the early studies on 2 Thess. 2 written in the
beginning years of this century refer to two epoch-making books.
They are Schöpfung und Chaos (1895) by H. Gunkel, and Der
Antichrist in der Überlieferung des Judenthums, des Neuen
Testamentes, und der alten Kirche by W. Bousset, published in the
same year. The former work asserts that the roots of the Jewish
Antichrist doctrine are to be found in the primitive Babylonian
dragon myth regarding the conflict between the chaos monster

Tiamat and the Creator Marduk. Bousset expresses similar views, after working along independent lines, but he is more cautious in his use of the ancient Babylonian myths than Gunkel. The evidence indicates that such legends were familiar to the Jews in Old Testament times, but many scholars have come to think that their influence has been exaggerated. As regards ὁ ἄνομος Bousset asserts that this term is the equivalent of Belial (otherwise occurring as Beliar, Belian, Beliab, Belias, Belier, Belchor), familiar to apocryphal and pseudepigraphical works. All the assumptions of the religionsgeschichtliche school are implicit in this position. To Bousset, the descriptions of Antichrist found in the eschatological commentaries of Iranaeus, Hippolytus, and other patristic writers, must spring from non-biblical sources rather than from their own meditation upon the scriptural data.[58]

The word for Beliar occurs often in the Old Testament,[59] but it is never the case that it applies as a name directly given to a person. Rather it is linked with prefixes in such a way as to give an evil connotation to persons or things.[60] The situation however, is quite different in the non-canonical Jewish writings. These became familiar to scholars in the 18th and 19th centuries, and particularly through the diligence of R.H. Charles the large reservoir of such materials was made available for the buckets or thimbles of commentators. Qumran has now added to the store. Immediately the belief in the essential identity and continuity of all Oriental religion made the myth of the contest between Marduk and the Chaos-dragon a probably origin for the Antichrist myth.

In the period between the Old and the New Testaments, the already existing belief of the Jews in an eschatological God-opposing power[61] burgeoned through the influence of the Beliar-myth. Later pseudepigraphical literature shows that a demonizing process affected the earlier belief till the title of Beliar became a synonym for Satan or one of his chief representatives. The question is, how much of the New Testament picture of Antichrist springs from non-canonical sources? Many today agree with the conclusions reached by Geerhardus Vos of Princeton over forty years ago. He wrote:

> This recurrence upon the apocalyptic and pseudepigraphi-
> cal literature to discover the antecedents of the Antichrist
> figure does not carry much convincing force. Of course,
> it cannot a priori be denied that an amount of supersti-
> tious folklore was current in Jewish circles before the
> Pauline epistles were written. Only that these current
> beliefs of such gross and rudimentary form were the
> source from which the N.T. Antichrist doctrine was drawn
> and from which it can be satisfactorily explained is hard

to believe.[62]

Mere assertion, such as this by Vos, is not enough to settle the question. We must ask concerning the verbal relationships of Paul's words. 'Are these to be found paralleling canonical or non-canonical sources?' The answer is obvious to all who have closely studied that ancient apocalypse which proved so influential upon the Jewish milieu of the first century. The key features of Paul's description of the great adversary are drawn from the book of Daniel. They can be listed as follows:

"The man of lawlessness", cf. Dan. 7:25; 8:25; 11:36-37;
"The son of perdition", cf. Dan. 7:11,26; 8:25;11:45;
"who opposes and exalts himself against every so-called god. . . ." cf. Dan. 7:8,20,25; 8:4,10,11,23-25; 11:36-39;
"he takes his seat in the temple of God. . . ." cf. Dan. 8:9-14; 9:26-27; 11:31,45.

Other scriptures alluded to by this passage from 2 Thess. 2 include Isa. 14:13-15, Eze. 28:2,8, and Deut. 13:1-3. Undoubtedly there are also other less obvious allusions, but the ones already listed are undeniably related. Vos is correct in saying that "No clearly traceable and safe road leads back into the past to discover the man-of-sin concept except that via the prophecy of Daniel."[63]

The reason for Paul's use of the passages from Daniel is not difficult to find. His predecessors and contemporaries firmly believed that Antiochus Ephiphanes, the adversary sketched in Daniel, was the type or symbol of a God-opposing figure yet to come. Christ Himself had endorsed this concept in His eschatological discourse, and Paul claimed that his own views of the end were derived from "the word of the Lord."[64] While Bousset assumed that "the distinctly apocalyptic part" of Christ's Olivet sermon was "a fragment of foreign origin", others already listed[65] believe with H.A.A. Kennedy that this view of Bousset's "is an assumption which we have already seen grave reasons to doubt."[66] And while Bousset used 2 Thess. 2 to explain Matt. 24, Kennedy, on the contrary, declared that "it seems much more probable. . .that echoes of a genuine tradition of Jesus' words are to be found in the statements of St. Paul."[67]

So far in our study of Paul's man of lawlessness we have found that he parallels both Satan and Christ, and that the terms descriptive of his activities are drawn primarily from Old Testament sources. The evidence indicates that long before Beliar became a popular figure in non-canonical writings, the notion of a mighty eschatological opponent of Yahweh and His people existed. Ps. 2; Eze.38-39; Joel 3; Zech. 14; as well as "Daniel the prophet"[68] testify to this.

We have noticed also that the lawless one appears only at the
end of time. Not only his parody of Christ indicates this, but
the whole context of the passage. He is the center of
ἡ ἀποστασια and the time-location of this phenomenon automatically limits his own chronological possibilities. ". . . the
ἀποστασία implies the separation of the good and the wicked,
the ultimate divergence of two opposed lines of development[69]. ."
The fact that he is to be "revealed" could not but remind the
first readers that the same term had just been used of the
coming advent of Christ.[70]

Next we would enquire as to the particular nature of the
"lawlessness" to be manifested by this being, and whether,
as most commentators suggest, he is to be considered as a member
of the human species. One striking impression received as one
reads Paul here is that this godless character he is presenting
is ascetic in nature. There are no hints of any sins of the
flesh. His are the sins of the spirit. To illustrate, a zealous
Christian on the basis of Scripture could accuse the devil of
craft, envy, pride, blasphemy and the like, but not of gluttony,
impurity, or sloth. The present case seems similar. At this
point we are reminded of what has already been stated, that
ἀνομία points more to rebellion than the transgression of some
norm. The lawless one is primarily a rebel against his Maker,
rather than a criminal or profligate. His particular fault lies
in his self-deification. In 2 Thess. 2 we seem to have arrived
at the opposite pole to Genesis 3![71] There the desire to be as
God was indulged lightly, but here that particular sin has
burgeoned and flowered. It seems that Paul is saying that the
response of faith and the response of disbelief are finally to
issue in the purest form of the true cult of God, and the
contrasting idolatrous cult of self at its worst.[72]

Not the least puzzling of the verses in this chapter is v.4
with its reference concerning the Antichrist that "he takes his
seat in the temple of God, proclaiming himself to be God." The
meaning of ναός here is much debated. As Findlay points out,
more literally this passage runs "so that he in the temple of
God takes his seat, showing off himself, to the effect that
he is God."[73] This implies a formal claim to occupy the central
seat in men's minds which belongs to God alone. Ἀποδείκνυμι
literally means to "show off", or "exhibit". It is of frequent
occurrence in later Greek, and there means "nominate" or
"proclaim".[74] As Frame declares, "The session in the sanctuary
of God is tantamount to the assumption of divine honours."[75]
The purpose of the powerful display of signs and wonders is to
substantiate his claim to deity.[76] It may also be implied that
his exalting of himself against God will involve his legislating
of decrees which will be an attempt "to change the times and the
law" of Yahweh.[77] His own religion must be distinguished from
that of the One against whom he rebels, and counterfeits of

divine institutions are to be expected. So much for the work of "the man of lawlessness" but what of his nature? Is he really a man, and only a man?

Most commentators reply with a "yes" to this enquiry. Others admit that a complete parody would involve the incarnation of evil in the same way that Jesus was the incarnation of goodness. This would involve his "father" being Satan, as Christ's Father was God.[78]

The use of ἄνθρωπος in this regard need only show that this being **appears** as man. The Old Testament frequently uses "man" for spiritual beings.[79] Furthermore, we have noted above that his sinfulness by no means smacks of physical, bodily indulgence. It is certainly the sins of spirit which are brought to view. Again he is spoken of as being "revealed", almost as though implying that he already existed but was not yet manifested. This implication is certainly not compulsive, but should be taken into account. Far more significant is the concentration of power invested in this personage. He works with πάσῃ δυνάμει To Paul and his contemporaries, it would have appeared much more likely that Satan would manifest himself through spirit beings in various places as an angel of light, than that Antichrist would be merely a fellow human.[80] The writer of the Apocalypse expected the manifestation of Antichrist in the form of "demonic spirits, performing signs" going "abroad to the kings of the whole world, to assemble them for battle on the great day of God the Almighty."[81] The best that moderns could do in expressing such ideas would be to press into service such "catch-alls" as the word "Spiritism".[82]

Opinion may never be uniform on the matter of the exact nature of the being contemplated by Paul, but as we have seen, some important factors regarding him are quite clear. He is an eschatological personage, in character and power similar to Satan, but in work he endeavours to parody Christ. His basic lawlessness lies in his self-deification. To this end he endeavours to authenticate his own system of worship by means of miracles.

We have also noticed that many things can be said with certainty regarding what Antichrist is not. He is not any past personage.[83] He belongs to the future and not to history, although figures from history such as Antiochus and Caligula may have influenced Paul's description. He is not a Jewish pseudo-messiah, or a Jewish antichrist.[84] Jewish misdirected zeal might lead to persecution of the true representatives of Yahweh, but it is difficult to see how Judaism could ever acknowledge opposition to Yahweh, or countenance violation of His temple. Neither is there any validation for the claim that the Antichrist

is primarily a political tyrant.[85] Despite the events of 40-41
A.D., Paul "situe nettement l'impie dans le domaine religieux".[86]
The absence of political specifications is even more striking in
view of the fact that both in Daniel and the pseudpigrapha, the
Antichrist bears the colours of a political oppressor. And
lastly, Antichrist is not a power that exalts itself against God
by denying the supernatural. He is not related to present-day
atheists who, in terms of the history of the world, are a
comparatively recent phenomenon. Rather we find him "proclaiming
himself to be God".

One other thing should be said concerning the relationship
between the eschatological discourse and our present passage.
The latter presents "as a single phenomenon what the eschatological discourse divides into three."[87] Those who possessed
only the Gospels would anticipate in the future that some would
come saying, "I am." They would also expect the advent of
"the abomination of desolation" and then the appearance of
miracle-working false prophets. Paul seems to unite the three.
After studying both his presentation and that of the Synoptic
writers, a first century Christian could have drawn the
conclusion that the anticipatory phenomena associated with the
fall of Jerusalem was to be shortly re-enacted on a vaster scale.
The writer of the Apocalypse was one such Christian, who incorporated the distinguishing elements of the end offered by Christ
and Paul and applied them on a global scale.[88] A final period
of tribulation and testing, great apostasy, supernatural signs
and wonders, and an idolatrous Antichrist, [89] characterize New
Testament eschatology from first to last.

ὁ ναός

To what does Paul here refer? Does he intend the reader to
think of Jerusalem's present temple, or an eschatological temple,
or the heavenly temple, or the Christian church, or. . . .?

He does not speak of ἱερόν but of ναός. Thus it is not an
entire temple complex that is alluded to, but an inner shrine.
Furthermore, the repeated article points to a temple well-known.
In view of the apostle's use of the βδέλυγμα τῆς ἐρημώσεως
passages in Daniel, and the parallel in Mk. 13:14, it is clear
that the temple at Jerusalem is once more in focus. This would
not necessitate, however, that Paul employs the well-known site
in a literal sense. It could in this setting be a metaphor.[90]
His rather contemptuous reference to the existing Jerusalem
in Galatians 4:25, and his neglect of that place elsewhere in
his writings, argues for the case that Jerusalem's temple is not
his real concern in 2 Thess. 2.[91] Neither does the eschatological temple concept, based on a peculiar interpretation of
Eze. chs. 40-48, find countenance anywhere in the Pauline

corpus.

Neil assumes that it is "not likely that the actual Temple at Jerusalem is in Paul's mind at all, but that he is thinking rather in the sense of Ps. xi.5. . .of the Temple of God in heaven".[92] But there is nothing in the context to support this assumption. On the contrary, the context affords the strongest arguments against this position. The ἄνομος functions on earth. There he claims to be God and seeks the homage of all men, until those who have not earlier received the love of the truth now are infatuated by "the lie". He is destroyed on earth by the advent of Christ.

Paul's normal use of ναός is with reference to the Christian church.[93] In a bygone polemical era Protestants assumed this usage in 2 Thessalonians, and thereby found an effective club to batter the papal antichrist.[94] This view, however, ignored not only the eschatological setting of 2 Thess. 2, but also the truth that the Christian church must cease to be such once the Antichrist becomes its tenant.[95]

There is only one view which fully accommodates the context. The remainder of the sentence concerning the temple has too often been neglected by exegetes when expounding ὁ ναός It is this καθίσαι, ἀποδεικνύντα ἑαυτον ὅτι ἐστιν θεός which itself interprets the word in question. The temple session finds its equivalent in Antichrist's proclamation of Deity. This is his ἀποκάλυψις In other words, the whole section regarding the establishment in the temple is a poetical description of the usurpation of divine prerogatives generally.[96] It may well be that Paul has in mind not only the actions of Antiochus Epiphanes but also the threat of Caligula. But the central fact regarding both was their blasphemy, and it is this attitude which Paul projects to the end of Time, (not necessarily more distant than the fall of the temple), rather than the exact location affected by earlier profanities. C.J. Riggenbach sums the matter up admirably when he says: ". . . in colors of his own time, Paul depicts an act which, as a symbol of permanent spiritual significance, is confined to no locality, and means to say: He places himself in God's room, and forces himself on mankind as a Divine ruler."[97]

ὁ κατέχων

"Who now is the κατέχων is really the darkest point in the whole passage."[98] Most exegetes would agree with this judgment. Because of this obscurity it is correct to say, as does Giblin, that the κατέχων has become more famous than Antichrist himself.[99]

Right at the outset one is struck with a phenomenon found also in other esoteric portions of the New Testament. In Mk. 13;14 and in Rev. chs. 13 and 17, as well as in 2 Thess. 2, a power is referred to by use of both neuter and masculine terms. In two out of these three instances, the reader is called upon to exercise wisdom in order to rightly identify the entity depicted. And all acknowledge that that same wisdom is required for the third instance, the one now under our survey. Because these similarities may be only superficial they should not prejudice the issue of the present enquiry. Furthermore, in Mk. and in Rev. the power in question is viewed as one antagonistic to God, whereas in 2 Thess. most exegetes consider the κατέχων to be beneficient. But if we are warranted in extending this caveat, we are also justified in extending another, namely that the phenomenon of parallelism between the three sources should not be overlooked.

Until recently, the main positions held with reference to the κατέχων could be listed as follows: (1) the contemporary-historical view; (2) the traditional view; (3) the mythological view; (4) the "gospel" view. The first links the words of the apostle with contemporaries such as Caligula or Nero, seeing in the restrainer the predecessors or inhibitors of such "Antichrists". The second position holds that the Roman Empire is the κατέχων and the Emperor the κατέχων. The third view has been earlier alluded to, and is represented by the exegesis of Dibelius who sees ὁ κατέχων as some mythological spiritual being, restraining some equivalent of the chaos monster.[100] As for the fourth position it has been revived in modern times by Oscar Cullmann, and J. Munck.[101] These scholars believe that the necessity for the world-wide proclamation of the gospel is the restraining factor. About five years ago another interpretation was offered by Charles H. Giblin. This new view should not be linked with the other four as though it paralleled them in popularity or enduring nature, but because of its claim to displace alternative views, its elaborately argued presentation must be taken into account. Giblin applies the linguistic data differently to the majority of exegetes.[102] In particular he thinks of the κατέχων as a malevolent rather than beneficent entity. He sees in it a charismatic manifestation, a pseudo-prophetic gift, the exercise of which had produced an unruly element into the Thessalonian congregation. The ἄτακτοι are regarded as those adversely affected.[103]

As one reviews exegetical analyses of the κατέχων, one is tempted at times to think that the commentator sometimes reveals more about himself, his methods and his presuppositions, than about the hinderer, as opposing positions come under review. While some follow the humility of Augustine and reflect his wise caution, others have seized upon a particular interpretation with dogmatic certainty, and scorned alternatives. This is

212

particularly true of some who hold to the Roman Empire as the restraining power, and of some who categorically reject that idea. Giblin says of the traditional view (he calls it the historical or political opinion, a nomenclature which is just as appropriate as the alternative) that "in quite recent times no one has maintained it enthusiastically or even very seriously."[104] Beare has asserted that this position (the traditional one) is "nothing more than a conjecture and one that will not stand up under scrutiny."[105] And Gunkel much earlier claimed that the solution by recourse to the empire is so arbitrary that it escapes refutation."[106] Some who cherish the scorned viewpoint will feel that such summary rejections are arbitrary and evince unfounded prejudice. Others will feel that the judgments in question merely state the obvious, despite the appraisal of those who, like Milligan, claim that the Empire view has "won the support of the great majority of ancient and modern scholars."[107]

Those who hold to the zeitgeschichtliche hypothesis usually place the great Rebel and his restrainer within the same circle. Thus Claudius could be the κατέχων of Nero, and the Proconsul Vitellius of Caligula. Others have seen in Nero the κατέχων of Titus. All such views founder on the rock of fact earlier mentioned, namely that the discussion of Paul's has to do with the maturing of evil at the end of time, and not with any lesser crisis.[108] While Paul undoubtedly believed that the End could come in his day, he likewise must have believed that the final throes of Satan would cause more "fireworks" than Caligula or Titus. At the time Paul wrote, Caligula was ten years in the past, and Nero and Titus yet in the future. The apostle also is picturing events essentially religious rather than political. Few modern commentators have recourse to what we have here called the contemporary-historical view (not to be confused with the traditional view, though contemporary history is likewise there envisaged, but on a vaster scale).[109]

A large number of exegetes believe that the mythological school, best represented by Dibelius, holds the key to the present passage. Thus Neil can write that "there is much to be said in favour of looking for the clue to the restraining power, not in history, but in some kind of theological or even mythological speculation."[110] He adds, "The 'restraining power' is therefore probably supernatural. The Lawless One is held in check meantime by some angelic power appointed by God."[111] Leon Morris, on the other hand, says about this explanation, "there seems no point in postulating this as the solution to our problem."[112] Frame, reviewing the various hypotheses summarizes his own stance by concluding: "This brief review of conjectures only serves to emphasize the fact that we do not know what Paul had in mind, whether the Roman Empire, or a supernatural being that keeps the Anomos in detention. . .or something else quite

different."113 Rigaux seems closer to Dibelius than to other
commentators, but he refuses to pronounce a definite conclusion.
In sympathy with Augustine's position of agnosticism he confesses
"Nous nous avouons incapable de découvrir en quoi elle consiste."114
Thus, a review of recent commentators upon Thessalonians shows
that the mythological view, though better supported than the
zeitgeschichtliche hypotheses, is still expressed with a stammer-
ing tongue. The note of certainty is absent from most exegetes
who vouchsafe space to it.

The traditional view that the Roman Empire constituted the
hindrance should not be dismissed as summarily as is done by
most of its critics. Its supporters are significant in quality
and quantity, and therefore the same is probably true of the
arguments employed. Some, arguing from apologetical prejudice
rather than from exegetical grounds, point out that the Roman
Empire has gone, and that Antichrist is still not with us. We
reject this type of argumentation. The simplest answer to
such a prejudiced exegesis would be to say with Neil, "Paul was
mistaken."115 Rather than deciding from the testimony of the
centuries, we must decide from the words of the passage itself.
Did Paul have the Roman Empire in mind? This is the first
question. Whether he was right or wrong lies outside our purview.

Rigaux is more to the point when he criticizes the Empire view
by declaring "La pensée de l'apôtre n'est pas politique ni
historique: elle est théologique et eschatologique."116

To dispose of the opinion in question, we will need to be more
precise than with the first two hypotheses. The most obvious
question must be asked in this connection, though its yields
are not demonstrative. What is the meaning, that is, the literal
meaning of κατέχων? Obviously it would be presumptuous of the
present writer to endeavour to gild or contradict the philological researches of scholars such as Milligan, Hanse and
Rigaux in this connection.117 Giblin has essayed the case of
κατέχων meaning "to seize", intending a type of demonic-
possession in the instance of certain of the Thessalonians. It
is true that some scholars have called for renewed investigation
to determine whether the traditional meaning of "restrain" is
the most accurate determination of the term in question in
2 Thess. 2.118 On the other hand, reviewers of Giblin have
noticed that his contention largely depends on what he elsewhere
says about the ἄτακτοι.

The defence of the belief that a false prophetic ecstasy at
Thessalonica provoked Paul's passage about the Antichrist and
the κατέχων is at best tenuous, and therefore the nuance of
meaning which Giblin wishes to attribute to the key term is
likewise only a possibility and by no means a probability. There

are many good things in Giblin's study of 2 Thess. 2, but we would not rank his exegesis of vv. 6-7 among these. The disorderly ones rebuked by the apostle were not necessarily those who had been seized by some experience analogous to prophets of the cult of Dionysus. And this being the case, the evidence is not conclusive enough to warrant rejecting the majority interpretation of κατέχων as meaning in 2 Thess. 2:6 "to restrain."

Two other grammatical and exegetical issues pertinent to the κατέχων should be at least mentioned. Fifty years ago, N.F. Freese suggested that the revelation spoken of in v.6 could be that of Christ's own coming, and that therefore the ταῦτα was the Antichrist. His faulty grammatical arguments led to Rigaux's almost contemptuous dismissal of his position.[119] The case for the restrainer being the Antichrist has never know much favour. A second issue is whether the hindering power is to be understood as included in the ταῦτα referred to in v. 5. That is, can we be certain that Paul had included this mysterious figure in his eschatological instruction of the new converts at Thessalonica? Rigaux differs from Bornemann, Milligan, Frame, and Dibelius in this matter, and sides with Hilgenfeld and von Döbschutz. With considerable hesitation (which he acknowledges), Rigaux supposes that the hindering power is an entity concerning which Paul had not previously spoken.[120] In this instance we feel that Giblin is correct when he argues that one has a right "to presume that το κατέχων is somehow related to ταῦτα provided subsequent study of the κατέχων and its relation to others elements explicitly contained under may be expected to bear out one's hypothesis."[121] In reply to Rigaux and von Döbschutz et al., we would argue that regardless of how one construes the temporal or logical meaning of νῦν in v. 6, and irrespective of the words in the passage to which we wish to relate it, the vital fact is, that apart from the debatable usage of this one word, there is no hint that Paul is for the first time making mention of a highly significant yet unknown entity. The entire tenor of the pericope implies that the Thessalonians were familiar with both the Antichrist and Hinderer concepts, and that therefore Paul now needs only to allude to these.[122]

Our digression on the philological significance of κατέχων leads us to agree with Rigaux that such an examination yields nothing which is absolutely demonstrative for any exegetical position.[123] Therefore on linguistic grounds alone, we can neither endorse nor repudiate the viewpoint that sees in the Roman Empire the hinderer.

The usual evidence for seeing in the Empire the κατέχων and the Emperor as the κατέχων consists of (1) The secrecy

215

surrounding the allusions, (2) the double description, as of a power invested in a person, (3) the understanding of Daniel's fourth beast as the Roman Empire. According to the seer, the blasphemous little horn (Antichrist) would come into prominence in connection with the "dreadful and terrible" kingdom. (4) Paul himself had found in the Roman magistracy an "unfailing refuge against Jewish malice and persecution."[124] Both Acts and the Epistles testify to this. "Could anything be more intelligible than that St Paul should see in this impartial State the main bulwark against the forces of injustice and impiety which menaced his work at every turn?"[125] But the conviction did not belong to the apostle alone. Bousset reminds us that: "The mention of one distinct premonitory sign occurs in nearly all the sources. The end is at hand when the Roman Empire perishes."[126]

The greatest difficulty usually offered against this position is the one already referred to in the criticism by Rigaux. Paul is not in the habit of making political references. If the Empire interpretation is correct, then it constitutes the only political reference in Paul's apocalyptic utterances as a whole. As Frame says, "a theory which is not open to this objection would be distinctly preferable."[127]

We now proceed to offer such a theory. To rest content with the "something somewhere"[128] offered by many exegetes may be a course of wisdom but it could possibly spring from lesser causes. With this suspicion we tentatively make some observations.

The pericope itself offers some characteristics of the entity we seek. (1) It is a <u>present</u> force. κατέχων is a present participle, thus the obstacle was already a barrier at the time Paul was writing. (2) It is a <u>beneficent</u> force. The κατέχων restrains the full burgeoning of the mystery of iniquity into the Antichrist. It is the removal or withdrawal of this beneficent power from the midst that enables Satan to lead his representative to success. (3) Thus on the principle of opposites, it would seem that this power is itself in harmony with the government of God. It is a <u>law-abiding</u> force, and <u>law-upholding</u>, in contrast to the lawless one. It is ἔννομος rather than ἄνομος. (4) This power has <u>a divine time-mission</u>. As Antichrist is to be revealed "in his time", so will the hinderer hinder till his time has been fulfilled. (5) It is a power that <u>actively withdraws</u>, rather than one which is passively acted upon. There is no hint that it is to meet with any fate similar to that of the Antichrist. It is neither to be "consumed" or "destroyed". It is merely moved out of the midst.[129] (6) This power <u>spans the ages</u>, from the beginning of time to the end. We would emphasize a truth which most commentators fail to give adequate attention and weight. It is implied throughout this passage that the eschatological rebellion

216

is Satan's crowning effort. It is his master-plan, or so thinks
the apostle, and it is his mind that we seek to represent. This
ultimate rebellion, with its dramatic claim to deity by the
lawless one masquerading as Lord of the divine temple, has not
been postponed willingly from age to age by the great Adversary.
Rather he has been foiled by God's power, the hinderer, and it
has been so from the beginning. There are no grounds for
believing that the Rebellion has just been conceived in Paul's
time by Satan, and therefore there are no grounds for believing
that the hindrance and hinderer belong only to Paul's
yesterday. There is every reason for understanding the passage
as teaching that for as long as there has been a Satan active
upn the inhabitants of this globe, just so long has his key-
weapon, the Antichrist, been restrained by God's opposing
agency. We should look for an entity whose existence at least
measures with the existence of evil itself. We submit that this
has not been taken fully into account in the study of this
problem. (7) We add a seventh, not merely to fit in with the
thinking of Paul's time, but because the facts demand it. This
power, of necessity, must be an <u>extraordinarily great and mighty</u>
one, if it is able to withstand a being supernaturally endowed.
A feather could crush a mosquito, but if we wish to
exterminate Hiroshima we use something of greater proportions.
What alone could withstand the one whom Paul believed to be
"the prince of the power of the air", a wicked spirit from the
heavenly places, who could send storm and tempest, and destroy
with no boundary other than the permitted will of God?

Of lesser importance than any of the preceding is yet another
characteristic which should be kept in mind. This power, or the
sphere of its operations, can only be discussed with reserve.[130]
Had Paul merely meant his own ministry, or the proclamation of
the gospel, or the influence of the Holy Spirit, it is not
apparent why he could not have said so plainly. As mentioned at
the beginning of our discussion of the κατέχων, this feature is
something which is shared with other esoteric passages of the New
Testament. However, while the κατέχων is referred to with
mystery, and is applied both to a power and seemingly to a
person, as is the case with the βδέλυγμα τῆς ἐρημώσεως
of Mk. 13:14, a great difference also confronts us. The κατέχων
is benign, while the entity of Mk. 13:14 is malign. Thus the
vagueness with which the apostle speaks in this instance suggests
that the entity concerned probably has political connotations.

Does any single theory reconcile all these characteristics
suggested by 2 Thess. 2? Certainly, the Roman Empire was both
present and benign. It was also law-upholding, and it could be
said that in God's providence it has a specific time-mission.
Likewise if Paul intended to refer to its passing, it is
obvious why he is purposely restrained in his description of the

restrainer.131 But the Roman Empire, it seems to us, does not comply with specifications six and seven. Compared with the ages Paul would have attributed to Satan, Rome was only of yesterday. And compared with the might of one who had stood by the throne of God, even the mighty Roman Empire paled into insignificance. Furthermore, the most obvious of all questions is to ask "in what sense could the Empire hinder the appearance of Antichrist?" "Why could not the Antichrist successfully venture on the scene during the reign of the Emperors?" It does not seem enough to answer that in the book of God's providence, Rome filled the last sheet prior to the page of Antichrist. There needs to be some logical connection demonstrated between the work of hindering and the nature of the object hindered. If the system of law in the realm of Caesar be pointed to, then the question must follow "Why should a mere civil code and its enforcement officers prevent the revelation of the lawless one any more than the law against taking life prevents war?" Law has no strength on its own, and other factors must be introduced to account for its efficacy besides that of wages to an established officialdom. In summary, it seems to us that the view of the Roman Empire as the κατέχων is far from self-authenticating, but it remains an option.

Can any alternative solution be found which meets with fewer objections? We believe so. Our own suggestion is one that smacks somewhat of placation, and may seem to be in this issue of exegesis what Erasmus was in the religious controversy centuries ago --representative of compromise rather than emblematic of a clear-cut position. Some will consider that it strives to make the best of more than two worlds. We think, however, that these "seemings" do not ring true upon close examination.

The reviewer of the positions taken in this matter of the κατέχων becomes aware of some obvious and significant facts. (1) Several of them date from practically the beginning of the history of exegesis. (2) These positions, for the most part, did not spring from exegetical axes requiring grinding, but rather were originated to meet the facts of the case. (3) As one studies these, he finds that, as with most heresies, they seem to err in what they deny, rather than in what they affirm, and criticism frequently attacks them on this negative flank. (4) Therefore, the strongest case may be capable of being fashioned from a combination of the "strengths" of the respective positions.

A coherent explanation of τὸ κατέχον and ὁ κατέχων is obtainable by a <u>Gestalt</u> of all the key elements and requirements of the pericope. Paul's presentation to the Thessalonians was almost certainly that of a complex, rather than that of one or two parts. We think that the evidence indicates that he discussed a situation rather than merely a power or a person, but a situation with certain basic emphases. We submit that, in harmony with positions taken elsewhere by Paul and other New Testament writers, <u>the Thessalonians were taught that civil law would restrain the natural rebellion of human depravity for as long as the Holy Spirit moved on men's hearts urging them to yield to the gospel.</u> It is perfectly clear that the great apostasy surrounding the coming Antichrist would constitute a unique event in the history of mankind. And therefore some factor or factors would be missing at that time which had prevailed hitherto throughout the entire history of the world. Logically it is this factor, or factors, which constitute the hindrance to the threatening rebellion.

Paul was aware that the Old Testament presented occasions when the pleading of the divine Spirit ceased, and with that event the closing of human probation for some, leading to experiences of unmitigated rebellion ending in hopelessness, despair, and perdition. When Yahweh pronounced "Ephraim is joined to idols, let him alone",[132] then the next event to be expected was that those who had sown to the wind would reap the whirlwind. In the Writings it was found:

> Because I have called and you refused to listen,
>   have stretched out my hand and no one has heeded,
>   and you have ignored all my counsel
>   and would have none of my reproof,
> I also will laugh at your calamity;
>   I will mock when panic strikes you,
>   when panic strikes you like a storm,
>   and your calamity comes like a whirlwind,
>   when distress and anguish come upon you.
> Then they will call upon me, but I will not answer. . . .
>   Because they . . . did not choose the fear of the Lord,
>   would have none of my counsel. . .
>   therefore they shall eat the fruit of their way.[133]

Paul himself had undoubtedly preached, as he was to later write in Romans, that God "gave up" those who remained stubbornly impenitent.[134] They were given over to a reprobate mind. And no doubt Paul's understanding of the future was patterned somewhat according to what he believed about the past. He understood the Torah as teaching that, not only at the time of the Flood but on repeated occasions when the warnings of the prophets had been rejected, then the people had been left alone, to fall into incurable rebellion against God. Had not Jeremiah been told, "Pray not for this people. . . ."[135]

Paul was also aware that in his own day Christ had spoken of the sin against the Holy Spirit which would leave the guilty defenceless against the assaults and temptations of Satan.[136]

219

The same Christ who had pronounced doom upon the race which rejected Him, also warned that Israel would find themselves the victim of seven devils worse than the devil of external idolatry which they had successfully exorcized.[137] And it had also been said by Christ that after the gospel had been preached in the power of the Spirit to all the world then would come a time of great iniquity, trial, and deceptive miracles.[138] Therefore, it was as clear as day to Paul that the worst rebellion could not possibly take place till mankind as a whole had rejected the good news of grace.[139] Meanwhile the Holy Spirit, working through all benign institutions of the race such as civil law, would restrain man's natural wickedness. Man would not fall to the lowest depths until the pleading Spirit ceased to move upon resisting hearts. It was this factor of the moving of the Spirit upon all men, (albeit with limited power until Pentecost) which alone had prevented the race from sinking into abysmal depravity from the very beginning. Or so Paul, the child of rabbinic schools, believed.[140]

This gazing into the mind of Paul reveals nothing foreign to the pericope we are studying. It is all too consonant with his expressions there. 2 Thess. 2:10-12 points to the ultimate flowering of righteousness and iniquity, the maturing of the two groups those being saved and those who are perishing. It is made plain that it is those who have refused to receive the love of the truth who will partake in the apostasy. Those who reject the gospel of truth consent to "the lie" of Antichrist. They are without the divine panoply of the Spirit and thus are deceived by devilish signs and wonders. Twice in these three verses it is asserted that it is the failure to accept the gospel ("the truth") which renders the race ripe for the ultimate rebellion. This same emphasis is found in the preceding chapter. Rest is promised to those who believed Paul's testimony to the gospel, but vengeance is threatened against those "who do not obey the gospel of our Lord Jesus."[141] And in his previous letter Paul spoke of wrath coming upon the Jews because of their rejection of that gospel which alone could save them and the Gentiles.[142]

This interpretation fits the requirements drawn from 2 Thess. 2, but only as all aspects of the Gestalt are taken into consideration. Let it be noted that in the following "trial fitting" no one element is being considered as truly on its own. For example, the function of civil law is viewed as dependent upon the working of God's gracious Spirit, and this in turn is regarded as dependent upon the gospel's still being proclaimed.

(1) Civil law was a present force. (2) Its operations were beneficent for those proclaiming and receiving the gospel.

(3) Civil law was in harmony with the foundation principles

of the divine government. It was itself the natural
barrier to ἀνομία. The rebellion pictured in 2 Thess. 2,
with its rampage of lying wonders and the conceivable
results of wide-spread license, the frantic actions of men
who are perishing -- all suggest that first the restraints
of law must be dissolved. Civil government was ἔννομος
rather than ἄνομος.

(4) Civil law had <u>a divine time-mission</u>. Rom. 13 shows that
it has been appointed by God for His purposes of good,
restraining evil while grace is being offered to men
through the gospel.

(5) The power giving efficacy to civil law, the Holy Spirit,
will <u>actively withdraw</u> as human probation ceases. When
the fiat is proclaimed in heaven: "Let the evildoer still
do evil, and the filthy still be filthy, and the
righteous still do right, and the holy still be holy",[143]
then men's sides are determined and sealed, and the Spirit
ceases to influence those who have rejected Him.
Automatically, to Paul's thinking, civil law will crumble.
Its influence will restrain no longer. The fear of God
is absent from the hearts of those who have sided against
Him, and lawlessness becomes the rule of their existence.[144]

(6) Civil law, in the form of human government, <u>has spanned</u>
<u>the ages</u>. Acknowledged right and wrong were recognized
by men from the earliest times, according to the first
records of the Torah.

(7) The power of civil law has been <u>extraordinarily great and</u>
<u>mighty</u>, but only because of its alliances with the
restraining influence of the Holy Spirit acting upon that
residue of the image of God still present in lost mankind.

The ancillary specification suggested earlier, the necessity
for mysterious rather than open reference, is also fulfilled in
this interpretation. Because the civil law functioned through
the Empire, to speak of its dissolution would imply that also of
the ruling government. Such would have been accounted treason by
some.

Let us think again on Rigaux's objections to the interpretation
concerning the Roman Empire, for it is obvious that the solution
just offered embraces this interpretation, though it also
transcends it. Rigaux rightly argues that Paul's thought is not
political or historical, but rather it is theological and
eschatological. And he adds that moreover the Empire is a patent
thing and not secret. ". . .et l'empire romain est la chose la
plus patente qui soit."[145] Rigaux also quotes Dibelius

approvingly: "Si κατέχων se rapporte à l'empire romain, seul peut le découvrir dans le texte celui qui le sait déjà auparavant."[146] What can be said with reference to these criticisms?

It is true that the thought of the apostle is <u>primarily</u> not political but religious. As for whether his thinking be historical or eschatological the reply must be as with the parallel case of the Olivet discourse. Paul, like the prophets, does not separate history and eschatology.[147] To him, it is the same God Who works all in all. As both the Speaker and the recorders of the Advent sermon believed that history could swiftly move into eschatology if the conditions were fulfilled, so likewise the apostle. And while Paul's concern was not with matters political, again it must be urged that he considered such things as the sphere wherein divine providence continually moved. He would have felt towards Rome as Christ towards Pilate, Rome's representative, "You would have no power. . . unless it had been given you from above [i.e. from God] "148 The apostle knew no absolute dividing line between the secular and the sacred, for all things were alike tributary to the divine purposes. Everything in existence was under God's control and for His glory. Of Him, to Him, and through Him were all things.

When the criticism is made that the Roman Empire was a patent rather than a secret entity, we feel that the apostle's thought may here be represented with a twist. Paul is not necessarily saying that the hindrance is a secret thing. Rather he intimates that he is under obligation to speak of it with reserve, that is, he dare not let his meaning be as patent as the reality. During World War II many in Germany or occupied zones wrote to friends making reference to Hitler and the Gestapo. These were real and not mysterious entities, but undoubtedly many of the references in such letters were of necessity akin to Paul's mode of expression in 2 Thess. 2:5-7. And as for the criticism of Dibelius, that only the one aware of Paul's meaning already could understand his epistolary reference, this is the very point we are at present asserting. The Thessalonians <u>did</u> know what Paul was talking about. He says so. It was not intended that Roman officials should understand the esoteric references. Of course, Dibelius means that of <u>modern</u> readers, none will be able to decode Paul's communication unless they possess the key. This is true, but we have the key in what we know of Paul's thinking (based as it was on the Torah and Christian tradition), and of his experience and situation.

The matter of similarity between 2 Thess. 2:6-7, Mk. 13:14, and Rev. 17:8-11 must now be glanced at afresh in view of the interpretation that has been given of the hindrance and the hinderer. How is it, if these entities are related, that Paul can picture as benign the Empire through which law functions in his day, and yet Mark and John picture it oppositely? The answer lies in the difference between their respective situations. From mid-way through Nero's reign, the Empire changed its face as far as Christians were concerned.[149] The law which had protected them[150] was now invoked against them. A second question which grows out of the likeness of the terms in Mk., 2 Thess., and Rev., is: "If the βδέλυγμα τῆς ἐρημώσεως applied to the armies of the Roman Empire in A.D. 70, how can a relationship be affirmed to exist between this βδέλυγμα and both the hindrance and the Antichrist in 2 Thess.? The answer is included in the former one, but we will spell it out in greater detail.

Firstly, it is clear that there is a linguistic and contextual similarity between the βδέλυγμα τῆς ἐρημώσεως of Mk. 13:14 and the Antichrist of 2 Thess. 2. Both powers are an abomination to God, both powers are a threat to His people, both menace the temple of God, both constitute the sign of the end, both are displaced by the avenging Christ. Even the expressions βδέλυγμα τῆς ἐρημώσεως, ἄνθρωπος τῆς ἀνομίας and υἱὸς τῆς ἀπωλείας have some things in common. In the Septuagint βδέλυγμα is sometimes the equivalent of ἀνομία and ἐρημώσις of ἀπώλεια.[151]

Secondly, it is likewise clear that there _is_ a linguistic similarity between the βδέλυγμα τῆς ἐρημώσεως of Mk. 13:14 and the hinderer of 2 Thess. 2. The entity is presented as both a power and a person. Both are connected with government, and both are linked with the necessity of mystical reference. Both are eschatological.

Thirdly, the key to the puzzle lies in the fact that, as many scholars have recognized, Mk. 13:14 "transcends a limited historical reference to the destruction of Jerusalem", though "the historical reference is undeniably present."[152] Two levels of meaning exist in Mk. 13. The first has reference to the attack on the holy city in A.D. 70, and the second to the attack on the Israel of God immediately prior to the end. The one could have quickly have merged into the other, had the early Christians met with greater success in their proclamation of the gospel to the Jews and the world. Because of these two levels of meaning, and because of the Empire's change of attitude to Christians with the Neronic persecutions, it is possible to see how the Roman Empire could be part of the hindrance complex in A.D. 50, and yet in A.D. 70 be found as a prefiguration of Antichrist.[153]

The interpretation thus offered of the hindrance and the hinderer comprehends within it several of the main positions taken by commentators in such a way as to avoid contradiction and to harmonize with the pericope. In one sense the Holy Spirit is the hinderer, because only while He moves upon men by the gift of "common" grace does law retain its influence, and thus at a lower level the human law-enforcement officers, made thus willing to maintain law themselves, become the κατέχων. In another sense the preachers of the gospel are the personal restraining influence, and the gospel preached becomes itself the hindrance for so long as its task of witness is incomplete. This is not to contradict what has just been said regarding the Holy Spirit, for it is He Who empowers the preachers, and enables the gospel to be received by willing hearers. For those who wish to invoke a divine Decree as the hindrance, Mk. 13:10 and Mt. 24:14 exist, and such a position becomes identical with what has already been described.

Neither does the position of Hofmann[154] lie far from what is here favored. He argues that since Paul appealed to his oral instruction which, so far as the man of lawlessness is concerned, depended on Daniel, it is to be expected that the same source may also yield the solution to the problem of the κατέχων. Hofmann referred his readers to Dan. 10:5,13,20, and reasoned that angelic beings act as restraining powers among human governments. The angel tells Daniel that after he departs (compare Dan. 10:20 with ἐκ μέσου γενέσθαι of 2 Thess. 2:7) then will come Antiochus, the Old Testament Antichrist. "The very same prospect Paul holds out for the period of the Christian church: through the conservative action of a good spirit opportunity is given for the Spirit of Christ; when the former is compelled to withdraw, then will Antichrist come."[155] This comment of Riggenbach, it will be noticed, comprehends the interpretation advocated in this thesis. He implies that the Christian church has opportunity for its work of proclaiming the gospel for as long as angels, as the instruments of the Holy Spirit, move upon the leaders of governments.

It is objected that the Holy Spirit is nowhere called ὁ κατέχων. But because the Holy Spirit is but one key element in a Gestalt, and because Paul's teaching may have stressed the human elements as much as the divine, we are not justified in upholding this objection. Certainly, the concept of the work of the Holy Spirit restraining the last great apostasy, is to be found throughout Scripture. And it is just as certain that the Spirit is represented as working through human agencies such as preachers of the gospel, or government officials. "For there is no authority except from God. . . ."[156] ". . .he [him who is in authority -- v.3] is the servant of God. . . ."[157]

The view taken by Hofmann, Luthardt, Baumgarten, Auberlen, Von Oettingen, and some modern writers[158] linking the restrainer with the ministry of benign spirits (reflected in Daniel 10) may find a partial reflection in the connexion between angelic beings and the restraint of evil pictured in the last Apocalypse. As John adapts his pictures of Antichrist to the time wherein he lived, some forty years after Paul, when the attitude of the Empire had changed, so his imagery for the restraint of evil is also adapted. While his presentations cannot be used to interpret Paul's in any strict sense, they nevertheless cast light on the thinking of Christians of that day, and thus indirectly aid interpretation.

In Rev. 9 we read two versions of wickedness restrained and bound, and in Rev. 20 a final instance. In 9:1-3 a star from heaven has the key to the abyss which imprisons the demons of chaos, and when the key is used, it is the King of destruction (perdition) who issues forth with his hosts. The same concept is echoed in v. 14ff. Again bound angels of death are released from restraint, and they unleash a plague "such as never was" upon mankind. The final fling of demons and men is described in Rev. 20. It is preceded once again by the removal of divine restraint. A spirit from God unlocks the abyss and the greatest of all antichrists, recovered of his deadly wound, ascends to battle. Gog and Magog and their abominable multitudes are gathered to stand where they ought not, in their endeavour to desolate the holy city. But their end is perdition, and restraint is needed no more.

In the presentation of John, Paul, and Daniel, as with other Bible writers, evil is never an independent power. It is Yahweh who ever must grant permission before the winds of strife and rebellion are loosed. Certainly, in the thinking of Paul, before the great apostasy could transpire, the gospel in the power of the Spirit must have finished its work. Evil would not be allowed to dominate until Truth had been offered to all men. Then and then only, would those institutions among men which best represented and maintained the elements of divine government be allowed to crumble. With the ultimate rejection of the pleadings of the Spirit of God would come the dissolution of civil law, and then the enactments of the ἄνθρωπος τῆς ἀνομίας would lead men to war against the holy. Such a view is not only consonant with 2 Thess. 2., but with all that Paul has written, and with those scriptures from which his own ideology was hewn. It likewise agrees with those λόγοι κυρίου handed down by tradition. Almost all commentators have recognized part of the picture, and what so often has appeared as difference and contradiction may only be the failure to recognize the Gestalt in which truth often comes.

We have now completed our study of the key-terms of 2 Thess. 2: 1-12, and we submit that the interpretation here suggested is self-consistent, true to the original meaning of the text, and in harmony with the pattern of the βδέλυγμα τῆς ἐρημώσεως prophecy previously elucidated.

225

1. This is not to say that the concept of Antichrist is always embodied in a human figure. Not only their own sacred books, but the myths of surrounding nations influenced the eschatological presentations of the writers of the pseudepigrapha. Thus Beliar is sometimes a demonic figure, and sometimes humanized. The more general presentation of apostasy is prominent in the descriptions of the end written after Daniel, but the picture is gradually sharpened until Antichrist as Satan or one of his lieutenants, either demonic or human, becomes a regular feature. See Testaments of the Twelve Patriarchs, Reuben 4:7; 6:3; Levi 3:3; 18:12; Dan. 5:10-11; Judah 25:3; Psalms of Solomon 2:1,29 (re: Pompey); Book of Jubilees 1:20; 15:33; Sibylline Oracles 3:63ff.; 2:167f. (Whether such passages as this one had originally a Jewish rather than a Christian origin is not certain.) The role of Belial in the Qumran document, The War of the Sons of Light with the Sons of Darkness (chs. 1,13,16) should be compared with the foregoing.

Later sources include IV Ezra 11-12; II Baruch 40; Sibylline Oracles 5:93-110.

Because of difficulties regarding dating, and the possibility of Christian interpolation, it is not possible to place much stress on Jewish writings produced about the time of the early Christian era. However, we can say that at that time, the Jews in general held the idea of a coming powerful ruler born of the tribe of Dan, who would unite in himself enmity against God and hatred against Israel, but who would be destroyed by the Messiah. See Bousset, The Antichrist Legend; and Russell, Apocalyptic; Rowley, Apocalyptic; Milligan, Thessalonians (London, 1908), 158-162; Rigaux, L'Antéchrist, ch. 7.

Daniel 11:36, alluded to by Paul in 2 Thess. 2:4, has not been found in any extra-biblical text, but see Rigaux, Ép, 654: "À partir de ce moment-là. . . ."

2. Assuming, with most, the priority of Thessalonians over Galatians.

3. George G. Findlay, Thessalonians (CB)(Cambridge, 1914), 170.

4. Cf. William Neil, Thessalonians (MNTC)(London, 1950), 155. ". . .one of the most difficult passages in all the epistles -- and one which in the A.V. is quite incomprehensible."

5. Saint Paul: Les Épitres aux Thessaloniciens (Études Bibliques)(Paris, 1956), 279. (Hereinafter referred to as Ép.)

6. The Life and Work of St Paul (2 vols., N.Y., 1880), I, 617.

7. Findlay, Thessalonians, 172. But the same writer says of 2 Thess. 2:1-12, "This paragraph is the most obscure to us in St. Paul's Epistles". Ibid., 139.

8. Charles H. Giblin in The Threat to Faith (AB, XXXI)(Rome, 1967), 13, 15. (Hereinafter referred to as Threat.) 13-15 has listed Feuillet, Rigaux, W. Neil, Masson, Staab, etc., as expressing discontent with present positions. Cf. Leon Morris, Thessalonians (NIC)(Grand Rapids, 1959), 225.

9. See pages 6-11.

10. F. W. Beare, "Thessalonians", Interpreter's Dictionary of the Bible, ed. G. A. Buttrick et al. (4 vols., Nashville, 1962), IV, 625.

11. Kümmel, Introduction, 188. See also 27-29.
Donald Guthrie lists the supposed eschatological "contradiction" among the arguments most commonly presented against the authenticity of 2 Thess., but says: "The change is not in eschatology but in viewpoint due to changing circumstances." Introduction, 572. At the conclusion of his review he states, "Not one of these objections is seen to possess real substance." Ibid., 573.

12. Beare, "Thessalonians", 625.

13. Kümmel, Introduction, 190.

14. Beare, "Thessalonians", 626. J. Frame asserts similarly. ". . . the hypothesis of genuineness may be assumed as the best working hypothesis in spite of the difficulties suggested by the literary resemblances. . . ." Thessalonians (ICC)(Edinburgh, 1912), 53.

15. Threat, 148-150.

16. We do not mean by this that reviewers question Giblin's philological evidence, but that it is doubted whether his evidence is rightly applied for interpreting 2 Thess. 2:6-7. See further discussion on 212-215 of this chapter.

17, 2 Thess. 2:1-2. E. von Dobschütz entitles 2 Thess. 2:1-17 "Der Hauptteil des Briefes", Die Thessalonicher-Briefe (KEK) (Göttingen, 1909), ad loc.

18. "Thessalonians", 628. The passages here concerned are 2:3; 2:13; 3:6. Only the first is relevant for our study, and here the textual evidence is equivocal, though most critics favour the rendering we have followed.

19. See C.H. Dodd, The Apostolic Preaching and its Developments (London,[2]1944), 38-39; B.H. Streeter, The Four Gospels (London, 1924), 493; H.A.A. Kennedy, St Paul's Conceptions of the Last Things (London, 1904), (hereinafter referred to as Conceptions), 55-56, 166-68; Beasley-Murray, Jesus, 232; J.B. Orchard, "Thessalonians and the Synoptic Gospels", Bib, XIX (1938), 19-42; Torrey, Documents, 36-37; Giblin, Threat, 73; Rigaux, Ép., 95-105; Hartman, Prophecy, 178-205, et al.

20. Das Evangelium des Matthäus (KNT)(Leipzig, 1905), 651n.

21. Kennedy, Conceptions, 56.

22. "Thessalonians and the Synoptic Gospels", 19.

23. Rigaux, Ép., 95-105.

24. Hartman, Prophecy, 205.

25. "Thessalonians and the Synoptic Gospels", 37.

26. Cf. Giblin, Threat, 73.

27. Rigaux, Ép., 105. "Les nombreux cas de ressemblances soulignés plus haut entre les expressions pauliniennes et synoptiques sont une indication de valeur. Ils permettent de mésurer l'apport de la prédication chrétienne primitive en fait de doctrines, de formules, de fixation des thèmes, et de reconnaître la part d'originalité des différents auteurs."

28. 2 Cor. 15:3.

29. Hartman lists discussions, past and present, on this subject, Prophecy, 180.

30. See also 223f of this chapter.

31. Dan. 11:31-45.

32. Discussed on 190f of this volume. It seems that, in their anxiety to defend the historical application of Mk. 13 to the events of A.D. 70, such writers as Carrington have refused to recognize any other possible level of meaning. J. van Dodewaard, we believe, errs in this way. He contrasts the βδέλυγμα τῆς ἐρημώσεως of Matt. and Mk. with the ἄνθρωπος τῆς ἀνομίας of 2 Thess. 2 thus:

"Mt. en Mc.   II Thess.
βδέλυγμα --geen wonderen; eerst   vs. 9 De wonderbare teekenen
Mt 24,23 en Mc 13,21 wordt over   zijn karakteristiek voor den

Mt en Mc.	II Thess.
de wonderen der valsche Messiassen gesproken.	den Antichrist.

Mt en Mc.   II Thess.
de wonderen der valsche Messiassen   den Antichrist.
gesproken.
    Er is gavaar voor de bewoners   Gevaar voor alle geloovigen.
van Judea
    Men kan nog vluchten.   Vlucht is uitgesloten.
    Gevaar vooral voor het   Gevaar vooral voor de ziel
tijdelijke leven.   (vs. 10-11)."

    Prior to this series of contrasts, van Dodewaard says,
"Opvallend is, dat de zinspeling op 2 Thess. 2,3 vv bij alle
auteurs voorkomt, die onzen tekst eschatalogisch uitleggen.
Veel Protestanten verdedigen deze stelling en leggen dezen
Evangelietekst uit in vergelijking met den Paulustekst."
"De gruwel. . .", 131.
    We have already shown that it is not remarkable that "all
authors" link 2 Thess. 2 with Mk. 13:14. There are the best of
reasons for doing so. As for the supposed contrasts offered by
this writer, they dissolve once it is recognized that the
description of the tribulation in Mark transcends the event of
A.D. 70, although it includes them. (See Dodd, More N.T. Studies,
80, and also 76ff of this thesis.) In fairness to van
Dodewaard, however, it must be said that he concludes his protest
with an acknowledgement which, in effect enervates his previous
arguments. He says, "Er is dus niets tegen, dat men dit
gebeuren letterlijk van den val van Jerusalem uitlegt en in
typischen zin van den Antichrist." "De gruwel. . . .", 131.
    All such protesting writers acknowledge that Christ gave an
extension of meaning to Daniel's βδέλυγμα τῆς ἐρημώσεως.
In principle, Paul is doing the same to Christ's reference, and
yet not quite the same, for there is good reason for supposing
that Christ Himself intended the broader meaning for βδέλυγμα
τῆς ἐρημώσεως that later churchmen elaborated. A partial list
of those scholars who have linked the Antichrist of 2 Thess.
2 with the βδέλυγμα τῆς ἐρημώσεως of Mk. 13:14 is given on
184 of this thesis.

33. The attempt is made with the challenge and warning of Leon
Morris et al. in mind. "Many conjectures have been put forward.
Sometimes they have been supported by ingenious arguments. But we
cannot feel at all sure that we have the clue to the situation.
It is best to face the fact." Thessalonians, 224-25.

34. Hartman, Prophecy, 198.

35. The sense of political revolt is attached to the word in late
Greek, but the usage of the LXX and the N.T. is opposed to such
an interpretation. See Josh. 22:22; 1 Macc. 2:15; 2 Chron.
29:19; Jer. 2:19; Acts 21:21. Cf. Frame, Milligan, Neil,
Morris, ad loc.

36. Rom. 10:1-2. Pace Kennedy, Conceptions, 218.

37. Neil, Thessalonians, 160.

38. Giblin, Threat, 65.

39. "Entre les mains de l'ange des ténèbres se trouve le gouvernement des fils d'iniquité", 1 QS, III, 21 cited in Ép. 655.

40. Cf. Eph. 2:2.

41. Rigaux, Neil, Frame, Milligan, Morris, et al., ad loc.

42. Mt. 24:10,12.

43. Mt. 24:23-24.

44. Dan. 8:23.

45. See discussion in Rigaux, Ép. 253-255.

46. 1 Enoch 80:7; 91:5-9; 99:4-9; 100:1-2.

47. IV Esdras 56:1-2.

48. Eze. chs. 38-39.

49. Rev. 16:13-14; 19:19.

50. Rev. 20:7-9.

51. C.J. Riggenbach, "Thessalonians" Lange's Commentary, XI, 132. "The appearance of the Man of Sin must help to bring about the complete separation." Cf. Giblin, Threat, 84-85, ". . .another compatible meaning should not be ignored. It is conceivable that the ἀποστασία   implies the separation of the good and the wicked, the ultimate divergence of two opposed lines of development; viz., the response of faith and the response of disbelief, the true cult of God and the idolatrous cult of self."

52. Isa. 14:13-15.

53. Cf. Rev. chs. 11, 13, 17. John's Antichrist suffers death, but rises again. He, too, works signs and wonders, claiming worship, etc.

54. Threat, 69.

55. Ép., 271.

56. <u>Ibid</u>., 269.   56a. See Ford, <u>Daniel</u> (SPA), 155f, 187, 272.

57. See Neil, <u>Thessalonians</u>, 177-179, for an example. "Only when
the evil in men is overcome, when Antichrist is vanquished by
Christ, will the Kingly Rule of God be complete. Whether it
comes quickly and suddenly. . .or whether slowly. . .it is
still, as Paul would tell us, an Act of God. . . ." 179. Neil
recognizes that his homily does not really express Paul's thought
in this place, but some have presented similar moralizing as
exegesis. This, it is not.
      One of the best discussions of this matter is to be found
in Milligan's <u>Thessalonians</u>, 170-173. He says of one
interpretation which he considers to be merely idealistic:
". . . however true this may be as an <u>application</u> of the Apostle's
words, it contributes little or nothing to their <u>interpretation</u>,
or to the exact meaning they must have conveyed to their
first writer or readers." 171.
      Despite Denney's own vagaries in interpreting 2 Thess. 2:
1-12, he has at least seen clearly the principle here involved.
See Denney, <u>Thessalonians</u>, (Expositor's Bible)(London, 1892), 317f

58. But see Milligan, <u>Thessalonians</u>, 159. On Bousset's theory
as a whole see <u>ibid</u>., 173. "The data on which this theory is
built up are too uncertain to make it more than a very plausible
conjecture. . . nor, after all, even if it were more fully
established, would it have any direct bearing on our inquiry,
for certainly all thought of any such mythical origin of the
current imagery was wholly absent from St Paul's mind."

59. Deut. 13:13; Judg. 19:22; 20:13; 1 Sam. 1:16; 2:12; 10:27;
25:17,25; 30:22; 2 Sam. 16:7; 23:6; 1 Kings 21:10,13; 2 Chron.
13:7.

60. Geerhardus Vos, <u>The Pauline Eschatology</u> (Princeton, 1930),
(Hereinafter referred to as <u>Eschatology</u>.)

61. Passages such as Psalm 2, Eze. chs. 38 and 39, Zech. 14, and
above all, Dan. chs. 7, 8, 9, 11, were responsible for the
original Jewish belief.

62. Vos, <u>Eschatology</u>, 103.

63. Vos, <u>Eschatology</u>, 104-105. See also W. Hendriksen,
<u>Thessalonians</u>, 176. Hendriksen cites H.F. Hahn, <u>Old Testament in
Modern Research</u> (Philadelphia, 1954), 110-117 to the effect
that "the <u>distinctive</u> features of Old Testament were of greater
significance than those which it had in common with other
religions, and that even those elements which might be called
derivative had been transformed into vehicles for <u>distinctive</u>
beliefs." <u>Ibid</u>. These conclusions of Vos, Hendriksen, <u>et al</u>.,

are only a repetition of positions long held by others. Moses Stuart, for example, pointed out that ἀποστασία was an exact version of יעשפ in Dan. 8:13, and affirmed that this expression, and ὁ ἄνθρωπος τῆς ἁμαρτιας and ὁ ἄνομος all had their basis in this verse. See James Strong's editorial footnote in Otto Zöckler's commentary on "Daniel", Lange's Commentary, VII, 176.

64. 1 Thess. 4:15.

65. See 19 of this thesis.

66. Kennedy, Conceptions, 212.

67. Ibid.

68. This title was used by the Qumran community for the author of the popular model for all subsequent apocalyptic. See 4 Q 174, col. 2, line 3. Discoveries in the Judean Desert, V, ed. J.M. Allegro (Oxford, 1968), 54.

69. Giblin, Threat, 84-85.

70. 2 Thess. 1:7.

71. Riggenbach, "Thessalonians", 127.

72. Giblin, Threat, 84-85.

73. Thessalonians, 144.

74. Milligan, Thessalonians, 100.

75. Thessalonians, 256.

76. This is a parallel to the use of σημεῖον by John the evangelist, to exhibit Christ's deity.

77. Dan. 7:25.

78. A position that has been held by some commentators from the time of Theodore of Mopsuestia. Leon Morris does not believe that Paul here teaches the present existence of the man of lawlessness but says, "Paul speaks of this figure as being 'revealed', just as in 1:7 he has spoken of the revelation of the Lord Jesus. . . . It indicates that the Man of Lawlessness will exist before his manifestation to the world. It may also point to something supernatural about him." Thessalonians, 221. Rigaux seems most careful in this area. He says: "Si Paul a en vue un individu, peut-on le déterminer davantage?

"Ce n'est pas Satan lui-même. Paul l'en distingue explicite-
ment. Sa parousie se fait par l'énergie de Satan. . . .Quoi
qu'il en soit des origines lointaines des idées sur les demons
et leur chef, il n'y a point trace dans Paul d'une incarnation
du diable." Ép. 270. But having disavowed the idea of an
incarnation of the devil he proceeds to add: "Si l'on peut
estimer certain qu'il vise un individu, touchant la personne
même de l'Antéchrist, il ne dit rien de précis. . .Ibid., 271.
We think Giblin goes beyond the evidence and accommodates
Paul's thought for the sake of modern sophisticates. He says:
". . .the interpretation of the Man of Rebellion given above
will be more readily appreciated as a distinctively Pauline
characterization of an anti-God figure which could be basically
representational -- i.e., an imaginative representation of evil
that is not affirmed as both a physical and empirically-defined
entity. . . .the figure is represented in a cultic context,
but by Paul he is depicted more as an antithesis to faith than
as either a physical presence or a persecutor." Threat, 72.
We agree that the apostle presents this figure as a threat to
faith rather than as a persecutor, but we cannot see that he
does not intend his readers to understand a physical presence,
i.e. an "empirically-defined entity".

79. Judg. 13:6,8,9; Dan. 9:21; 10:16.

80. 2 Cor. 11:14.

81. Rev. 16:13-14. Neil writes: "So the Lawless One is now
hidden and will likewise soon be made manifest." Thessalonians,
161. Frame et al. take the same position. It is denied by
Riggenbach, Vos, Findlay, et al.

82. Rigaux says, "Enfin, l'opposition eschatologique terrestre,
phase de la lutte entre le bien et le mal, est dominée par le
jeu des puissances ténébreuses. Les premières pages de la Bible
annoncent une victoire des hommes sur l'esprit infernal. Les
dernières productions juives décrivent l'action du monde
invisible sur la terre et rangent les démons sous la dépendance
d'un chef. Elles prédisent pour les temps eschatologiques un
redoublement d'activité de la part des esprits et un triomphe
définitif de Dieu." L'Antéchrist, 204.

83. Rigaux, Ép., 269. See Ford, Daniel (SPA), 155,156,187,272.

84. "Il n'est guère probable que Paul ait pensé à un pseudo-
messie juif ou à un antéchrist juif." Ibid., 271. Rigaux says
that even Bousset abandoned this position. See also Vos,
Eschatology, 114f.

85. Rigaux, Ép., 271.

86. Ibid., 272.

87. Hartman, Prophecy, 202.

88. Rev. 13:1-8,12-18; 16:13,14; 17:8-11; 19:20.

89. We do not mean to imply by this statement that the New Testament view of Antichrist is solely that of an eschatological individual. The contrary is the case. Christ, Paul, and John give us a variety of aspects of the one concept. However, all three believe that an eschatological individual is to appear as the Antichrist par excellence. The initial use of the word indicates this: "Children, it is the last hour; and as you have heard that antichrist is coming, so now many antichrists have come. . . ." 1 John 2:18. John here (pace Bultmann) both affirms the coming Antichrist, and the existing fulfilment of the same genre.

90. We find it difficult to follow Leon Morris when he writes: "While the temple is not easy to identify, the best way of understanding the passage seems to be that it is some material building which will serve as the setting for the blasphemous claim. . . ." Thessalonians, 224. Morris recognizes the connection of the temple with the Antichrist's proclamation of deity, but does not see that this climax, by its very nature, indicates the metaphorical use of temple in this regard. See what follows in our discussion.

91. See G. Wohlenberg, Thessalonicherbrief (KNT)(Leipzig, 1903), 142.

92. Thessalonians, 164.

93. 1 Cor. 2:16-17; Eph. 2:20.

94. More recently than the Reformers we find a representative instance in the commentary of Bishop Christopher Wordsworth.

95. See Rigaux, Ép., 661. ". . . l'église qui mettrait un autre Christ à la tête de l'église ne pourrait plus se nommer l'église de Dieu." Likewise Morris, ad loc.

96. Rigaux perceives Paul's intention. "Siéger dans le temple est pour lui une attribution divine. Le Saint des saints est la propriété et la demeure inviolable de Dieu. Le sanctuaire est le lieu où les fidèles viennent l'adorer et solliciter ses faveurs. Usurper la place de Jahvé, le déloger de sa demeure, c'est l'acte le plus abominable que l'on puisse commettre contre lui 'afin de se faire passer pour Dieu'". Ép. 661. This is also the understanding of Knabenbauer, Voste, Steinmann, Amiot. Ibid.,

660. Cf. also A.J. Mason, ad loc.

97. "Thessalonians", 128. Cf. W.F. Adeney's comment regarding the ναός ". . .used in a wide allegorical sense, being, as Mr. Garrod suggests 'a forcible method of showing that the man of sin will by his own deliberate action usurp the dignity and prerogative of God'." Thessalonians (The New Century Bible) (Edinburgh, 1902), 238. In support of this position is the fact that "sitting" is often used in the N.T. in a figurative sense. See Col. 3:1; Heb. 1:3; 8:1; 10:12; 12:2; Rev. 3:21; 20:4.

98. Riggenbach, "Thessalonians", 130.

99. Threat, 14.

100. In his commentary, Dibelius asks: "Who is the κατέχων?" and replies, "In myth, saga, and fairy-tale is the monster bound with chains or secured behind strong doors." He proceeds to quote Job 40:26, and illustrates further from Russian folklore. He warns however against the interpretation of the κατέχων as Satan. Thessalonicher (HNT)(Tübingen, 1925), 43.

101. The most recent exegete to adopt the "gospel" view is A.L. Moore. See his Thessalonians (Century Bible, n.s.)(London, 1969), 103.

102. "κατέχων could be used in a doctrinal context and in a pejorative sense to denote a strong-handed action but probably one without the connotation 'control'. . .Its intransitive form, particularly in Pauline usage, is not well explained by 'hold sway' or 'prevent', or even 'restrain'. On the other hand, it could well connote a self-interested act of possession. . . . Unfavorable overtones of the term and its abrupt appearance could be grasped more concretely through an allusion to pagan cult practices, particularly that of pseudo-charismatic activity in which something or someone 'takes hold of' or 'seizes' another." Threat, 201-202.

103. ". . .the ἄτακτοι are contrasted to Paul in terms of apostolic enterprise, and their fault is one neither of simple idleness nore of indifference to the needs of earthly life. It seems more likely that the ἄτακτοι were those responsible for the deception on the topic of the parousia rather than victims of this deception. Paul does not make the connection, however, and we must have recourse to conjecture." Threat, 147. Giblin here mentions the chief objection to his position. Paul does not make the specific point upon which Giblin's case largely rests. Most readers of Giblin's work would feel that this is an "Achilles heel" for the author. Other major objections, however, can and have been marshalled against his case. Robert

J. Peterson says: "Giblin argues (pp. 169ff.) that ὁ κατέχων cannot be a restrainer of evil because 'the mystery of lawlessness is already at work.' The mysteries of sin at Qumran (1 QH 5:36, IQ 27 1:2, 1 QM 14:9) refer to the hidden activity of evil. If this is the background for the term in II Thess, there is no reason why ὁ κατέχων could not restrain evil by not allowing it to come into the open." JBL, LXXXVII (1968), 360. D.E.H. Whiteley, who himself holds to the traditional understanding of the κατέχων has said of Giblin's linguistic position that it is to some extent "powerful". But he points out that while Giblin suggests that there are no good lexicographical parallels for rendering κατέχων as 'restrain', Moulton and Milligan do give such instances. See JThSt, n.s., XXI (1970), 168-69. Charles Brutsch's key criticism is that Giblin's explanation of the κατέχων fails to explain why the disappearance of this force brings with it the coming of the great rebel. ThZ, XXVI (1970), 359-60. See also W. Schmithals, THLit LXV (1970), 200-202; J.D. Quinn, CathBibQ, XXX (1968), 612-14; W.J. Dalton, ThSt, XXIX (1968), 767-68; J. Murphy O'Connor, RB LXXVI (1969), 622-23.

104. Threat, 17.

105. "Thessalonians", 628.

106. Schöpfung und Chaos, 224-25, cited by Rigaux, Ép., 274.

107. Thessalonians, 101.

108. Wohlenberg wrote of the apostasy: "Es kann nur der in Verbindung mit der endgeschichtlichen Trübsal stehende gemeint sein." Thessalonicherbrief, 140.

109. See the discussion by Milligan, Thessalonians, 171-73.

110. Thessalonians, 169.

111. Ibid., 170.

112. Thessalonians, 226.

113. Thessalonians, 262.

114. Ép., 279.

115. Thessalonians, 177. "It is an historical fact that Paul was wrong."

116. Ep., 274.

117. See Rigaux, Ép., 593; J.H. Moulton and G. Milligan,
The Vocabulary of the Greek Testament Illustrated from the Papyri
and other Non-Literary Sources (London, 1930), 336-37; Milligan,
Thessalonians, 155-157; Hanse, "κατέχων " TDNT, II, 829ff.
Apart from the technical navigation use in Acts 27:40, κατέχων
is always transitive, applying ἔχειν. Because the concept is
broad, the meaning is variable and must be determined by the
context. In the Thessalonian epistles two distinct meanings
are usually assigned by commentators -- (1) Hold fast, 1 Thess.
5:21, (2) Hold back, 2 Thess. 2:6,7. Both are appropriate for
derivatives of ἔχω = possess, but whether they are the most
appropriate renderings is more a matter of interpretation than
of philology. Milligan shows that the linguistic basis for
Giblin's case is an option. He says: "And if we accept the
view, which has recently found strong support, that the
κάτοχοι of the Serapeum are to be regarded as those 'possessed'
by the spirit of the god, we have further evidence pointing in
the same direction." Thessalonians, 156. By this statement
Milligan alludes to the metaphorical use of the verb as
illustrated in some instances of Koiné usage in the second
century. Thus the objections to Giblin's position must be
primarily on grounds other than philology.

118. See Giblin, Threat, 16-17.

119. Ép., 665-66.

120. Ibid., 665.

121. Threat, 165.

122. Frame comments as follows regarding the position of those
who wish to understand νῦν of v.6 in the sense of "and now
to pass to a further point": "This explanation puts so great
a stress on the new point as such as to demand νῦν δέ (cf.
1 Cor. 12:20. . .). . . .it is more likely that the emphasis
is laid not on the new point as such but on the present
situation involved in κατέχον as contrasted with the future
situation when ὁ κατέχων ἄρτι will be removed, and the prophecy
of v.3 will be realised." Thessalonians, 262-263. The following
verse confirms Frame's position, for we have the same contrast
there. ἤδη is opposed to καὶ τότε and τ.μ.α to ὁ ἄνομος.
μόνον is to be connected with ἐνεργεῖται meaning 'works
inwardly', which is contrasted with ἀποκαλυφθήσεται the later
manifestation. Wohlenberg agrees. "Immer steht auch hier
als Zeitpartikel, mit Energie im Gegensatz zur Vergangenheit auf
die jeweilige Gegenwart hinweisend. An unserer Stelle den
Gegensatz des jetzigen Wissens zu der früher erfolgten
mündlichen Belehrung ausgesagt zu finden, geht nicht an."
Thessalonians, 143. He argues the case at length throughout most

of the following page.

123. Ép., 274.

124. Frame, Thessalonians, 260.

125. Kennedy, Conceptions, 219-220.

126. Bousset, The Antichrist Legend, 123.

127. Thessalonians, 260.

128. Rigaux, Ép., 665; Neil, Thessalonians, 173; Beare, "Thessalonians", 628. All use the same nebulous "something, or someone, somewhere" or close approximates.

129. Frame, Thessalonians, 265. "The fact, not the manner of the removal. . . is indicated." Milligan, Thessalonians, 102. "Nothing is said as to how the removal spoken of is to be affected." And Wohlenberg, "Es ist doch kaum der Nebenbegriff einer unfreiwilligen, gewaltsamen Hinwegräumung wegzudeuten." Thessalonians, 147.

130. Paul's epistles, at his own request, were read publicly and circulated widely. While they were to be rehearsed πᾶσιν τοῖς ἁγίοις ἀδελφοῖς 1 Thess. 5:27, there was always the possibility that some less "holy" than others might misuse statements by the apostle. We have an imperfect parallel in the case of proselytizing Christians who meet secretly in Communist countries.

131. In his discussion of "The Final Revelation of Antichrist", E. Stauffer says, "Under the assault of antichrist the last defences that the Creator has erected against the powers of chaos break down completely. Even political order collapses." New Testament Theology (E.T., London, 51955), 214. (Hereinafter referred to as Theology.) This correctly expresses the biblical concept that lawful government is a divinely ordained hinderer, restraining the anarchic tendencies of depraved man. However, Stauffer also points out that according to the N.T. "The nearer the Church comes to the end of its history, the more destructive will persecutions and the final 'offences' prove to be (Matt. 24:10; Did. 15:5; Barn. 4:3; 2 Thess. 2:3,10ff). Here the sifting of history reaches its climax, and there comes the revelation of the divine rejection, which is carried through in destruction." Theology, 220.
  This is an excellent commentary upon the Thessalonian reference offered by Stauffer.

132. Hos. 4:17.

133. Proverbs. 1:24-31.

134. Romans 1:24,26,28.

135. Jeremiah 7:16; 11:14; 14:11.

136. Matthew 12:28-36. It is significant that Christ's warning regarding tne unpardonable sin came as a result of a rejection so marked that the Jews concerned attributed Christ's work to Satan. Apparently, to the mind of Christ, total rejection of the movings of the Spirit (so as to ascribe divine work to Satan) would always be followed by the withdrawal of the Spirit, and the close of probation for those implicated. Does not Paul contemplate something of the sort of the entire world of unbelievers just before the end? He believed in a God, so well-mannered.as not to tarry where He was unwanted. Had not Christ walked out of the temple environs with the commentary that henceforth the "house" was "theirs" -- the Jews, and no longer God's? And had not the same Christ warned the Jews that as a result of their rejection of Him, they would be open to deception from a pretender to come? John 5:43.
It is interesting to note how Rigaux in his chapter "L'Homme du Péché et l'Ensemble de l'Eschatologie Paulinienne" in L'Antéchrist, 314-316.has much to say about the opposition of Satan and wicked spirits to Christ and the apostles in their spread of the gospel. He uses such terms as "empêcher" and "obstacle" in the same sense as we have above, but applies them to the opposite parties. That is, Rigaux clearly sees the hindering effect that Satan and evil angels have upon the propagation of "the truth". He also refers to Christ's mention of His vision regarding the expulsion of Satan from heavenly places as the apostles successfully preached. (Luke 10:17-18). Thus, it is obvious that the gospel is an obstacle to Satan's designs. Rigaux speaks of the hindering effect of wicked spirits in connexion with their endeavour to lead believers into apostasy. But the interaction is surely apparent, for if those who wish to purvey apostasy hinder the preachers of the gospel, it must also be true that the gospel, by its proclamatior and influence on the heart of men, is an obstacle or hindrance to apostasy. Only when preaching ceases, and the Holy Spirit moves no more on the hearts of unbelievers, can the ambition of Satan and his minions regarding world-wide apostasy be fulfilled.

137. Luke 11:23-26.

138. Mk. 13:10-22; Mt. 24:11-24.

139. 2 Thess. 2:9-12.

140. Paul believed that God desired the conversion of Israel,
and that to that end the Holy Spirit was continually working to
make effectual the preaching of the gospel. In this connexion
Cullmann's comments are of interest. "During the New Testament
period there arose a view, often expressed in the Talmud and in
the apocryphal books, that the Kingdom of God would not come
until Israel as a whole had repented. In this connection, this
question oftens appears in the Talmud: 'Who is preventing the
Messiah's appearing?'" "Eschatology and Missions in the New
Testament", The Background of the New Testament and its
Eschatology, eds. W.D. Davies, D. Daube, (Cambridge, 1956), 414.
"In both passages (Mk. 13:10 and Mt. 24:14) the mission is
mentioned as a divine 'sign' along with the eschatological woes:
wars, famines, cosmic catastrophes, persecutions, etc., and the
intensification of evil in men. Thus it appears that the coming
of the Kingdom does not depend upon the success of this
'preaching', but only upon the fact of the proclamation itself.

"We find further evidence for the same view in the Book
of Revelation (vi. 108). . . . .What then has the preaching of
the Gospel in the world in common with the task of the other
three riders? It also is a divine 'sign' (or 'promise') of the
end. . .Further, in other passages in this book the necessity
for the summons to repentance before the end is emphasized. In
xi.3 the 'two witnesses' are mentioned. . .who prophesy. In
xiv. 6-7 is the picture of the angel with the 'eternal Gospel',
who addresses a final appeal to repentance 'to every nation and
tongue and people'.

"The fact that the proclamation of the Gospel as an
eschatological 'sign' is not a peripheral phenomenon, comes out
very clearly in the passage in Acts i. 6-7. . . ." Ibid., 415-
416.

". . . a great deal could be said for the view, suggested
first of all by Theodore of Mopsuestia and by Theodoret, and
later on by Calvin, according to which 'the withholding thing'
in II Thess. ii. 6 is the eschatological missionary message.
At first the Greek verb for 'withholding' had a temporal meaning
in the sense of the 'retarding', 'delaying'. Here the allusion
is to the 'time' or 'date' of the coming of the Kingdom of God.
. .According to the Synoptic passages in Mark xiii.10-14 and
Matt. xxiv. 13-15 the Anti-Christ appears after the preaching
of the Gospel to the Gentiles, just as in II Thess. ii. 6ff.
he will appear after 'the withholding thing' has been removed.

"Further, this assumption is directly connected with that
Jewish Rabbinic question, 'Who is preventing the appearing
of the Messiah?'" Ibid., 419.

The last two lines link the arguments of Cullmann with
our suggestion as to what "Paul, the child of rabbinic schools,
believed."

141. 1:7-8.

142. 1 Thess. 2:14-16.

143. Rev. 22:11.

144. Cf. Rom. 1:21-32.

145. Ép. 275.

146. Ibid.

147. See 31 of this thesis.

148. Jn. 19:11.

149. Bo Reicke writes, "Only in one respect did the persecution
under Nero affect the one undertaken some thirty years later by
Domitian and even later persecutions; following the fire, the
authorities were aware of the difference between Christians and
Jews, so that Jewish privileges no longer furnished sure
protection for the Christian community." The New Testament Era,
(E.T., London, 1969), 251.

150. See Rom. 13:1-7.

151. It is well-known that Paul's terminology was influenced by
the Septuagint. The word ἀπώλεια   and its cognates occur often
in the LXX. Eze. 29:12 is an instance where ἀπωλείας is
used as a synonym for ἐρήμωσιν. The Hebrew root שׁמם exists three
times in this verse, and underlies both these words. While the
range of meaning for ἀπώλεια   in the Septuagint extends from
the idea of "calamity" to that of "death", the common conceptual
factor is always that of "ruin", which of course is also basic
to שׁמם. Thus the expression βδέλυγμα τῆς ἐρημώσεως   would have
many connotations to the reader of the LXX. While primarily
it would be reminiscent of the phrase in Daniel, its component
parts would carry the nuances of lawlessness in all its forms,
but particularly idolatry, and also the ruin which lawlessness
always brought in its train.
        It would appear, therefore, that the phrases ἄνθρωπος τῆς
ἀνομίας and υἱος τῆς ἀπωλείας do not stand a great way off in
meaning from the fearful and hateful βδέλυγμα τῆς ἐρημώσεως.
When it is remembered that the special sin of the man of lawlessness is the idolatry involved in his demand for worship, it is
evident that the thought of such a character would be a stench
in the nostrils of the pious, a βδέλυγμα indeed.
        ὁ κατέχων   of course, has no unsavoury connotations in
and of itself. Its contextual flavour here is benign. However,
the passage of time between Paul's writing of Thessalonians and
the destruction of Jerusalem brought changes which made civil
law and government at times a menace where once they had been

a protection. Thus after the events of Nero's reign Christians could read of both the κατέχων and the βδέλυγμα τῆς ἐρημώσεως and apply them to the same entity, but in contrasting senses. Cf. Alfred Plummer's comment. ". . .in LXX ἀνομία very often represented the Hebrew for 'abomination', and in Hebrew "the man of abomination" might mean one who claimed worship as an idol." A Commentary on St Paul's Second Epistle to the Thessalonians (London, 1918), 47. See also E.A. Abbott, The Son of Man, 347, referred to by Plummer.

152. Giblin, Threat, 73.

153. Beckwith's remarks are pertinent: "The identification of the Beast and Antichrist with the Roman emperors is held by some to be inconsistent with the Christian view as expressed elsewhere in the New Testament. St. Paul, Rom. 13:1 ff. declares the existing governmental power, the Roman, to be ordained by God; and in 2 Thess. 2:7 he sets the Roman power in opposition to Antichrist, saying that it is only the former that prevents the appearing of the latter. This latter passage is the only one in the New Testament expressing directly this opposition, and it is not difficult to account for it in view of the Apostle's experiences. To him the order and security of the world maintained by the Roman government represented a divine ordinance in contrast with the awful tyranny and hostility to God anticipated as to come in the reign of Antichrist. The persecutions of Nero and those of Domitian, in part already begun and in part yet threatening the Christians at the time of our book, and the growing rigor in enforcing the emperor-worship, are all subsequent to the writing of these epistles of Paul. It must also be borne in mind that to one familiar with the revolutions marking the course of Roman history it would not be difficult to conceive, as does the Apocalyptist, 17:16f., the present Roman order to be destroyed by one who had been a Roman emperor." The Apocalypse of John (New York, 1919), 396.

154. Die Heilige Scrift Neuen Testaments, I, 330ff., cited by Riggenbach, "Thessalonians", 130.

155. Ibid., 140.

156. Rom. 13:1.

157. Rom. 13:4.

158. O. Betz, "Der Katechon", NTS, IX (1963), 276-291.

CHAPTER SIX

THE APOCALYPSE AND THE
βδέλυγμα τῆς ἐρημώσεως

If the βδέλυγμα τῆς ἐρημώσεως   motif has its seed in the
book of Daniel, its "blade" is found in the Olivet discourse,
its "ear" in 2 Thess. 2, and the "full grain" in that book known
pre-eminently as the Apocalypse. It is doubtful, indeed,
whether the theme of Antichrist would ever have assumed more
than footnote attention, but for its prominence in the last
book of the New Testament.[1]

As T.D. Bernard pointed out in a notable work, the threatening
clouds grow thicker and darker as one reads the concluding
books of Scripture.[2] The meridian glory of Pentecost, and the
full flush of early Christian expectation, begin to gradually
diminish with the attrition of passing years. Several of Paul's
epistles warn of approaching troubles. In the letter commonly
called 2 Peter, the warning intensifies, while in John's
epistles and the missive of Jude it becomes still more shrill.
But in Revelation itself we have not only clouds, but storm
and tempest. At this juncture Antichrist comes into his own,
as the representative of "the prince of the power of the air"
who has great wrath knowing "that his time is short."

Of course, Antichrist is a genus as well as a specific
figure.[3] All who oppose by cruelty, or counterfeit by subtlety,
Christ and His church, come under this head. Though sometimes
left out of the reckoning by commentators, Satan himself, in
the eyes of the first century Christians, was the supreme
Antichrist. So Revelation 12 paints him. Better known by the
title is his chief henchman of the last days, one who will
employ signs and wonders, proclaim himself as God, and
precipitate a time of trouble such as never was, "the hour of
trial" which will "try them that dwell upon the earth."[4]

What relationships exist between the Antichrists of Revelation
and the βδέλυγμα τῆς ἐρημώσεως of Daniel, Mark and Matthew,
and the ἄνθρωπος τῆς ἀνομίας   of 2 Thess. 2?

It should first be said that such relationships should be
anticipated if for no other reason than that the final
apocalypse appears to be an expansion of all prior apocalyptic
found in Scripture. While the Olivet discourse is not apocalyptic
in form, it certainly embodies and reflects throughout
apocalyptic motifs of which the βδέλυγμα τῆς ἐρημώσεως
is one of the chief. And it is a truth that has impressed almost
all commentators that the book of Revelation is a thorough-going
development of Christ's sermon on "the last things". It is just
as certain that the writer has in view the forecast of Christ on
the last Tuesday of His life, as that Christ in that address
had the themes of Daniel in mind.[5]

In Mk. 13 and its parallels, the βδέλυγμα τῆς ἐρημώσεως

is linked with attack upon the holy city, precipitation of an
unparalleled time of trouble, miraculous signs and wonders,
counterfeit Christs and false prophets, and the ultimate
Parousia of the avenging and rescuing Christ. In Revelation,
the same theme of attack upon the holy city occurs and reoccurs.
It is synonymous with persecution, or "war" against the saints.
This "war" is the great subject of the concluding chapter of the
first half of the book, and of the entire second half.[6] It is
specifically referred to in chapters 11,12,13,16,17,19 and also
in other chapters which do not use the word πόλεμος. While
special attention to Armageddon has been discounted by some
on the ground that it is only mentioned once in the book, what
we actually have in this mention is the climax to a war which is
repeatedly alluded to, and which dominates the thinking of the
writer.

As the original βδέλυγμα τῆς ἐρημώσεως was not only a
desolating invader who wore out the saints, but also one who
claimed worship for himself, so it is with the chief earthly
manifestation of Antichrist in the book of Revelation. And
furthermore, as in Daniel, Mark, Matthew and 2 Thess., this
apparition was the immediate prelude to the setting up of the
kingdom of God in glory, such is also the case in the Apocalypse.

Preparatory to a closer look at the passages concerned, some
of the more obvious parallels pertinent to our subject will
be indicated.

Dan. 8:13: ". . .For how long is the vision concerning
the continual burnt offering, the transgression that makes desolate, and the giving
over of the sanctuary and host to be
trampled under foot?"

Mk. 13:14: "But when you see the desolating sacrilege
set up where it [he] ought not to be
. . . ."

2 Thess. 2:3,4: . . .the rebellion comes first, and the
man of lawlessness. . .takes his seat in
the temple of God. . . .

Rev. 11:2: ". . .the nations. . .will trample over
the holy city. . . ."[7]

In the first reference we have a desolating power "treading
down" the holy places and the worshippers. In the second, a
power similarly described "stands" "in the holy place" "where
it ought not", as a threat to the worshippers who must flee if
they are to be saved. The third reference characterizes the

profaning one as "sitting" in "the temple of God". When we reach
the parallel in the Apocalypse, again the temple and holy city
are in focus. Again the worshippers are threatened, even
"trampled", as in the initial reference. And again it is
invading Gentiles who are responsible for the aggression and
profanation, as was the case with Antiochus Epiphanes.[8] The
climax of devastation is reached when the beast from the
bottomless pit successfully makes war on the Two Witnesses. But
the triumph is brief, for vindication of the saints follows, and
with it the kingdom of God on earth. Here is the parallel to the
concept adjoining the verse in Daniel quoted above. After many
days the sanctuary was to be vindicated, and of course its true
worshippers.[9] Thus closely does the first chapter of Revelation
concerning the Antichrist cling to the initial apocalyptic
sketch in Daniel on the same topic.

The opening chapter of the second half of Revelation also
enshrines Danielic imagery concerning the work of Antichrist. We
read of a monster with seven heads and ten horns raking the stars
from the skies,[10] making war in heaven, and on earth pouring
out a devastating flood[11] to drown the escaping saints. The
battle wages for "one thousand two hundred and sixty days" even
"a time, times, and half a time."[12] Then for the final war on
the remnant, the monster stands on the sand of the sea summoning
a fearful henchman who will initiate the last slaughter.

All of this takes its rise from the Old Testament description
of the work of Antiochus.[13] He, too, was pictured as sky-
raking, and dashing the holy ones to the ground. He, too,
invaded the holy land like an overwhelming flood. He, too, was
pictured as the representative of a monster with ten horns. His
period of persecution also was represented as "a time, times,
and half a time."

The thirteenth chapter of Revelation continues the expansion
of the Danielic picture. The earthly twin of the heavenly
dragon, having the same number of heads and horns, and doing
the same work for the same length of time, appears. He blasphemes
the sanctuary of God and desolates its worshippers.[14] His
representatives perform miraculous signs and wonders to persuade
those on earth to adore his image which could both breathe and
speak.[15] Then comes the great martyrdom of the non-conformists,
an obvious parallel to the war upon, and the death of, the Two
Witnesses in the first Johannine presentation of the Antichrist
theme.[16] Many features of this chapter enhance the counterfeit
aspect of the adversary which had been stressed by the Olivet
discourse and by 2 Thess. 2.[17] The chief figure of Revelation
13 is the member of a trinity; he has been slaughtered but
revives to resurrection life; he calls forth authenticating
signs; he has witnesses who, like Christ's witnesses, can call

down fire from heaven; he demands worship. A new feature in
this chapter is the reference to an image which is to be the
object of reverence. This is a very definite allusion to the
βδέλυγμα τῆς ἐρημώσεως motif. Even the number 666 reflects
imagery found in Daniel 3.[18]

Chapter fourteen of Revelation contains a warning against
submission to Antichrist and promises special blessing to those
who are to be martyred. The entire book of Daniel had the
same purpose as this chapter of the Apocalypse. It also, from
the first chapter to the last, had a didactic and paraenetic
purpose.[19] The evils of the Gentile oppressor were sketched in
graphic pictures whose point was in every instance "beware of
this same mark in the beast now oppressing us."[20] And Daniel
is the prototype of martyrologies. Dan. 11:32-35 is the basis
for all later variations on the theme. Such admonitions as
Rev. 13:10 and 14:12-13 are but reminders of Dan. 12:2-3,10-13.'

Revelation 15 pictures the ultimate victory of those who
had refused to worship Antichrist and his image. The destruction
of the desolator is seen to issue from the heavenly temple of
which the desecrated one on earth was but a faint shadow. One
familiar with Daniel, reading this chapter, would be reminded
of many references in the Old Testament book coinciding with
this theme. Daniel had spoken of a heavenly Watcher Who marked
the pride of Israel's oppressor, and he had sketched the
judgment which weighed the impious adversary in the balances
and found it wanting. Catastrophic upheavals had brought old
Babylon to its end, and there had been none to help it.[21]
Dan. 9:27 had promised a "decreed end" for the desolator, and
this end was to be "poured out" when the divine indignation was
accomplished. Similarly Revelation 15 promises the pouring
out of the wrath of God upon Antichrist, even the emptying
of heaven's bowls of judgment plagues. Thus would the
consummation foretold by Isaiah and enlarged upon by Daniel be
fulfilled.[22] The message of Daniel and Rev. 15 is the same --
"It does not pay to submit to Antichrist. The desolator will
himself shortly be desolated."

The following chapter in Revelation still centers around the
work of Antichrist and the divine response. The seven plagues
are divided, as is usual with the sevens of Revelation, into
four and three.[23] Most attention is given to the second group
which describes the final battle in the war between the true
and false Christ. In ancient times Antiochus had compelled
men to be branded with the ivy leaf,[24] the mark of Bacchus,
but the writer of Daniel had warned that all who submitted
to receiving such would become subject to "shame and everlasting
contempt."[25] Revelation 16 pictures the divine wrath descending
upon "the men who bore the mark of the beast and worshipped its

image."[26] Those who have persecuted others are now persecuted,
and those who have shed blood, must now drink it.[27] But the
central emphasis in this chapter is upon the gathering of the
kings of the earth "for battle on the great day of God the
Almighty." The powers of chapters twelve and thirteen, namely
the dragon, the beast, and the false prophet, are the leaders
of this opposition.[28] In fact, Rev. 16:13-14 appears to be
descriptive of the same crisis mentioned in the last half of
Rev. 13. War is made upon God by compelling His people to
worship the beast and its image, or die. The same powers are
in view, and the same signs and wonders. The following chapter
enlarges the identical crisis by use of different imagery, but
the war motif remains. Concerning the ten horns of the beast
it is written that they "will make war on the Lamb", apparently
by antagonism to "those with him", who are "called and chosen
and faithful."[29]

The initial references to this "war", it should be kept in
mind, are found in Daniel's descriptions of the attack by the
Antichrist of his day. Commentators on Dan. 9:26 frequently
point out that the war here mentioned is a springboard for later
references to the final eschatological conflict.[30]

Revelation 17 describes Antichrist from another viewpoint,
when the one who has shed the blood of the saints is characterized
as a harlot arrayed in purple and scarlet, bedecked with gold and
jewels and pearls, and astride the now familiar beast with
seven heads and ten horns. The name "Babylon the great" is yet
another allusion to the Old Testament saga of Antiochus Epiphanes.
Nebuchadnezzar, who had boasted concerning the "great Babylon"
which he had built, thereby exemplified the pride of Antichrist.[31]
His kingdom city built upon the Euphrates becomes the symbol of
Rome and her allies, for the harlot is not only located upon
seven hills but also upon "many waters".[32] The writer of
Daniel had depicted the fall of ancient Babylon, an event
associated with the "drying up" of the river Euphrates, as
foretold by second Isaiah.[33] Even so, hints Daniel, shall the
flood of persecution unleashed by Antiochus be "dried up".[34]
As Isaiah's writings, well-known and repeatedly quoted by Daniel,
had predicted that Babylon would "come down and sit in the dust"
with "no one to save" her,[35] so the later seer said of the
eschatological adversary that he, upon attacking the glorious
holy mountain "would come to his end, with none to help him."[36]
Thus Revelation 17 continues the application of the βδέλυγμα
τῆς ἐρημώσεως "spoken of by the prophet Daniel."[37]

It is evident that Revelation 17 delineates the crisis which
calls forth the judgments of the preceding chapter. But it
does more. It, along with the following chapter, describes
those judgments by employing other symbols. The ten horns

desolating the harlot and burning her, and the holocaust of the
city, are but alternative expressions of the fate depicted in
the chapter concerning the seven last plagues. And all this
symbolism has its roots in passages of Isaiah and Daniel.[38]

It should be specially noted that the terms βδέλυγμα, ἔρημος,
and ἐρημόω are linked with the person and fate of Antichrist
in this chapter.[39] The power which had forced the saints into
the wilderness of a persecution experience is now itself to
endure the wilderness of persecution. The eighteenth chapter
reiterates this terminology.[40]

The parousia is symbolized in Revelation 19, but its
occurrence is seen as the climax to the battle of Armageddon.
The powers of Antichrist, the beast and the false prophet of Rev.
13, lead the kings of the earth and their armies.[41] But their
ultimate destination is the lake of fire. This latter symbol
is reminiscent of the fate assigned to Daniel's Antichrist which
"was given over to be burned with fire."[42] The angel's call to
the birds refers back to the similar call recorded in Ezekiel
when the powers of Gog and Magog, from the north, fell upon
the mountains of Israel.[43] Daniel's description of the last
attack upon "the holy mountain" by Antiochus is modelled
upon the Ezekiel passage. Thus the reference to "the north", etc.
The overwhelming inundation of 11:40-44 is reminiscent of
Eze. 38:14-16, and the fate of the king of the north in 11:45 is
identical with the fate of Gog and Magog upon the mountains of
Israel.[44] The Johannine reference to Armageddon incorporates
the imagery of the mountains mentioned by Ezekiel and Daniel.
Thus Rev. chs. 16,17,18,19 all enlarge upon the destruction of
Israel's attacker "in the latter days", "the time of the end".[45]
The fate wished upon Antiochus Epiphanes by the writer of
Daniel has become the destiny assigned to the eschatological
Antichrist of John.

There is yet another reference to the βδέλυγμα τῆς ἐρημώσεως
motif in the Apocalypse. It is a final, climactic allusion.
The attack made before the millennium is repeated after the
thousand years. Or, if we choose to follow the amillennial
view, the same attack is pictured anew. Rev. 20:7-10 describes
the hordes of Gog and Magog as coming, not now from the north,
but from the four quarters of earth after their resurrection,
and as led by the supreme Antichrist, Satan himself. Again the
holy city is menaced as in Dan. 11:45. Once more the βδέλυγμα
τῆς ἐρημώσεως stands "where it ought not", on the borders of
"the holy place". But once and for all "he shall come to his
end, with none to help him." He is "given over to be burned with
fire." And from the ashes of a desolated earth the seer beholds
arising "a new earth". Now the new covenant promise is fulfilled
and God descends to tabernacle with men. The kingdom has come
indeed, with the glory of its consummation. Shut out forever are

all those who have worked abomination.[46] The once desolated
saints are now vindicated as they bear on their forehead, not
the mark of Antichrist, but the name of Yahweh -- that ancient
priestly inscription of "holiness unto the Lord" -- figure of the
primeval image of the Creator borne by the original sinless
parents of the race.[47] Such is the symbolic vision of the seer
of Patmos, embodying and transforming "on a larger canvas"[48] all
that his predecessors had intimated.

Exegetical Summaries of Antichrist Passages in Revelation

We do not propose to give an exhaustive exegesis of all the
passages in the Apocalypse which reflect the βδέλυγμα τῆς
ἐρημώσεως motif. Any one of these passages could well occupy
an entire thesis if dealt with comprehensively. We plan rather
to indicate the basic meaning of the most important of these
passages, showing the relevance of such for the βδέλυγμα τῆς
ἐρημώσεως theme. Some suggestions regarding the special
hermeneutic to be applied to the book of Revelation will be
offered, and illustrations of their application will be made
in the instance of the first passage considered, and with
subsequent passages to a lesser extent. Preliminary matters
vital to the background of exegesis will also be treated, but
with brevity, because of the virtual unanimity of leading
scholars regarding them. The Book of Revelation -- Authorship,
Date, Text, Historical Setting, Interpretation.

Authorship

While a few scholars such as E. Stauffer believe that the five
Johannine writings are from one author, and that author the
apostle John,[49] the majority believe the issue must remain an
open question.[50] It is not possible to prove the identity
of the John of Rev. 1:4,9 with any other John of the New
Testament.[51]

Until the end of the 18th century the Apocalypse was
generally ascribed to the apostle John, but the following
century saw many scholars opposing this primitive tradition. The
great difference in language and style between John's Gospel and
the Revelation was the chief reason for this dissidence.
Furthermore, an increasing number viewed the fourth Gospel as
non-apostolic.

In recent years there appear to be hints of another possible
change of tide in critical opinion. Otto Piper has written as
follows in a noteworthy article.:

Anderseits sind die Argumente gegen die Tradition in
neuester Zeit beträchtlich geschwächt worden, seitdem

250

Forscher für einen gemeinsamen Verfasser der J. und
des JohEv eingetreten sind. Dass die Behauptung der
Unvereinbarkeit der beiden Bücher stark überstrieben ist,
ehrt ein Vergleich der Sprache. Beide haben gegenüber
dem übrigen NT eine ganze Anzahl zentraler Begriffe
gemeinsam. . . .[52]

But he concludes: "Zusammenfassend wird man sagen dürfen, dass
die Bestreitung der apostolischen Verfassershaft der J. noch
eine Reihe ungelöster Problems enthält."[53]

We think that for the present there is nothing to add to
these conclusions by Piper regarding the matter of authorship.

Date

It is quite clear from the book that it was penned during a
period of persecution for the infant church.[54] Thus most
critics have chosen either the reign of Nero or that of Domitian
as the time of composition. Against the former date is the fact
that the writer obviously considers the church to be in serious
danger of complacency and worldliness, beyond that which Paul
warned against in this time.[55] Arguments based on passages such
as Rev. 17:9f., and 17:11 are not conclusive as the divergent
interpretations testify. A number of early writers such as
Iranaeus assert with definiteness that the book originated at the
time of Domitian.[56] The fact that the threat of increasing
pressure towards emperor-worship is alluded to throughout
Revelation indicates at least that the book was probably
written at some time during the last third of the century, and
that Domitian's reign was a likely occasion.

In summary:

Die verschiedenen Versuche, aus dem Buche selbst
Indizien für das Datum zu finden, beruhen zT auf
fehlerhafter Exegese, zT sind die andezogenen Stellen nicht
eindeutig genug. Immerhin lassen die Erwähnung des
erneuten Erstarkens der jüdischen Feindschaft gegen die
Christen und die Hinweise auf --Christenverfolgungen
darauf schliessen, dass die Scrift, wie schon Irenäus
annahm, gegen Ende der Regierungzeit Domitians (+96)
geschrieben wurde.[57]

Text

Despite the fact that "the Greek text of Revelation is more
uncertain in some respects than that of other books of the
New Testament"[58] yet it raises "few major problems."[59]

The vast majority of the more than 1600 variants are minor
in character, consisting of the usual differences in word order,
the addition or omission of articles and connectives,
synonym substitution, and the "correction" of the writer's
grammatical "errors". Thus there does not exist any real
question regarding the significance of any given sentence or
paragraph which a better text could solve.[60]

Furthermore, it must be said, that despite the massive
learning and equally massive imagination of R.H. Charles there
are no good grounds for assuming dislocations or rearrangements
of the original text.[61]

Historical Setting

The main point to be made here has already been referred to
in the discussion of the dating for this book. The author
obviously believed that the great tribulation well-known to both
Jewish and Christian tradition was about to break. Apparently
he read the signs of the times as foretelling an increase in the
existing pressures towards emperor-worship, an increase finally
to be accelerated by the appearance of a demonic antichrist.
Kümmel expresses the thought of the majority of modern
commentators when he writes: ". . .to understand the message of
the Apocalypse a knowledge of the external circumstances of its
origin is especially indispensable."[62]

Interpretation

It has often been remarked that Calvin showed his extreme
good sense when he left this book of the Bible without a
commentary from his pen -- the sole exception. Jerome declared
that the Apocalypse "has as many secrets as words", and that it
is "beyond all praise; for multiple meanings lie hidden in each
single word."[63] This hyperbole has understandably left lesser
souls speechless, but others more self-confident have affirmed
that the ancient exegete must have been blinded by a penchant
for the allegorical exegetical methods of Origen. Luther wrote:
"My spirit cannot accommodate itself to this book. There is
one sufficient reason for the small esteem in which I hold it --
that Christ is neither taught in it nor recognized."[64] Zwingli
denounced it as an intrusion into the canon. In our own day
C.H. Dodd has been almost as severe. His judgment is that "if
we review the book as a whole, we must judge that this
excessive emphasis on the future has the effect of relegating
to a secondary place just those elements of the Gospel which
are most distinctive of Christianity. . . ." Neither does
Dodd stop here. He adds: ". . . we are bound to judge that in
its conception of the character of God and his attitude to man
the book falls far below the level not only of the teaching of
Jesus but of the best parts of the Old Testament."[65]

Loisy's verdict is similarly unfavourable. He pulls no punches when he says:

> The best that can be said of it is that for centuries men have taxed their wits to find in it a meaning which is NOT there, for the simple reason that the meaning which IS there was immediately contradicted by the course of events.[66]

Such a comment stands in strong contrast to other earlier appraisals. Take Bishop Wordsworth for an example of the opposite school.

> . . . Henry More observes 'that there never was a book penned with that artifice as this of the Apocalypse, as if every word were weighed in a balance before it was set down.' Those remarkable specimens of careful composition in its earlier chapters may have been designed to remind the reader that every sentence of it is pregnant with meaning, and that in order to understand its Visions, the best method is to examine diligently every word of the Apocalypse.[67]

In much more recent days Caird has summarized the situation aptly:

> No other book can have aroused such equally passionate love and hatred. It has been the inspiration of poetry, music, and art, the fountain of worship and devotion, the comfort of the bereaved, and the strength of the persecuted. But it has also been roundly denounced by more critics than Luther as a work of vindictive and unchristian spirit.[68]

Strangely enough, critic can be pitched against critic on almost every issue affecting its worth. While Dodd can assert that it fails to glorify Christ, others find that it exalts Him far and above most of the books of the New Testament.[69] While some declare it to be vindictive and unchristian, others attempt to show that its spirit is not alien to Christ's own rightous indignation when He voiced woes against the Pharisees, not because He hated them, but because they misrepresented God, and by slighting His love, caused the feet of others to stray.[70] While one can reject the book on the basis that "his [John's] prophecies did not come true, and that must affect our judgment of the book and the author",[71] others assert that such a judgment is a failure to recognize the nature of Hebraic prophecy. Such countering critics believe that the emphasis of prophets has ever been upon the issue of the times rather than upon the times themselves,[72] and that furthermore time was seen as qualitative rather than quantitative, with "nonentity" time being left out of the reckoning. Again, these writers suggest that such spans of mere chronological time in contrast to opportunity time could be long or short depending upon prior human response to the Divine initiative.[73] The element of contingency, undoubtedly characteristic of Hebrew prophecy, must be reckoned with, say they.[74]

Another factor leading to critical prejudice against the Apocalypse is the fact that millenarian fanatics in particular have run to extremes in their exegesis of this volume -- their happy hunting ground and paradise.[75] From the initial circulation of the book these excesses have been common, and they certainly explain in part the slowness of some regions to accept the book as canonical, and they also explain to some degree modern negative attitudes.

Thus we have returned to the same position where our study of the βδέλυγμα τῆς ἐρημώσεως began -- interpretation being far from uniform, not because of the facts of the case, but because of strong, often unrecognized prejudices. Human nature being as it is, even exegetical human nature, eschatological materials must ever encounter such bias -- from opposite sides of the fence. Favourable critics tend to blur the problems, and negative critics sometimes damn the whole because the problems appear to support existing pejorative attitudes. The situation with the Apocalypse is thus identical with what we have found earlier regarding approaches to Mk. 13 and 2 Thess. 2. One's own Weltanschauung can too easily interpenetrate one's application of the laws of grammatico-historical exegesis. As a result the reader of Revelation "is faced not only with a bewildering book, but with and ever more bewildering array of interpretations."[76]

All of which preamble has been to give point to the necessity of an adequate hermeneutical approach to Revelation. Commentators have always waxed eloquent in superlative vein, in describing the difficulty of interpreting the chapters they face and sometimes unwillingly.[77] Therefore we propose at this juncture to submit some hermeneutical principles which spring from the book itself, and which can therefore with safety be employed as a legitimate exegetical approach.[78] These are supplementary to, and not substitutionary for, well-known standard exegetical procedures. These supplementary principles will be outlined, and then illustrated by a concise exegesis of the relevant sections of Rev. 11. The same principles will later be applied to other key passages of the book. The objective throughout will not be the impossible one of giving an exhaustive commentary,[79] but rather the aim will be to indicate the basic concepts embodied and their relationship to the βδελυγμα της ερημωσεως motif.[80]

Supplementary Hermeneutical Principles for Interpreting the
Apocalypse

The first principle requiring attention is not supplementary.
It is basic for all interpretation, but doubly so for this
particular book. Inasmuch as all the writings of the New
Testament are occasional pieces, more representative of
persuasive oratory than of enduring literature, they are to be
recognized as Tracts for the Times, and the vital question
asked -- "What times?"[81]

The first page of Revelation gives an adequate answer. John
testifies that he was in the isle of Patmos "on account of the
word of God and the testimony of Jesus." The most obvious
meaning of the words is that as a result of the persuasion
of government the writer found himself in a new habitat.[82] That
this is the right interpretation seems evidenced by the
references to persecution and martyrdom which permeate the rest
of the book.

So much for the times. Now we ask, "What sort of tract is
this one? How does John meet the needs of the time?" And
again John himself gives us the answer. His work is an
ἀποκάλυψις. This classifies the book as within a certain class
of literature.[83] Writings of this kind describe the existing
crisis against the background of world history, and they
usually do so in the language of symbol.

It follows, therefore, that in order to explain an
apocalypse, we must first identify the earthly realities
to which the heavenly symbols correspond, and then see
how by the use of this symbolism the author has tried
to interpret earthly history.[84]

That this judgment of the symbolic nature of John's tract
for the times is correct is indicated at the close of his
introduction. There he says:

As for the mystery of the seven stars which you saw
in my right hand, and the seven golden lampstands, the
seven stars are the angels of the seven churches and
the seven lampstands are the seven churches.[85]

Thus John asserts: "In this my opening vision I saw stars
as the symbol of angels, and lampstands as the symbol for
churches." The literary context adds its endorsement, for
the following verse speaks of one who holds the seven stars in
his right hand and who walks among the seven golden lampstands.
It is certain that the literal meaning is unintended. Incongruous indeed would be the mental image of one large enough to

255

hold stars like the sun in his palm, and yet small enough to thread his way between lampstands.

Thus the book is full of symbols.[86] But do the symbols chiefly belong to a common source or do they have diversified origins? The answer again is found on the first page. Here we have frequent references to the Hebrew prophets, and to Hebrew ritual and history. Daniel, Zechariah, Isaiah et al, are repeatedly cited, as if designed to lead the reader to regard the Apocalypse "as a sequel to, and continuation of, Hebrew prophecy. . . ." Israel's experience when called to become a nation of kings and priests, and the institution of the sanctuary and the priesthood are also alluded to.

W. Milligan has it right when he sums up his conclusions regarding the symbols of Revelation. He says:

(1) They are for the most part suggested by the religious position, training, and habits both of the writer and his readers. The Apostle had been a Jew, in all the noblest elements of Judaism a Jew to the very core. . . .We may expect that what is written from such a point of view will breathe the very essence of Old Testament prophecy, more especially in its apocalyptic parts, will be moulded by its spirit, be at home amidst its pictures, and be familiar with its words.

(2) . . . .Similar remarks may be made with regard to the historical events referred to in the Apocalypse. Such events often lie at the bottom of its symbols, but it may be doubted if there be a single instance in which the incident taken advantage of by the Seer was not both well known and of the deepest interest to his readers. . . .But the symbolism of the Revelation is wholly and exclusively Jewish.

(3) The symbols of the Apocalypse are to be judged of with the feelings of a Jew, and not with those of our own country or age.[87]

Many, of course, will contend that Milligan does not give due right to pagan myths incorporated by John. Otto Piper, however, says:

Die Bilder und Symbole sind ferner nicht nach ihrem ursprünglichen mythologischen Sinn zu deuten, sondern einerseits im Lichte ihres Gebrauches in der israelitisch-jüdischen Literatur . . . .Im Hinblick auf ihren visionären Charakter sind sie auch nicht als Bescreibungen zu behandeln, die wörtlich zu verstehen sind. . . .[88]

Austin Farrer tells us that he began his work on the
Apocalypse in reaction against the commentators he had read. To
him it appeared that they assumed too easily that much of the
book could be interpeted by reference to what existed outside
of John's work, such as pagan myths. Farrer's own conclusion was
that "there appeared to be in several parts of his book a more
continuous, hard-headed and systematic working-out of Old
Testament themes than had been recognized. . . ."[89]

Beckwith, in commenting upon the imagery of Rev. 12, reminds
us that "the Apocalyptist has clothed his thought here in a
form adopted from some legend or myth familiar in Jewish folklore."[90] He continues by saying that as part of their
common Semitic heritage the Jews retained legends which they
more or less transformed. Thus pagan myths adopted by John have
passed through a Jewish crucible, and to keep this in mind is
vital for interpretation of the Apocalypse.

Having said that the symbolism of this book is primarily
Jewish, we must next enquire whether John was now applying the
things of Israel to that nation still, or to the Christian
church as the new Israel. Our conclusion here, also, will
vitally affect our interpretation of many passages.

We believe that the whole trend of the book, from the
introductory reference to the Christian churches in Asia under
Jewish sanctuary symbolism, to the final vision of the New
Jerusalem, testifies to the fact that in the thinking of the
seer, the Christian church has taken the place of literal Israel.[91]
This fact may be the explanation for the phenomenon often
commented upon -- the strange Hebraic Greek used by the seer --
"unlike any Greek that was ever penned by mortal man"[92] according to R.H. Charles. This Greek, however, "is not the
product of incompetence, for he handles it with brilliant
lucidity and compelling power. . . ."[93] One has commented thus:

> The diction of the Book of Revelation is more Hebraistic
> than that of any other portion of the New Testament. It
> adopts Hebrew Idioms and Hebrew words. It studiously
> disregards the laws of Gentile Syntax, and even courts
> anomalies and solecisms; it christianizes Hebrew words
> and sentiments, and clothes them in an Evangelical dress,
> and consecrates them to Christ.[94]

We do not find in John's book the evidence that we have in
Paul's epistles of a hope for Israel's conversion to Christ.
He seems rather to look upon those who were circumcised as
part of "the synagogue of Satan". They have become
tormentors of Christ's followers, and as such they now belong to
the great city of Babylon responsible for the crucifixion of

Christ and the martyrdom of His followers. In John's eyes "the
proud name of Jew, with all its ancient associations, had become
the prerogative of those who gave allegiance to the true
Messiah."[95] Commenting upon Rev. 7, Kiddle says:

> . . .John makes what amounts to a twelvefold assertion
> that the Christian churches are the chosen people,
> complete heirs to the ancient Jewish heritage (cf. Jas. 1:1;
> 1 Pet. 1:1); it was as the elect nation that they must
> both suffer persecution and enjoy vindication.[96]

Carpenter sums up the matter:

> The Christian Church absorbs the Jewish, inherits her
> privileges, and adopts, with wider and nobler meaning, her
> phraseology.
> The historical basis of the Apocalypse is the past history
> of the chosen people; God's dealings with men always
> follow the same lines. The Apocalypse shows us the
> principle working higher levels and in a wider arena. The
> Israel of God, the church of Christ, takes the place of the
> national Israel.[97]

We feel that the principle here expressed is mandatory for a
correct exegesis of Revelation. For failure to observe it
consistently many have made shipwreck of their task. Even such
a classic commentary as Beckwith's forgets it to some extent
when commenting on the key chapter of Revelation concerning the
Two Witnesses. Ladd, more recently, has followed his example.[98]

From this principle emerges yet another. If the things of
Israel are now applied to the Christian church they must
thereby automatically have a world-wide application rather than
merely a local.[99] The true Israel is scattered throughout every
nation, and similarly Babylon also has become world-wide. The
seven lamp-stands point to a world-wide body of believers, but
the original seven-branched candlestick resided in a Palestinian
holy place.[100] Throughout this book John takes materials from
the visions of the Old Testament prophets originally couched
in a local setting, and he applies them to world-wide events.
For example, Rev. 1:7 applies the original mourning of some in
the land of Palestine, and gives it an eschatological universal
application. In Rev. 3:4,5 the "white raiment" of Israel's
priests is promised to the faithful in all the world. Rev. 6:14
takes a passage from Isaiah's description of the destruction of
Idumea and applies it to the end of the world. The following
verse alludes to Isa. 2:10-22, originally levelled at impenitent
Judah, but in its new setting the significance has reference
to an impenitent world at the time of the second advent of Christ.
And Rev. 6:16 similarly takes words of threatened judgment upon

Samaria and refers them to the wicked of all the world at the end of time. The following chapter of Revelation uses the vision of Ezekiel regarding the marking of some in Jerusalem, but now its usage applies to protection for Christians in the four quarters of the earth. Examples could be multiplied, but these are sufficient to illustrate the principle.

What has already been said underlines the fact that the entire book of Revelation is a mosaic of Old Testament passages, and therefore any solitary interpretation which ignores this fact must inevitably founder.[101]

Closely integrated with the foregoing is the usage in the Apocalypse of the ritual and festivals of Israel's sanctuary.[102] This too is not without significance for interpretation of the book.

A vital principle for any hermeneutic of Revelation is the Christ-centered nature of the work, and this in ways beyond the obvious. The life of Christ, particularly His ministry from the baptism on, is a vital key to the visions.[103] John assumes the truth of the New Testament teaching that the church is the body of Christ, and therefore it is to be expected that the body will share the experience of the Head. Chapter 11, in particular, illustrates this.

But not only the life of Christ as regards events is significant for the interpreter. His teachings also play their part. It cannot be too strongly stressed that Christ's sermon on the Mount of Olives is the seed-bed of the Apocalypse in a special sense.[104] All the key concepts of Mark 13 are also to be found in an enlarged form in this book. The spread of the gospel, the persecution of its adherents, international disasters such as war, famine, and earthquake, the time of trouble such as never was, the appearance of Antichrist including false Christs and false prophets, and His own return in glory to rescue and reward the saints -- all these which figure so prominently in the Olivet discourse are found again in symbolic yet more detailed form in the Apocalypse.

Most of what has been said in the immediately preceding pages amounts to the fact that the book with which we are concerned revolves around Christ,[105] His ancient testimony through the prophets, and His own more recent revelation, and His world-wide church -- the new Israel. Note how Piper has summarized these emphases.

> Was steht im Mittelpunkt der _Botschaft_, die der Seher verkündigen will? Negative kann man sagen: nicht Gott. . . tätig ist nicht er, sondern Christus oder Jesus, wie ihn

Johannes mit Vorliebe nennt. . . .Mit gleichem Recht könnte
man aber auch sagen, die J. Beschäftige sich in erster Linie
mit dem Gottesvolk. . . .Genauer aber wird man sagen müssen,
dass die J. die Wechselbeziehung zwischen dem himmlischen
Herrn und seinem Volk auf Erden beschreibt, wobei das
letztere alle Auserwählten durch die ganze Geschichte
hindurch umschliesst. Das zentrale Geheimnis, das Johannes
zu verkundigen hat, ist das Teilhaben der Gläubigen an
Christus und seinem Wirken und Leiden, und daher auch an
seinem schliesslichen Triumph.[106]

Thus Piper rightly sees that in this book the church is seen doing
the same work of proclamation as Her Lord, and as sharing His
sufferings and victory. This truth casts light not only on the
symbols of the people of God such as the Temple, the Witnesses,
the twelve tribes of Israel, the Woman clothed with the Sun, the
New Jerusalem etc., but also on the opponents of Christ and His
church -- the Dragon, Beast, and False Prophet, and Babylon. Thus
the interpreter can be saved from novel and erroneous applications
of the symbols.

While it has been emphasized that the recognition of the book
as apocalyptic literature is a guiding principle, it should also
be pointed out that the book claims to be more than just a
typical apocalypse.[107] Its oft-repeated claim is that it is also
prophecy.[108] It is not for us to endeavour to analyze John's
psychical state while illuminated, but it is for us to recognize
the nature of the claims he makes.[109] According to his own
statements the book is not the product of coolly reasoned literary
art. He believed himself to have been "in the Spirit" and to have
received from heaven such vital messages that all who dare to
tamper with them are anathematized.[110]

Similarly, John claims that his book has for its theme the
eschatological crisis.[111] G.B. Caird translates the last sentence
of Rev. 1:3: "For the crisis is near", and thereby he does
justice to the constant implications of John's assertions.
Beasley-Murray goes further than some in making reference to this
matter, but in essence his words reflect the claims of the
Apocalyptist himself.

John was more than a poet setting forth in vague images
the triumph of God over all evil. He wrote for the churches
under his care with a practical situation in view, viz.,
the prospect of the popular Caesar-worship of his day
being enforced on all Christians. . . .Grasping the
principles involved, John was given to see the logical
consummation of the tendencies at work, mankind divided to
the obedience of Christ or antichrist. On the canvas of
John's age, therefore, and in the colours of his environ-

ment, he pictured the last great crisis of the world, not
merely because from a psychological viewpoint, he could
do no other, but because of the real correspondence between
his crisis and that of the last days. . . . this 'foreshort-
ened perspective' no more invalidates his utterances than it
does those of the OT prophets and of our Lord Himself, for
it is characteristic of all prophecy.[112]

It seems to us that only the recognition of these features,
which characterize the book, can lead to an adequate exegesis of
its contents.[113]

Revelation 11 -- The Two Witnesses and Antichrist

In the light of the foregoing principles it is proposed to
examine the first passage of Revelation to embody in detail the
βδέλυγμα τῆς ἐρημώσεως   motif.[114] This examination must be
done with brevity, so far as its results are here presented,
in order to keep within the proportions necessitated by the
scope of the present thesis.

The eleventh chapter of Revelation is both a conclusion and an
introduction.[115] It concludes the first half of the book but
introduces the second. Most of the key elements which are to
characterize chapters 12-22 here find enunciation -- the attack
upon the church as it proclaims the gospel during the final
crisis, the rising of the Antichrist from a state of apparent
death, the real safety and ultimate vindication of believers, and
the ushering in of the eternal kingdom in glory accompanied by
judgments upon those who reject the gospel -- all are here set
forth.

The chapter has often been declared the most difficult of the
book,[116] but as Caird has said, a faithful interpretation of its
symbols in harmony with legitimate exegetical principles makes
its meaning "free from any sort of ambiguity."[117]

To detach the chapter from its own introduction in ch. 10 is to
fail in rightly interpreting it.[118] There we read of an angel
astride land and sea with a little scroll open, proclaiming that
there is to be no more delay, and that the mystery of God is now
to be fulfilled as predicted by the prophets. John takes the
open scroll, and on eating finds it sweet to the palate but
bitter upon digestion. Then he is told "You must again prophesy
about many peoples and nations and tongues and kings." At this
point our present chapter commences, as John is given a measuring
rod and commanded to measure the temple of God, its altar, and
its worshippers. He is instructed -- ". . . .do not measure the
court outside the temple; leave that out, for it is given over
to the nations, and they will trample over the holy city for

forty-two months. And I will grant my two witnesses power to prophesy for one thousand two hundred and sixty days, clothed in sackcloth."

It seems then that the contents of the open scroll are identical with the matter set forth in the eleventh chapter of John's book.[119] Thus the bitterness indicates the suffering coming to those who proclaim the sweet tidings of the gospel. And this suffering is to be world-wide, for the message goes to "many people and nations and tongues and kings."[120] Furthermore, it is suffering during the final crisis, for there is now to be no more delay, but the mystery of the kingdom is to be consummated.[121] Thus we have in chapter 10 clues to the meaning of the following chapter.

The temple of God, the holy city, the two witnesses, the two olive trees, and the lampstands all symbolize the witnessing church.[122] They witness to the truths contained in the law and the prophets (alluded to by references from the experiences of Moses and Elijah in vs. 6-7), and they, like Joshua and Zerubbabel of old, have priestly and royal prerogatives and duties. It would be impossible for "men from the people and tribes and tongues and nations" to "gaze at their dead bodies"[123] were these two literal corpses in the literal street of literal Jerusalem. THe world-wide church is signified.

The sources of this passage are basically the following:

(1) Daniel's βδέλυγμα τῆς ἐρημώσεως passages, particularly 7:25; 8:13; 9:26; 11:31-35.

(2) Ezekiel passages regarding eschatological events. See particularly chapters 40 and 37.

(3) Zechariah passages. See particularly chs. 12 and 4.

(4) The Old Testament narratives regarding Elijah and Moses.

(5) The records of Christ's ministry, which may indicate that He prophesied for 1260 days rejected of men, and then was crucified prior to His vindication in resurrection and ascension. Even v.10 seems to be an allusion to the Gospel record. See Luke 23:12.

Thus this chapter gives John's understanding of what the future holds for believers in Christ. Soon they are to enter upon the great tribulation, similar to that of the days of Antiochus Epiphanes.[124] Those who refuse to "worship the beast and his image" will be slain by the beast from the abyss, just as those who refused to receive the mark of the ivy branch and conform

to the false worship surrounding the image of Antiochus were
martyred in the 2nd century B.C. "But," says John in effect, "
remember you are kings and priests like Christ your Master.
You will not be treated worse than He. You are to be partakers
of Christ's sufferings as certainly as you are to partake of His
glory. Your inmost life cannot be touched. God has measured
you, secured you, sealed you. In the courtyard of earth where
the Lord suffered, you may lose this earthly life, but the life
hidden with Christ in God cannot be hurt. Ultimately you will
be vindicated before all in the kingdom of glory, while your
oppressors must suffer judgment."

Verse 8 is of great significance. Here John tells us plainly
that he is using metaphor and symbol.[125] He also makes it clear
that the spirit of Jewry which crucified Christ is to be the
spirit of the entire world in their opposition to the church. It
seems likely that the court outside the temple, referred to in
v.2 is a symbol of the Babylonian world. ἔκβαλε is stronger
than merely "leave that out".[126] Elsewhere it has the thought
of excommunication, i.e. casting out. Only the believers are
safe, but all others are cast out. The believer's earthly life
is indeed in the world, and there it must suffer from all who
echo the unbelief of apostate Israel. Thus the court points to
the same as "the great city which is allegorically called Sodom
and Egypt, where their Lord was crucified." The court was the
place for sacrifice and thus aptly typifies the persecuting
world.

Verse 7 is similarly important. Here we find the article
linked with the beast which is now mentioned for the first time.
This is in harmoney with John's frequent usage of prolepsis. The
beast is Antichrist, as the later chapters also make clear. Like
the βδέλυγμα τῆς ἐρημώσεως in Daniel, the beast persecutes
the saints because their worship is not of him. He is victor-
ious for 1260 days, and during that time he treads down the
worshippers in the sanctuary. Thus both Daniel's visions and
the prophecy of Christ in Mk. 13:14 and Lu. 21:24 are referred to.
The beast, because of its desolation of the true worship, is
indeedan abomination to the seer who portrayed him. Thus later
he will portray the fact that the desolator will himself be
desolated.[127] The abyss is significant in pointing to the
nether world of desolation as his origin and destiny.[128] He is
from the abyss in the sense that Christ by His victory on Calvary
has inflicted upon Satan and his representatives a mortal wound[129]
and hence they have no real right to attempt to coerce the people
of God. This is spelled out more clearly in the twelfth chapter,
but for the present we should note that rising from the abyss
is to be equated with a show of life manifested by persecution.
This gives the clue to the real nature of the healing of the
mortal wound referred to in chapters 13 and 17. The same theme

reoccurs in the chapter on the millennium. If R.H. Charles, G.E.
Ladd, and similar exegetes are correct, Satan is wounded afresh
at the second advent of Christ and consigned to the grave for
a thousand years. But after that time the wound is apparently
healed, and as of old he goes forth to make war on the saints.

Thus Rev. 11 sets forth in seed form all that is to be
enlarged in the following chapters, and in doing so it indicates
the manner in which these later chapters are to be interpreted.
And throughout the whole story the reader can ever hear ringing
echoes from from the days of the original Antichrist, Antiochus
Epiphanes, the βδέλυγμα τῆς ἐρημώσεως   in the first great
apocalypse.

Revelation 13

This can be called "the Antichrist chapter" of the book, for
although other chapters make reference to the same power and
the crisis initiated by it, none give so much detail to the
climactic time of trouble as is here to be found. Ernst rightly
refers to the passage as "the high-point of the whole
eschatological drama."[130]

Again our interpretation is aided by taking into account the
preceding chapter. There the Atonement of Christ had been
graphically pictured as the expulsion of Satan from the heavenly
places. The defeated adversary has "great wrath, because he
knows that his time is short." He stands on the sand of the sea
watching for his last representatives who will set on foot his
final desperate efforts to spite and spoil the people and plans
of the Lamb his conqueror.

Then is described the well-known beast with its ten horns and
seven heads, and modern commentators are agreed in recognizing
therein an allusion to the Empire of John's day, lately become
vicious in its attitude to Christ's followers.[131] However, in
harmony with the hermeneutical principles earlier outlined, it
must be said that it is the Empire as viewed by John through
the lens of the visions of Daniel. What he sees is not civil
government as such about its lawful business. Rather, he
beholds the Antichrist foretold by the prophets.[132] What is
then happening in the Asian province of the Empire is but the
breaking of the waters. The real attack has yet to be launched,
and when it comes, a demonic potentate will be its leader, one
from the abyss of death. At this point reference must be made
again to the popular interpretation regarding Nero redivivus.
It is indeed possible that John alludes to the current myth,
but it is not possible that he is here giving it credence. He
does not expect a revived Nero. But he does expect revived pers-
cution on a world-wide scale, reminiscent of what took place in

Rome during the days of the mad fiddler. And almost certainly John sees in the legend about Nero a caricature of the tremendous truth that Satan, the chief Antichrist, has been mortally wounded by Christ's Atonement, yet will essay his strength once more by a final attack on the church. He believes that what is coming is the final death throes of the serpent whose swirling tail will launch the earth-dwellers to perdition, and many of the saints to rest.

Allusions to the βδέλυγμα τῆς ἐρημώσεως pattern are many.[133] Most commentators refer not only to the familiar Antichrist prophecies of Daniel 7,8,11, but also to the story of the image recorded in Daniel 3 which undoubtedly pointed to the idolatry of the Syrian king as well as that of the Babylonian monarch. Once more we have the well-known period of trial, "forty-two months", the same therefore as indicated in Rev. 11:2-3. Again we have reference to "war" upon the saints, as in Rev. 11:7.[134]

What seems to be new is the symbol of the two-horned beast who hereafter is known as the false prophet. But even here the theme of Rev. 11 is being reiterated, for the two-horned beast is an obvious counterfeit of the two witnesses. He also calls down fire from heaven and works mighty signs.[135] He also is the representative of another, indeed, his publicity and propaganda officer. One cannot help being reminded, not only of Rev. 11, but of the eschatological discourse of Christ which foretold not only false Christs but also false prophets. We have both brought to view in the present chapter. While John's thought took its point of departure from the pagan priesthood of Asia minor, it does not linger there. He sees false religious leaders on a world-wide scale, apostate to God and in league with the dragon, being thus enabled to work the wonders of Spiritism. He has in mind the eschatological fulfillment of Deut. 13:1-3. Church and state will yoke as in Christ's day when opposing religious parties united over their hatred to the popular Rabbi and linked with the State in order to destroy Him. The union will be aided by miracles through the power of the dragon, and thus all men will be enlisted to make war on the Lamb, all that is, save those whose names are in the book of life. This combination of the beast and the false prophet and their ensuing activities is discussed again in Rev. 16,17,19. No better commentary on chapter 13 can be found that John's own words:

> And I saw, issuing from the mouth of the dragon and from the mouth of the beast and from the mouth of the false prophet, three foul spirits like frogs; for they are demonic spirits, performing signs, who go abroad to the kings of the whole world, to assemble them for battle on the great day of God the Almighty. . .And they assembled

them at the place which is called in Hebrew Armageddon.

Revelation 13 is thus the gathering for Armageddon -- the final conflict in the controversy between good and evil, a conflict to be ended by the Parousia of Christ.[136] John is saying that the last conflict like the first (Cain and Abel) will be about worship, and will involve death. As in the original instance there will also be a marking of separation. So severe will be the struggle that the majority of earth will join the dragon and his associates. While a warning message from the witnessing church strives to save men from worshipping the beast and his image, and endeavours to turn them to the worship of the Creator, the multitudes instead will become subject to the Adversary of God and receive his mark, his likeness. The mystic number has ever been associated with the serpent. It is the number of sin and imperfection, attenuated to a trinity as if to indicate evil to the nth degree. It represents all that belongs to man when separated from God. It is truly "the number of man" -- man under the serpent's control.[137] And even here are overtones from the original βδέλυγμα τῆς ἐρημώσεως pattern, for in that source too the number six is repeated in connection with false worship.[138]

Revelation 14 and 16

According to Lohmeyer, Rev. 14 is the high point of the Apocalypse. Certainly here is pictured the outcome of the last battle. The victors stand with Christ upon Mount Zion. But having given that glimpse of triumph, the seer then proceeds to present the final warning to the world about its last fatal choice. Rev. 14:-6-12 pictures the fulfilment of Mk. 13:10. It places earth-dwellers in a dilemma. They stand indeed between the devil and the deep crystal sea of God. While the beast threatens death to those who refuse to worship him, heaven thunders a pause to all who contemplate submission. The fall of Babylon the oppressor is foretold in order that men might not consider it invincible. The obedient are characterized as possessing endurance and the faith of Jesus. Upon them who risk martyrdom by their loyalty, a special blessing is pronounced. Then appears the sign of the Son of Man in heaven, as He comes to garner His own and destroy their persecutors.

We are particularly interested in the last verse which contains an additional allusion to the βδέλυγμα τῆς ἐρημώσεως motif. Here we read that the wine-press of the wrath of God is trodden ἔξωθεν τῆς πόλεως We cannot agree with the laboured exegesis of those who, like Caird, endeavour to prove that both the harvest of the wheat and the later vintage apply to the ingathering of God's servants.[139] Rather, the evidence supports the contrary.[140] The symbolism of the vintage has been gleaned from Old Testament pictures of divine indignation against the wicked. But let us enquire -- "Why is the scene of destruction placed outside the city?"[141]

Here we have another illustration of the homogeneity of the biblical eschatological themes. The time of trouble such as never was is to be launched by the βδέλυγμα τῆς ἐρημώσεως (also called "the king of the north") surrounding the holy city, according to the climactic presentation of Daniel. Then Michael comes and delivers His menaced saints. This view is similar to Joel 3 and Eze. 38-39, which also picture the attack upon the city of the saints "in the latter days". John uses the same idea in Rev. 20:8 where the final employment of this symbolism occurs. In Rev. 14:20, John comforts the church with the assurance that in the last onslaught (Rev. 13) the saints will be secure. John knew that Joel 2:32 promised deliverance from the foes gathered outside the city.[142] Similarly, Joel 3 pictured a harvest in the valley of Jehoshaphat (= Judgment) which lay outside Zion. It is this same harvest which John describes as the harvest of the earth. He also applies the treading referred to in Joel 3:13. Those, who in days past have trodden down the holy city, are now themselves trodden, while the saints composing the city of God are secure. The 1600 furlongs is the circuit of "the holy oblation" of Ezekiel's vision wherein figured a mighty temple and city on the "very high mountain" "in the land of Israel."[143] The writer of the Apocalypse applies Ezekiel's "oblation" to the world-wide church -- outside of which the enemies of the church perish in Armageddon's slaughter. Thus the treading of the wine-press in Rev. 14, the bringing of the βδέλυγμα τῆς ἐρημώσεως (i.e. the king of the north) to his end, the harvest in the valley of Jehoshaphat, the feast upon the slain of Gog and Magog, and the desolation accomplished at Armageddon, all point to the same event -- judgment and destruction upon those who seek to destroy the people of God. Rev. 14:20 constitutes another excellent example of the hermeneutical principles suggested as specially applicable for this book.

In Revelation 16, the drying up of the river Euphrates, the kings of the east,[144] the gathering of the kings of the whole world, and Armageddon, are symbols which call for particular attention. The first two symbols are borrowed from second Isaiah which foretells a drought upon Babylon's waters in order that Babylon might be overthrown by Cyrus, God's Anointed, the "one from the east". Such was the preliminary to the deliverance of Israel from Babylon. The last Apocalypse thus asserts that when the ten horns turn upon the whore "the people and multitudes and nations and tongues" represented by the waters of Euphrates cease to be her support.

267

Then Christ comes from the east, i.e. from heaven, as King of Kings and Lord of lords. Almost all modern commentators see in this passage an allusion to the Parthians from the east, whom, according to legend, Nero would lead against Rome. It is indeed possible that this myth lies at the back of John's mind, but here again, as with Rev. 13:3, he may have something more Christ-centred than that to convey.[145] He speaks of Christ and His church, and other powers only enter the picture when they have some relationship with the people of God. Ἀνατολή was a familiar symbol for the Messiah in New Testament times. It pointed to something or Someone of heavenly origin. Elsewhere the Apocalypse used the term in this manner, and it is hardly likely that a book so carefully written should change the meaning of this symbol in the later chapter. To literalize "east" is to depart from all sound principles of exegesis when dealing with this book of metaphors. The "kings of the east" may be intended as a direct contrast to "the kings of the whole world" mentioned in the same paragraph, and could represent heavenly beings who come to deliver the saints, as the Median kings from the east came with Cyrus to deliver Israel of old from Babylon. Possibly John also had in mind Eze. 41:2, which pictured the divine glory as coming from the east, ever the route of entrance to the sanctuary. These symbols are of particular interest to the student of the βδέλυγμα τῆς ἐρημώσεως because the attacks of the latter upon Israel are often represented as a "flood". Many scholars have pointed out that Euphrates is used in Scripture as a symbol of an invading force.[146] Daniel probably borrowed his use of the term from Isaiah's reference to the overflowing Euphrates. It is clear from Revelation that the Euphrates represents the multitudes supporting Babylon, and it is also clear that it is these multitudes who are gathered by the dragon, beast, and false prophet, to make war on Christ by attacking His church. Thus as surely as the ultimate βδέλυγμα τῆς ἐρημώσεως is the Antichrist of Revelation, so surely is the drying up of the Euphrates the symbol of the beginning of the end for this persecuting (desolating) power. It is vital to remember that the Euphrates and Babylon are part and parcel of Antichrist.

It has already been pointed out that the "battle" mentioned in Rev. 16:14 is but another phase of the "war" referred to so often in the chapters of Revelation dealing with the Antichrist. Chapters 11,12,13,17,19,20 specifically mention it. The primary source of this motif is found in the Danielic references to the war made upon Israel by Antiochus Epiphanes.

The symbol of Armageddon thus becomes exceedingly appropriate. It conjoins the memories associated with Megiddo with the prediction of Ezekiel that the enemies "upon the mountains of Israel."[147] Beckwith not only declares Armageddon to be "an

imaginary name for designating the scene of the great battle
between Antichrist and the Messiah", but shows that Ezekiel's
prophecy about the overthrow of Israel's enemies "upon the
mountains" is the source.[148] It is quite likely that the writer
of Daniel has Megiddo in mind when he speaks of the king of the
north coming to his end "between the sea and the glorious holy
mountain."[149] The location fits Megiddo, across which plain
floods of invading armies poured when en route to attack
Jerusalem. Thus both concepts of πόλεμος and 'Αρμαγεδών link
with Daniel's presentation of the βδέλυγμα τῆς ἐρημώσεως
and the συναγών of the kings of the whole earth is identical with
the compulsion towards false worship described in Rev. 13, which
chapter is also based on Daniel's imagery concerning the
Antichrist of his day.

Revelation 17

In Revelation 17, Antichrist is depicted as the "mother of
harlots and of earth's abominations."[150] It is declared that
ultimately she who has desolated others by martyrdom will
herself be made "desolate and naked".[151]

There can be no dodging the allusion to Rome, the city upon
seven hills, which had dominion over the kings of the earth.[152]
But again it must be said that John, though fully aware of the
current political and even economic scene is not primarily
interested in either. To him Babylon is essentially religious
and personifies the whole world's apostasy from God. His use
of the title tells us that he has Babel in mind, and also the
kingdom of Nebuchadnezzar. John goes out of the way to say that
Babylon is "a name of mystery".[153] The first conclusion may not
be the truth, or at least not the whole truth.

Babylon the whore stands in obvious contrast to the woman
clothed with the sun.[154] This woman is the consort of Satan --
the very opposite of the church of Christ, encompassing all of
all ages who have rebelled against the Most High. As the woman
of Rev. 12 obviously is a figure for the people of God in all
times, so the woman of Rev. 17 encompasses the rebels of every
era. But as John particularly applies the bride eschatologically,
so with the harlot. Paul had spoken of ἡ ἀποστασία and Babylon
to John summarizes the rebellion spoken of by the apostle to the
Gentiles. Babel had originated in rebellion, and thus it will
end.

Too often emphasis has been placed solely upon the secular
significance of this figure as applied to the city of Rome.
Certainly this metropolis of the Empire is in view but does it
exhaust John's meaning? He sees only in black and white. Either
one is numbered with the woman clothed with the sun, or one is

part of Babylon. And his purpose remains parenetic to the last.[155] Throughout the letters to the seven churches his objective has been to save his flock from compromise. He warns them against the synagogue of Satan,[156] and against those who like Balak and Balaam seduce God's people.[157] False teachers are styled as Jezebel,[158] and John's desire is to save "half-baked" Christians from becoming Ahabs. All this must be kept in mind as we contemplate the picture in Rev. 17. It is succeeded by a call to separate from Babylon (18:1-4), and thus indicates that if the Christians of the seven churches in Asia were to come out of the seven-hilled city, more than geographical locations are in focus.

While it is true that Scripture uses the harlot symbol for cities such as Tyre and Nineveh it is much more frequently applied to the apostatizing people of God.[159] "Harlot" and not "adulteress" is the most appropriate figure, for the emphasis is upon the many lovers and the wages gained. The literary origin of the symbolism in Rev. 17 is to be found in Jer. 2:33-34 and 3:1-11, where Judah is a harlot (Jer. 2:20) with a sign upon her forehead (Jer. 3:3), who causes transgression in others (Jer. 2:33), and "on whose skirts is found the lifeblood of guiltless poor" (Jer. 2:34). She is clothed in crimson (Jer. 4:30) and golden ornaments. Her lovers will despise her (Jer. 4:30) and seek her life. We are reminded too that the same thing is written of Babylon as was addressed to faithless Jerusalem -- "in her was found the blood of prophets and of saints, and of all who have been slain on earth." Compare Mt. 23:35. These references should be kept in mind as well as Nahum 3:4ff.; Isa. 23:15, which are the texts most often cited in support of the undoubted fact that John initially thinks of the city of Rome.

These references to βδελυγμάτων and ἠρημωμένην ἠρημώθη and ἔρεμον in chs. 17 and 18 by no means exhaust the connections of Babylon with our main theme. The call to flee from Babylon has often been linked by commentators to Christ's admonition to flee from the βδέλυγμα τῆς ἐρημώσεως.[160] Only such withdrawal can save the soul. How appropriate the admonition, how artistically placed by John, when we recall that Rev. 18 is the fifth consecutive chapter dealing with the destruction of the rebellious worldlings. In ch. 14, the theme began with the announcement: "Fallen, fallen is Babylon the great. . . ." The destruction by the treading of the winepress tells the same story. In the following chapter, a solemn pause accompanies the preparation for the outpouring of God's unmingled wrath upon Babylon. Chapter 16 describes Babylon's plagues. Chapter 17 shows why Babylon deserves such punishment -- it is because of her rebellion against God, her idolatry, her pride, her persecution of the saints. Chapter 18 enlarges what was commenced in the preceding chapter which foretold that the ten horns would desolate the whore and burn her with fire. Such was the fate of a priest's daughter if she played the harlot, and such would be the fate of a world to whom Christ came, but who received Him not. Her failure to recognize the divine Lover would be her undoing, and the burning of the city is only another metaphor for expressing the fate already suggested in the preceding chapters. Therefore, says John, therefore FLEE! And all who read it would be reminded of Christ's admonition to flee from the guilty city of Jerusalem as Antichrist, the βδέλυγμα τῆς ἐρημώσεως drew near.

Also in chapter 17 we find a parallel to Rev. 13 and its description of the healing of the mortal wound. John says that the beast upon which the woman is borne has seven heads, and of these, five are fallen and one is and the other is not yet come. The beast finds its identity in each of the successive heads. Thus it can be said to be not, though it once was, and that it shortly will be again. We doubt if there is any need to count Emperors.[161] John was not primarily interested in that. Seven in this place has the same symbolic meaning as elsewhere, and there are about fifty-three other cases. Arithmetical calculation is not the primary significance, rather it is the symbolism of completeness.

Thus the five heads represent all who have gone before as Satan's representatives, including the emperors of Rome. The number six refers to the existing evil time about to give birth to the final Antichrist, the seventh head of the beast. The number eight is the symbol of resurrection and new beginning, to remind the readers that the beast would yet again ascend the abyss and demonstrate his revived life by a flood of persecution.[162] All the powers of earth united under the ultimate demonic Antichrist by the spirits of demons constitute the seventh head. There are not eight heads, only seven, but the seventh is also called the eighth to show its parody of Him who is the Resurrection and the Life, and whose number is 888.[163] John may indeed think of the Nero myth, but if used at all, it is only a mask for a face much more demonic. There is no precise parallel to this in the Danielic presentation because He of whom the parody is given had not yet come to die and rise again.

Revelation 20

Into the problems of this much-debated chapter it is not our purpose to enter. Suffice to say that here most of the motifs of the preceding chapters recur once more for their final outworking. Again the beast rises from the abyss, again he assembles by deception the kings of the earth, again the object of attack is the holy city, but this time the doom that falls upon the abomination of desolation is complete.[164]

271

The great rebel who sought to make all men worship him, and who employed force to do so, "comes to his end, with none to help him."[165] He returns forever to the desolation of the grave's abyss. Simultaneously, the objects of his attack become aware that the unending conflict has at last ended, and that temptation and trial will be no more. They luxuriate in the joy of their Lord, bearing His mark and basking in His glory throughout the ages. Such is John's story, John's painting, John's undying music.

1. This is not to deny the plethora of references to key figures of evil which exist in the pseudepigraphical writings and elsewhere. But for the Apocalypse, these references might have been explained as merely the natural development of dualistic philosophy. Similarly, the O.T. antagonists of Israel, such as Antiochus, Gog and Magog, et al., might never have achieved eschatological status but for the expanded treatment of such a final adversary in the last book of the New Testament. Christ's references could have been brushed aside as mere literary and homiletic use of an old theme and inasmuch as 2 Thess. 2 is an isolated phenomenon in the Pauline corpus, it is doubtful whether it would have achieved its present prominence but for the recurrence of the same motif in the Revelation. The term Antichrist is purely a Christian neologism, so far as available evidence indicates.

2. The Progress of Doctrine in the New Testament (London, 1864), passim.

3. "Es ist sicher auch nicht zufällig, wenn man immer wieder versucht war und versucht hat, eine bestimmte geschichtliche Gestalt als den A. anzuprangern. -- Ob night dieses Wort -- man denke an den Wechsel von Sing. und Plur.! -- vielleicht eher eine Art Chiffre ist, ein Gattungsbegriff, eine Umschreibung eines Typs, immer wieder konkretisiert und aktualisiert in den Epochen zwischen der Auffahrt und Wiederkunft des Herrn?" L. Coenen, "Antichrist", TBNT, 30. "Antichrist. . .strictly defined, a mythical demonic or demonic-human adversary of Christ who will appear before the Second Advent. . . .More broadly, the term is also applied to a historical or mythical potentate who wages war against the faithful." N. Rist, "Antichrist", IBD, I, 140. ". . . καὶ νῦν ἀντίχριστοι πολλοὶ γεγόνασιν." 1 Jn. 2:18.

4. Rev. 3:10.

5. For example, R. H. Charles says: "The more closely we study the Seals in connection with Mark xiii., Matt. xxiv., Luke xxi., the more strongly we shall be convinced that our author finds his chief and controlling authority in the eschatological scheme there set forth." The Revelation of St. John (ICC, Edinburgh, 1920), I, 158. (Hereinafter referred to as Revelation.)

6. Commenting on Rev. 16:16, W. Hendriksen says: "Here very little is said about this final battle. But we must remember that this same conflict of Har-Medgedon is described in Rev. 11: 7ff. . . .; and especially in Revelation 19:11ff.; 20:7ff." More Than Conquerors (London, 1962), 164. (Hereinafter referred to as Conquerors.)

7. Lu. 21:24: ". . .and Jerusalem will be trodden down by the
Gentiles.

8. See T.F. Glasson, The Revelation of John (The Cambridge Bible
Commentary, Cambridge, 1965), 67-70; Isbon T. Beckwith, The
Apocalypse of John (New York, 1919, 252; Charles, Revelation, I)
279; W. Milligan, The Book of Revelation (London, 1898), 176-77.
(Hereinafter referred to as Revelation.)

9. Dan. 8:14: ". . . then the sanctuary shall be restored to
its rightful estate."

10. Rev. 12:4, cf. Dan. 8:10.

11. Rev. 12:15, cf. Dan. 9:26; 11:40.

12. Rev. 12:6,14.

13. Dan. 8:10; 9:26; 7:7-8; 7:25.

14. Rev. 13:5, cf. Dan. 8:13.

15. Rev. 13:13, cf. Dan. 8:25.

16. See Martin Kiddle, The Revelation of St. John (MNTC, London,
1940), 242-244, (hereinafter referred to as Revelation); Austin
Farrer, The Revelation of St. John the Divine (Oxford, 1964),
151-55 (hereinafter referred to as Revelation); Charles,
Revelation, I, 333; Hendriksen, Conquerors, 144-46; G.B. Caird,
A Commentary on the Revelation of St. John the Divine (London,
1966), 162 (hereinafter referred to as Revelation); Ronald H.
Preston and Anthony T. Hanson, The Revelation of St. John the
Divine (London, 1949), 95 (hereinafter referred to as Revelation):
"The symbolism of this chapter is taken mostly from Daniel. . . ."
Glasson, The Revelation of John, 79 (hereinafter referred to as
Revelation): "The imagery comes from Daniel 7. . . ."

17. See Caird, Revelation, 164, "The monster is a parody of
Christ. Previously John had seen the Lamb 'bearing the marks of
slaughter'; now he sees one of the monster's heads bearing the
deadly marks of slaughter, and its death had been followed
by something that could pass for a resurrection." Preston and
Hanson, Revelation, 96. "As we study the details of this chapter
there is one astonishing feature which gradually becomes apparent:
Satan has produced a parody of the divine dispensation." Farrer,
Revelation, 152,". . . .a parody of Christianity. . . ." Kiddle,
Revelation, 252-53.

18. The image erected by Nebuchadnezzar is said to have
measured sixty cubits by six cubits. Emphasis on the symbolism of

numbers (which is foolish to the Western mind) was taken quite seriously by the ancients. The number six in ancient Egypt was understood to be the combination of the solar disk and the sacred serpent. See the remarks of E. Lohmeyer, Die Offenbarung des Johannes (HNT, Tübingen, 1926), 118-119. (Hereinafter referred to as Offenbarung.)

19. Rowley, Servant, 279.

20. See comments in Ibid., 276.

21. Dan. 4:13-14; 5:5,25-30.

22. See Isa. 10:22-23, cf. Dan. 9:27, 11:45.

23. Austin Farrer, A Rebirth of Images (Westminster, 1949), 42; (hereinafter referred to as Rebirth); Hendriksen, Conquerors, 23, "The author of the Apocalypse is constantly speaking in terms of seven. This number occurs fifty-four times. What is even more striking is the fact that he again and again arranges his sevens in groups of three and four or four and three." See also Beckwith, The Apocalypse of John, 254,523. (Hereinafter referred to as Apocalypse.)

24. 2 Macc. 6:7; 3 Macc. 2:29.

25. Dan. 12:2.

26. Rev. 16:2.

27. Rev. 16:4-6.

28. Rev. 16:13-14.

29. Rev. 17:14.

30. Jeffery, "Daniel", 497-98. Porteous, Daniel, 143: "The war which the writer anticipates is no doubt conceived of by him as the final eschatological struggle between good and evil (cf. Ezek. 38 and 39; Rev. 16:6 and The War of the Sons of Light and the Sons of Darkness)."

31. Dan. 4:30.

32. Rev. 17:1.

33. Isa. 44:27. Cf. Jer. 50:38; 51:36.

34. It is even possible that the symbolism employed by the writer of Daniel in 12:6 is related to this theme. Frequently

the Old Testament writers liken oppression and persecution to an overflowing river. It is also a standard symbol for invasion. See Jer. 46:6-10; 47:2; 25:9-11,15-26; Isa. 8:7,8; 2 Sam. 22:5; Ps. 69:1,2,14,15; Dan. 9:26; 11:22,40. Dan. 12:6 could well be intended as a pictorial presentation of the truth expressed in Ps. 29:10, "The Lord sits enthroned over the flood; the Lord sits enthroned as king for ever." Compare Ps. 93:3-4, which stresses that Yahweh is mightier than flooding waters, and able to control them.

35. Isa. 47:1,15.

36. Dan. 11:45.

37. Mt. 24:15.

38. We refer specifically to the symbolism of the drying up of the Euphrates, the coming of the kings from the east, and the references to the beast and the ten horns. The description of the weeping over of the city, of course, is taken from Ezekiel's passage on the lamentation over fallen Tyre, but the references to "Babylon the great" reflect Dan. 4:30. Probably the use of fire as the destroying emblem also comes from the same book. See Dan. 7:11.

39. Rev. 17:5,3,16.

40. Rev. 18:19.

41. Rev. 19:19. We read here of "τον πόλεμον", the article being present as in the cases of Rev. 16:14 and 20:8.

42. Dan. 7:11.

43. Eze. 39:4,17-20.

44. Eze. 39:2-4. Kiddle, Revelation, 330, ". . .there was a tradition, exemplified in such passages as Ezek. xxxix.1ff. and Dan. xi.45 that the final conflict was to be among the mountains of Israel." See also Russell, Apocalyptic, 192.

45. Eze. 38:16; Dan. 11:40.

46. Rev. 21:17.

47. Rev. 22:4; Ex. 28:36; Rev. 14:1; Gen. 1:26.

48. Preston and Hanson, Revelation, 10.

49. Theology, 40,41.

50. "All that we can say with fair certainty is that the book
was written by a Christian named John, who was for a time ban-
ished to the island of Patmos." Glasson, Revelation, 4. Kiddle's
statement is well-known: "No subject of Biblical studies has
provoked such elaborate and prolonged discussion among scholars
as that of the authorship of the five books of the New Testament
which are traditionally ascribed to 'John' (the Fourth Gospel,
the three Epistles of John, and Revelation). And no discussion
has been so bewildering, disappointing, and unprofitable. The
student who attempts to follow the innumerable lines of enquiry
is soon caught in a maze of conflicting arguments brought
forward to support the rival theories, and invariably finds
himself unable to reach any definite conclusion concerning the
authorship of at least some, if not all, of the books concerned.
In fact, it is quite impossible to determine the authorship
of any of these books from the available evidence." Revelation,
xxxiii.

KÜmmel says: "We know nothing more about the author of the
Apocalypse than that he was a Jewish-Christian prophet by the
name of John. For he cannot be identical with John the son of
Zebedee, if the son of Zebedee died as a martyr long before the
end of the first century. . . ." Introduction, 331.

Preston and Hanson agree. They ask the question, "Who
wrote Revelation?" and reply, "The answer must be simply --
John." Revelation, 23.

Despite this uniformity of opinion some recent scholars
seem to have second thoughts about the possibility of improving
upon mere "John" as the answer to the quest. See Caird,
Revelation, 4-5; Farrer, Revelation, 1-3. (Caird thinks that the
weight of the evidence is against the common authorship of the
gospel and the Apocalypse but records his conviction that the
language difference is not decisive. Farrer, characteristically,
is more thorough-going in voting for the Apostle.) Leon Morris
believes the evidence for KÜmmel's objection to be scanty, and
inclines towards Stauffer's position. See The Revelation of St.
John (London, 1969), 25-34.

51. But see Morris, Ibid., 27f.

52. "Johannesapokalypse", RGG (3rd edn.), col. 829.

53. Ibid., col. 830.

54. Rev. 1:9; 2:13; 2:10; 6:9; 3:10; 17:6; 18:24; 19:2; 16:6;
20:4.

55. See Rev. chs. 2 and 3.

56. Adv. Haer. v. 30:3.

57. Piper, Ibid., col. 830. Cf. Guthrie, Introduction, 949: "although the main purpose of the book may be considered apart from the question of date, this question is not unimportant in the quest to ascertain the precise historical background, nor is it entirely irrelevant for arriving at a satisfactory interpretation of the book. The most widely held view is that this Apocalypse was written during the reign of Domitian, more precisely towards the end of that reign, i.e. AD 90-95. . . ." See also Morris, Revelation, 34-40; Kümmel, Introduction, 327-29; Preston and Hanson, Revelation, 25-27; Caird, Revelation, 5-6; et al., all of whom agree with the preceding references. A. Feuillet believes that the book was written in Domitian's reign but issued as though produced in the time of Vespasian. See NTS, IV (1957-58), 183ff. The position of C.C. Torrey regarding authorship during the days of Galba is not widely held today. See his The Apocalypse of John (New Haven, 1958), 58ff.

58. M. Rist, "The Revelation of St John the Divine" (IB), XII, 357.

59. Caird, Revelation, v.

60. "It is surprising how seldom these divergences create any serious doubt about the sense intended, or affect the English rendering." Farrer, Revelation, 51. "On the whole, the text of Revelation is fairly certain. A majority of the variants appear to deal with the curious solecisms in which the book abounds. . .; scribes from time to time endeavoured particularly to correct the author's grammar in the matter of gender, number, and case of noun and adjective, and in that of mood and tense of the verb." J. W. Bowman, "Revelation, Book of", IBD IV, 70.

61. Similarly there are no certain grounds for holding that the book contains fragments of other works incorporated into its own structure. Such theories are handicapped by "overprecision and arbitrary canons of literary criticism", according to Moffatt. See Introduction to the Literature of the New Testament (Edinburgh, 1918), 491. According to Kiddle: ". . . many other unhelpful and unnecessary theories, and the unconvincing attempts to mutilate the text which commonly accompany them, can be avoided when John's mind and purpose are correctly understood." Revelation, xxxii. For a very thorough discussion of such questions, see Beckwith, Apocalypse, 216-239.

62. Introduction, 327.

63. Ep. liii.9.

64. Cited by Caird, Revelation, 2.

65. The Apostolic Preaching and its Developments (London, 1936), 86ff.

66. The Origins of the New Testament (E.T., 1950), 11, cited by N. Turner, "Revelation" (Peake new edn.), 1044.

67. Commentary on the New Testament (London, 1872), II, 172. Wordsworth waxes quite lyrical in expressing his evaluation of the book. His comment is worthy of study as a contrast to more modern expressions. "It reveals a long train of future sufferings, failings, and chastisements in the History of the Church. And yet it cheers the reader with the consolatory assurance, that Christ is mightier than His enemies; that He went forth in the first age of the Gospel like a royal warrior, 'conquering and to conquer', and that He enables all His faithful servants to overcome; that they who die for Him, live; that they who suffer for Him, reign; and that the course of the Church of Christ upon Earth, is like the course of Christ Himself; that she is here as a Witness of the Truth, that her office is to teach the world; that she will be fed by the Divine hand, like the Ancient Church with manna in the wilderness; that she will be borne on eagles' wings in her missionary career throughout the world; and yet that she must expect to suffer injuries from enemies and from friends; that she too must look to have her Gethsemane and her Calvary, but that she will also have her Olivet; that through the pains of Agony and Suffering, and through the darkness of the Grave, she will rise to the glories of a triumphant Ascension, and to the everlasting joys of the new Jerusalem; that she, who has been for a time 'the Woman wandering in the wilderness,'" will be for ever and ever 'the Bride' glorified in heaven.

"It will be readily acknowledged by those who contemplate the course of the Church from the days of St John to the present age that such a representation of it is in perfect accordance with the facts of the case; that it bears evidence of divine foresight; and that it was well adapted to serve the purpose of rescuing the minds of Christians in every age from the dangers of despondency and unbelief, and also from the snare of indulging in illusory hopes and visionary dreams of perfect spiritual unity, and religious purity upon earth; and that it was admirably framed to instruct and prepare them to encounter trials and afflictions with constancy and courage, and to endure hardness as good soldiers of Christ; and to strengthen their faith, and quicken their hope even by those trials and afflictions, as having been foretold by Christ in this Book; and that it thus affords a pledge that the other predictions of this same Book, which reveals the full and final Triumph of Christ and the eternal Felicity and Glory of all His faithful servants, and the destruction of all His Enemies, will not fail of their accomplishment.

"The Apocalypse is therefore a Manual of Consolation to the Church in her pilgrimage through this world to the heavenly Canaan of her rest." Ibid., 148.

There have been and are modern scholars who would agree with Wordsworth regarding the skill, artistry, and abiding value of the book, though not many would express themselves as he does. See, for example, W. Milligan's three books on The Apocalypse; and Kiddle's Moffatt Commentary (xxv. f.); Merrill C. Tenney's Interpreting Revelation (Grand Rapids, 1957), 194f.; J.B. Phillips, The Book of Revelation (London, 1960), 9; A. Wikenhauser, New Testament Introduction (New York, 1958), 545f; G.E. Ladd, "Revelation", Baker's Dictionary of Theology (London, 1960), 53; Austin Farrer, Rebirth, 6.

On the other hand there are commentators who view the book differently. While Hendriksen can tell us in his opening sentence that "in form, symbolism, purpose and meaning the book of Revelation is beautiful beyond description", (Conquerors, 7), N. Turner suggests that in the book, "There is too much unassimilated second-hand material, and often it is employed pointlessly -- obscure to us, to many early Christians, and to vast numbers of readers who decline to make it support their peculiar notions. . . .the relevance of Rev. today can hardly be as great as it was in the 1st century. . . .John does not really live and move in our intellectual sphere. We sometimes experience what we think may be symbolically described in his word-pictures, but that does not tell us what his symbols mean. Did he really know himself? The number three means heaven, four means the earth, and the number seven is the blending of these two, or God dwelling with man: but most of the rest is as obscure as the Jewish literature on which it is based." "Revelation" (Peake, new edn.), 1043-44. When commenting upon Rev. 16, Turner refers to the fact that Megiddo was the battle-ground of kings in the OT but then adds, "nothing so subtle could have been in the author's mind." Ibid., 1054. (Our own opinion is that the writer of Revelation was considerably more subtle than Turner gives him credit for, yet considerably less subtle than Farrer makes him out to be in his Rebirth. This conclusion may say as much about Turner and Farrer as it does about John, but critical research is useless without conclusions. An open mind exists for the same purpose as an open mouth, that it might shortly seize upon something worth digesting.)

But the main point is that we should observe the contrary evaluations of the book. This certainly suggests, not that the book itself is chameleon, but that another factor is present. This factor is the invariable prejudice against eschatological literature (which ever postulates supernaturalism) in an age when the supernatural has been dissipated before the rising sun of science.

68. Caird, _Revelation_, 2.

69. See Piper, "Johannesapokalypse", col. 832.

70. E.g. Morris, _Revelation_, 221-22. "The call to rejoice at
the destruction of the city appalls some modern students. But
we should notice in the first place that this is not a vindictive
outcry. It is a longing that justice be done. And in the
second, John and his readers were not armchair critics
pedantically discussing rights and wrongs in an academic fashion.
They were existentially committed. . . .It is a passionate cry
uttered out of the deep conviction that right must triumph and
which eagerly welcomes that triumph." See also Caird, _Revelation_,
230.

71. Turner, "Revelation", 1044.

72. Beasley-Murray, "A Conservative Thinks Again About Daniel",
Baptist Quarterly, XII (1948), 367.

73. See 75ff.

74. See 98f. of this volume. Caird writes: "All oracles of
doom, whether prophetic or apocalyptic, are expressed in
unconditional terms, but carry an unarticulated condition:
unless they repent." _Revelation_, 177.

75. These extreme interpreters are not yet all dead. Partic-
larly writers of futurist persuasion such as Walvoord have
expressed some fantastic positions regarding the meaning of
Revelation.

76. Caird, _Revelation_, 2.

77. Caird, _Revelation_, 2.

78. E.g. Turner, "Revelation", 1044. "It is certainly very
difficult to interpret the book in detail to the modern
Christian. Assuming that the first readers knew the meaning of
the details, the secret perished with them and cannot be
recovered." See also Preston and Hanson, _Revelation_, 9f., and
W. Milligan, _Lectures on the Apocalypse_ (London, 1892), 7-10.
(Hereinafter referred to as _Lectures_.) Milligan protests
against the neglect of the book due to its difficulties and says:
"That it should be obscure or mysterious would in no way startle
us. Obscurity and mystery meet us everywhere. We have no reason
to complain of such arrangements. It is an altogether different
thing when we are told, not that a part of Revelation is difficult, but that it is from its very nature unintelligible, and
that it is constructed with so little reference to common

processes of thought and rules of language as to place a
distinct conception of its meaning beyond our reach. . . .Man may
not immediately comprehend it, just as thousands of years
passed before he comprehended the structure of the earth, or
the movements of the heavenly bodies. But the voice both of the
earth and of the heavens was never in itself less fixed or
certain than it is now. They were capable of being interpreted;
and at last they received their interpretation. It is the
same with the book before us." 9.

79. It is a matter of regret that so few commentators have
prefaced their work with a rationale of their subsequent
procedures. W. Milligan is a welcome exception, though we may
still differ with him concerning some conclusions.

80. In most cases, argument and evidence are left for the
footnotes.

81. This is axiomatic, and scarcely needs documenting. However
for excellent treatment see introductory materials in Beckwith
(Apocalypse, 197-208); Kiddle (Revelation, xxxvi-xliii);
H.B. Swete (The Apocalypse of St. John (London, 1911), lxvi-xcviii
xcviii); Charles (Revelation, I, xci-xcvii). Every modern
commentary asks the question we have asked. Reicke's The N.T.
Era is helpful in answering it.

82. See Beckwith, Apocalypse, 434-35.

83. In addition to 11ff. of this volume, see the same topic
amply discussed in the volumes listed under footnote 1 of this
page.

84. Caird, Revelation, 10.

85. Rev. 1:20.

86. See Milligan, Lectures, 14-40. Charles writes: "A literal
description would only be possible in the case of the simplest
visions, in which the things seen were already more or less
within the range of actual human experience. . . .in our
author the visions are of an elaborate and complicated nature,
and the more exalted and intense the experience, the more
incapable it becomes of literal description. Moreover, if we
believe, as the present writer does, that behind these visions
there is an actual substratum of reality belonging to the
higher spiritual world, then the seer could grasp the things
seen and heard in such visions, only in so far as he was equipped
for the task by his psychical powers and the spiritual
development behind him. In other words, he could at the best only
partially apprehend the significance of the heavenly vision

vouchsafed him. To the things seen he perforce attached the symbols more or less transformed that these naturally evoked in his mind, symbols that he owed to his own waking experience of the tradition of the past; and the sounds he heard naturally clothed themselves in the literary forms with which his memory was stored. Thus the seer laboured under a twofold disability. His psychical powers were generally unequal to the task of apprehending the full meaning of the heavenly vision, and his powers of expression were frequently unable to set forth the things he had apprehended." Revelation, I, cvi-cvii.

87. Milligan, Lectures, 25-30.

88. "Johannesapokalypse", col. 831.

89. Rebirth, 7.

90. Apocalypse, 613. Otto Piper on this subject has written: "Die Religionsgeschichtliche Schule hat auf die Fülle mythologischer Stoffe hingewiesen, die in der J. auftauchen. Wenn aber das Buch nicht völlig falsch gedeutet werden soll, wie das bes. bei Boll der Fall ist, muss man zwei Gesichtspunkte im Auge behalten: Zu einem grossen Teil handelt es sich bei diesen 'Mythen'. . .um gemeinsemitisches Material, das der Seher im AT vorgefunden hat und das ihm deshalb bereits in einer israelitischen Deutung gegeben war(zB das Tier als Symbol der gottfeindlichen politischen Macht) Auch kann von einer einheitlichen Gnosis, in der damals die Mythologien des Nahen Ostens und Persiens zu einer Art Weltreligion vereinigt waren, keine Rede sein. Die Siebenerreihen zB haben ihren astrologischen Ursprung in der J. völlig verloren, und wenn auch der Gedanke einer eschatologischen Schlacht seine Wurzel in einem babylonischen Mythos von der Götterschlacht haben mag, so kam er dem Seher durch das Medium des AT zu. Die Weise, in der die mythologischen Bilder in der J. benutzt werden, zeigt, wie sehr sie dem Verfasser ausschliesslich als Ausdrucksmittel für seine christlichen Gedanken dienen." "Johannesapokalypse", col. 829.

91. See Caird, Revelation, 131-32; Farrer, Revelation, 109-110, says: "Now this picture (xxi.9-xxii.2) taken literally, is sheer Judaism. . . .St John keeps the picture, because it is in the prophets; he does not take it literally. The pouring in of the nations does not await the world to come; the cadres of God's Israel were filled out with Gentile recruits. . . ." "Such is St John's way of saying that the triumph of God's people and their blessed future are secured by his promises to Israel, and that the Gentiles are nevertheless brought in to share the promises. How purely symbolical such a way of speaking is can be judged from the equalization of numbers sealed from the

twelve tribes." The best test case for commentators in this regard is their exegesis of Rev. 7.

92. _Revelation_, I, xliv. Charles affirms that "no literary document of the Greek world exhibits such a vast multitude of solecism. It would almost seem that the author of the Apocalypse deliberately set at defiance the grammarian and the ordinary rules of syntax. . . .The reason clearly is that, while he writes in Greek, he thinks in Hebrew. . . ." _Ibid._, I, cxliii.

93. Caird, _Revelation_, 5.

94. Christopher Wordsworth, "Revelation", _Commentary on the New Testament_, 149.

95. Kiddle, _Revelation_, 26. See also John Wick Bowman, _The Drama of the Book of Revelation_ (Philadelphia, 1955), 29.

96. _Ibid._, 136.

97. W. Boyd Carpenter, "Revelation", _Ellicott's Commentary_, VIII, 526, 578.

98. _A Commentary on the Revelation of John_ (Grand Rapids, 1972), ad loc. (Hereinafter referred to as _John_.) See Zahn also.

99. For a typical example of the application of this principle see Farrer, _Revelation_, 178. In every case where commentators have applied the things of Israel to the church this principle is implied.

100. It should be stressed that John's initial and primary purpose was to address seven specific local churches. All conjectures based on John's most comprehensive levels of meaning should issue from the sure "pegs" of the local, historical, situations to which he alludes. Thus later when Rev. 17-18 is considered, the basic application to the Capital of the Empire must not be overlooked despite some consequent legitimate extension of John's meaning.

101. "It is impossible to enlarge without going over every chapter, verse, and clause of the book, which is a perfect mosaic of passages from the Old Testament, at one time quoted verbally, at another referred to by distinct allusion, now taken from one scene in Jewish history, and now again from two or three together." Milligan, _Lectures_, 76.

102. Sir Isaac Newton recognized this feature and employed it in his commentary. In more recent times it has been stressed by Farrer. He says that the apocalyptic week runs "from Christ the

birth of light (Apoc. 1) to Christ the fulness of light (Apoc. XXII). On the way, however, it runs through all the quarters of the year, and this brings within St John's scheme all the symbolical riches of the Jewish sacred calendar." Rebirth, 93. See also D.T. Niles, Seeing the Invisible (London, 1962), 108-111.
     Not quite as strongly supported is the possibility that behind the structure of this book is to be found a primitive form of the Paschal Vigil. See Massey H. Shepherd's The Paschal Liturgy and the Apocalypse (London, 1960).

103. Milligan, Lectures, 61. ". . . the life of Christ, remembered as St John remembered it, supplies the type to which the history of His people shall be conformed. . . ." And on 69 we read: ". . '. the Apocalypse is penetrated in a remarkable manner by the tendency to present the history of the Church as corresponding in every respect to the history of the Church's Lord."

104. See Charles, Revelation, I, 158; Farrer, Revelation, 4-13; Milligan, Lectures, 42f.

105. Thus even what is said about Christ's enemies, and the foes of His church, is related to Him by way of parody.

106. "Johannesapokalypse", col. 832.

107. See G. E. Ladd, "The Revelation and Jewish Apocalyptic", EQ, XXIX (1957), 94-100; Zahn, Introduction to the New Testament (E.T. Edinburgh, 1909), 437. (Hereinafter referred to as Introduction.) This apocalypse is not pseudonymous, neither does it retrace history under the guise of prophecy. It is not pessimistic, but rings with prophetic hope.

108. Rev. 1:3; 22:7,10,18,19. Says Piper: "Der Verfasser will göttliche Offenbarungen mitteilen, nicht nur seine persönlichen Ansichten. . . . in der J. beschreibt der Verfasser seine pneumatischen Erlebnisse, in denen ohne bewusste Vorbereitung die Gesichte plötzlich in sein Bewusstsein eintraten. Sie sind nicht als des Verfassers religiöse Deutung zeitgeschichtlicher Ereignisse zu verstehen." "Johannesapokalypse", cols. 830-831.

109. But see Charles, Revelation, I, ciii -- cix.

110. Rev. 22:18-19.

111. See Charles, Revelation, I, clxxxiii-clxxxiv; Beckwith, Apocalypse, 208-213; Farrer, Revelation, 4f. et al.

112. "Revelation" (NBCR), 1280.

113.   Other minor principles to guide exegesis of this book could
be listed, particularly as regards stylistic forms such as
contrast, prolepsis, recapitulation, etc. As one of these, in
particular, is vital for our study in these pages, reference to
it, in the words of another, will be made. "The principle of
contrast. In their broader features the contrasts of the
Apocalypse at once strike the eye. No reader can fail for a
moment to perceive that, like Aaron when he stood between the
dead and the living, St John stands in this book between two
antithetical and contrasted worlds. On the one hand he sees
Christ, life, light, love, the Church of the living God, heaven,
and the inhabitants of heaven; on the other he sees Satan, death,
darkness, hatred, the synagogue of Satan, earth, and the dwellers
upon earth. . . .It is not enough, however, to observe this. The
contrasts of the book are carried out in almost every particular
that meets us, whether great or small, whether in connexion with
the persons, the objects, or the actions of which it speaks.
      "If, at one time, we have an ever blessed and holy Trinity,
the Father, the Son, and the Holy Spirit, at another we have that
"great antitrinity of hell,' the Devil, the Beast, and the False
Prophet. If we have God Himself, even the Father, commissioning
the first beast and giving him 'his power. . . .' If the Son. . .
appears as a Lamb with seven horns, the dragon. . .has two horns
like a lamb, though he speaks as a dragon. If the name of the
one is Jesus or Saviour, the name of the other is Apollyon or
Destroyer. If the one is the bright, the morning star shining
in the heavens, the other is a star fallen out of heaven into
the earth." "If the one in carrying out his great work on earth
is the Lamb 'as though it had been slaughtered,' the other, as
we are told by the use of the very same word. . . has one of his
heads 'as though it had been slaughtered unto death.' If the one
rises from the grave and lives, there cannot be a doubt, when
we read in precisely the same language of the beast that he
hath the stroke of a sword and lived, that here also is a
resurrection from the dead. If the description given of the
Divine Being is 'He which is, and which was, and which is to
come,' that given of diabolic agency is that it 'was, and is
not,·and is about to come up out of the abyss';. . . .
      "Many other particulars meet us in which the same
principle of contrast rules. Believers are sealed with the seal
of the Living God; unbelievers are marked with the mark of the
beast. . . .The 'tribes of the earth' are in contrast with the
tribes of Israel. . . .and the harlot Babylon with the bride. . .
in the binding of Satan. . .in the casting him into the abyss,
in shutting it, and sealing it over him, we have a counterpart
of the binding and burial of our Lord, and of the sealing of
His tomb." Milligan, Lectures, 110-114.

114.   The relationship between Dan. 8:13; Mk. 13:14; Luke 21:24;
2 Thess. 2:4 and Rev. 11:2 is intimate. In each instance an

anti-God power menaces the sanctuary and its worshippers. The
very language of the first reference has been incorporated into
the last. While Rev. 6:9-11, with its references to the
sanctuary, martyrdom, the cry for vindication and its answer,
may also point back to Dan. 8:13,14, the presentation of Rev. 11
is much more particular and less general.

Revelation 11 is part of the interlude between the sixth
and seventh trumpets. As such it is somewhat analogous to the
similar interlude between the sixth and seventh seals. We
think the remarks of Farrer on this latter passage also have
bearing on the former which certainly has to do with the final
proclamation of the gospel on the eve of Antichrist's final
rising, and thus is related to Mk. 13 and 2 Thess. 2.

"St John's way of saying that Antichrist cannot be
manifested, nor the end come, until the Gospel has been preached
to all nations (Matt. xxiv.14) will be to say that the
predestined number of the elect must be stamped with the Name,
before the persecution of Antichrist gives them the
opportunity to merit their eternal reward. St Paul reminded
the Thessalonians that a caretaker power, or person, delaying
the accession of Antichrist, was a part of the Christian scheme
(2 Thess. ii. 6-7); Antichrist cannot come 'until this power
is out of the way'. In spite of all that has been written to
the contrary, the most natural interpretation of St Paul is
that which follows the lines of Revelation vii. An angel of God,
or a commandment of God (it is all one) restraining the
appearance of Antichrist, holds sway until the apostolic
mission has run its course; then 'the obstacle will be removed'."
Revelation, 105-106.

Josef Ernst is representative of most modern commentators
when he links Rev. 11 with Mk. 13:14 and 2 Thess. 2. A
connection with Dan. 7,8,9,11 is also made by equating the beast
from the abyss with the beast from the sea in Rev. 13, and
tracing the genealogy of the latter to the portrayal of Dan. 7.
See Die Eschatologischen Gegenspieler in den Schriften des
Neuen Testaments (Regensburg, 1967), 123, 125, 126, 127, 132.
(Hereinafter referred to as Gegenspieler.)

115. T.S. Kepler says on this chapter: ". . . a key to the
book's basic meaning. It acts as a sort of prologue which
interprets all to which the remaining chapters of the book are
leading." The Book of Revelation (New York, 1957), 117.

Preston and Hanson introduce their comments on the section
10-11.13 by saying: "The whole parenthesis seems to be intended
to prepare us for the ultimate appearance of the Beast."
Revelation, 87.

116. "Chap. xi. is at once the most difficult and the most
important in the whole book of Revelation. . . . in many
respects this chapter is the key to John's central theme. . . ."

Kiddle, Revelation, 174.
"The chapter is extraordinarily difficult to interpret, and the most diverse solutions have been proposed." Morris, Revelation, 144. Josef Ernst characterizes this chapter as belonging to the darkest and most difficult portions of Scripture. See Gegenspieler, 124.

117. Caird, Revelation, 133-34.

118. See Morris, Revelation, 136; Caird, Revelation, 128; Farrer, Revelation, 127; Milligan, Revelation, 166-67 for typical statements regarding the connection between these two chapters. The little scroll contains the description of the coming tribulation for the church. Beasley-Murray says: "The little scroll seems to include the rest of the visions of this book." "Revelation" (NBCR), 1292. "The persecution of the church is. . .the content of the little scroll." Caird, Revelation, 128.

119. See note 3 on p. 312. Hendriksen comments on the same theme as follows: "In very close connection with 10:8-11, chapter 11 now gives us a description of the 'bitter' experiences which the true Church must endure when it preaches the 'sweet' gospel of salvation." Conquerors, 126.

120. Rev. 10:11.

121. Rev. 10:6-7.

122. "The first figure that we meet with in this chapter could scarcely be plainer; nothing save a lapse into the misapprehensive literal conception could, from this passage, ch. xi. 1,2, draw the conclusion that the Temple in Jerusalem was still standing at the time of these visions. The Temple has always been a symbol of the visible form under which the Kingdom of God has appeared, i.e. the Theocracy at first, and later, the Church . . . ." Lange, "Revelation", Commentary, XII, 223.
There is no absolute necessity for the theory that John here incorporated an oracle of a Jewish prophet, uttered during the siege of A.D. 70, with reference to the inner courts of the temple. Caird says that "there has been a remarkable amount of scholarly support for the idea", but he adds, "In spite of the eminence of its advocates this theory must be judged improbable, useless, and absurd: improbable, because, once the outer court had fallen to the army of Titus, not even the most rabid fanatic could have supposed that he would be content to occupy it for three and a half years and leave the sanctuary itself inviolate; useless, because, whatever these words might have meant to a hypothetical Zealot, they certainly meant something quite different to John twenty-five years after the siege; and absurd, because of the underlying assumption that

John could not have intended these words to be taken figuratively unless someone else had previously used them in their literal sense. Indeed, it is hardly too much to say that, in a book in which all things are expressed in symbols, the very last things the temple and holy city could mean would be the physical temple and the earthly Jerusalem. If John had wanted to speak about them, he would have found some imagery to convey his meaning without lapsing into the inconsistency of literalism. But in fact John regarded the Jews as the synagogue of Satan, and was not interested in the preservation of their religious institutions." Revelation, 131. Despite the fact that Caird could be wrong in rejecting the idea of an incorporated apocalypse, he is certainly right in the Christian meaning he ascribes to the passage. We include his long quotation because of its exemplification of the hermeneutical principles suggested at the commencement of our exposition. Caird clearly sees that the church has taken the place of literal Israel, and he likewise is strongly aware of the symbolism employed throughout which, though based on the tangible things of literal Israel, is now applied spiritually to the church.

Caird echoes Kiddle to some extent, for the latter too assures his readers that the conjecture of sources being employed here is impossible of demonstration. "Can we then believe that John was so far removed from reality as to insert a meaningless passage into his Apocalypse? Surely not. He was writing for Christians in days of extreme urgency, when every word was precious." Revelation, 174-75. See also Morris, Revelation, 144. The reasons adduced by these writers may suggest that the great majority of recent commentators have climbed too precipitately upon the contemporary "band-wagon" of exegesis in this matter, when asserting an original reference to the literal temple from a non-johannine source.

Feuillet stresses that the theory that the writer of Revelation has incorporated a separate Jewish document has not been demonstrated, and he proceeds to show that the symbolism of the Temple should not be interpreted in a Jewish sense.

". . . qu'elle n'a pas été suffisamment démontrée. . . .la signification de l'ensemble du chaptre est chrétienne. En particulier, la préservation partielle du temple de Jérusalem, dont Jésus avait annoncé la ruine totale, n'est pas à interpreter, comme on l'a fait, en un sens juif; le langage symbolique est utilisé implique un sense chrétien." "Essai D'Interpretation Du Chapitre XI De L'Apocalypse", NTS, IV (1958), 184.

"À la suite de Swete, Allo, Lohmeyer, Charles, Wikenhauser, etc., nous croyons en outre que le temple de Jérusalem, dont doit être épargnée la partie intérieure avec 'ceux qui y adorent", ne peut être ici qu'une figure et ne saurait être pris au sens propre. Il est impossible de le faire si Jean écrit après 70. Et même, à supposer que le morceau soit antérieur à cette date, comment l'auteur de l'Apocalypse eût-il pu aller à l'encontre de

la parole de Jésus: du temple "il ne restera pas pierre sur pierre
qui ne soit renversée". . .?" Ibid., 184-85. This endorsement
of these early statements by Feuillet does not imply endorsement
of the exegesis offered for other symbols by him. He is
inconsistent, and believes the measuring has to do with merely
converted Jews. To him, those measured are the Jews spoken of
in chapter 7. If Feuillet understood by "Jews" Christians only,
and not necessarily converted Israelites, he would be on firmer
ground. Commenting on 11:1 he can say regarding the measuring
of the worshippers with a reed "Un tel langage montre clairement
que nous sommes en présence d'un pur symbole: l'auteur ne
s'intéresse qu'aux authentiques adorateurs du vrai Dieu, et non
à la construction matérielle." Ibid., 185. These words represent
exegetical sanity, but Feuillet departs from his own premises and
makes a similar error to Beckwith who also wishes to drag in
literal Israel while interpreting this chapter. One's
convictions about Paul's promise of penitence and conversion yet
to be seen among the race which crucified Christ is not to be
made the basis of exegesis of this chapter. Lagrange has erred
the same way, applying this chapter eschatologically to events
in Palestine and in special connection with literal Israel. Josef
Ernst sees that the contemporary-historical interpretation of
11:1-2 is not necessary, but he also wishes to invoke the fate
of believing Jews in the last crisis. See Gegenspieler, 130.
This error would be unnecessary if the meaning assigned by
John to the tribes of Israel in Rev. 7 were understood. John
symbolizes what Paul plainly states in Gal. 3:28-29; 6:16; Rom.
2:28-29.
     Lohmeyer emphasizes the adaptation by John of the things of
Israel to the world-wide Christian church. Before setting forth
this view he declares concerning the Wellhausen view of an
embodied Jewish oracular fragment that: "Diese Ansicht scheint
nicht genügend begründet." Offenbarung, 88. And later this
thought is repeated. "So wird es nicht mehr notwendig, c. 11
durch Annahme von Interpolationem oder Zuweisung an verschiedene
Quelle verständlicher zu machen. . . ." Ibid., 90. It is
necessary to recognize his viewpoint on this matter, because elsewhere he speaks of Jewish traditions John has incorporated, but
by such he means not the Wellhausen oracle, but chiefly those of
the Old Testament, such as found in Daniel, Ezekiel, and
Zechariah. In interpreting 11:1-2 he says: ". . .es ist dann
möglich und notwendig, sie auch als christliches Orakel zu
verstehen. 'Der Tempel' und 'die in ihn anbeten' sind dann die
urchristlichen 'Gläubigen'; und das 'Messen' bedeutet nichts
anderes als das 'Versiegeln' in 7:3-8. . .Dan aber sind diese
Verse eine Art 'pneumatischer' Interpretation und Adaption der
ezechielischen Vision. . . Damit ist dann auch eine sachliche
Verbindung zwischen 1f. und 3-13 angedeutet." He points out that
whereas Rev. 11, at first glance seems to speak of Jerusalem as
the show-place of the Antichrist and of his triumph over the

witnesses, ch. 12f. "wissen nichts von solcher Lokalisation."
Ibid., 89. The seer recognizes, says Lohmeyer, that the beast
out of the abyss represents the unbelieving world, and that his
appearance "nicht an Jerusalem gebunden." Ibid. "Um einen
Ausgleich dieser widersprechenden Vorstellungen, einer jüdisch-
partikularen und einer universalen handelt es sich in dieser
Vision. . . . So gibt die alte jüdisch-urchristliche Erwartung,
und sie gilt auch nicht. Es ist notwendig von ihr zu reden, und
doch hat sie nicht mehr die Bedeutung, die man früher an sie
knüpfte." Ibid. This view-point is much more homogenous with the
whole trend of Revelation than that of Lagrange who wishes to
retain literal Jerusalem in the eschatological picture. See
also Kiddle, Revelation, 175-180, who is close to Lohmeyer,
Morris, and Caird, and who protests against such views on the
conversion of the Jews as expressed by Charles, Beckwith, and
Lagrange, et al. Caird says: ". . . the outer court, and the
holy city, no less than the temple, symbolize the church in part
of its existence." Revelation, 132. He also refuses to accept
that Jerusalem is to be taken in its literal sense, and affirms
rather the application to the whole Roman world. He says:
". . .the gloating crowds are not restricted to Jews; they are
the inhabitants of earth. The ancient world had no Cook's Tours
capable of assembling in Jerusalem the international audience
John here envisages."

"Our conclusion about the city incidentally confirms what
we have said about the witnesses. If the witnesses were two
individual Christians, the city in which they died would have
to be a city in the narrow, literal sense; and this hypothesis
leads, as we have seen to a reductio ad absurdum." Ibid., 138.

Morris shows exegetical good sense when he writes: "It
seems to me important that the whole section (verses 1-13) is to
be taken symbolically. It is plain enough that the sanctuary
of verse 1 is symbolical, but most expositors proceed to take
the witnesses and the holy city literally. Then difficulties
multiply. They are fewer when we see all as symbolism and a
coherent pattern emerges. John has already used the lampstand
symbol and explained that it refers to churches (1:20). Thus
it seems best to take the witnesses as symbolizing the witnessing
church or some part of it. . . . What John is doing then is
outlining the function of the witnessing church. Its lot will be
hard, but its eventual triumph is sure." Revelation, 144-45.

123. See Caird, Revelation, 138, and particularly Kiddle
(Revelation, 176) who says: "What a strange phrase to use of
the death of two individuals, though they have been divinely
protected -- 'make war on them and kill them' (a phrase which
is quite natural and appropriate in the similar and, as we hope
to show, parallel passage in xiii.7, where the Beast 'wages war'
on the saints in general). Stranger still is what happens after
their death. This was no parochial affair of interest only to

the small circle of those who had been obliged to listen to their
unpleasant prophecy, or had witnessed their slaying by the Beast;
no ordinary event calculated to attract the attention of their
own local city. It was nothing less than universal in its
significance. The whole world was moved -- John stresses the
fact three times over. . . . The whole world is concerned, the
whole world gazes at their bodies (though John says nothing to
suggest that they come to the City to do so - - that would be
awkward indeed!). . . ."

124. ". . . he (John) was writing in a time of supreme and
urgent crisis. . .he was passionately convinced that the Church
was about to face the great Distress of ruthless persecution
. . . ." Kiddle, Revelation, 178. See also Preston and Hanson,
Revelation, 89; Glasson, Revelation, 68-70; Farrer, Revelation,
128-130 et al. Note Farrer's rebuttal of those who wish to read
literal Jerusalem into the chapter's application. "St John
cannot be deeply interested in what happened to Jerusalem in
A.D. 70. Evidently the end of the world was not implicated in
the event, as it had looked like being. . . St John is too far
away from the event, and his Church is fighting on a different
front. He hurries on into a description of the position of the
Gospel in the intermediate age between the fall of the Holy City
and the coming of Antichrist; that is to say, in the time of
St John." Ibid., 130.

125. Sehr lehrreich ist das Wörtchen πνευματικῶς. . . das wohl
nur nach 1 Cor. 2:13f. zu erklären ist. Aber hier ist, anders
als bei Pls, das "pneumatische" Urteil auf das konkrete
Verhältnis zu "Jerusalem" angewandt; es begründet die Schärfe
des Gegensatzes, aber ebenso auch die Tiefe der Verbundenheit
mit dem Judentum, weil es das Recht zu einer "pneumatischen"
jüdischer Tradition gibt. . .Darüber hinaus liegt in dem Wort
vielleicht eine Andeutung, dass die Bilder der Apc "pneumatisch"
zu verstanden sind. Das ist nicht unwichtig für die Frage nach
der "Bildlichkeit" der apokalyptischen Visionen." Lohmeyer,
Offenbarung, 93.

126. See Feuillet's extended discussion on this point. "Essai",
186.

127. Rev. 17:3. Beckwith says: "The wilderness is taken by many
com. to be typical of the utter destruction to which Rome is
to be reduced." Apocalypse, 692. Beckwith himself does not agree
with this application and contends that "the actual destruction
of Rome, or the desolation following, is not exhibited in this
vision. . . ." Ibid. However, it is difficult to understand
how such a position can be taken in view of the plain statement
in v. 16 that the harlot is to be made desolate, and the
similar allusion in 18:19 "in one hour she has been laid waste."

Moses Stuart comments: ". . . desert, appropriate to symbolize the future condition of the beast." A Commentary on the Apocalypse (Edinburgh, 1847), 675.

128. The demons looked on the ἄβυσσος as their home. See Luke 8:31. Paul's solitary use of the term applies it to the abode of the dead. Rom. 10:7. All other N.T. usages of the word are found in Revelation where it appears as the habitation of beings hostile to God and His Church. The angel of the abyss is called the Destroyer. See Rev. 9:11. The Greek term here employed is sometimes used in the LXX as a synonym for שׁאול See Kennedy, Conceptions, 121ff. In Job 28:22 it is "the pair and forerunner of Death." Farrer, Revelation, 119. This is the original Abgrund of Semitic mythology.

129. This application does not deny that John entertained also an allusion to Nero, but we contend that his main application is not thus superficial. Commentators have too readily followed Bousset in this matter. The interwoven parody present throughout the presentation of Christ's opponents suggests that we should look for an event overtaking Satan himself similar to Christ's reception of a mortal wound. Indeed, it is the same event, and is symbolized also by the casting down to earth of Satan (Rev. 12). "The smiting of the head is not simply an historical allusion. . . it rests on Scripture. Because the serpent has attacked the woman, he is flung down grovelling on the earth, to carry on a feud with the woman, which is continued between his seed and the woman's seed: the serpent (in himself, or in his seed?) shall have his head ambushed, the woman's seed, his heel (Gen. 3:13-15). We have witnessed the fulfill-ment of this oracle point by point; and now that the serpent takes up the feud with 'the rest of the woman's seed' through the instrumentality of his own 'seed', the beast, we are not to be surprised to see that the head of the serpent's 'seed' is smitten." Farrer, Revelation, 153. Farrer has so many concepts unique to himself, we might not be persuaded by his exposition here, did he stand alone. However, commentators well-known for their sobriety of exegesis have affirmed similarly, despite the majority trend in favour of Nero. Even were it not so, the facts in and of themselves cry out. To rise out of the bottom-less pit is, to John, the symbol of resurrection. It is identical with the healing of the wound of death. Compare Rev. 11:7; 13:3; 17:8; 20:1-3,7. Wherever we read of a rising out of the pit in Revelation, the renewal of a desolating policy by a resurrected power is spoken of. It is this very fact of the renewal of persecution which proves the resurrection state of the beast to those whose names are not written in the book of life. ". . . the beast has already once existed and will again come up out of the abyss -- i.e. the world of the dead (cf. ix.1f., 11) -- (xvii. 8,11 three times ἦν καὶ οὐκ

ἔστιν). The antichrist and his kingdom are a power which had
already appeared once in history, had then disappeared, and at
the end of the times is to appear again in life. This is a
fundamental thought of early Christian prophecy. . . The same
thought is expressed, xiii.3,12,14, in the statement that one of
the seven heads of the beast had received a mortal wound, which
healed again. This means that the beast itself had received a
death-stroke, and had come to life again. . . ." Zahn,
Introduction, 440.

"By the death of Nero, or any other one of the emperors,
before the time of Revelation, the continued existence of the
Roman kingdom had never been questioned, much less had it
ever ceased to exist. . . If a Caesar dies, there is another
Caesar who immediately lives and reigns." "The idea, however,
that the representation of the revivification of the fatally
smitten beast or of one of its heads. . . rests upon the myth
of the return of Nero, is irreconcilable with the history of
this myth. . . .The notion, which arose soon after the suicide
of Nero and at first among his heathen admirers, that he had
not died, but had fled to the Parthians, and would return from
that country to Rome to take vengeance on his enemies and to
assume the throne again, existed unchanged until the beginning
of the second century -- namely, until the time when it was no
longer probable that Nero, who was born in 37 A.D., was still
alive." Ibid., 443. "Moreover, the interpretation of the
number 666 as the alleged Hebrew form. . . of the name of Nero
. . . is extremely improbable Revelation was written for
Greek Christians, for whom it would be necessary to translate
a Hebrew name. . . ." Ibid.

Guthrie discusses the Nero myth and the interpretation
derived from it and then proceeds as follows: "But does
the Apocalypse itself really demand this? The Beast with
the mortal wound which has now been healed (xiii.3) may be
illustrated by the current Nero myth, but in its later forms
that myth involved Nero returning at the head of a Parthian army
to recapture his lost throne, with the consequent destruction
of Rome. Yet there is no reference to Parthians, either in
chapter xiii or xvii. The Beast represents the embodiment of
evil, a conception quite comprehensible without recourse to a
Nero myth, which, according to Tacitus, had become a 'joke'
(ludibrium) by Domitian's time. Moreover, since the Apocalypse
represents the Beast as returning from the dead, this could only
refer to Nero after a period when the idea that he had not
really died had ceased to be believed because too great an
interval had elapsed since his supposed disappearance."
Introduction, 953-54.

The first Christian writer to refer to the returning of Nero
from the dead was Augustine. But he does not link this in any
way with the prophecies of Revelation. See Civ. Dei. xx. 19.3.

Paul Minear points out that twice in Revelation the wound

is assigned to the beast itself, and that a wound inflicted on a
former rejected ruler is not a wound on the empire. Furthermore
to the prophet John "this mortal blow which affected the sea-
beast injured the dragon as well. . . . A mortal wound
simultaneously destroyed the authority of head, beast, and
dragon by terminating the blasphemous adoration by men. It is
difficult to maintain that Nero's suicide fulfilled such
specifications." I saw A New Earth (Washington D.C., 1968), 250-
51. He also says: "The cure also impelled men to worship the
dragon by the greater devotion and fear which they accorded to
the beast. Now there is absolutely no evidence that the rumored
resuscitation of Nero actually had such effects as these."
Ibid. Minear places great stress on the fact that πληγὴ
translated "wound" in Rev. 13 is everywhere else translated
"plague". Therefore, he concludes that the wound is as elsewhere
the symbol of a divine punishment. "The wound was a God-
inflicted plague which simultaneously destroyed the authority of
the head, the beast, and the dragon. It was a wound from which
the beast could recover only by using deception, by succeeding
in that deception, and by making absolute his blasphemous claims
to ultimate power over human destiny." Ibid., 253-54. Minear
then makes the same application of Rev. 12 as does Farrer,
making the Atonement the infliction of the deadly wound. "Such
an interpretation is in line with other New Testament
descriptions of the war between the servants of God and 'the
principalities and powers'. . . ." Ibid., 254. Texts such as
Luke 10:17-24; 11:14-22 and Col. 2:15 support this view. Minear,
of course, rejects the application of 666 to Nero, and we
consider that this rejection as elaborated by Zahn, Lohmeyer, et
al., is a water-tight case. While Bousset's work on the
Apocalypse was tremendously important as showing the relationship
between the book and the times, a good case was somewhat spoiled
by being overdone. This has resulted in retarding progressive
exegesis of Revelation. On the issue of the Nero interpretation
see also Lohmeyer's commentary on Rev. 17 which is prepared to
grant allusions to the Nero legends, but chooses to interpret
on the basis of apocalyptic symbolism rather than from history.
He may overdo this, as he overdoes his emphasis on the seven-
fold structure, etc. of the book, but his case is worthy of
study. Loisy, on the other hand, follows Bousset closely.
    It may be necessary, in order to do justice to all the
facts, to keep in mind that John sometimes works on more than
one level. It is possible to acknowledge that the seer is aware
of and employs the legend of Nero without being committed to
the position that sees in such allusions the full meaning of his
references. The safe place to begin all attempts at interpretation in depth is with the local historical application which was
immediately apparent to both John and his readers. Thus Rigaux
says: "Il nous semble donc probable que Jean a connu et
employé la légende de Néron redivivus dans sa description de la

Bête. Rien ne prouve cependant qu'il ait cru à la légende.
C'est même fort improbable. Tout est symbole dans la description
des bêtes." L'Antéchrist, 353.
　　Articles on the topic include:　P. Minear, "The Wounded
Beast", JBL, LXXII (1953), 93-102;　B. Newman, "The Fallacy of
the Domitian Hypothesis", NTS, X (1963-64), 133-39;　C. Clemen,
"Die Zahl des Tieres Apc. 13,18"; "Nochmals die Zahl des
Tieres Apc. 13,18." ZNTW, II (1901), 109-114;　XI (1910), 204-
223.

130.　Gegenspieler, 131.

131.　See Beckwith, Apocalypse, 633f.; Charles, Revelation, I,
333;　Caird, Revelation, 162;　Preston and Hanson, Revelation,
95, et al.

132.　Morris comments:　"Many modern scholars see in the beast
a reference to the Roman Empire.　This seems too simple.　We may
well see in the Empire a preliminary manifestation of the evil
that will one day be realized to the full in the antichrist.　But
there is much more to the beast than ancient Rome." Revelation,
165.　Hendriksen takes a similar position.　"Chapter 13 shows
us the agents, instruments, or tools which the dragon uses in
his attack upon the Church.　Two beasts are described. . .The
first represents the persecuting power of Satan operating in and
through the nations of this world and their governments.　The
second symbolizes the false religions and philosophies of this
world.　Both these beasts oppose the Church throughout this
dispensation;　yet the apostle describes them in terms that
indicate the form which they assumed during the closing decade
of the first century A.D." Conquerors, 144. Farrer says
concerning the first beast ". . .he is for obvious symbolical
reasons the figure of Antichrist. . . ." Revelation, 151.
Milligan, who shies clear from any historical applications such
as Nero, etc., writes: "The whole description of the beast is
thus, in multiplied particulars a travesty of the Lord Jesus
Christ Himself. . . . Like the latter, the former is the
representative, the 'sent' of an unseen power, by whom all
authority is 'given' him;　he has his death and his resurrection
from the dead;　he has his throngs of marvelling and
enthusiastic worshippers;　his authority over those who own
his sway is limited by no national boundaries, but is
conterminous with the whole world;　he gathers up and unites in
himself all the scattered elements of darkness and enmity to the
truth which had previously existed among men, and from which the
Church of God had suffered." Revelation, 224. Milligan
proceeds to assert that the beast is not Rome, either pagan
or papal, but "the general influence of the world, in so far as
it is opposed to God. . . ." Ibid. This is making too much of
a good thing.　It is certain that for John the beast represented

historical realities more specific than merely the antagonistic
world. However, Milligan's words regarding the beast being a
travesty of Christ are well spoken. As such they fit the
concept of an Antichrist to be manifested in history but particularly at the end of time. Ernst stresses the fact that the
political meaning of Rev. 13 will not suffice, but requires the
complementary consummation of a demonic eschatological power.
Gegenspieler, 133.

133. Commenting upon the first beast of Rev. 13, Rigaux writes:
". . . car ni les Juifs, ni les chrétiens ne considéraient les
prophéties daniéliques comme accomplies par les exploits d'
Antiochus Épiphane. Pour les Synoptiques, l'abomination de la
désolation doit encore se produire. Il n'est pas douteux que
Josèphe, l'Apocalypse d'Esdras et celle de Baruch, les rabbins
et les Pères apostoliques ne considèrent la quatrième bête de
Daniel comme le symbole de l'empire romain. Par conséquent,
dans saint Jean comme dans Daniel, le symbole des Bêtes s'applique
à des empires. De plus, puisque le règne de la quatrième Bête
n'est pas envisagé comme passé, mais est regardé comme se
réalisant dans l'empire romain. . . Jean a voulu décrire, sous
le symbole de sa première Bête, l'action persécutrice de Rome."
L'Antéchrist, 347.
        Glasson well says: "As in Dan. 7, the king and the kingdom
tend to be identified; at first the monster is the Roman empire
but as the chapter develops it comes to stand for a single
ruler with supernatural powers and with a deadly hate against
the servants of God." Revelation, 79.
        "The ten horns no doubt come from Dan. 7:7 where they
represent ten kings." Ibid., 80.
        On v. 14 the same writer comments: "One is reminded of the
similar situation in Dan. 3 and Nebuchadnezzar's image of gold
which all his subjects were to worship." Ibid., 82.
        Caird links Rev. 13 with Mk. 13:14 as do many others. "John
does not actually use the title Antichrist for the monster,
though he might well have done. Jesus had prophesied the
coming of 'false Christs and false prophets' (Mark 13:22); and,
since John calls the second of his two monsters 'the false
prophets'. . . . it is a reasonable inference that he thought of
the first as a false Christ. . . .Other traces of the same
tradition may be found in two other New Testament books. In Mark
xiii.14 there is a reference to a new 'desecrating horror', which
was to pollute the temple. . . . Mark personifies it. . . ."
Revelation, 165. Caird thinks of the myth of Antichrist as a
genuine myth "capable of re-enactment in varying circumstances."
Ibid., 166.
        Loisy, too, makes several connections between this chapter
and Daniel. He sees the beast as "une incarnation de Satan, et
par elle va réaliser le règne de l'Antéchrist. . . ." Apocalypse
de Jean (Paris, 1923), 245. Commenting upon the blasphemous

mouth of the beast he writes: "Trait emprunté à Daniel. . .où il concerne Antiochus Épiphane." "L'auteur va insister sur les blasphèmes en paraphrasant Daniel; l'utilisation qu'il fait de ce prophète donne à croire qu'il ne voyait aucunement l'empire des Séleucides dans la quatrième bête et qu'il regardait la prédiction de Daniel touchant le quatrième empire, les trois ans et demi d'oppression et le règne des saints, comme restant à accomplir; c'est pourquoi il ne se fait aucun scrupule de la rééditer." Ibid., 250. And again later he speaks of John as "préoccupé de suivre Daniel en l'interprétant, et ne voulent pas abandonner son formulaire plus ou moins mystérieux. . . ." Ibid. Rare indeed is the commentary which does not link Rev. 13 with the βδέλυγμα τῆς ἐρημώσεως of Daniel.

134. The "war" references in Revelation concerning the activities of the Antichrist all have their rise in Daniel. See Dan. 7:21; 9:26.

135. The second beast emphasizes the great cunning of Antichrist, as the first stresses his great power. This also is a glance backwards at Daniel. See particularly Dan. 8:23-25; 11:21-23. Stauffer writes: "These two weapons of antichrist, great power and much cunning, appear combined into a system in Rev. 13ff.: The antichrist is the eschatological world power that takes the lying spirit into his service!" ". . .the military, political and economic alliance is consummated in a religious united front -- the devil's counterpart to the universal mission of the civitas dei (cf. Mark 13:10). This religious united front is the work of the false prophet, who looks like a lamb, but talks like a dragon. . . .He is the religious and political herald of antichrist, for whom he recruits adherents by mislead-ing miracles. His favourite theme is a perverted Good Friday, of antichrist's mortal wounds and their miraculous healing. . . ." Theology, 214-15.

136. Stauffer and many other scholars have seen the close relationship between Rev. 13 and Armageddon. He also links both with the fulfilment of 2 Thess. 2. Theology, 214-15. And Armageddon is inevitably associated with Dan. 11:45 and the βδέλυγμα τῆς ἐρημώσεως.

137. Cataracts of nonsense have been written concerning the mystical number 666. Almost all of it pours from thought-forms quite removed from those of John. An adequate interpretation must take into account the rabbinical currents in the Judaism of John's day which were not altogether lacking in the early church. Milligan here is on the right track. "The number six itself awakened a feeling of dread in the breast of the Jew who felt the significance of numbers. It fell well below the sacred number seven just as much as eight went beyond it.

This last number denoted more than the simple possession of the Divine. As in the case of circumcision on the eighth day, of the 'great day' of the feast on the eighth day, or of the resurrection of our Lord on the first day of the week, following the previous seven days, it expressed a new beginning in active power. By a similar process the number six was held to signify inability to reach the sacred point and hopeless falling short of it. To the Jew there was thus a doom upon the number six even when it stood alone. Triple it; let there be a multiple of it by ten and then a second time by ten until you obtain three mysterious sixes following one another, 666; and we have represented a potency of evil than which there can be none greater, a direfulness of fate than which there can be none worse." Revelation, 235. We are not certain that Milligan's claims can be entirely substantiated but we believe that they lean in the right direction.

Caird criticizes most approaches to the interpretation of 666, but offers no positive solution of his own. See Revelation, 174-76. The comments of Morris are more helpful. Revelation, 174. ". . . translate 'it is the number of man" . . . ."

The variant reading of 616 probably arose out of a partisan application, such as to Gaius, and should not divert us from the problem of this trinity of six.

Regarding the Nero solution G.E. Ladd has voiced the doubts of many as follows: ". . . the numberical total of Neron Kaisar in Greek is not 666, but 1005. The problem is solved by transplanting Neron Kaisar into Hebrew, which does indeed total 666. This is achieved, however, by a slight variation in the spelling of the Hebrew word for Caesar. Furthermore, no one has explained why John, writing to a Greek-reading public, would have used the elaborate symbolism of gematria with a Hebrew instead of a Greek form of the name. It is also significant that none of the ancient interpreters of Revelation recognized this solution." John, 186. The same writer suggests that "it is possible that the number was intended to be altogether symbolic." Ibid., 187.

138. See Dan. 3:1.

139   Revelation, 189-195.

140. "In the vision of the vintage which now follows, vv. 17-20, the principal feature, as in its original, Joel 3:13, is contained, not in the ingathering of the grapes, but in the treading of the winepress. The crushing of the grapes in the press, and especially the staining of the feet and garments of the treaders with the red juices, the 'blood of the grapes'. . . became a familiar figure for the utter trampling down of enemies and furious vengeance. Hence this symbol of God's wrath visited upon the wicked; cf. Is. 63:2-4. . .cf. Joel 3:13;

299

Lam. 1:15; Rev. 19:15. The meaning of the second vision is
clear; it pictures not the judgement as a whole, but God's
vengeance visited upon the wicked. It is then not parallel
with the first, which. . . figures the whole judgment, as it
affects the righteous and the wicked alike. We have in the
two visions, as often with the author, first a general fact or
statement, then a detail or part. . . ." Beckwith, Apocalypse,
663. See also Morris, Revelation, 185. Hendriksen, Conquerors,
155-56; Farrer, Revelation, 165-68, et al.

141. "The vintage is trodden outside the city. St John accepts
the symbolism of Joel. Joel describes under the metaphor of a
ghastly vintage a battle in which the nations, attacking
Jerusalem, are smashed outside the walls. St John no more
supposes the act of judgement to be confined within the valley
of Jehoshaphat than he supposes the blessed harvest to be reaped
in a field of barley on the Judean hills. The value of the
phrase 'outside the city' is that it links Joel's prophecy with
the last chapters of Isaiah and Zechariah respectively, both of
which describe a final slaughter of enemies outside of Jerusalem."
Farrer, Revelation, 167. Beckwith reminds us that "A final
assault upon God's people by the assembled forces of their
enemies, and the overthrow of these, are the common predictions
of the apocalyptic writings. . . and this event is thought of
as taking place near Jerusalem. The Apocalyptist appears to
have this tradition in mind in the use of the words 'without
the city.'" Apocalypse, 664-65. This is nearer the mark than
Morris's more general application. Revelation, 186. Kiddle would
have us believe that the city mentioned is Babylon, but he has
missed the allusion to Old Testament passages about the final
slaughter outside Jerusalem. Carpenter is nearer the mark when
he says that those who fall "have refused the defence of the
true city and sanctuary." "Revelation", 604.

142. See Beckwith, Revelation, 665. R.H. Charles differs
with Beckwith regarding the issue of whether the earthly or
heavenly Jerusalem is meant. He says in contrast to Kiddle and
Beasley-Murray, "There can be no question as to the identity of
'the city.' It is not Rome (for its destruction has already been
announced in the hearing of the Seer in 9) but Jerusalem. It is,
moreover, most probably not the earthly Jerusalem but the
heavenly Jerusalem which is to descend from heaven to be the
centre of the Kingdom of Christ for the 1000 years. . . If xiv.
14,18-20 is a proleptic summary of xix. 11-21 only, then the
city referred to might be the historic Jerusalem, or rather its
ruined site; but if this is a summary of xix. 11-21 and also
xx. 7-10, then the city can be none other than the city that came
down from heaven--the seat of the Messianic Kingdom." Revelation,
II, 25. We think Charles is mainly right, but wrong in his
reference to "the historic Jerusalem, or rather its ruined site".

John by the holy city means the church, at least in all references
prior to chapter 20. Whether in picturing a subsequent era to
the Parousia, when faith gives place to sight, he replaces
the emblems of ancient Israel by more material representations
is another question.

143. See Eze. 40:2; 45:1-5; 48:9f.

144. On the commonly received interpretation of the passage
Ladd says: "Many commentators assert--as though it were a
self-evident fact in the text--that the 'kings from the east'
represent the Parthians who now invade the civilized world under
the leadership of Nero redivivus. This, however, is sheer
speculation." John, 213. However, we view Ladd's own interpretation (regarding "the pagan hordes") as just as speculative.
This type of interpretation came into modern favour when
journalists "puffed" the "yellow peril" about the turn of the
century. While it is true that John interweaves some current
myths of his day into his work, and may here have the Parthians
in mind, it is even more true that the main source of his
imagery is the Old Testament. As in the case of Christ's
teachings where for every local allusion several Old Testament
references can be found, even so it is with the author of
Revelation. Older commentaries were wont to point out that the
language of Rev. 16:12 has been drawn from expressions in
Isaiah having reference to Israel's deliverance from ancient
Babylon.   For example, note that the phrases "from the east"
(Isa. 41:2; 43:5; 46:11) and "from the rising of the sun"
(Isa. 41:25; 45:6; 59:19) are each employed three times in
Isaiah in connection with Israel's redemption from the captor
nation. Similarly, the drying up of Euphrates is there
mentioned. See Isa. 44:27. Milligan has expressed himself at
length upon this matter, and should be closely studied. He
says: "Probably no part of the Apocalypse has received more
varied interpretation than the first statement of this Bowl.
Who are these kings that come from the sun-rising is the
point to be determined; and the answer usually given is, that
they are part of the anti-christian host, part of those
afterwards spoken of as the kings of the whole inhabited earth,
before whom God dries up the Euphrates in order that they may
pursue an uninterrupted march to the spot on which they are to
be overwhelmed with a final and complete destruction. Something
may certainly be said on behalf of such a view; yet it is
exposed to serious objections.
        "1. We have already at chap. ix. 14,. . . been made
acquainted with the river Euphrates; and, so far from being a
hindrance to the progress of Christ's enemies, it is rather the
symbol of their overflowing and destructive might.
        "2. We have also met at chap. vii.2 with the expression
'from the sun-rising,' and it is there applied to the quarter from

301

which the angel comes by whom the people of God are sealed. . . .
it is not easy to think of anti-christian foes coming from a
quarter described in the same term.
"3. These kings 'from the sun-rising' are not said to be
a part of 'the kings of the whole inhabited earth' immediately
afterwards referred to. They are rather distinguished from them.
"4. The 'preparing of the way' connects itself with the
thought of Him whose way was prepared by the coming of the
Baptist.
"5. The type of drying up the waters of a river, takes us
back, alike in the historical and prophetic writings of the Old
Testament, to the means by which the Almighty secures the
deliverance of His people, not the destruction of His enemies."
Revelation, 269-70
A. Plummer says similarly. "The 'kings of the east' are
certainly the forces ranged on the side of God. Many writers
see an allusion to Christ and the saints. The sun is a frequent
figure of Christ in Scripture (cf. Mal. iv. 4; Zech. iii.8 and
vi. 12 LXX; Luke 1. 78 also ch. vii. 2; xii. 1; xxii. 16).
The kings of the east may thus be identified with the armies
of ch. xix. 11-16." Revelation, (PC), 395.

145. To be consistent in applying the literary principle of
parody which John continually uses is a safeguard against
erroneous interpretations. He makes even Christ's enemies to
speak for Christ in so far as he describes them in terms
reminiscent of Him. Thus many commentators point out that
". . . die Worte: 'es war und ist nicht und wird wieder sein'
klingen wie eine dämonische Nachäffung des Gottestitels; 'der
war und der ist und der kommt'." Lohmeyer, Offenbarung, 145.
Similarly the principle of contrast whereby John places the
beast against the Lamb, and the whore against the woman
clothed with the sun, and Babylon against Jerusalem, also makes
for safety of interpretation. In Rev. 16:12, this principle is
used by John to place "the kings of the east" in opposition
to "the kings of the whole world". It is not an instance of
parody. Such cases are clearly shown to be such by their
context.

146. Euphrates is first referred to as נהר in Joshua 24. The
word itself means a stream, sea, flood, or river. Many verses
describe the Euphrates as the boundary line between Israel's
land and Babylon. See Joshua 24:2-3,14-15; Gen. 15:18, etc.
See Isa. 8:7,8 as a typical example of the use of the word with
reference to a catastrophic invasion by Assyria. The same
symbolism is used by Daniel and by John. See Dan. 9:26;
11:40 and Rev. 12:15-16. Thus it is not unlikely that the writer
of Revelation by his reference to Euphrates in Rev. 16 points
to the same war as mentioned in 17:14. The waters are distinctly
declared to be "people and multitudes and nations and tongues"

who are hostile to the people of God. Rev. 17:15.

147. See Kiddle, Revelation, 324. Farrer sums up the symbolism
aptly: "The spirits bring the kings to Har-Megedon, that is,
Mount Megiddo. No such mountain-name was ever current.
Megiddo is a town on the southern side of the Esdraelon Plain,
the nearest of known cities to the foothills of Carmel.
'Mount Megiddo' would have to designate Carmel. . . .St. John
wants to refer to Megiddo and to Carmel in one breath. Ahab,
a renegade Anointed, or Antichrist, and husband of Jezebel (see
ii.20) 'sent unto all the children of Israel and gathered the
prophets' of Baal and Ashtaroth 'together unto Mount Carmel'
. . . there to try their strength against the Lord God of
Elijah, and to perish by the sword. And. . . Ahab was himself to
perish likewise on the day when a lying spirit in the mouths of
false prophets enticed him and his allies. . . .The author of
Chronicles transfers the exact circumstances of Ahab's death to
the death of Josiah. He defied a true warning, he fought against
God. . .he was shot by archers at Megiddo. . . .There was a
great lamentation for him. . . .The lamentation of Megiddo
appears to be taken up by Zechariah. . . where 'all the families
of the land mourn', because they have 'looked on him whom they
pierced'. Now we know from Rev. 1:7 (cf. xi.9) what St. John
made of this text. So in sum, Mt. Megiddo stands in his mind
for a place where lying prophecy and its dupes go to meet their
doom; where kings and their armies are misled to their
destruction; and where all the tribes of the earth mourn, to
see him in power, whom in weakness they had pierced. For there
the stars in their courses fight against princes, and the
floods of destruction sweep them away (Judges v.19-21)."
Revelation, 178.

148. Apocalypse, 685.

149. Kiddle, Revelation, 324. ". . .Daniel mentions the hill
too--between Jerusalem and the sea. . . ." Morris also refers
to Dan. xi.45, when interpreting this passage. Revelation, 200.
Daniel probably had Ezekiel's Gog and Magog in mind.

150. Rev. 17:5.

151. Rev. 17:16.

152. Rev. 17:18.

153. Rev. 17:5. See Ladd, John, 222.

154. This is another illustration of the use of John's
principle of contrast. If he can represent the church of all
ages by the symbol of a pure woman, it is unlikely that the

303

antithesis he pictures applies only to certain unbelievers in
a certain city, or even to those in a particular empire at one
point of time only.

155. Thus flight from Babylon is enjoined upon all who have not
taken their stand in the holy city. See Rev. 18:1-4.

156. Rev. 2:9; 3:9.

157. Rev. 2:14.

158. Rev. 2:20.

159. Isa. 1:21; Jer. 2:20; 3:1; 13:27; Eze. 16:15,22,33,35;
23:7,8,11,14,17,18,19,29,35,43,45; 43:7,9; Hos. 2:2,4,5,10;
4:12,15,18; 5:4; 6:10; 9:1; Mic. 1:7. πόρνη, or its derivatives,
is used in the LXX at least fifty times to describe the spiritual
fornication of Israel and Judah. It may be significant also that
μυστήριον, which occurs more than twenty times in the New
Testament, is never applied to anything openly unbelieving, but
always to things sacred or professing religious characteristics.
    Such contentions as these, as used in this study, are not
meant to deny the well-known arguments for Rome such as are
found in Rigaux's L'Antéchrist, 348-350. They are meant rather
to indicate that John saw more than just Rome, and that he was
particularly concerned with the final apostasy which will have
as its centre the issue of relationship to God rather than
political matters. Furthermore, he was writing for professing
Christians, not for unbelieving citizens of Rome. Therefore,
he intends by his portrayal to admonish the flock, lest its
members be led by Antichrist into spiritual fornication. Rev.
18:1-4 with its admonition to forsake Babylon strengthens these
contentions. Kiddle admonishes: "But we must not forget that
in Isaiah, Jeremiah, and Ezekiel it is pre-eminently Jerusalem
who is the harlot-city. We have already seen (see excursus
on ch. xi) how John's picture of Babylon the great was
fashioned with the thought constantly in mind of Jerusalem as
the city of doom." Revelation, 341.

160. ". . . our Lord also gave a similar command to depart
from Judea in the times of the abomination. . . . Jesus warned
the people of great wickedness and persecution which would be
present in the Judean area. . . .Moreover, false prophets shall
arise and attempt to deceive even the people of God. . . . When
such wickedness prevails in the city and when the false
prophets are attempting to lead God's people astray there is
only one way to escape. . . .And that is to leave the city. . . .
Many of these thoughts lie behind the command in Rev. 18:4 to
flee from Babylon. This city is likewise full of wickedness. . .
her hands are stained with the blood of martyred Christians. . .

Moreover. . . there is the implicit association of Babylon and
the false prophet. Thus the two situations which our Lord
pictures in his apocalyptic discourse, and which John relates in
the vision of Rev.17-18 are, mutatis mutandis, rather similar.
And the command of Christ to leave Judea in view of the
tribulation and wickedness undoubtedly contributes to the form
of the thought and expression in Rev. 18:4." Louis A. Vos,
The Synoptic Traditions in the Apocalypse (Kampen, 1965), 161.
"So ist der himmlische Befehl an die Christen zum Auszug aus
Babylon Apk 18,4 einerseits durch Js 48,20; 52:11; Jer. 50:8;
51,6 ud vorgebildet anderseits aber auch sicher durch Mt. 24:15ff.
par mitbestimmt." Kuhn, "βαβυλων ", TWNT, I, 513. These
suggestions from Vos and Kuhn also throw light on the identity
of the woman of Rev. 17, particularly when we take into account
the principle for exegeting this book which is found in
recognition of Revelation's close kinship with the eschatological
discourse of Mk. 13.

161. Kiddle discusses the troubles of those who attempt to do
so and then adds: "The fact is that those who seek in the
reference to seven kings a list of seven individual monarchs must
admit that the text is enigmatic beyond hope, and that a mere
approximation to intelligibility is to be reached only by the
arbitrary mutilation of the text or the performance of
extraordinary mental gymnastics."
    "No, the number seven has here its symbolical force--as
always in Revelation. . . .we shall insist that in their present
form his words admit of no exact historical reference: verse 10
is a general statement, and John's readers can have no temptation
to read it as anything else." Revelation, 350-51
    Beckwith writes with much good sense on this topic. See
706-707 of his Apocalypse. He says in part: "What kings have
preceded is for the Apocalyptist's message to his readers
unimportant; it is enough for them to know that only one is to
follow before the end of the then present world-kingdom is
reached." 707. And on the following page he summarizes: "In
view of these considerations we are brought to the conclusion
that the number seven here is purely symbolical, that the
Apocalyptist means to represent the Roman power as a historic
whole."
    Ladd speaks similarly and then proceeds to discuss vv. 9-11
to excellent effect. "It is difficult to see any connection
between the seven hills of Rome and seven of its emperors." 222.
"The second and final manfestation of the beast is an eighth
king; but it is not the eighth king for there are only seven;
it is an eighth king which is one of the seven. This suggests
that one of the seven is to experience two stages of his
existence." John, 231. Zahn also takes this position. See
Offenbarung, II, 553ff.
    Our own suggestion is that a key is provided in Rev. 20:

3-10 where we see that the slain dragon, as with the beast, has a resurrection experience for "a little while". Cf. Rev. 17:10. The sixth head is the wounded one (thus it both "is" and yet "is not"). When the beast revives it is manifested in the seventh head and because this seventh head represents the beast rising up after having been slain it is also called the eighth. The latter number symbolizes resurrection. See Lohmeyer, ad loc. There is no reference to eight heads. The beast himself is declared to be "the eighth" because he, like Jesus (the 888 name) has experienced resurrection. If this is the true meaning of the enigma, the significance of "five have fallen, one is, the other is not yet come" has nothing to do with calculating emperors, but only with the fact that the Antichrist is about to enter the scene as earth's final demonstration of Satanic power.

162. Milligan, Revelation, 286. ". . . the number eight marks the beginning of a new life, with quickened and heightened powers." See also Farrer, Revelation, 158. "For eight signifying resurrection, see 1 Peter iii.20-21, and 2 Peter ii.5."
    Carpenter writes: ". . . no eighth empire shall rise, but the wild beast, now smitten in all the seven heads of his power, will, in the convulsive death-throe, seem an eighth power, in which the ebbing life of all the seven finds expression. . . . This fierce and last flickering up of the doomed power of evil is dwelt on again in chap. xx. 7-10." "Revelation", 613.

163. See Morris, Revelation, 174.

164. Nikolaus Walter ("Tempelzerstörung und synoptische Apokalypse", 45) links the βδέλυγμα τῆς ἐρημώσεως with this event. We do not agree with either his dating for Mark, or his exposition of Mark 13, but we agree with him that there is a relationship between the Mk. 13:14 passage and Rev. 20:7-10. Says Walter ". . . setzt er (Mk.) an die Stelle des Übergangs zur letzten Periode der Geschichte, an der nach der aus Dan 9 gespeisten Erwartung die Entweihung des Tempels stehen sollte, jenes halb mythische Bild vom Auftreten des Antichrists (vgl. Apc. 20:7-10)."

165. Dan. 11:45.

CONCLUSION

Our study has been an attempt to interpret "the most difficult section" of that chapter in the Synoptic Gospels most commented upon in modern times.[1] Our conclusions are as follows.

In confirmation of the then revolutionary viewpoint offered sixty years ago, the present study indicates that the New Testament is indeed inescapably and unashamedly apocalyptic in some of its basic concepts. This can be said also of its key figures such as Christ, Paul, and the writer of Revelation. Eschatology itself is no mere addendum to the New Testament but "the very fibre of the living strand",[2] and the type of eschatology mirrored by apocalyptic, with its concepts of the kingdom of God and the Son of Man, has rightly been called "the mother of Christian theology".[3] The recent emphasis by Pannenberg in this regard is exegetically sound. However distasteful now, as in 1910, this acknowledgement is to the twentieth-century mind, the evidence is compelling.

Much of the scholarly work done to prove that the records we have of the Olivet discourse consist largely of unauthentic insertions appears instead to prove that prejudices die hard, and that such positions are the outgrowth of philosophical attitudes inimical to all that apocalyptic implies, rather than the result of impartial study.[4] For example, there are no conclusive grounds for rejecting the dominical nature of the βδέλυγμα τῆς ἐρημώσεως saying. The eschatological sermon, and Mk. 13:14 in particular, reflect the same attitude of concord with the contents of "Daniel the prophet" as other genuine logia of the Gospels. The same Old Testament book which furnished the springboard for most apocalyptic notions, and especially the terminology of "the kingdom" and its representative "Son of Man" is the originator of the βδέλυγμα τῆς ἐρημώσεως and the primary Gospel does not hold any of these concepts in isolation.[5] Furthermore, as certainly as Christ accepted the teaching of Daniel regarding the expected dramatic events of the near future, so did His followers, including the writers of 2 Thess. and Revelation.

The latter writings contain overtones, not only of the Passion but of the eschatological sermon which embodies Passion motifs. Thus the study of Mark 13:14 has value for the exegesis of 2 Thess. 2 and the Apocalypse, both of which have been subject to such innumerable vagaries of interpretation. There exists a remarkable homogeneity in the New Testament presentation of Danielic themes, and there is little need to look outside the Old Testament itself for the main elements of New Testament eschatology and apocalyptic.

This study has endeavoured to show that hitherto the βδέλυγμα τῆς ἐρημώσεως has been given too narrow a context.

The usual references to Daniel, 1 and 2 Maccabees, 2 Thess.,
and Josephus are all pertinent but they are not exhaustive. The
elements of the phrase are to be traced back much earlier than
Daniel. They are found in the Pentateuch and reoccur in the
historical and prophetic writings. Daniel's presentation of the
שקוץ שמם is a welding of elements already existing in the
historical and prophetic books. He merely consummates themes
emphasized long before. And what Daniel did with motifs from
his predecessors, Christ did with Daniel. Nestle's interpretation
of the שקוץ שמם is correct as far as it goes, but it is not
complete. As certainly as the translators of the LXX were
influenced by Jeremiah's use of שמם and thus were simultaneously influenced by some of Jeremiah's predecessors, so Christ,
motivated by similar sources as well as by the results of His
own creativity, could utilize the same concept. Luke also
interweaves ἐρημώσις into his alternative presentation of Mk.
13:14 in 21:20. There is a growing awareness among recent
scholars that ἐρημώσεως in Mk. 13 is to be understood in its
own right, and not merely as part of a phrase signifying
desecration only. This understanding dissolves the long-
standing difficulty echoed and re-echoed since Wellhausen that
if Mk. 13:1-2 are authentic, then vv. 3-37 are not, because in
the former the temple's destruction is spoken of, while in the
latter only desecration is predicted. The riddle as to why
there should be such panic-characterized flight because of an
event at the temple is also solved. Furthermore, the solution
harmonizes with the Markan context of ch. 13, which emphasizes
judgment and desolation, rather than approaching sacrilege.
As several exegetes have pointed out, Christ in Mk. 13 is giving
Daniel 9:24-27 a much wider application than the events
connected with Antiochus Epiphanes.[6] He apparently anticipated
that in the near future the idolatrous Romans would react against
the insurrectionists by devastating the holy land, the holy city
and temple, and the holy people. This crisis, commencing in
Palestine, would ultimately involve the whole world, particularly
the Christian elect. The spreading tribulation would find its
terminus in His own return as the Vindicator of His oppressed
saints. As the time of trouble was to swell from the initial
Judean episode to a global one, so it is likely that Christ
anticipated a similar development in the nature and actions
of Antichrist, the βδέλυγμα τῆς ἐρημώσεως. Hints of just such
a tradition remain in 2 Thess., 1 John, and the Apocalypse.

The 2 Thess. 2 presentation of Antichrist, modelled on the
Olivet discourse, has reference to an eschatological adversary
attended by miraculous signs, who would display himself as God
and claim universal homage. The βδέλυγμα τῆς ἐρημώσεως
standing in the holy place, and the ἀνθρώπος τῆς ἀνομίας
sitting in the temple of God, on one level of interpretation at
least, point to the same phenomenon. One marked difference,

however, exists. In 2 Thess. 2, the Empire is seen as part of
a providential complex which hinders the coming of the final
antagonist.

The pictures in John's Apocalypse of the varied manifestations
of Antichrist embody the characteristic features found in Daniel,
Mark, and 2 Thess. 2. Pagan Rome is certainly in focus, though
the writer seems to anticipate eschatological events which will
include supernatural manifestations. Antichrist is a genus as
well as a specific figure, and all who oppose by cruelty, or
counterfeit by subtlety Christ and His church, come under this
head.

A strong philological link, as well as conceptual ones,
connects together Daniel, Mark, 2 Thess. 2, and Revelation. It
has been noted that ἐρήμωσις is not unrelated to ἀπώλεια as used
by Paul in his description of the Antichrist, (just as in the
later Old Testament שקוץ is often a parallel to ἀνομία) and to
some extent it is synonymous with שאול and ἄβυσσος. Thus the
language itself of Mk. 13:14 (including the masculine ἑστηκότα)
implies that the eschatological adversary would be characterized
not only by idolatrous worship but by a destructive effect upon
all in his wake. He would drag down to physical destruction
those who resisted him and destroy spiritually all who did not.
Ultimately, the destroyer himself would be destroyed as foretold
by Daniel, and thus be revealed as a son of perdition indeed.

The intimate link between the abomination and the sanctuary
as forged by Daniel remains in the New Testament. The two
are coupled in Mt. 24:1-3,15; Mk. 13:1-4,14; 2 Thess. 2:4, and
the symbolism of Revelation. Throughout the Old and the New
Testaments the sanctuary is seen as a microcosm of the kingdom
of God, and both the exploits of Antichrist and the ultimate
vindication of his victims are portrayed in sanctuary imagery.
Mk. 13, as certainly as Daniel, has the destiny of the holy
places in focus but also the vindication of "the holy ones".
The presence of the Son of man motif in Daniel and Mark betoken
the same -- i.e. uplifting for the downtrodden worshippers,
rescue and praise for the oppressed and hated "priests" of the
Most High. Several scholars have recognized that the picture
of judgment being given in favour of the saints (Dan. 7:22) is
synonymous with the "restoral to its rightful estate" of the
sanctuary (8:14), and the anointing of the "most holy place"
(9:24). Similarly, the coming of the Son of Man in Mk. 13:26
parallels Dan. 7:13 and is as surely the counterpart of the
abomination of Mk. 13:14 as the same figure is of the little
horn in Dan. 7. The return of "great power and glory" (13:26)
hints that the Shekinah, once withdrawn, is to be restored. Thus
the chapter, far from being a hodge-podge of disparate elements,
is a well-integrated midrash on the chief themes of Daniel,

namely the reign of God and the opposition thereto.

The same portrayal of the kingdom of God under the imagery of
the sanctuary, and of the Antichrist under the symbolism of a
destructive invader of the temple, is prominent in the final
canonical apocalypse. The closing chapters of Revelation
picture the destruction of the world power which had blasphemed
the tabernacle of God and its worshippers (13:6-7). Those who
have trampled underfoot the holy city housing the temple are
destroyed by the treading of the great wine press outside the
city. Their destiny is the ἔρημος (17:3,16; 18:19) and the
ἄβυσσος (20:1-3). The coming of One "like a son of man" (1:7,13;
14:14) brings vindication for the saints (6:9-11; 16:4-6; 20:4),
and the subsequent tabernacling of God with those who hitherto
have been "living stones" and "pillars" of the church-temple
yet counted as refuse by the world, and with men in general.
Now the covenant promise "I will dwell with you", typically
realized in the wilderness sanctuary, is completely fulfilled.
Glorification brings that restoration of the divine image
symbolized by the inscription of the sacred name. Each believer,
like the high priest of old, has "holiness to the Lord" beaming
from his forehead. The reign of God is thus consummated as the
holiness betokened by the holy places prevails from sun to sun.
Earth's sanctuary, once defiled by wickedness incarnate in
Antichrist, has been cleansed and vindicated by the act of the
Son of Man who once tabernacled among men in the days of His
flesh, and Who will continue so to do in His glorified body
throughout the ages to come.

In view of the modern emphases upon the kingdom of God and
the Son of Man themes, this study of the relationship between
the βδέλυγμα τῆς ἐρημώσεως   and the sanctuary microcosm
of the divine reign suggests the need for closer study of Daniel
and Mark 13 from those standpoints. Lagrange, Congar, McKelvey,
Grässner, Cole, and Gaston have pointed the way, though not all
deal with Mark 13. Dodd's contention that the underlying pattern
of Scripture is that of death and resurrection finds emphatic
support in these particular portions of the canon.

All that has been written in this volume to date posits that
the New Testament affirms the doctrine of Christ's future Parousia.
While not all eschatology is apocalyptic, all apocalyptic is
eschatological. With Cullmann, Matthew Black, H.H. Rowley,
et al. it must be said that the belief in the return of Christ,
as pictured in Mark 13, is not a delusion of primitive
Christianity but something inherent in fundamental Christian
doctrine and "to reject this hope is to mutilate the New Testament
message of salvation." To the N.T. writers such a belief was
an essential part of the theodicy they offered. It vindicated
the divine silence and apparent non-intervention to salve a

world's gaping sores. Apart from this, as Kuyper has shown, every other locus leaves some questions unanswered which eschatology alone can satisfy.[7] Thus our study of Mk. 13:14 is intimately related to vital issues of Biblical Theology as well as to matters of Biblical criticism and exegesis.

In summary, we should think of J.A.T. Robinson's reminder that "the eschatology of the Gospel of Mark as it now stands is dominated and must be interpreted by the apocalypse in chapter 13, . . . And what is true of Mark is true both of Matthew and Luke: any reference to the End must be understood in the light of their concluding apocalypse."[8] Having granted this, it should next be added that what is thus said concerning the eschatology of the Synoptic Gospels is true of the New Testament as a whole.[9] Furthermore, whether the disparate nature of the Old Testament is affirmed or denied, it is difficult to avoid seeing that the apocalyptic eschatology presented in the New Testament is modelled on that of the Old, though the height and depth of the former transcend the latter. The study of the βδέλυγμα τῆς ἐρημώσεως   motif, as herein attempted, documents this fact.

The words of Pannenberg and Barry are appropriate in epilogue:

   . . . He . . . was not an apocalyptic, although the views of the apocalyptic tradition are everywhere the presuppositions of what He said and did. Jesus certainly thought in apocalyptic categories.[10]

   His message can only be understood within the horizon of apocalyptic expectations.[11]

   The whole story [the life of Jesus] moves in an atmosphere of wonder, fringed, as it were, with a numinous corona, whose flames leap up in immeasurable splendour into spaces which we cannot chart. We cannot tear it out of that setting. Apart from it there is no story to tell. And it is the triumph of the eschatologists to have recovered that atmosphere.[12]

1. See Gaston, No Stone on Another, 8,23.

2. H.R. Mackintosh.

3. E. Käsemann.

4. "An inadequate critical methodology and/or a theological or philosophical bias has vitiated the conclusions of modern biblical critics nearly as often as those of pre-critical exegetes. As a substitute for the older dogmatic approach to the problems of criticism and exegesis, the student of the New Testament has often been offered another 'key' to guide him in his criticism; in many cases the point of reference has had little foundation in strictly historical study and exegesis, but rather has been based upon philosophical and theological prior judgments." W.W. Gasque, "A Study of the History of the Criticism of the Acts of the Apostles", unpublished Ph.D. thesis (Manchester, 1969), 372.

5. W.C. Allen, Saint Mark, 163. ". . . even in St. Mark we have the following apocalyptic ideas:- 'the kingdom of God,' 'the Son of Man,' 'the coming of the Son of Man in glory with the angels,' 'life' 9:45; 'the world to come,' 10:30; 'the resurrection,' 12:25; 'the Son of Man coming with the clouds of heaven,' 14:62; 'inheriting eternal life,' 19:17; 'the nearness of the coming kingdom,' 9:1."

6. See Gaston, No Stone on Another, 118. See also 162ff.

7. "Eschatology is the crown and the capstone of dogmatic theology. . . . It is the one locus of theology, in which all the other loci must come to a head, to a final conclusion. . . . every locus left some questions unanswered, to which eschatology should supply the answer. In theology it is the question, how God is finally perfectly glorified in the work of His hands, and how the counsel of God is fully realized; in anthropology, the question, how the disrupting influence of sin is completely overcome; in christology, the question, how the work of the Holy Spirit at last issues in the complete redemption and glorification of the people of God; and in ecclesiology, the question of the final apotheosis of the Church. All these questions must find their answer in the last locus of dogmatics, making it the real capstone of dogmatic theology." A. Kuyper, cited by L. Berkhof, Systematic Theology (Grand Rapids, 1949), 665-66.

8. Jesus and His Coming, 118.

9. Streeter asserted that "the Christian hope, first finding

its expression in crude apocalyptic like that of the Epistles to the Thessalonians, insensibly changes its emphasis, passes through the mysticism of the Epistles of the Captivity, and culminates in the Johannine doctrines of the Spirit and Eternal life." Oxford Studies, 426. But this same Streeter urges that during the identical period there was "an evolution in the contrary direction" in the Gospel literature, beginning with an uneschatological Q followed by Mark's admission of the 'little apocalypse', and ultimately the whole is heightened by Matthew. In other words, according to Streeter, the tendency of the Gospel literature of the church was the opposite of the church's movement in theology. But this surely demands too much. It is more accurate to say that the emphasis upon the immediate coming of Christ gave way to an emphasis that the present Christian life is right now of the same essential quality and blessedness that Christ will bestow at His return. "The truth rather is that there are two aspects of religion which are present throughout the whole New Testament side by side, the thought of Eternal Life or of the kingdom as present, and the conception of it as future." W.C. Allen, Saint Mark, 166.

10. W. Pannenberg, Jesus--God and Man (E.T., London, 1968), 217.

11. Ibid., 32.

12. F.R. Barry, The Relevance of Christianity (London, 1931), 98.

BIBLIOGRAPHY

315

SELECT BIBLIOGRAPHY

Aalders, G. C., "De 'Gruwel der verwoesting', Mt. 24:15, par.," GerThT, LX (1960), 1-5.

Adenay, W. F., Thessalonians (Century Bible), Edinburgh, 1902.

Allegro, J. M., and Anderson, A. A., Discoveries in the Judean Desert of Jordan, V, Oxford, 1968.

Allen, W. C., A Critical and Exegetical Commentary on the Gospel according to S. Matthew, (ICC), Edinburgh, ³1912.

Allen, W. C., The Gospel according to Saint Mark, London, 1915.

Bacon, B. W., The Gospel of Mark: its Composition and Date, New Haven-London-Oxford, 1925.

Barclay, W., Matthew, 2 vols., Daily Study Bible, Edinburgh, ²1958.

Barr, J., The Semantics of Biblical Language, Oxford, 1961.

Barrett, C. K., The Holy Spirit and the Gospel Tradition, London, ²1966.

Barrett, C. K., "New Testament Eschatology," SJTh, VI (1953), 136-55, 225-43.

Barry, F. R., The Relevance of Christianity, London, 1931.

Bartsch, H-W., "Early Christian Eschatology", NTS, XI (1964-65), 387-397.

Baumgartner, W., "Ein Viertejahrhundert Danielforschung", ThRs (NF), XI (1939), 59-83, 125-144, 201-228.

Beare, F. W., The Earliest Records of Jesus, Nashville, 1962.

Beasley-Murray, G. R., "A Century of Eschatological Discussion", ET, LXIV (1952/53), 312-16.

Beasley-Murray, G. R., "The Rise and Fall of the Little Apocalypse Theory", ET, LXIV (1952/53), 346-49

Beasley-Murray, G. R., Jesus and the Future. An Examination of the Criticism of the Eschatological Discourse, Mark 13, with Special Reference to the Little Apocalypse Theory, London-New York, 1954.

Beasley-Murray, G. R., A Commentary on Mark Thirteen, London, 1957

Beckwith, I. T., The Apocalypse of John: Studies in Introduction, New York, 1919.

Bentzen, A., Daniel (HAT), Tübingen, 1952.

Berkhof, H., Well-Founded Hope, Richmond, 1968.

Berkhof, L., Systematic Theology, London, ²1949.

Bernard, T.H., The Progress of Doctrine in the New Testament, London, 1864.

Best, E., The Temptation and the Passion, London, 1966.

Betz, H. D., "The Concept of Apocalyptic in the Theology of the Pannenberg Group", JThCh, VI (1969), 192-207.

Betz, H. D., "On the Problem of the Religio-Historical Understanding of Apocalypticism", JThCh, VI (1969), 134-156.

Betz, O., "Der Katechon", NTS, IX (1963), 276-291.

Bevan, A. A., A Short Commentary on the Book of Daniel, Cambridge, 1892.

Bickermann, E., Der Gott Der Makkabäer, Berlin, 1937.

Bicknell, E. J., The First and Second Epistles to the Thessalonians (WC), London, 1932.

Black, M., An Aramaic Approach to the Gospels and Acts, Oxford, 21954. "The Son of Man in the Teaching of Jesus", ET, LX (1948), 32-36.

Black, M., and Rowley, H. H., edd., Peake's Commentary on the Bible, London, ²1962.

Blass, P., Philology of the Gospels, London, 1898.

Bousset, W., The Antichrist Legend, E.T., London, 1896.

Boutflower, C., In and Around the Book of Daniel, London, 1923.

Bowman, J. W., The Drama of the Book of Revelation, Philadelphia, 1955.

Bowman, J. W., "The Life and Teaching of Jesus", Peake's Commentary on the Bible, rev. ed., ed. M. Black, London, '62, 733f

317

Bowman, J. W., _The Religion of Maturity_, Nashville, 1948.

Brandon, S., _The Fall of Jerusalem and the Christian Church_, 1951.

Branscombe, B. H., _The Gospel of Mark_ (MC), London, 1937.

Bratcher, Robert G., and Nida, Eugene, A., _A Translator's Handbook on the Gospel of Mark_, Leiden, 1961.

Bright, J., _The Kingdom of God._, New York, 1953.

Brown, J. P., "Synoptic Parallels in the Epistles and Form-History", _NTS_, X (1963-64), 27-48.

Brown, R. E., _Jesus, God and Man_, London, 1968.

Browning, W. R., _The Gospel According to Saint Luke_, London, 1960.

Bruce, A. B., "The Synoptic Gospels", _The Expositor's Greek Testament_, I, ed. W. Robertson-Nicoll, 4 vols., London, 1897, 3-651.

Bruce, F. F., _Biblical Exegesis in the Qumran Texts_, London, 1960.

Bruce, F. F., "The Book of Daniel and the Qumran Community" in _Neotestamentica et Semitica_ (Festschrift for M. Black), Edinburgh, 1969, 221-235.

Bruce, F. F., _New Testament History_, London, 1969.

Bruce, F. F., _Tradition Old and New_, Exeter, 1970.

Bruce, F. F., ed., _Promise and Fulfilment, Essays Presented to Professor S. H. Hooke_, Edinburgh, 1963.

Buhl, F., "Daniel", _The New Schaff-Herzog Encyclopaedia of Religious Knowledge_, III, ed. S. M. Jackson, 15 vols., Funk and Wagnall's original 1907 edn. reprinted by Baker Book House, Grand Rapids, 1949-55, 347-50.

Bultmann, R., _The History of the Synoptic Tradition_, E.T., Oxford, 1963.

Bultmann, R., "Is Exegesis Without Presuppositions Possible?" _Encounter_, XXI (1960), 194-200.

Bultmann, R., _Jesus and the Word_, E.T., London, ^{2}1958.

Bultmann, R., _Theology of the New Testament_, London, I, 1952; II

Burkill, T. A., _Mysterious Revelation: An examination of the Philosophy of Mark's Gospel_, Ithaca, 1963.

Burkitt, F. C., _The Gospel History and Its Transmission_, Edinburgh, 1911.

Burkitt, F. C., "The Use of Mark in the Gospel According to Luke", _The Beginnings of Christianity_, ed. by F. J. Foakes-Jackson and K. Lake, II, 106-120.

Buttrick, G. A., ed. _The Interpreter's Bible_, 12 vols., New York-Nashville, 1952-57.

Caird, G. B., _The Apostolic Age_, London, 1958.

Caird, G. B., _The Revelation of St. John the Divine_ (BC), New York, 1966.

Caird, G. B., _Saint Luke_, Harmondsworth, 1965.

Calvin, J. _Daniel_, reprinted from Calvin Translation Society edition of 1852-53, London, 1966.

Carpenter, W. P., "The Revelation of St. John the Divine", _Ellicott's Bible Commentary_, VIII, 8 vols., Grand Rapids, 1959, 523-641.

Carrington, P., _According to Mark. A Running Commentary on the Oldest Gospel_, Cambridge, 1960.

Carrington, P., _The Meaning of Revelation_, London, 1931.

Charles, R. H. ed., _The Apocrypha and Pseudepigrapha in English_, 2 vols., Oxford, 1913.

Charles, R. H., _Commentary on the Revelation of St. John_ (ICC), 2 vols., 1920.

Charles, R. H., _The Book of Daniel_, Oxford, 1929.

Cheyne, T. K., and Black, J. S., edd., _Encyclopaedia Biblica_, 4 vols., London, 1899.

Cheyne, T. K., "Abomination of Desolation", _Encyclopaedia Biblica_, I, 21-23 (cols.).

Clemen, C., "Die Zahl des Tieres Apc. 13,18"; _ZNTW_, II (1901), 109-14.

Clemen, C., "Nochmals die Zahl des Tieres Apc. 13,18", _ZNTW_, XI

(1910), 204-23.

Cole, R. A., The Gospel According to St. Mark, Grand Rapids, 1961

Cole, R. A., The New Temple, London, 1950.

Colpe, C., "ὁ υἱὸς τοῦ ἀνθρώπου ", TWNT, ed. Kittel, G., Friedrich, G., Stuttgart, vols. I-VII, 1933-64; VIII, 403-81.

Congar, Y. M., The Mystery of the Temple, E. T., London, 1962.

Conzelmann, H., "Gegenwart und Zukunft in der synoptisches Tradition", ZThK, LIV (1957), 277-296.

Conzelmann, H., "Geschichte und Eschaton nach Mc 13", ZNTW, L (1959), 210-21.

Conzelmann, H., The Theology of St. Luke, E.T., New York, 1960.

Cotter, G., "Abomination of Desolation", CJT, III (1957), 159-64.

Cousar, C. B., "Eschatology and Mark's Theologia Crucis", Interpretation, XXIV (1970), 321-35.

Cranfield, C. E. B., "St. Mark 13", SJTh, VI (1953), 189-96; 287-303; VII (1954), 284-303.

Cranfield, C. E. B., The Gospel according to St. Mark, (CGT, n.s.) Cambridge, 1959.

Creed, J. M., The Gospel according to St. Luke, London, 1930.

Cullmann, O., Christ and Time, London, 1951.

Cullmann, O., Christology of the New Testament, London, 1963.

Cullmann, O., "Eschatology and Mission in the New Testament", The Background of the New Testament and its Eschatology, Cambridge, 1956.

Cullmann, O., "L'opposition contre le temple de Jérusalem, motif commun de la théologie johannique et du monde ambiant", NTS, V (1958-59), 157-73.

Cullmann, O., "Parusieverzögerung und Urchristentum. Der gegenwärtige Stand der Diskussion", ThLZ, LXXXIII (1958), 1-12 (cols.).

Cullmann, O., Le retour du Christ, esperance de l'Église, selon le Nouveau Testament, Neuchâtel-Paris, 1945.

Daube, D., _Christian Origins and Judaism_, London, 1962.

Daube, D., _The New Testament and Rabbinic Judaism_, London, 1956.

Davies, W. D., and Daube, D., edd., _The Background of the New Testament and its Eschatology_, Cambridge, 1956.

Denney, J., _Thessalonians_ (Expositor's Bible), London, 1892.

De Young, J. C., _Jerusalem in the New Testament_, Kampen, 1960.

Dibelius, M., _An die Thessalonicher I und II_, Tübingen, 21923.

Dobschutz, E., von, _Die Thessalonicher Briefe_ (KEK), Göttingen, 1909.
Dodd, C. H., _According to the Scriptures_, London, 1952.

Dodd, C. H., _The Apostolic Preaching and its Developments_, London, 1936.

Dodd, C. H., _The Coming of Christ_, Cambridge, 1951.

Dodd, C. H., _More New Testament Studies_, Manchester, 1968.

Dodd, C. H., _The Parables of the Kingdom_, London, 21936.

Driver, S. R., "Abomination of Desolation", _Dictionary of the Bible_, I, ed. J. Hastings, 5 vols., Edinburgh, 1898-1904, 12-13.

Driver, S. R., _The Book of Daniel_ (CB), Cambridge, 1912.

Earle, R., _The Gospel According to Mark_, Grand Rapids, 1957.

Easton, B. S, _Christ in the Gospels_, London, 1930.

Easton, B. S., _The Gospel according to St. Luke_, Edinburgh, 1926.

Easton, B. S., _The Gospel before the Gospels_, New York, 1928.

Eisfeldt, O., _The Old Testament_, E.T., Oxford, 1965.

Ellicott, C. J., _Commentary on the Whole Bible_, 8 vols., Grand Rapids reprint, 1959.

Ellis, E. E., _The Gospel of Luke_ (Century Bible, n.s.), London, 1966.

Fairbairn, P., _The Interpretation of Prophecy_, Edinburgh, 1856.

Farrar, F., _The Bible, Its Meaning and Supremacy_, London-New York

Bombay, 1897.

Farrar, F., History of Interpretation, London, 1886.

Farrar, F., Life and Work of St. Paul, 2 vols., New York, 1880.

Farrer, A., A Rebirth of Images, London, 1949.

Farrer, A., The Revelation of St. John the Divine, Oxford, 1964.

Farrer, A., St. Matthew and St. Mark, London, 1954.

Farrer, A., A Study in St. Mark, London, 1951.

Feuillet, A., L'Apocalypse. État de la question. (Studia neotest. subsidia 3.), Paris-Bruges, 1963.

Feuillet, A.,"Le discours de Jesus sur la ruine du temple d'après Marc XIII et Luc XXI, 5-36", RB, LV (1948), 481-502; LVI (1949), 61-92.

Feuillet, A., "Essai D'interpretation Du Chapitre XI De L'Apocalypse", NTS, IV (1958), 183-200.

Feuillet, A., "Le Fils de l'homme de Daniel et la tradition biblique", RB, LX (1953), 170-202, 321-46.

Feuillet, A., "La synthèse eschatologique de saint Matthieu XXIV-XXV", RB, LVI (1949), 340-64, LVII (1950), 62-91, 180-211.

Filson, F. V., A Commentary on the Gospel according to St. Matthew (BC), London, 1960.

Findlay, G. F., The Epistles to the Thessalonians (CGT), Cambridge, 1914.

Fison, J. E., The Christian Hope. The Presence and the Parousia, London, 1954.

Flückiger, F., "Der Redaktion der Zukunftsrede in Mark 13", ThZ, XXVI (1970), 395-409.

Foakes-Jackson, F. J., and Lake, K., The Beginnings of Christianity, 5 vols., London, 1920-33.

Foerster, W., "βδελύσσομαι . . . .", TDNT, I, 657-660.

Ford, Desmond, Daniel (S.P.A., Nashville, 1978).

Frame, J. E., A Critical and Exegetical Commentary on the Epistles of St. Paul to the Thessalonians (ICC), Edinburgh, 1912.

Freedman, D. N., "The Flowering of Apocalyptic", <u>JThCh</u>, VI (1969) 166-174.

Froom, L. E., <u>The Prophetic Faith of Our Fathers</u>, 4 vols., Washington D. C., 1950-54.

Frost, S. B., <u>Old Testament Apocalyptic - Its Origin and Growth</u>, London, 1952.

Funk, R. W., "Apocalyptic as an Historical and Theological Problem in Current N. T. Scholarship", <u>JThCh</u>, VI (1969), 175-91.

Gärtner, B., <u>The Temple and the Community in Qumran and the New Testament</u>, Cambridge, 1965.

Gaston, L., <u>No Stone on Another. Studies in the Significance of the Fall of Jerusalem in the Synoptic Gospels</u>, Supplements to N. T., Vol. XXIII, Leiden, 1970.

Gasque, W. W., "A Study of the History of the Criticism of the Acts of the Apostles", unpublished Ph.D. dissertation, University of Manchester, 1969.

Geldenhuys, J. N., <u>Commentary on the Gospel of Luke</u> (NLC ET), London, 1950.

Ginsberg, H. L., <u>Studies in Daniel</u>, New York, 1948.

Glasson, T. F., <u>The Second Advent. The Origin of the New Testament Doctrine</u>, London, [2]1947.

Gould, E. P., <u>A Critical and Exegetical Commentary on the Gospel according to St. Mark</u> (ICC), Edinburgh, 1896.

Grant, F. C., <u>The Gospels, their Origin and their Growth</u>, London, 1957.

Grundmann, W., <u>Das Evangelium nach Markus</u>, Berlin, 1959.

Grundmann, W., <u>Das Evangelium des Lukas</u>, Berlin, [2]1964.

Gunkel, H., <u>Schöpfung und Chaos in Urzeit und Endzeit</u>, Göttingen, 1895.

Guthrie, D., <u>New Testament Introduction</u>, London, [3]1970.

Guy, H. A., <u>The New Testament Doctrine of the Last Things</u>, London, 1948.

Haenchen, E., <u>Der Weg Jesu</u>, Berlin, 1968.

Hance, H., "$\kappa\alpha\tau\acute{\epsilon}\chi\omega$ ", TDNT, II, 829-30.

Harder, G., "Das eschatologische Gesichtsbild der sogenannten kleinen Apokalypse Markus 13", ThV, IV (1952), 71-107.

Harrington, W. J., Understanding the Apocalypse, Washington D.C., 1969.

Hartman, L., Prophecy Interpreted. The Formation of some Jewish Apocalyptic Texts and of the Eschatological Discourse Mark 13 Par., Gleerup, 1966.

Heaton, E. W., The Book of Daniel (TBC), London, 1956.

Heim, K., Jesus, the World's Perfector, E. T., London, 1959.

Hempel, J., Die Mehrdeutigkeit der Geschichte als Problem der prophetischen Theologie, Neue Folge, I, Nr. I, Göttingen, 1936.

Hendriksen, W., Lectures on the Last Things, Grand Rapids, 1951.

Hendriksen, W., Thessalonians, Baker N.T., Commentary, Grand Rapids, 1955.

Hendriksen, W., More Than Conquerors, London, 1962.

Hiers, R. H., "Purification of the Temple", JBL, XC (1971), 82-90.

Higgins, A. J. B., Jesus and the Son of Man, London, 1964.

Hill, D., Greek Words and Hebrew Meanings, Cambridge, 1967.

Hobbs, E. C., An Exposition of the Gospel of Mark, Chicago, 1958.

Hooker, M., Jesus and the Servant, London, 1958.

Hooker, M., The Son of Man in Mark, London, 1967.

Hoskyns, Sir E. C., and Davey, F. N., The Riddle of the New Testament, London, 1947.

Hunter, A. M., The Gospel According to St. Mark (TBC), London, 1949.

Hunter, A. M., The Work and Words of Jesus, London, 1950.

Jeffery, A., "Daniel", IB, VI, New York-Nashville, 1956, 341-549.

Jeremias, J., Jesus als Weltvollender, Gütersloh, 1930.

Jeremias, J., "Kennzeichen der ipsissima vox Jesu", Synoptische Studien, ed. J. Schmid, München, 1953, 86-93.

Jeremias, J., The Parables of Jesus, E.T., London, 1963.

Johnson, S. E., The Gospel According to St. Mark (BC), London, 1960.

Johnson, S. E., "The Gospel according to St. Matthew", IB, VII, Nashville, 1951.

Jones, A., The Gospel According to St. Mark, New York, 1963.

Jones, N. W., The Function of the Gospel of Mark, Chicago, 1945.

Josephus, Works, tr. H. St. J. Thackeray, R. Marcus, A. Wikgren, and L. H. Feldmann, Vol. I-IX, London, 1926-65.

Käsemann, E., "The Beginnings of Christian Theology", JThCh, VI (1969), 17-47.

Käsemann, E., "On the Topic of Primitive Christian Apocalyptic", JThCh, VI (1969), 99-133.

Kennedy, H. A. A., St. Paul's Conception of the Last Things, London, 1904.

Kepler, T. S., The Book of Revelation, New York, 1957.

Kiddle, M., The Revelation of St. John (MC), London, 1940.

Kittel, G., "ἔρημος. . . . ", TDNT, II, 598-600.

Kittel, G. and Friedrich, G. edd., Theologisches Worterbuch zum Neuen Testament, Stuttgart, 1933-.

Kittel, G., and Friedrich, G. edd., Theological Dictionary of the New Testament, E.T. of TWNT, trans. and ed. by G. W. Bromiley, Grand Rapids, 1964.

Klostermann, E., Das Markusevangelium (LHB), Tübingen, 1950.

Knox, R. A., A New Testament Commentary, 3 vols., London, 1952.

Knox, W. L., The Sources of the Synoptic Gospels, Cambridge, I, 1953; II, 1957.

Kraeling, E., Commentary on the Prophets, II, Dan.-Mal., Camden, N.J., 1966.

Kuhn, "βαβυλὼν", TWNT, I, 514-17.

Kümmel, W. G., Introduction to the New Testament, E.T., of the 14th revised edn. (1965) of Feine-Behm's Einleitung in das Neue Testament, London, 1965.

Ladd, G. E., A Commentary on the Revelation of John, Grand Rapids 1972.

Ladd, G. E., Jesus and the Kingdom, London, 1966.

Ladd, G. E., "The Revelation and Jewish Apocalyptic", EQ, XXIX (1957), 94-100.

Lagrange, M-J., Évangile selon saint Matthieu, Paris, 1927.

Lagrange, M-J., Évangile selon St. Luc, Paris, 1927.

Lagrange, M-J., Évangile selon St. Marc, Paris, 1929.

Lambrecht, J., Die Redaktion der Markus-Apocalypse (AB 28), Rome, 1967.

Lange, J. P., A Commentary on the Holy Scriptures, Critical, Doctrinal and Homiletical, 12 vols., trans. and ed. by P. Schaff, E.T. of 2nd German edn. reprinted by Grand Rapids, 1960, VIII, 40-564.

LaSor, W. S., The Amazing Dead Sea Scrolls, Chicago, 1956.

Lattey, C., The Book of Daniel, Dublin, 1948.

Leaney, A. R. C., A Commentary on the Gospel according to St. Luke, London, 1958.

Leupold, H. C., Exposition of Daniel, Ohio, 1949.

Lewis, C. S., Transposition and Other Addresses, London, 1949.

Lightfoot, J. B., Notes on the Epistles of St. Paul (Grand Rapids, 1957, reprint of 1895 edn.).

Lightfoot, R. H., The Gospel Message of St. Mark, Oxford, 1950.

Lohmeyer, E., Das Evangelium des Markus, Göttingen, 1960.

Lohmeyer, E., Lord of the Temple, Edinburgh, 1961.

Lohmeyer, E., and Bornkamm, G., Die Offenbarung des Johannes (LHB), 1953.

Lohse, E., Mark's Witness to Jesus Christ, E.T., New York, 1955.

Loisy, A., Les Évangiles synoptiques, 2 vols., Paris, 1907-1908.

Loisy, A., L'Apocalypse de Jean, Paris, 1923.

Lundström, G., The Kingdom of God on the Teaching of Jesus, Edinburgh-London, 1963.

Manson, T. W., The Sayings of Jesus, London, 1949.

Manson, T. W., Studies in the Gospels and Epistles, ed. M. Black, Manchester, 1962.

Manson, T. W., The Teachings of Jesus; Studies of its Form and Content, Cambridge, 1931.

Marshall, H., Luke: Historian and Theologian, London, 1970.

Marshall, H., "Tradition and Theology in Luke (Luke 8:5-15)", TB, XX (1960).

Martin, James, P., The Last Judgment, Grand Rapids, 1963.

Martin, R. P., "A Gospel in Search of a Life-Setting", ET, LXXX (1969), 361-64.

Martindale, C. C., The Gospel According to Mark, Westminster, 1956.

Marxsen, W., Der Evangelist Markus, Göttingen, 1956.

Mason, A. J., "Thessalonians", Ellicott's Bible Commentary, VIII, Grand Rapids reprint, 1959, 149-170.

McDowell, E. A., The Meaning and Message of the Book of Revelation, Nashville, 1951.

McKelvey, R. J., The New Temple, London, 1969.

Menzies, A., The Earliest Gospel, London, 1901.

Milligan, G., St Paul's Epistles to the Thessalonians, London, 1908.

Milligan, W., The Book of Revelation (Expositor's Bible), London, 1898.

Milligan, W., Discussions on the Apocalypse, London, 1893.

Milligan, W., Lectures on the Apocalypse, London, 1893.

Milligan, W., The Revelation of St John, London, 1887.

Minear, P. S., The Christian Hope and the Second Coming, Westminster, Md., 1954.

Minear, P., I Saw a New Earth, Washington D. C., 1968.

Minear, P. S., "The Wounded Beast", JBL, LXXII (1953), 93-102.

M'Neile, A. H., The Gospel According to St Matthew, London, 1915.

Montefiore, C. G., The Synoptic Gospels, 2 vols., London, 21927.

Montgomery, J. A., A Critical and Exegetical Commentary on the Book of Daniel (ICC), Edinburgh, 1927.

Moore, A. L., The Parousia in the New Testament, Supplements to N.T. Vol. XIII, Leiden, 1966.

Morison, J., A Commentary on the Gospel According to Mark, London, 1873.

Morris, L., The Epistles of Paul to the Thessalonians (TNT), London, 1956.

Morris, L., The Revelation of St. John (TNT), London, 1969.

Moule, C. F. D., The Birth of the New Testament, New York, 1962.

Moule, C. F. D., "From Defendant to Judge -- and Deliverer", SNTS Bulletin, III (1952), 40-53.

Moulton, J. H., and Milligan, G., The Vocabulary of the Greek Testament Illustrated from the Papyri and other Non-Literary Sources, London, 1930.

Mowinckel, S., He that Cometh; the Messiah Concept in the Old Testament and Later Judaism, Oxford, 1956.

Muller, E. F. K., "Wiederkunft Christi", Real-Encyclopädie Für Protestantische Theologie und Kirche, 3rd. edn. XXI, 256-266.

Nairne, A., The Epistle of Priesthood: Studies in the Epistle to the Hebrews, Edinburgh, 1913.

Nast, W., Commentary on the Gospels of Matthew and Mark, Cincinnati, 1864.

Neil, W., Commentary on I and II Thessalonians, London, 1950.

Neill, S., The Interpretation of the New Testament, 1861-1961, London, 1966.

Nestle, E., "Der Greuel der Verwüstung, Dan. 9:27; 11:31; 12:11", ZAW, IV (1884), 248.

Neville, G., The Advent Hope, A Study of the Content of Mark 13, London, 1961.

Newman, B., "The Fallacy of the Domitian Hypothesis", NTS, X (1963-64), 133-39.

Nicoll, W. R., ed., The Expositor's Greek Testament, 5 vols., London, 1905 f.

Nineham, D. E., The Gospel of Saint Mark, London, 1963.

Oepke, A., Die Briefe an die Thessalonicher, Gottingen, [8]1959.

O'Callaghan, J., "Papiros neotestamentarios en la LIII:I Cueva de Qumran", Bib, LIII (1972), 91-100.

Olshausen, H., Matthew, Commentary on the New Testament, E.T., New York, 1857.

Orchard, J. B., "Thessalonians and the Synoptic Gospels", Bib, XIX (1938), 19-42.

Otto, R., The Kingdom of God and the Son of Man, E.T., London, 1938.

Pannenberg, W., Jesus - God and Man, E.T., London, 1968.

Peake, A. S., The Revelation of John, London, 1920.

Perrin, N., The Kingdom of God in the Teaching of Jesus, London, 1963.
Perrin, N., Rediscovering the Teaching of Jesus, London, 1967.

Perrot, C., "Essai sur le discours eschatologique (Mk. 13,1-37 parr; Mt. 24,1-36; Lc. 21,5-36)", RSR, XLVII (1959), 481-514.

Perry, A. M., The Sources of Luke's Passion Narrative, Chicago, 1920.

Pesch, R., Naherwartungen. Tradition und Redaktion in Mk. 13, Düsseldorf, 1968.

Pfeiffer, R. H., Introduction to the Old Testament, London, 1952.

Pinnock, C. H., "The Structure of Pauline Eschatology", EQ, XXXVII (1965), 9-20.

Piper, O., "Principles of New Testament Interpretation", TT, III (1946-47).

Piper, O., "Johannesapokalypse", RGG, Tubingen, ^{3}1956-65, col. 822-840.

Plummer, A., Commentary on St. Luke (ICC), Edinburgh, 1896.

Plummer, A., Commentary on Revelation (Pulpit Commentary), edd. H. D. M. Spence, J. S. Excell, London-New York, 1909.

Porteous, N., Daniel, London, 1965.

Preston, R. H., and Hanson, A. T., The Revelation of St. John the Divine, London, 1949.

Rawlinson, A. E. J., The Gospel according to St. Mark (WC), 1949.

Rad, G. von, The Message of the Prophets, E.T., London, 1968.

Rad, G. von, The Theology of the Old Testament, 2 vols., E.T., London, Edinburgh, I, 1962; II, 1965.

Reicke, B., The New Testament Era, E.T., London, 1969.

Riesenfeld, H., The Gospel Tradition and its Beginning, London, 1957.

Rigaux, B., L'Antéchrist et l'Opposition au Royaume Messianique dans l'Ancien et le Nouveau Testament. (Univ. Cath. Lovan. Diss. ad grad. mag. Facult. Theol. II:24), Paris, 1932.

Rigaux, B., Les Épîtres aux Thessaloniciens, Paris, 1956.

Rigaux, B., "βδέλυγμα τῆς ἐρημώσεως (Mc 13,14; Mt 24,15)", Bib, XL (1959), 675-83.

Riggenbach, C. J., "Thessalonians", Lange's Commentary on the Holy Scriptures, XI, 1-163.

Rist, M., "Antichrist", Interpreter's Bible Dictionary, I, 140-43.

Robinson, J. A. T., Jesus and His Coming; The Emergence of a Doctrine, London, 1957.

Rohde, J., Rediscovering the Teaching of the Evangelists, London, 1968.

Rowley, H. H., The Faith of Israel, London, 1956.

Rowley, H. H., The Relevance of Apocalyptic, London, [3]1963.

Rowley, H. H., The Servant of the Lord, Oxford, [2]1965.

Russell, D. S., The Method and Message of Jewish Apocalyptic, London, 1964.

Russell, J. S., The Parousia: a critical enquiry into the N.T. doctrine of our Lord's Second Coming, London, 1878.

Sanday, W., ed., Studies in the Synoptic Problem, Oxford, 1911.

Schlatter, A., Die Evangelien nach Markus und Lukas, Erläuterungen zum Neuen Testament, vol. II, Stuttgart, 1947.

Schlatter, A., Matthew, Stuttgart, 1963.

Schmid, J., Das Evangelium nach Markus, Regensburg, [2]1958.

Schniewind, J., Das Evangelium nach Markus, Göttingen, [6]1952.

Schniewind, J., Das Evangelium nach Matthäus, Göttingen, [7]1954.

Schweitzer, A., The Quest of the Historical Jesus: A Critical Study of its Progress from Reimarus to Wrede, New York, 1910.

Schweizer, E., Lordship and Discipleship, London, 1960.

Schweizer, E., "Eschatology in Mark's Gospel" in Neotestamentica et Semitica (Festschrift for M. Black) ed. E. Earle Ellis and Max Wilcox, Edinburgh, 1969, 114-118.

Schweizer, E., The Good News According to Mark, E.T., London, 1971.

Schweizer, E., "Der Menschensohn", ZNW L (1959), 185-209.

Schrenk, G., "ἱερός. . . . .", TDNT, III, 221-83.

Scott, C. A., Revelation (Century Bible) Edinburgh, n.d.

Shires, H. M., The Eschatology of Paul in the Light of Modern Scholarship, Philadelphia, 1966.

Sjöberg, E., Der verborgene Menschensohn in den Evangelien, Lund,

1955.

Smith, W. R., The Prophets of Israel, Edinburgh, 1882.

Stauffer, E., New Testament Theology, London, [5]1963.

Stein, R. H., "The Propher Methodology for ascertaining a Markan Redaktiongeschichte", unpublished Ph.D. dissertation, Princeton, 1968.

Stein, R. H., "The Proper Methodology for ascertaining a Markan Redaktiongeschichte", NovT, XIII (3, 1971), 181-198.

Stonehouse, N. B., Origins of the Synoptic Gospels, London, 1964.

Stonehouse, N. B., The Witness of Matthew and Mark to Christ, Grand Rapids, [2]1958.

Streeter, B. H., The Four Gospels, London, 1924.

Streeter, B. H., "St. Mark's Knowledge and Use of Q", in Studies in the Synoptic Problem. . . , ed. W. Sanday, Oxford, 1911, 165-83.

Suhl, A., Die Funktion der Alttestamentlichen Zitate und Anspielungen in Markusevangelium, Gerd Mohn, 1965.

Swete, H. B., The Apocalypse of St. John, London, 1907.

Swete, H. B., The Gospel according to St. Mark, London, 1902.

Taylor, V., "The Apocalyptic Discourse of Mark XIII", ET, LX (1948/9), 94-98.

Taylor, V., Behind the Third Gospel: A Study of the Proto-Luke Hypothesis, Oxford, 1926.

Taylor, V., The Gospel according to St Mark, London, 1952.

Tenney, M. C., Interpreting Revelation, Grand Rapids, 1957.

Thompson, E.T., The Gospel According to Mark and its Meaning for Today, Richmond, 1962.

Tödt, H. E., Der Menschensohn in der synoptischen Überlieferung, Gutersloh, 1959.

Torrance, T. F., The Apocalypse Today, 1959.

Torrey, C. C., The Apocalypse of John, New Haven, 1958.

Torrey, C. C., Documents of the Primitive Church, New York-London, 1941.

Trocmé, E., La Formation de l'Évangile selon Marc (Études d' HPhR, 57), Paris, 1963.

Turner, C. H., The Gospel according to St. Mark, London, 1929.

van Dodewaard, J., "De gruwel der verwoesting (Mt 24:15 = Mc 13, 14)", StCathXX (1944), 125-35.

van Oosterlee, J. J., "Luke", Lange's Commentary on the Holy Scriptures, VIII, 1-405.

Vawter, B., The Four Gospels, Dublin, 1967.

Vielhauer, P., "Gottesreich und Menschensohn in der Verkündigung Jesu", Aufsätze zum Neuen Testament, München, 1965, 55-91.

Vos, G., The Pauline Eschatology, Grand Rapids, 1953.

Vos, L. A., The Synoptic Tradition in the Apocalypse Kampen, 1965.

Walter, N., "Tempelzerstörung und synoptische Apokalypse", ZNTW, LVII (1966), 38-49.

Weiss, J., "Die Drei älteren Evangelien", Die Scriften des Neuen Testaments, I, ed. J. Weiss, 4 vols., Göttingen, [2]1906, 31-525.

Welch, A. C., Visions of the End: a Study of Daniel and Revelation, London, 1922.

Wellhausen, J., Das Evangelium Marci, Berlin, [2]1909.

Wikenhauser, A., New Testament Introduction, E.T., New York, 1967.

Wilder, A. N., Eschatology and Ethics in the Teaching of Jesus, New York, [2]1950.

Williams, C. S. C., "The Synoptic Problem", Peake's Commentary on the Bible, rev. edn. London, 1962.

Williams, N. P., "A Recent Theory of the Origin of St. Mark's Gospel", in Studies in the Synoptic Problem by members of the University of Oxford, ed. W. Sanday, Oxford, 1911, 389-424.

Wilson, R. McL., "Mark", Peake's Commentary on the Bible, revised edn., London, 1962.

Wohlenberg, G., Thessalonicherbrief (KNT), Leipzig, 1903.

Wordsworth, C., Commentary on the New Testament, 2 vols., London, ²1872.
Worsley, F. W., The Apocalypse of Jesus, London, 1912.

Yadin, Y., The Scroll of the War of the Sons of Light against the Sons of Darkness, Oxford, 1962.

Young, E. J., The Prophecy of Daniel, Grand Rapids, 1949.

Young, J. C., de, Jerusalem in the New Testament: The Significance of the City in the History of Redemption and in Eschatology, Kampen, 1960.

Zahn, T., Introduction to the New Testament, E.T., Edinburgh, 1909.

Zahn, T., Die Offenbarung des Johannes (Komm. zum N.T.), Leipzig, 1924-26.

Zöckler, O., "Daniel", Lange's Commentary on the Holy Scriptures, Grand Rapids reprint of 2nd German edn., 1960, VII, 1-273.